GUERNSEY UNDER OCCUPATION

The Second World War Diaries
of
Violet Carey

Violet Carey, late 1940s.

GUERNSEY UNDER OCCUPATION

THE SECOND WORLD WAR DIARIES

OF

VIOLET CAREY

Edited by
Alice Evans

PHILLIMORE

First published in 2009 by
PHILLIMORE & CO. LTD

Reprinted 2014

The History Press
The Mill, Brimscombe Port,
Stroud, Gloucestershire, GL5 2QG
www.thehistorypress.co.uk

© Alice Evans, 2009

ISBN 978-1-86077-581-9

Printed and bound in Great Britain

Contents

Acknowledgements	vii
Introduction	ix
The View of one who was there: A Biography of Violet Carey	xxiv
What the Diaries tell us	xxx
The Diaries of Violet Carey, 1940	1
The Diaries of Violet Carey, 1941	33
The Diaries of Violet Carey, 1942	69
The Diaries of Violet Carey, 1943	117
The Diaries of Violet Carey, 1944	155
The Diaries of Violet Carey, 1945	195
Appendix: Index of People mentioned in Violet Carey's Diaries	219
Bibliogaphy	223
Index	227

Acknowledgements

A number of people have given me their assistance or expertise and have helped to bring this work to publication. Firstly, I am grateful to the committee of the Lord Rootes Memorial Fund at the University of Warwick who sponsored my first research trip to Guernsey in 1999. Secondly, Professor Carolyn Steedman, my supervisor for my Masters degree who directed my research and helped me formulate my argument. I would also like to mention Kate Chilton who presented with me a joint paper about the Occupation at a conference in Liverpool in 2001.

Thank you to the many people (too many to mention individually) who were willing to talk to me about the Occupation and Violet Carey; these conversations were inspiring and deepened my understanding of the subject in a way no book can. I am also grateful to the individuals in Guernsey who shared valuable knowledge and resources. In particular my thanks go to Dr Darryl Ogier and the staff at the Island Archives. Mr Richard Heaume of the German Occupation Museum in Guernsey has also been helpful and generous, allowing me to include in the book photographs from his collection. Similarly, I would like to thank Sir de Vic Carey for his encouragement and also for permission to use pictures.

This work would probably never have begun without the assistance of my parents, Ross and Pat Paxton; thank you for your help, encouragement, funding and nagging! Finally, I would like to remember Violet Carey's daughter, my Granny Guernsey, who was an inspiration to me. She would have been delighted to see these diaries in print.

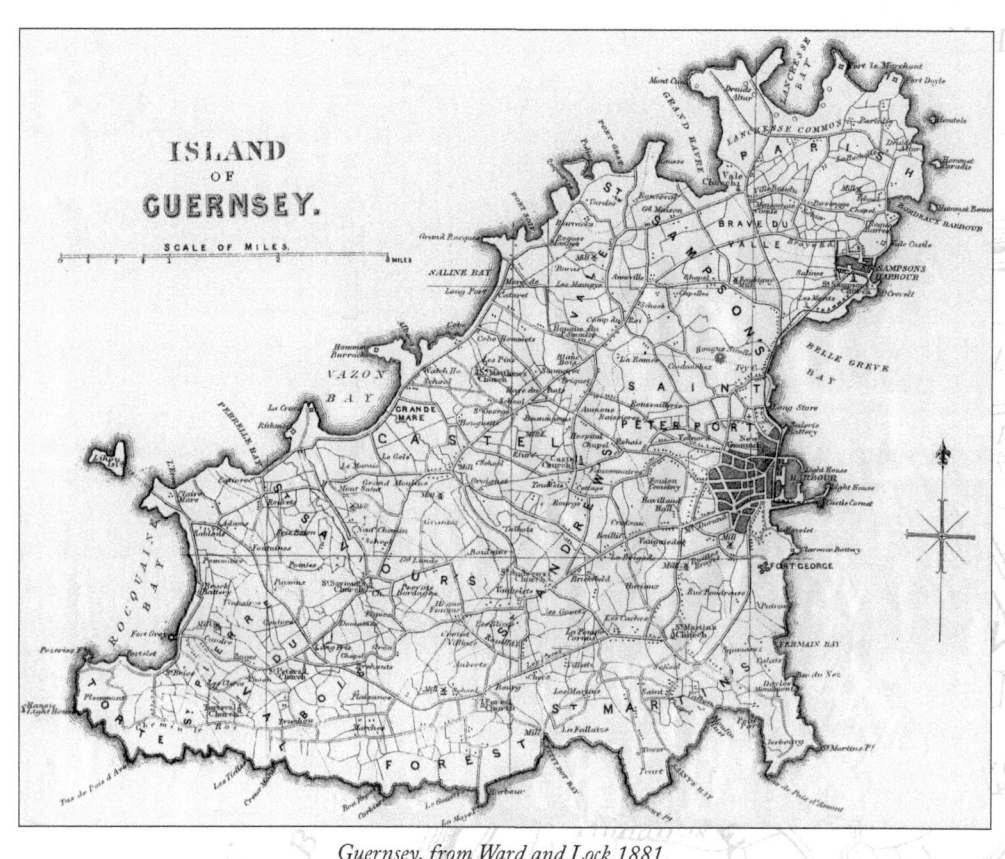

Guernsey, from Ward and Lock 1881.

Introduction

Guernsey is the second largest of the Channel Islands. It forms a triangle of 24 square miles and lies approximately 75 miles from its nearest English seaport, Weymouth. The Channel Islands are neither a part of the United Kingdom nor are they colonies. Their relationship with Britain is derived from their integration into the Duchy of Normandy in the mid-tenth century; they became linked to England when William the Conqueror came to the throne in 1066. Although England lost Normandy in the 13th century, the Channel Islands have remained loyal to the Crown to the present day. However, they have never been incorporated into the Kingdom of England.

Due to its Norman origin, Guernsey has always maintained a certain level of independence and has kept many of its own laws, customs and names. In particular it remains free from English taxation. Guernsey has an independent system of government based on the ancient Norman Law. The Bailiff of the Island holds a unique position as the President of the Island Parliament and the senior Judge in its Courts.

In 1939 the system of government in Guernsey was administered through the States of Deliberation and the Royal Court. The States usually met at monthly intervals to consider proposals made by the committees responsible for the day-to-day administration of the Island.[1] However, the States had no formal capacity to make byelaws or laws. The Royal Court had both judicial and quasi-legislative functions, and had full power to determine civil and criminal cases. They also had the power to make regulations, usually in response to proposals made by the States, by means of registering *Ordonnances* which encompassed a wide range of issues that can be broadly defined as low level internal legislation.[2]

However, the government bodies within the Islands were subject to a degree of intervention from the Privy Council. This body was responsible for actual legislation that made or modified the law of the Island. A further role of Her Majesty's Government was to take responsibility for the Island's defence and international relations.[3] The link between Britain and Guernsey was maintained by a Lieutenant-Governor who was appointed as the representative of the Crown and was the official channel of communication between the Island and British government.[4]

The inhabitants of Guernsey, amounting to some 40,000 in 1939, have traditionally been staunchly independent. The great majority of the population at this time were natives of the Island whose families could be traced back for centuries. Many families still spoke the local patois, Guernsey-French. Writing of the Channel Islanders in 1904, Edith Carey described an attitude among native Islanders that exists to this day:

---

[1] Ken Tough, 'The States of Guernsey, 1939-1945', *Channel Island Occupation Review*, Vol. 6, 1978, p.45
[2] Interview with HM.Greffier Mr Ken Tough, 23 May 2001.
[3] Sir John Loveridge, *The Constitution and Law of Guernsey*, second edition, edited by J.H. Loveridge Junior (Guernsey, 1997), p.1.
[4] Charles Cruickshank, *The German Occupation of the Channel Islands* (Guernsey, 1975), pp.1-2.

> There still lingers a certain individuality about the thoroughbred Channel Islander; to the world in general he asserts himself an Englishman, but in the presence of the English he boasts of being a Jerseyman or a Guernseyman.[5]

Many of these native Islanders were descended from medieval farming communities and still based their livelihoods on the traditional trades of farming and fishing. However, there were increasing numbers of settlers from Britain who came to live in the Island. Furthermore, due to the increasing popularity of Guernsey as a tourist resort, there was a seasonal influx of people of other nationalities who came to the Island to work.[6]

By 1939 tourism had become an important source of income for the Island and many Guernsey residents were financially dependent on visitors from the UK. Traditional forms of farming had also gradually given way to a thriving economy based on agriculture and horticulture, consisting mainly of exporting Guernsey cattle, flowers, fruit and vegetables, particularly the famous Guernsey tomato for which the Island was highly reputed. Thus, in 1939, the Island was not self-sufficient and was dependent on the UK for supplies and to support trade.

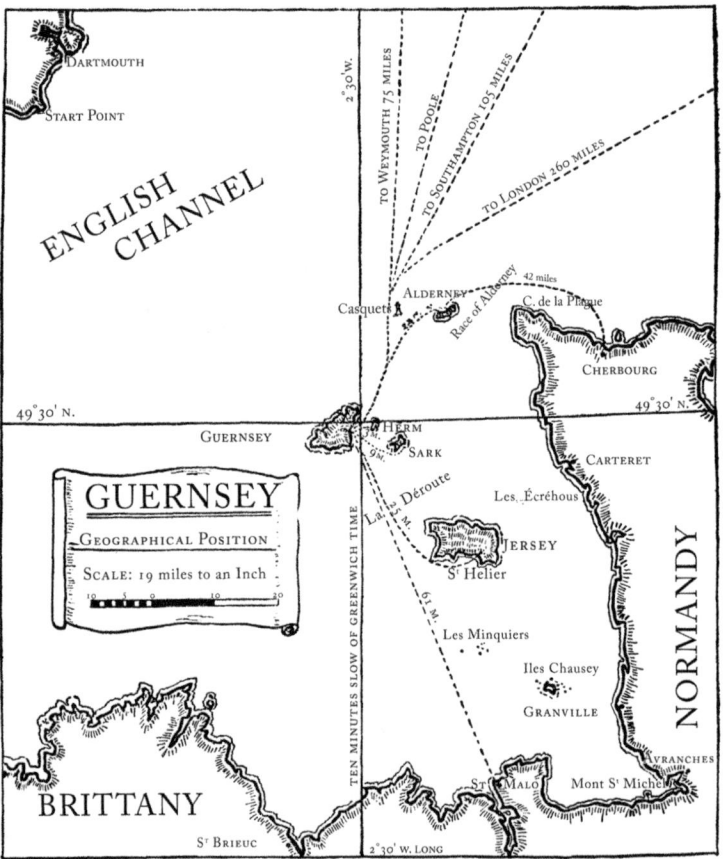

The Channel Islands (from J.P. Warren, Our Own Island, *Guernsey 1926, p.3).*

---

[5] Edith Carey, *The Channel Islands* (London, 1904), p.228.
[6] Cruickshank, *The German Occupation*, p.2.

Charles Cruickshank gives an admirable summary of the situation of the Channel Islands at the outbreak of the Second World War in *The German Occupation of the Channel Islands*:

> So it was that the Channel Islands awaited the Second World War. Two densely-populated bailiwicks, close to France, still using French for some purposes, and patois in the country districts, but loyal to the United Kingdom for a thousand years; virtually self-governing, except for the King in Council standing benevolently in the wings, and taking the stage only to consider the wishes of the Island legislature; each with the machinery of an independent state, but sometimes incapable of making quick decisions because of their relationship with the Privy Council; dependent on selling their produce to Britain, and on visitors from Britain.[7]

The Outbreak of War

With the exception of some men and women of military age who left to join the Armed Forces, the approach and outbreak of the war made little impact on Guernsey, and the Island was only disrupted by wartime precautions. However, in May 1940 Hitler's successes in Europe and his rapid advances towards the Normandy coast posed a great threat to the Channel Islands, the closest of which (Alderney) was less than ten miles away. On 16 June the Home Office withdrew the Lieutenant-Governor from the Island and his powers and duties, except those relating to military matters, were conferred on the Bailiff.[8] On 19 June the War Cabinet decided to demilitarise the Channel Islands as it believed they had no strategic importance and the possibility of attack was 'somewhat remote'; the military strength required to defend them was needed more urgently elsewhere and so the Royal Militia and Defence Volunteers were disbanded.[9] This decision threw the Islanders into confusion and panic as it was impossible to know what to do for the best. All were given the opportunity to evacuate and 17,000 people, mostly mothers and children, left Guernsey in the next few days.[10] In spite of the opportunity to leave, however, many Islanders, aided by an unofficial anti-evacuation campaign, preferred to stick firmly to their roots.

At this point the situation of the Channel Islands in relation to Britain and the war against Germany was very confused and the Islanders were in grave danger. They were undefended and the States of each Island had complete responsibility but no guidance from England. To make matters worse, Britain had decided the Islands should be demilitarised but the fact they were undefended was not publicised, and consequently they were exposed to any form of enemy attack. The Germans were under the impression the Islands were defended and on 28 June they bombed the main towns of Guernsey and Jersey, killing a total of 44 people.[11] On 30 June German planes landed in Guernsey, and then in Jersey the following day. Both Islands had no choice but to surrender.

---

[7] Cruickshank, *The German Occupation*, p.7.
[8] On 21 June 1940 the *Star* reported that, 'Owing to His Excellency the Lieutenant-Governor being recalled from the Island, the Bailiff was yesterday sworn in by Jurat A. Drake as Lieutenant-Governor insofar as civil duties only pertain.'
[9] Cruickshank, *The German Occupation*, pp.23, 27, 31.
[10] Cruickshank, *The German Occupation*, p.59.
[11] Cruickshank, *The German Occupation*, p.69.

Occupation Government

The Second World War precipitated unique modifications to the system of government in Guernsey. On 21 June 1940, following the demilitarisation and evacuation of the Island, the Bailiff called for a special meeting of the States, where Jurat Leale outlined a proposal for a new form of government designed to cope with the emergency. There was no doubt that as there was no means of defence the Island would have to submit to occupation: 'The military have gone, we are civilians ... it must be realised that as at present constituted, our system does not work. ... The only way out I know is to appoint a small Executive Committee with very large executive powers.'[12] Thus the Controlling Committee was created and given the authority to make quick decisions and meet in private rather that in the public context of the States. The Attorney-General, Ambrose Sherwill, was appointed as President and he selected seven other members to be responsible for particular aspects of civilian life, including agriculture, horticulture and health.

When the Germans invaded and occupied Guernsey, the Commandant, Dr Lanz, decided that the Island courts and civil administration should continue to function under his supervision, although he retained the authority to issue his own orders and register them on the Island records. At the first States meeting of the Occupation on 7 August 1940, at which Dr Lanz was present, the function of the Controlling Committee was formally defined. It was given

> the right and power to do and cause to be done all executive and administrative acts which the States have authorised or could authorise whenever such acts appear to such Emergency Committee to require any early decision ...[13]

Throughout the Occupation the Controlling Committee met frequently and issued orders relating to the day-to-day administration of the Island, which were published in the local papers once approved by the Commandant.

Another change in the legislative processes occurred as a result of the severance of all communication with Britain. The Privy Council could not sanction legislation and therefore new laws could not be made, repealed or amended. In his memoirs, Sherwill described how he 'used the Kommandant to raise the British Civil Lieutenant-Governor (the Bailiff) to the "throne" instead'.[14] At the States meeting on 7 August 1940 the legal relationship between the German and Island authorities was formalised:

> Seeing that by Order dated the second day of July 1940, the Commandant of the German forces in occupation of the Bailiwick of Guernsey declared that such legislation as in the past required the sanction of His Britannic Majesty in Council for its validity should thenceforth be valid on being approved by the German Commandant and thereafter sanctioned by the British Civil Lieutenant-Governor of this Island of Guernsey.[15]

The States continued to meet throughout the Occupation but their meetings were generally a formality, to examine the annual budget for example. There were also circumstances when the States met to deal with a sudden emergency such as the sabotage of telephone wires in March

---

[12] *Guernsey Evening Press*, 22 June 1940.
[13] *Billet d'Etat 1940*, 7 August 1940.
[14] Sherwill, Ambrose, *A fair and Honest Book* (Lulu, 2006), p.100.
[15] *Billet d'Etat 1940*, 7 August 1940.

1941.[16] The Royal Court retained more of its pre-war functions. It continued to introduce and register ordinances; in August 1940, for example, an *Ordonnance* was rushed through to make injudicious speech against the Germans an offence liable to punishment through the Island courts as opposed to the German courts.[17] The Royal Court also maintained its judicial role and tried the majority of civil and criminal civilian cases throughout the Occupation. With the Germans in occupation, however, there were four other courts: the Feldkommandant's court, which tried members of the civilian population who committed offences against German orders, and three sections of the Wehrmacht's legal administration, which dealt with the Luftwaffe, the Army and the Navy. Which court civilians were tried in often depended on who had convicted them.[18]

Although the Island government was permitted to function it did not have a free rein, as the Germans imposed their own system of command. In August 1940 Feldkommandantur 515 was set up in Jersey with a Nebenstelle (branch) in Guernsey. This body was designed to ensure the government of the Island was carried out efficiently and was separate from the military commanders who remained responsible for military affairs.[19] An agreement was made at a meeting at area headquarters in St Germain, France, that the 'Feldkommandantur must at all costs be enabled to be the dominant partner in the government of the Islands'.[20] The Geheime Feldpolizei was assigned to Feldkommandantur 515 to ensure that the occupying power was not undermined.

Living under German Rule

On 1 July 1940 the German Commandant of the Occupying Forces issued orders which imposed restrictions on the civilian population regarding the security of the Island and the Germans' control. These included the imposition of a curfew, which restricted Islanders' social lives, and the prohibition of the use of private cars and the sale of spirits. Contact with the UK was severed: the telephone cable was cut and contact by mail stopped, with the later exception of Red Cross messages. As the Occupation continued, other orders impinged further on the Islanders' normal ways of life. In October 1940 an order was issued which forbade 'gatherings in the streets, the publication and distribution of leaflets, the organisation of and participation in public meetings'.[21] Islanders were issued with identity cards which they had to carry at all times and were prosecuted if found without. In June 1941 everyone was ordered to drive on the right hand side of the road.[22] In June 1942 all radios were requisitioned, which limited sources of information from outside the Island and also deprived the Islanders of a major form of entertainment.[23]

One of the worst problems that affected Guernsey during the Occupation was the shortage of food. As the Island had been dependent on the UK for most of its supplies, other means of feeding the population had to be found. Rationing was imposed and orders were issued to

---

[16] Tough, 'The States of Guernsey', p.53.
[17] *Ordonnances 28*, 23 December 1939 – 14 June 1941, p.439.
[18] Cruickshank, *The German Occupation*, pp.103, 114.
[19] Cruickshank, *The German Occupation*, p.106.
[20] Cruickshank, *The German Occupation*, p.112.
[21] The *Star*, 14 October 1940.
[22] Cruickshank, *The German Occupation*, p.127.
[23] The *Star*, 8 June 1942.

maximise the use of farmland and greenhouses for growing crops and vegetables. Fearing that Islanders would attempt to escape, the German authorities forbade fishermen to fish in the waters further away from the shore, which were more lucrative, thus depriving the Islanders of a substantial food source.[24] Whilst the Germans still occupied France, the Feldkommandant allowed representatives to go to France with a purchasing commission to buy seeds, flour, wheat and barley, which diminished the problem until the D-Day landings and the liberation of France in June 1944,[25] but in the last year of the Occupation the food shortage became extremely serious. Repeated SOS messages were sent to Britain via the International Red Cross, and eventually the desperate Island was relieved by the arrival of a Red Cross ship, the *Vega*, in December 1944, which brought 100,000 food parcels and medical supplies.[26] From then until May 1945 the Islanders depended on the parcels the *Vega* brought. However, the situation became even more grim when the supply of flour was exhausted in February 1945. The ship which was supposed to bring flour was delayed and the Islands were without bread for a month.[27] This increased the number of cases of malnutrition in the hospitals and resulted in several deaths caused by starvation.

The Germans caused great disruption to many Islanders' lives. Soldiers were billeted on private homes and people were evicted from their houses at short notice. Burglary and theft by both Germans and civilians became increasingly common, especially in the last desperate months before Liberation. Farmers found their cows milked in the night and crops were stolen from farms and the growers' greenhouses. Islanders also lived in perpetual fear of their houses being searched for stores of food and radios; if either of these were found, the victim was liable to be punished by heavy fines, imprisonment, or even deportation. Possibly the most disruptive incident that occurred during the Occupation was the order that all British-born Islanders be deported. In September 1942, 825 men, women and children were sent to internment camps in Germany. A further 200 followed them in January 1943.[28]

As the Royal Guernsey Militia had been disbanded and the British garrison withdrawn prior to the Occupation, the Channel Islands did not have the military strength or resources to resist the Germans. It is doubtful that the Islands could, in any case, have been defended successfully, at least not without tremendous loss of life and property. So the authorities adopted a policy of 'passive co-operation'. They advised civilians to wait patiently for liberation, maintaining an attitude of obedience and courtesy towards but not collaboration with the Germans.[29] This attitude was promoted by the Controlling Committee in a notice published in the *Star* on 2 July 1940 in conjunction with the Commandant's first orders:

> The public are notified that no resistance whatever is to be offered to those in military occupation of this Island. The public are asked to be calm, carry on their lives and work in the usual way and to obey the orders of the German Commandant.[30]

The Islanders reacted to the presence of the Germans in a variety of ways. Most resented their presence, some attempted to escape to England and a few succeeded, while others made

---

[24] Cruickshank, *The German Occupation*, p.121.
[25] Cruickshank, *The German Occupation*, p.123.
[26] Bell, William, *Guernsey Occupied but Never Conquered* (Exeter, 2002), pp.325-7.
[27] Bell, *Guernsey Occupied*, p.341.
[28] Cruickshank, *The German Occupation*, pp.219, 220.
[29] Cruickshank, *The German Occupation*, p.157.
[30] The *Star*, 1 July 1940.

outward attempts at resistance by spreading anti-German propaganda and participating in the 'V for Victory' campaign promoted in Europe. Such resistance invariably resulted in severe punishment and reprisals. Most Islanders chose to obey the Germans, but many delighted in petty attempts of resistance, like the farmers who defied the system by reporting their food stocks inaccurately. Others, though relatively few, did collaborate; some of these were motivated by a belief that Hitler would win the war or that their conduct would go unnoticed, and others by desperate circumstances such as unemployment and starvation.[31]

German Activity

Initially the Germans saw the invasion of the Channel Islands as a great triumph. However, once their value as propaganda had diminished, instead of giving the Germans a military advantage by facilitating the invasion of England, the Islands became a liability as they had to be defended. Fearing the British would attempt to recapture the Islands, Hitler ordered Count Graf von Schmettow, the Befehlshaber (Fortress Kommandant), to devise and implement a fortification programme to strengthen the Islands' defences.[32] Existing Napoleonic forts on the Islands were extended and new fortifications constructed. The beaches were heavily mined, coastal defence guns were installed and more troops were imported. In August 1942 the troops amounted to as many as 37,000 between the five main Islands.[33] The fortifications were constructed by the Organisation Todt, which put German and foreign labour at the disposal of German contractors for military construction. They were supplemented by the importation of political prisoners and prisoners of war who were essentially slave workers and treated 'little better than animals'.[34] Islanders were protected against forced labour on military constructions intended for use against their fellow countrymen by the Hague Convention and although some, tempted by the offer of high wages and better rations, did work for the Germans, the majority of the population resented the fact that the appearance of their beautiful Island was being ruined.[35]

The Debate on the Occupation of Guernsey

Since the Liberation of the Channel Islands in 1945, the German Occupation of Guernsey has attracted a great deal of interest. Much of this interest has concentrated on the events and the military aspect of the Occupation and the lifestyle of the Islanders. Collections of relics have been put on display in numerous museums and the Germans' underground hospitals and fortifications have been opened to the public, making this historical event into a public story. Within the Island, certain aspects of the Occupation have been emphasised in the public memory and have developed into a discourse of cheerful determination and community spirit in a time of severe hardship. Liberation Day is a clear illustration of this attitude. This annual public holiday, exclusive to the Channel Islands, is a joyful celebration of the Islanders' triumph of enduring and surviving five years of hardship under the rule of the enemy.

---

[31] Cruickshank, *The German Occupation*, pp.133-4.
[32] Cruickshank, *The German Occupation*, p.186.
[33] Cruickshank, *The German Occupation*, p.193.
[34] Cruickshank, *The German Occupation*, p.201.
[35] Cruickshank, *The German Occupation*, pp.130-1.

There has also been interest in how the Islanders behaved and coped under enemy rule, and a lot of attention has been paid to the issue of collaboration with the Germans, particularly from people outside the Islands. Different versions of the Occupation have developed within public memory and formed discourses which Islanders have drawn on and contributed to in order to think and talk about the situation they experienced. This process has been made more complex by the opinions of Islanders who did not experience the Occupation themselves, either because they were absent from the Island or because they belong to a younger generation. The fact that different versions of the Occupation are familiar to younger generations suggests something of the strength of feeling Islanders attach towards this part of their history. This strength of feeling and the differences of opinion have made the Occupation a complex and contoversial subject.

The historiography of the Occupation is extensive and illustrates the differing and at times conflicting versions of the period. Charles Cruickshank, commissioned by the States of Guernsey and Jersey to write the official history of the Occupation, published *The German Occupation of the Channel Islands* in 1975. This history focuses mainly on the events and the military aspect of the Occupation but also addresses issues of loyalty and culpability. Cruickshank defends the Islanders and the Island authorities:

> There was no precedent for the occupation, a fact which critics of the Island Administrations would do well to remember. They had no experience of conducting friendly negotiations with a great power, since the United Kingdom had been responsible for their external relations. Overnight they were abandoned to their fate ... It is not that they made some mistakes that is surprising, but that they did so much that was right in circumstances of the greatest possible difficulty.[36]

Various Islanders have researched and published books concerning certain aspects of the Occupation. These include Frank Falla's *The Silent War* which describes the impact of the war on the local press, and Beryl Ozanne's *A Peep Behind the Screens* describes how the Occupation affected the hospital. Frederick Cohen has written an account of the few Islanders with Jewish connections and of the Jewish people who were transported to the Islands to work on the Germans' fortification program. William Bell has published a number of detailed studies, including *I Beg to Report*, which is a thorough report on the role of the police, and *The Commando Who Came Home to Spy*, which describes the story of two Island men who had joined up and were sent back to the Island to gather intelligence.

In addition, many personal testimonies in the form of diaries and memoirs have been published and are an important part of the historiography of the Occupation. In general, both the testimonies and documentaries focus on the hardships of the Occupation and portray Islanders as heroically doing their best in an extraordinary and difficult situation when life became a mere struggle for survival. The published letters written (but not sent) by K.M. Bachmann to her mother throughout the war are predominantly concerned with the struggle to find food for her sickly new-born child. She describes her lifestyle as a 'trivial round of common tasks, while not furnishing all we need to ask, keep the body mobilised while the brain, in constant ferment, flits from one subject to another. Food, baby, war, tennis,

---

[36] Cruickshank, *The German Occupation*, p.329.

... local chaos, ... billeting of soldiers, loss of wireless and the growing catalogue of rumours afflict our already cluttered minds'.[37] Molly Bihet was a child during the Occupation. She expresses this preoccupation with survival in her memoirs, with a description of her mother's struggle to feed an extended family and comments: 'FOOD! That's the main topic I seem to remember.'[38] Winifred Harvey sums up the attitudes of many Islanders in her diary with her comment, 'I find that as in the case of Antarctic expeditions our conversation is now largely about food.'[39]

Alongside this, a recurrent theme in the testimonies is a sense of determined endurance, optimism and wartime camaraderie and a feeling that the Island community were united against the enemy. Violet Carey wrote in her diary, 'If ever any people were an eloquent example of the "brave old wisdom of endurance", the Guernsey people are that now. They are going on with their work doggedly and uncomplainingly, outwardly cheerful, resisting nothing, giving in with a dignity that is remarkable.'[40] Noting an increased sense of community spirit, K.M. Bachmann wrote that 'The esprit-de-corps of the Guernsey people has never been more pronounced. The joy of walking through Town and seeing one friendly face after another among the thick sprinkling of Germans is truly comforting.'[41] Comments such as these have contributed to the representation of the Occupation which has dominated public memory.

More recently, other histories of the Occupation have been published which are far more critical of the Islanders' conduct, and particularly of the conduct of the Island authorities. David Fraser, a legal historian, published an extensive study of the Jews who were deported to Auschwitz and claims that the prevalent discourse is a cover up for controversial issues:[42]

> The Occupation was officially constructed as a difficult period in which the local officials did their utmost to protect and preserve the local inhabitants of the Channel Islands. This remains the dominant historical mythology today as many Islanders continue to construct the Occupation as little more than a tourist attraction. It can hardly be surprising that the fate of the Jews in the Channel Islands has not figured prominently in collective memory and history of those years.[43]

Fraser tries to break through this 'dominant historical mythology' by tracing the fate of these Jews. He uses the documentation surrounding the registration of orders against Jews to argue that the Island authorities were guilty of anti-Semitism, measures introduced against Jews becoming a legal normality. In this way he has uncovered the tragic stories of three individuals, stories which cannot be reconciled with the dominant discourse.

In a similarly critical vein, Madeleine Bunting published *The Model Occupation*, a journalistic examination of the Occupation. She uncovered oral testimonies of women who fraternised with German soldiers and some foreign workers, and suggests there is a great deal of hidden history beneath a 'collective memory which eschews all controversy and provides a version

---

[37] K.M. Bachmann, *The Prey of an Eagle: A Personal Record of Family Life written throughout the German Occupation of Guernsey, 1940-1945* (Guernsey, 1972), p.129.
[38] Molly Bihet, *A Child's War* (Guernsey, 1985), pp.10-12.
[39] Winifred Harvey, *The Battle of Newlands: The Wartime Diaries of Winifred Harvey* (Guernsey, 1995), p.51.
[40] Diaries of Violet Carey, 3 August 1940.
[41] K.M. Bachmann, *The Prey of an Eagle*, p.42.
[42] David Fraser, *The Jews of the Channel Islands and the Rule of Law* (Brighton, 2000), pp.145-7.
[43] Fraser, *The Fate of the Jews in the Channel Islands*, p.150.

of the Occupation behind which all Islanders – whatever their experience, be it evacuation, deportation or occupation – can rally'. As Fraser has done, she claims that the public collective memory which says 'everyone suffered and "did their bit" for the war effort'[44] is a myth and does not tell the whole truth'.[45] Bunting dismisses testimonies such as K.M. Bachmann's by claiming that they 'abide by clearly defined conventions'.[46]

More recently still, in 2007, a further study of the Occupation has been published by Dr Hazel Knowles Smith which has been described as the 'antidote to Madeleine Bunting's book'.[47] In *The Changing Face of the Channel Islands' Occupation*, Dr Knowles Smith seeks to 'take a balanced view at the set of circumstances'[48] as she examines the contentious issues that have arisen since Liberation. Her work is based on detailed research into a great deal of unpublished and published material, including many diaries, and gives credit to the Islanders and Island leaders for the way they coped with their ordeal.

This brief description of the historiography of the Occupation makes it clear that the question of collaboration has been and remains a much discussed and controversial issue. Since Liberation there has been a deeply troubled relationship between different representations of the Occupation of Guernsey and the tension has increased as certain individuals have published what they claim to be the 'truth'.

However, different versions of Occupation experience cannot be divided so simply into those which complement what Bunting calls the 'collective memory' and those which do not. Although the testimonies I have quoted show a preoccupation with the hardships of the Occupation, and the stoic way in which the Islanders coped, they are not confined entirely to the conventions of the discourse. In contrast to the depiction of Islanders as enduring the Occupation with heroic cheerfulness, feelings of desolation and depression are also recorded. Violet Carey wrote, 'I have the dismal feeling that England is always so casual and callous about her own people … We simply feel abandoned. How I sympathise with the unemployed, that awful feeling of being cast aside, not wanted, of no use.'[49] Other issues are recorded which are not generally discussed. Bachmann expresses compassion and yet helplessness about the foreign workers in the Island. She writes:

> The innocent victims of forced labour, these poor, half starved slaves roam the streets, bereft of human rights and human dignity. One provides a couple of them with a bowl of soup one day, only to find on the morrow a dozen on the doorstep when charity has ceased for lack of provisions. It is heart-breaking to have to send them slouching away empty and to know they will meet with a similar fate from house to house.[50]

Violet Carey mentions Islanders who collaborated with the Germans:

> Mrs Renault told me the woman next door has had her clothes stolen off the line, silk underwear. She washes for the Germans and they are always at the house, one walked into Mrs Renault's kitchen.[51]

---

[44] Madeleine Bunting, *The Model Occupation* (London, 1995), p.61.
[45] Bunting, *Model Occupation*, p.320.
[46] Bunting, *Model Occupation*, p.320.
[47] *Guernsey Press*, 10 February 2007.
[48] Hazel R. Knowles Smith, *The Changing Face of the Channel Islands Occupation: Record, Memory, Myth* (Basingstoke and New York, 2007)
[49] Violet Carey, 11 November 1944.
[50] Bachmann, *Prey of an Eagle*, p.109.
[51] Violet Carey, 3 December 1941.

There are also references in the personal sources to the anti-Jewish legislation ordered by the German authorities and registered by the Royal Court. In October 1940 Winifred Harvey recorded in her diary, 'The last order that made me feel quite sick was all the regulations against Jews which had to be passed and registered by the Royal Court this week.'[52] There are other clear examples of testimony which deviate from the public voice. John Dalmau was a Spanish prisoner of war forced to work as a slave under the Nazis in the Channel Islands, and he published his recollections of his experiences in a pamphlet.[53] Thus the voice that comes from individual stories does not fit quite so neatly into the collective memory. At times it endorses the echoes of cheerfulness that are displayed in the public discourse, but feelings of despair and sincere concern for the fate of others is also indicated.

It is noticeable that most of the well-known testimonies were written by upper-middle-class married women. This suggests that the dominant discourse does not encompass all types of Occupation experience. Until recently there has been an absence of accounts of working-class Islanders, many of whom were faced with the choice of starvation or work serving the German forces. Those women who chose to fraternise with German soldiers had every reason to conceal their experiences once the Islands were liberated and many chose to leave the Islands altogether. It is known that various Islanders collaborated, but their memories are rarely heard and their motivations can only be guessed at. The Occupation discourse that is on display is incomplete and represents only the dominant voices, the voices that want to be heard.

However, dismissing some experiences and implying that others are the truth, as Bunting has done in uncovering stories of collaboration, exposes problems in the use of personal testimony as a source of historical evidence. We must not allow any form of testimony to be seen as 'better' or 'purer' versions of the past, even though it comes from the very people who experienced it.[54] This is particularly problematic when the testimony in question is oral history, because one is dealing with 'the discolourations and encrustations of thirty odd years on'.[55] It must not be assumed that oral history can penetrate the 'heart of truth'[56] and that memories can have a clear space in which to speak. A better question is to ask why this controversy has arisen.

After Liberation, most Islanders simply wanted to reconstruct their devastated Island and return to normality. The Occupation had been a deeply distressing experience and the majority of Islanders simply did not want to remember it. Richard Heaume, now Director of the German Occupation Museum, grew up in the post-Occupation years and developed an interest in the Occupation after finding relics whilst working on the family farm. He remembers that most people who lived through the Occupation wanted to forget about it, which meant he managed to collect an impressive collection of artefacts the Germans had left behind because no one else wanted them.[57] The old Guernseyman, Ebenezer Le Page, in G.B. Edwards' fictional tale of Island life, illustrates this reluctance to speak about the Occupation and the desire to forget certain aspects of it when he says, 'There is a lot I don't remember, or only remember all mixed up; and some things I want to forget. I don't like people asking me questions about the Occupation, the way the visitors do. I say I don't know.'[58]

---

[52] Winifred Harvey, *The Battle of Newlands*, p.37.
[53] John Dalmau, *Slave Worker in the Channel Islands*.
[54] Joan Sangster, 'Telling our stories: feminist debates and the use of history', in Richard Perks and Alistair Thompson (eds), *Oral History Reader* (London and New York, 1998), p.88.
[55] Denise Riley, *War in the Nursery: Theories of Child and Mother* (London, 1983) p.191.
[56] Ibid.
[57] Interview with Richard Heaume, Director of the German Occupation Museum, Guernsey, 19 October 2001.
[58] G.B. Edwards, *The Book of Ebenezer Le Page* (London, 1982), p.338.

However, since the Islands were liberated there has been intense public interest from abroad in the behaviour of Island officials and individual Guernsey residents. As the Channel Islands were the only part of the United Kingdom to be occupied, this has been largely motivated by British people's fascination with how they might have behaved in the situation. Many Islanders have been made to feel that their memories are somehow on trial. Rollo Sherwill, a boy during the Occupation, has commented, 'Since the war we have felt like a woman must feel in a rape trial. People accuse her of having led the rapist on. But just as a woman might co-operate for fear of not surviving, so did we.'[59] Consequently a tone of justification has developed in Islanders' testimonies of the Occupation, creating an uneasy dichotomy of accusation and defence.

The Channel Islands stood uncomfortably, both metaphorically and literally, between Britain, the 'heroic' nation which prided itself on standing firm against the Nazi threat, and the countries of Occupied Europe which had fallen to the Nazi forces. Although Guernsey and the other Channel Islands had shared the experience of the defeated and occupied Continent, British and Guernsey people were keen to emphasise their shared national identity. In the immediate aftermath of the Occupation, investigations and statements were made about the conduct of the Islanders, and particularly the Authorities, during the period of occupation. The language of the statements reflects the tone of defence. At the first meeting of the States, John Leale, who had been the President of the Controlling Committee in the latter years of the Occupation, made a speech justifying how they had dealt with the circumstances, and emphasised that 'We were not trained as diplomats. We were simply pitch-forked into the task of adjusting the Island to a situation from which we, one and all, believed we were for all time safe ... Our policy was based on a realistic acceptance of a situation which we all deplored, but which we were powerless to prevent. Our task was not an inspiring one: the most we could do was make the best of a bad job.'[60] Following thorough investigations by the Home Office, a statement made in the House of Commons by the Home Secretary shortly after Liberation claimed that 'The Channel Islands have every reason to be proud of themselves and we have every reason to be proud of them.'[61]

However, at the same time there was a great deal of attention in the national media which scandalised the situation. Headlines cried, 'COLLABORATORS GET OFF SCOT FREE'[62] and 'PURGE NEEDED'.[63] Similarly, an MI5 report accused Island officials and civilians of collaboration, claiming, 'It seems beyond doubt that many of them went out of their way to be friendly, co-operative and helpful to the Germans, and there is no excuse for their behaviour.'[64] In defence of the two Islanders, Brigadier Snow, commander of the liberating forces, wrote, 'Generally speaking the report is merely a rehash of the tittle tattle prevalent in the Islands but which nobody is prepared to come forward and substantiate.'[65]

It is clear that, in an attempt to retain their sense of honour, dignity, and Island identity, Islanders became defensive about aspects of the Occupation which are in any way controversial, or which jeopardise their integrity. Defensive attitudes have created an etiquette of the

---

[59] Cited in Madeleine Bunting, *Model Occupation*, p.3.
[60] John Leale, *Report of Five Years of German Occupation*, Jurat Leale's address to the States of Guernsey on 23 May 1945. Also published in *Guernsey Evening Press*, 23 May 1945.
[61] PRO: HO 45/25844, Mr J. Chunter Ede, the Home Secretary's statement about the Channel Islands in the House of Commons, 17 August 1945.
[62] *Daily Herald*, 28 July 1945.
[63] *Daily Worker*, 11 July 1945.
[64] PRO: HO 45/22399, MI5 Report, 'The Channel Islands Under German Occupation'.
[65] PRO: HO 45/22399, Letter from Brigadier Snow to the Home Office in response to the MI5 report.

Occupation, a language within which memories can be expressed without dwelling on the painful or controversial experiences.

In recent years, however, the public representation of the Occupation has gradually changed, and the passing of time has produced a more complex perspective, particularly among people who did not experience the Occupation directly. This has enabled a development of public understanding. In the most recent published study of the Occupation, Dr Knowles Smith acknowledges that the perception of the past can be changed by the influence of others. She argues that the collective memory of the Occupation has been affected by information laid over the facts. In addition, it has been altered by factors such as literature, discussion of shared experience, and political requirements of the time.

Although Bunting's revelations of some of the private stories of fraternisation and collaboration has provoked intense controversy, she has brought these stories into the public sphere. Islanders have been forced to examine the implications, if only to defend themselves. The more controversial aspects of the Occupation have also been brought into the public sphere through the plots and themes of popular fiction. In 1991 Michael Couch published a trilogy which recalled a dying man's memories of a forbidden friendship with an enemy soldier. In 1999 Tim Binding's *Island Madness* depicted the social world of German officers and some Guernsey girls; intertwined with a love story and a thriller is an exploration of the moral choices that arise in a situation of occupation. Along with the opening of documents in the National Archives and the Island Archives in the mid '90s, this literature has contributed to the creation of a forum, indeed a language, within which the more controversial stories can be told. Consequently there has been more acceptance that acts of wrongdoing and collaboration occurred. A significant mark of this change in attitude is the recent public recognition of the suffering of certain groups of people. For example, on Holocaust Memorial Day in the year 2000, a plaque was dedicated in memory of the three Jews deported to Auschwitz. Similarly, in 2001 a memorial room was opened in the German Occupation Museum to acknowledge Islanders who suffered because they stood up to the Germans.

But attitudes of accusation and defence have not been eradicated. In January 1993, in response to reports in the national media of wholesale collaboration and black marketeering following the opening of the Guernsey war files in the National Archives, the Bailiff, Graham Dorey, claimed, 'These accusations grossly distort the whole character of life and of the civil administrations of Guernsey during the German Occupation.'[66] Similarly, the Holocaust Education Trust published a document which states that 'in Jersey and Guernsey co-operation and fraternisation with the Germans was the rule'.[67] An article in the *Guernsey Evening Press* responded with 'Don't rewrite our history' and commented that Islanders must fight for their reputations.[68] Miriam Mahy indignantly wrote to the *Guernsey Evening Press* and stated:

> Those responsible for compiling the new educational booklet are living in peacetime Britain. It is evident that they have no idea of the responsibilities and decisions that had to be made by Island leaders in time of war and enemy occupation, with the enemy always having the last word. I wish to add that the vast majority of Islanders

---

[66] *Guernsey Evening Press*, 6 January 1993.
[67] David Cesarini, *Britain and the Holocaust* (London, 1998), p.15.
[68] *Guernsey Evening Press*, 12 February 2001.

never collaborated or fraternised with the German occupying forces. To say otherwise is a downright lie. It must be of concern that these allegations are being presented as facts in the recorded history of Guernsey.[69]

Even Dr Knowles Smith's book continues the theme of accusation and defence as one of her aims was to set the record straight. Dr Knowles Smith is reported to have said that during her research she 'began to feel an injustice had been done ... it soon became clear to me that more recent representations were plainly wrong'.[70] Following publication of her book she was warned to expect controversy, and an examiner who took the opposite view to hers demanded that she change her argument or sacrifice her PhD. The emphasis on the controversy is also evident in a review of the book in the *Guernsey Press*. Headlines reported that 'Author risked her PhD to tell the truth' and claimed 'Islanders cleared of collaboration'.[71] The extent of the research and the balanced perspective of the author makes this study an important and commendable development in Occupation history, acknowledging as it does the existence of varying and contradictory experiences, but the dichotomy of accusation and defence is continued by the conclusion of the book, which defends the Islanders with a tone of justification: 'The Islanders' contemporary views and records, most primary source material, as well as the testimony of survivor-witnesses today, overwhelmingly support an honourable narrative of the Occupation history with a few blemishes.'[72]

Examination of the historiography of this period and the process that has caused the controversy highlights the sensitivity of the Occupation. Although recent historical study has diminished the conflict between Islanders trying to retain their sense of honour and accusations of collaboration, the issue has not been eradicated and it has been difficult to take historical understanding further and look at how the Occupation affected life and society.

By looking at Occupation testimonies and considering the discourses which influenced them, it is possible to learn more about this period of history as it increases our understanding of why Islanders expressed themselves or behaved in certain ways.[73] An influential discourse is the attitudes of the Island Authorities towards the situation and the language employed to promote a national image for the Islanders to adopt. The lack of military strength and resources meant there was no way of creating any kind of resistance movement in the Island. The only option was some kind of relationship with the Germans enabling the civilian population to co-exist with the enemy. Sherwill, the Attorney-General in Guernsey, announced at the first States meeting of the Occupation, attended by the German Commandant Dr Lanz, that this was to be a 'model occupation': 'on the one hand tolerance on the part of the military authority and courtesy and correctness on the part of the occupying forces, and, on the other, dignity and courtesy and exemplary behaviour on the part of the civilian population'.[74] The language of 'dignity and courtesy' on the part of the civilian population is evident in several personal accounts. For example, on 17 April 1941 Violet Carey wrote:

> Prince von Oettingen called on the Countess Blucher, he knew a number of her people ... When he was going, he asked if he could call again. She said, 'No, when

---

[69] *Guernsey Evening Press*, 21 February 2001.
[70] *Guernsey Press*, 10 February 2007.
[71] Ibid.
[72] Knowles Smith, *The Changing Face of the Channel Islands Occupation*, p.254.
[73] This idea is proposed by Penny Summerfield in *Reconstructing Women's Wartime Lives: Discourse and Subjectivity in Oral Histories of the Second World War* (Manchester,1998).
[74] *Billet d'Etat 1940*, 7 August 1940, The Greffe, Guernsey.

peace was declared and happier times came again she would welcome him warmly, but until then, she could not receive him.' I do *like* her dignified attitude. So different from some of the people who accept cigarettes and cigarette coupons from them.[75]

However, courtesy can be interpreted differently and could be exploited to extend to fraternisation, which is likely to have been the way that the 'people who accept cigarettes ... from them' interpreted the word. One example of Bunting's illustrates the different interpretation of courtesy:

> Don Guilbert ... recounts the story of a local musician who suffered from a skin disease on his hands. 'A German gave him some ointment and in order to thank him the musician invited the German to his home. The musician's teenage daughter met the German and started going to concerts with him – but it was no more than that. Was that wrong? The German was a musician and the girl was something of a singer. The German went to the family to make music. What should the man have done? Not accept the ointment?'[76]

In many circumstances, courtesy was irrelevant. Dr Knowles Smith claims that far from being a 'model' occupation, the Islanders had no choice but to obey the Germans. 'Any serious resistance or disobedience would have ... carried the risk, as it did on the Continent ... of imprisonment or execution for sabotage, or inclusion on the list of undesirables, ready to be used as potential hostages or candidates for deportation.[77] Indeed, this did not remain just a threat, as in September 1942 and again in February 1943 a number of Islanders were deported to Germany. Clearly, fear and uncertainty influenced the way the Islanders understood and dealt with their situation.

Memories can also be influenced by the discourses of later years. Guernsey people have incorporated the spirit of the British war effort and the idea of the war as 'Britain's finest hour' into their memories. Beryl Ozanne, who worked as a nurse throughout the Occupation, wrote in the introduction to her memoir, 'Every man, woman and child just *had* to make the best of things.'[78] This is again contradicted by the circumstances which caused people to collaborate or fraternise, such as the sheer desperation for food. The loneliness among women whose men had joined up was a factor, and another influence was the attraction of being on good terms with the Germans; being associated with a German gave both security and privileges such as being allowed out after curfew and access to luxury goods.

The different representations of the German Occupation are intimately entangled, and even when the contradictions of accusation and defence cannot be reconciled, all versions are valid. The existence of these contradictions must be acknowledged, along with the understanding that individuals experienced the Occupation in different ways. As Ebenezer Le Page says:

> The visitors who come over to Guernsey nowadays know more about the German Occupation than I do. They have read the books. They know exactly what happened and what didn't, and the whys and the wherefores, and who was wrong and who was

---

[75] The Prince von Oettingen was one of the German officers. The Countess Blucher was of German origin but her family had moved to Guernsey in the time of Bismarck because they did not agree with his policies. She was an acquaintance of Violet Carey's.
[76] Bunting, *Model Occupation*, p.55.
[77] Knowles Smith, *The Changing Face of the Channel Islands Occupation*, p.46.
[78] Beryl Ozanne, *A Peep Behind the Screens* (Guernsey, 1994), p.2.

right. I don't. There are those who say, 'Oh you poor things! It must have been an awful time,' and I say 'Well it was and it wasn't.' There are those who say, 'After all, you didn't have such a bad time hob-nobbing with the Germans,' and I say, 'Well some did and some didn't.'[79]

It is imperative to acknowledge that actions, attitudes and remembrances, both during the Occupation and after it, form a complicated and varied mosaic. So much attention has been paid to the question of collaboration that questions about how the Occupation affected Island society have barely been discussed. Whether the Occupation changed individual Islanders' perspectives, and their opinions and values, is yet to be investigated.

I am in a privileged position as I am in possession of Violet Carey's detailed diary which spans the whole of the Occupation period. While I am affected by the complex arguments that surround the history of the Occupation today, and cannot escape from prejudices that I have developed in response to the controversy, Violet Carey's diary is not. Analysis of her diary will help us look at the Occupation in new ways by examining how it affected her life and her values.

In attempting to use one diary to further historical understanding of the Occupation, I could be accused of hypocrisy, having criticised Madeleine Bunting for dismissing some forms of testimony and prioritising others. However, I acknowledge that the study of one woman's experience will not account for all the experiences of the Occupation. The public memory will always remain controversial and contradictory accounts will always exist. In the analysis of one story, I do not dismiss the validity of other stories. But I hope that the diaries of Violet Carey will help to change the way that historians, particularly those from outside the Islands, look at the Occupation.

The View of one who was there: A Biography of Violet Carey

Violet Carey was one of many Islanders who recorded her experiences of the Occupation in a diary. She wrote almost every day for the duration of the Occupation and has provided a document which gives an illuminating insight into one woman's experience of the alien situation that the people of Guernsey endured in the Second World War. It has been difficult to gather information about Violet Carey's early life, as her surviving family now succeed her by two generations, but the fragments that I have collected and the memories of the few people alive today who remember her give the impression of high social status in the Island community and a strong personality.

The people who remember Violet have said that their most lasting impressions are of her sense of humour and her slightly eccentric nature. I had a wonderful conversation with three Islanders who knew her: Diana de Jersey, Liz McIntyre and Pam Browne.[80] One memory that provoked much laughter was about how Violet used to think it terribly funny to stand in the Arcade in St Peter Port and gaze intently up at the sky, as though she was looking at something incredibly interesting. People would gather round and look up to see what was so fascinating and Violet would promptly walk away leaving them looking rather bewildered! This sense of humour is one of the most delightful characteristics of the diaries. One of many examples is a comment made on *29 May 1943*:

---

[79] G.B. Edwards, *The Book of Ebenezer Le Page*, p.333.
[80] Interview with Diana de Jersey, Liz McIntyre and Pam Browne, 20 October 2001.

Katty came to fetch her bread. She was talking in a loud voice in the yard and the Rhode Island Red cock was beside her. Every time she spoke loudly, he crowed loudly, he *was* going to be cock in his own yard. It was too funny for words. Katty had to stop talking. She was completely defeated.

Violet's appearance also seems to have given the impression that she was slightly eccentric. Pam Browne remembers her cottage loaf hairstyle and rather odd attire. She said that Violet was 'no dresser', and 'looked like nothing on earth'! This impression is also conveyed in the diaries:

August 19th 1940
Whenever any of us are depressed and we are together, we always discuss what our feelings would be like when we hear the first phone call! … then we discuss the arrival of the boat and what we shall wear. It won't matter in the least whether it is pouring with rain, or brilliant sunshine. Katty has a whole length of pale pink satin to have made up! I can't make up my mind whether I shall be a sweet young thing in blue, or a perfect darling in brown! I think it will be brown because I have a beautiful scarf covered all over with Union Jacks, a bright red handkerchief with a crown on it, an exceedingly vulgar taste red, white and blue brooch, and a pair of gloves with the King and Queen on the fasteners; all these I wore on Coronation Day.

Although Violet was obviously a little eccentric, however, she was far from dotty. There is a sense of self-awareness in this mild eccentricity and some of her descriptions of herself have a gentle tone of self-mockery:

October 19th 1941
Booty Ozanne was very funny at bridge the other day. She was playing with Olive and Vera and Maud Drake. Booty looked at Vera and, in a voice of sincere admiration, Booty said, 'What a blessing it is to see a double chin nowadays!' Vera didn't know whether to be pleased or annoyed. Booty and Olive always muffle up their necks in scarves, they 'can't bear seeing scraggy necks,' says Olive severely to me. I maintain I have *not* a scraggy neck, but a firm chin and a well defined jawbone, denoting the innate strength of my character and the perfect oval of my face! Katty is always telling me what a beautiful figure she has now, so I am going to tell people what a beautiful face *I* have!

It is unlikely that it was Violet's face that denoted the strength of her character, but perhaps it was her self-confidence. This is another aspect of her personality that she is remembered for. Violet's daughter, the late Mrs Michelle Nixon, describes her as strong-minded, wilful and indomitable.[81] Indeed the only clear memory that another relative, Susan Marks, has of her is that she was absolutely terrifying![82] Although she was intimidating at times, Violet's strength of character also seems to have inspired confidence in those who knew her. This is demonstrated by the response of some of her neighbours to her firm resolution to stay in the Island despite the opportunity to evacuate when the German advances in France became a serious threat to the Channel Islands:

It went all round the Parish that I had said I had had a very good breakfast and I was blowed if I was going away. A great many said as long as I stayed in the Parish, they would stay and they still say it.[83]

---

[81] Interview with Michelle Nixon (Violet Carey's daughter), 26 July 2000.
[82] Interview with Susan Marks, 23 August 2001.
[83] Actually written in retrospect on 20 June 1941.

Violet Mary Carey was a well-respected member of the Island community and belonged to one of the upper-middle-class Island families. She was born into the de Sausmarez family on 23 August 1880, at Le Granges de Beauvoir in St Peter Port. Her parents were Thomas de Sausmarez and Mary née Mallock and she had one older brother, Arthur, who was known as 'Teddy'.[84] Violet spent her early life at 'Springfield' in Queen's Road, St Peter Port.

Violet was a founder pupil at the Ladies' College in Guernsey, a school modelled on Cheltenham Ladies' College, and she was educated there until she was eighteen. While she was not particularly academic, Violet was undoubtedly intelligent and her diaries and letters show a remarkable ability to write well. She took great pleasure in literature and poetry and was extremely well read. Indeed the enjoyment that reading gave her is evident from the frequent references to literature she made in her diaries.

The early part of Violet's wartime diaries give a sense of her lifestyle before the Germans invaded the Island. It would seem that she led a leisurely life; much of her time was spent in visiting friends, playing mah jong, reading, writing letters and receiving visitors at home. Her two earlier diaries, which she only managed to keep up for a few months of 1906 and 1907, are filled with descriptions of riding, cycling and walking around the Island and climbing and scrambling along the coastline with friends. The diaries also record some of the parties and dances she went to, although, according to her daughter, 'she wasn't madly social and got quite bored with that sort of thing'.[85] Sport was another pastime she enjoyed. The early diaries mention frequent games of tennis and badminton. In approximately 1906 she captained Guernsey's first ladies cricket team.

Violet Carey and her Ladies Cricket Team (Violet is the lady in the centre holding the bat).

---

[84] 'L'Enseigne De Noble Homme De Sausmarez Fût Dressé Sur Le Pinacle De St Martin AD 1199'. Family tree of the de Sausmarez family, consulted by kind permission of Patricia Paxton.
[85] Interview with Michelle Nixon, 26 July 2000.

James Frederick Carey.

On 29 October 1913 Violet married a Guernseyman, James Frederick Carey, whom she had met at kindergarten. He had been educated at Elizabeth College in Guernsey and then at Wellingore Hall in Lincolnshire, 'a school for the sons of gentlemen to prepare them for life in the colonies'.[86] At the age of 18 he was sent to Canada as a 'greenhorn' and eventually set up a ranch with another Guernseyman, Eugène Carey, in the town of Greenshan, Alberta. However, he had been engaged to Violet before he went to Canada and he gave up everything to return to Guernsey and marry her. On his return to Guernsey, James started up a farm at Les Merriennes in the Forest parish and became a successful farmer and cattle breeder. In 1935 he was elected a Jurat of the Royal Court, an appointment of great prestige in the Island. He was also the President of the Guernsey Farmers' Association and a member of various other States' Committees.

James and Violet Carey lived at Les Merriennes throughout their married life. They had two children: Michelle, known as 'Baba', and Jim, known as 'Boy'. Both children joined the services in the Second World War and so were absent from the Island during the Occupation. Michelle had trained as a nurse and joined the QAIMNS. She was posted on HMHC *Worthing*, a hospital carrier, and was sent to West Africa later in the war. Jim joined the Army and was a gunner. Violet herself rarely left Guernsey and was very protective of the Island and its community. She hated people who were critical of the Island and seems to have been rather insular; her eldest granddaughter, Patricia Paxton, remembers being told how Violet refused to 'know' a person until they had lived in the Island for at least five years.[87]

---

[86] William Wilfred Carey, Edith Frances Carey and Spencer Carey Curtis, *The History of the Careys of Guernsey* (London, 1938), p.206.
[87] Interview with Patricia Paxton, 31 December 2000.

Michelle Carey

Jim Carey – 'Boy'.

As a member of one of the most prominent Guernsey families, Violet had grown up in a house with staff and had never had to do household duties. As a married woman in her own home she ran her household, but had little to do with domestic duties as the family were in a position to have maids to do the cooking and cleaning. Indeed, it has been a source of amusement in the family that Violet did not know how to do most household tasks. Even during the Occupation she had Mrs Mauger, a char lady, and Mrs Renault, a daily maid, to do the housework. Surprisingly, given the social milieu, Violet's husband James, who had learnt how to live on the bare essentials whilst on his ranch in Canada, did most of the cooking.

Although little substantial evidence survives, Violet seems to have been involved with various Island committees. In her 1940 diary she describes being on a panel for choosing the new headmistress for the Guernsey Ladies' College, which suggests she was a school governor and a shareholder. She was a member of the Ladies' College Old Girls' Committee and the Mothers' Union. She was also involved with the Nicholas Carey Trust, a fund left by the late Nicholas Carey for the purpose of helping 'fallen' women. According to Sheila James, she had a great social conscience and was concerned for the welfare of others, regardless of their class status.[88] Michelle Nixon explained how Violet had a store of medicines which she would administer to people in need.[89]

Violet started to write her diary regularly in May 1940. She wrote detailed descriptions of her own activities and weekly routine which mainly comprised fetching the bread and the groceries and visiting people. In August 1940 she started to walk into St Peter Port on a weekly basis to visit friends and relatives and to do shopping in town. The people she spoke to inspired many of the stories and rumours that she recorded. She also related any new orders that were publicised, news

---

[88] Interview with Sheila James, 28 December 2000.
[89] Interview with Michelle Nixon, 26 July 2000.

that she heard on the radio or read in the paper, and her own opinions. It should be remembered that Violet would not often have known exactly what was happening, especially as rumour and speculation were rife. She did, however, often give further explanation of events as she heard more information. She also corrected herself if she found she had written something incorrect.

Violet Carey's diaries give us an insight into how the Occupation changed the lifestyle of an upper-middle-class lady in Guernsey. They depict the hardships of life under the conditions imposed by the arrival of the enemy and the generally dignified reaction amongst the Guernsey people towards their invaders. The general attitude of the Islanders she portrays is a valiant acceptance of circumstances and refusal to give up hope. Violet wrote with a remarkably down to earth style, which serves to highlight both her strong character and her optimistic, yet realistic, attitude to her situation. At times the diary entries are light-hearted and illustrate the humour and delight that she and many of her friends and acquaintances took in defying the Germans by politely, but firmly, sticking to their principles. Yet, whilst never indulging in self-pity, Violet does describe the misery that Islanders experienced as prisoners on their own Island. With an eloquent and poignant turn of phrase, she expresses the lethargy and depression that many, including herself, suffered, intensified by fear of the unknown and the terrible feeling of isolation from England, relatives and the rest of the war.

The diaries seem to be an honest account of events and do not disguise incidents of scandal and misconduct on the part of the Islanders, or the humanity of the Germans. Similarly, Violet displays a strong sense of approval towards what she saw as good conduct, and disapproval towards any incident or behaviour she considered to be unwise. Indeed, she was remarkably outspoken and there are occasions when she was very critical of others. Mr Finey, the rector of the Forest parish church, prompted some barbed comments in relation to the closure of the church in 1940. However, it should be pointed out that Violet was not always aware of other people's circumstances and, to her credit, if she discovered her critical words had been unfair, she would say so; she spoke very highly of Mr Finey later on in the Occupation when the church re-opened. Similarly, Violet was critical of Mr Sherwill, the President of the Controlling Committee, at the beginning of the Occupation, but later claimed that 'after cursing Mr Sherwill up and down I will have to put him on my honours list'.[90]

It is interesting to speculate about the Germans' reaction should these diaries have been found during the Occupation. Certainly there is a sense of fear of this, and Violet mentions that she actually slept on the diaries to keep them hidden. In 1945 her bedroom was ransacked and some food supplies stolen, but on hearing of the break-in she said her Red Cross parcel was the least of her worries; she thought first of her jewellery and her diaries. I suspect that had these diaries fallen into the wrong hands, Violet may well have found herself in serious trouble.[91]

Due to the sheer amount that Violet wrote, this is a heavily edited version of the original diaries. I have tried to ensure the entries I have included retain the sense of her character and represent the range of topics she wrote about. Much that has been omitted is simply more of the same, or lengthy transcriptions of letters and newspaper and radio reports. Where there is too little explanation of the events that Violet refers to, I have included explanatory footnotes based on my own research in the published histories, newspapers and archive records. I have also included a description of the principal people mentioned in the diaries to give more information about the main characters. I hope this will help readers understand the diaries more clearly.

---

[90] See entry for 19 October 1940.
[91] See entry for 19 January 1945 and 11 December 1943.

What the Diaries tell us

It is quickly apparent when reading Violet Carey's diaries that one of her reasons for writing was to record the events of the time. She went to great effort to transcribe notices, orders and articles from the paper and wrote detailed descriptions of her daily activities and the stories she heard. Violet's daughter, the late Michelle Nixon, commented that Violet wanted her diaries to be read by others and went as far as reading sections of it to people herself.

The diary shows that its author was highly educated and well read and the way events are described and characters depicted show she had a certain skill for writing. Indeed there is a sense of the dramatic in the way Violet inscribes herself into a story and depicts herself and other Islanders as triumphant victors. She seems to have used the diary to make her experience of the Occupation into a literary form; this enabled her to keep her sense of identity and champion normal life.

The uncertainty and threat that the invasion caused to Islanders' lives must have challenged the meanings they had traditionally assumed. Islanders had to find new meanings to attach to their present circumstances and this involved finding new forms of language to express themselves. Certain types of language were adopted in the way Islanders talked about and wrote about the Occupation. In the same way that certain discourses have developed and dominated since Liberation, these forms of language developed into linguistic frameworks, or discourses, which provided comfortable and acceptable modes of expression at the time. I suggest that by drawing on and contributing to these modes of expression, Islanders were able to express and make sense of their circumstances, and maintain a level of control.

Violet Carey's diary reveals a variety of such modes of expression and gives an insight into how Islanders discussed the Occupation at the time. An entry written shortly after the Red Cross ship relieved the Islands from the desperate food shortage reflects on the past four years of occupation and illustrates two dominant modes of expression which Islanders used to help maintain a spirit of optimism and to hide feelings of depression and desolation.

> *December 31st 1944*
> And 1944 has come to an end and we are still in captivity. But what a difference the arrival of that ship has made to our morale. No longer do we feel utterly desolate and deserted, apart from the horror of starvation, we felt that no one cared a scrap about us. This year has been very very grim, but our hopes are high for 1945. And that is one of the most striking examples of God's love for us. Every time we were more depressed, something happened, a rumour, whether it was false or true, would come and lift us out of depression. Or we would hear a piece of good news. We were always being carried along like that. And yet *everybody* felt on no account must they show their feelings.
>
> Everybody laughed and was as bright as anything in Town or when they were together. Nobody grumbled, everybody made the best of our really appalling conditions. The universal motto has been right through the Occupation, 'We will show the Germans we can take it.'

The fact that 'everybody laughed' implies that humour was an important aspect of conversation. The emphatic statement that '*everybody* felt on no account must they show their feelings', and the apparent determination to 'show the Germans we can take it', suggest that maintaining a brave face was a matter of honour and became the accepted way to behave.

Conversation conformed to an etiquette within her social circle, and by developing an understanding of what these discourses meant to Violet an analysis of the diaries might also reflect deeper social issues faced by Islanders.

The importance of humour to Violet Carey during the war is illustrated by the frequent anecdotes and jokes she relates in describing her daily activities and the way that she depicts observations in a light-hearted tone. In an environment where normal life was repressed, these anecdotes provided light relief:

> *April 7th 1943*
> Peggy told me a story that has come from German sources. Goering thought London was razed to the ground by his Luftwaffe and wanted to see for himself, so he went in a plane to London. They passed over a town which was flattened and he rubbed his hands and said, 'Gut! Gut! My Luftwaffe has done well indeed.' The pilot got very red and said, 'I am sorry your Excellency, we have half an hour more to go, that town is Wilhelmshaven!'

> *September 24th 1943*
> A perfect day. Hot, sunny and no wind. Mary and Violet came out to tea. Mary told me a lovely story about the doctors. Five of them drove out to Grande Rocque. Dressed in singlets and shorts they marched past the sentry singing a German song lustily, they were led by Dr Rose. They had a lovely bathe, formed up again and marched past the sentry again singing more loudly than ever. The sentry took no notice of them and let them go by.[92]

However, these jokes are not simply light relief. They reflect an attitude of non-confrontational resistance which united Islanders against the enemy in a way that protected their identity and insularity. To Violet, even the animals in Guernsey were superior to the Germans:

> *October 10th 1942*
> Mrs Mauger said Mrs Hazell's cow goes nearly mad with fright when they pass her in the road. That is understandable, a self-respecting aristocratic Guernsey cow, who is probably a connoisseur of smells, objecting to the odour she meets![93]

The humour serves to reinforce boundaries between 'them' and 'us', by setting apart and invalidating the behaviour and ideas of those 'not like us'.

Many of the humorous anecdotes in Violet Carey's diaries are not about the Germans, but about the effects of the Occupation on Islanders' way of life, habits and appearance:

> *August 23rd 1944*
> Peggy, Micque and Mrs Sherbrooke came to M-J. How hilarious and joyous we were, our play was almost erratic … How we all enjoyed it. We were discussing what our behaviour will be like when we go out to dinner or lunch parties again. After we have had our soup, we will automatically retain our spoons, exclaiming, 'I must use this again.' We have to wash up in cold water, then we will ignore our knives and use our spoons. Also we will watch each other all the time and if anybody leaves anything, we will say, 'Are you going to leave that, I will finish it up.' If we see anybody crumbing

---

[92] Mary and Violet were Hedley Hamon's daughters and had worked for Violet before the Occupation.
[93] Mrs Mauger was Violet's char lady. Mrs Hazell was a neighbour.

white bread, we will scream at them, 'Don't do *that*, bread is more precious than gold.' Then we will look at the food and say, 'O ... h, don't talk, I want to get down to this and enjoy it,' and then the only sounds we shall hear will be 'O ... .h, u ... m!' At tea we shall say, 'Let me smell the tea pot, what a delicious smell' and to each other we shall say politely, 'Do lick your knife, would you care to lick the jam spoon, of course, lick up your crumbs!' I'm sure that is the way we shall go on. Mrs Sherbrooke said her husband will go to her mantelpiece and say, 'What is all this muck?' and she will meekly say, 'Those are my cigarette ends dear, I am drying them!'[94]

The humour is also reflected in the way Violet described herself:

September 27th 1943
I am now suffering from occupational dottiness. James was out in the evening, I fetched my water and I said firmly to myself, 'I must *not* lock the door,' and was only brought to my senses later by an indignant James shouting outside my window to be let in. I place things so I fall over them to remind myself either to carry them up or downstairs. I fall over them all right, swear hard and leave them where they are!

December 4th 1943
I am feeling full of mortification. My pride is in the dust. For over 62 years I have boasted that I have never had *a chilblain*, that I have never known what it was like to suffer from chilblains, and privately and silently hoped that I *should* never have the ugly things on my hands! Today I have three chilblains on my hands, they are as ugly as possible as well as being painful.

These humorous anecdotes give an interesting insight into the detrimental effect of the Occupation on Violet and other Islanders. The way it caused Islanders to live in a more primitive manner was an assault on the dignity that Violet and her acquaintances had learned from their upper-middle-class social education. Violet's self-deprecating tone and the image of herself as a dotty old lady frantically licking up crumbs suggest that making these pathetic and pitiful afflictions funny enabled her to cope with them. Humour masks the offence that forgetting things and licking up crumbs gave to her dignity.

The discourse of humour does, however, have wider implications, and reflects the stories of heroic endurance that have become a part of the dominant public memory since Liberation. Indeed, the attitude of humour is likely to have contributed to the creation of the 'heroic' story that has been written off as a cover-up. However, this was simply a mode of thinking, a way of talking about, and a means of coping with the Occupation.

Another influence on Violet Carey's writing which served to maintain the sense of Island identity is the principle of honour. The importance of honour in the situation whereby people of one nationality are occupied by people of an enemy nationality is demonstrated in Ambrose Sherwill's speech to the States at the beginning of the Occupation. Sherwill announced that this was to be a 'model occupation', 'on the one hand tolerance on the part of the military authority and courtesy and correctness on the part of the occupying forces, and, on the other, dignity and courtesy and exemplary behaviour on the part of the civilian population'.[95] This is a clear example of how the Island authorities expected the Islanders to behave. The principle of

---

[94] 'M-J' refers to mah-jong. Peggy, Micque and Mrs Sherbrooke were friends of Violet's.
[95] *Billet d'Etat 1940*, The Greffe, Guernsey, 7 August 1940.

honour and correct conduct became an etiquette, another linguistic framework, within which the German Occupation and the whole war could be discussed in an acceptable way.

The following extracts illustrate the role of honour in Violet Carey's narrative:

> *May 8th 1942*
> Bobbie told me that Cissie would only see the German soldiers who were billeted on them in the kitchen, she would not allow them to go anywhere else. I do admire Cissie for that. She did not accept anything from them.[96]

> *October 24th 1942*
> Mrs Mauger told me of a family who have a soldier billeted on them and with whom they have become very friendly. They have a little girl with whom he is very friendly. He was stroking her hair one day and he said, 'If Hitler ordered me to shoot this little girl I would shoot her.' I am glad to say they had the spunk to turn him out of their room and to have nothing more to do with him.

These extracts give a strong sense of Violet's opinion of correct behaviour. Comments such as 'I am glad to say' and 'I do like her dignified attitude' show an appreciation and approval for people who responded to the Germans in an honourable and dignified manner. She also showed disapproval towards those who behaved dishonourably and a desire that such people should be brought to justice:

> *March 6th 1941*
> Olive had three tables of Bridge, the usual people. I had tea with them and then I went to see Aunt Edith and Vera. Vera told me that the 'Black Hand' had three down on the list. She said with much relish, they are all going to be thrown into the harbour with bricks round their necks so they won't come up again![97]

> *May 18th 1941*
> Yves Cattaroche came to see James to try and get James to help him, of course James couldn't help him. He had got drunk last night at the Caves de Bordeaux and he had brought a bottle of spirits through a German soldier, he had it in his pocket and went out, met a policeman who snatched the bottle out of his pocket, and he knocked the policeman down! So of course he is for it. James said to him, 'What can I do to help you? You were in the wrong, and what I *can't* understand is how you men can accept favours from the German soldiers, and you fought in the last war too!' I *was* so glad James said that. Yves said, 'They all give the German soldiers 1s. and they get the spirits for us.' The Guernseymen are not allowed to buy spirits. It is not only poor workmen who accept favours from the German soldiers, quite decent people accept cigarette coupons from [them], even though their own men are away fighting. It is annoying.

> *December 24th 1942*
> James came home with the rumour that the German Civil Authorities have received over 100 anonymous letters from people in Guernsey telling them of hidden wireless, and that they have said they must take notice and that is why the notice about the wireless has appeared in the paper. The Gadarene swine. Oh! I do hope somebody will find out who sent the letters.

---

[96] Bobbie Seabrooke and Cissie Brock were friends of Violet.
[97] Edith Carey was James' sister-in-law. Vera was her daughter. The 'Black Hand' was someone making a list of collaborators.

The attitude of maintaining honour and not befriending the Germans becomes particularly interesting in an anecdote which shows recognition of the social values of one of the enemy:

> *October 23rd 1942*
> I went to Le Noury's at 11.20am, they were all there. They had the most amazing story to tell about Mrs Sherbrooke. In the flat above her lives a German Naval Officer, a man about 60, she had never spoken to him. One day this week he sent his servant to ask her if he could come and see her; she said, 'Yes,' and wondered what on earth he wanted to see her for. He came, she said if he hadn't been an enemy, she would have described him as a charming man. He saluted and said, 'I have just come back from Paris, this parcel is for you. Ask me no questions and don't tell anybody,' saluted and departed. She opened the parcel and it contained a perfect photograph of her husband in uniform, a lovely photograph of her youngest son who is 15 at school. She can't get over it and has told everybody and shown the photograph to everybody.

Despite the inference that this German was a charming man and probably had a social status that would have commanded respect from Violet Carey and her contemporaries, he was not respected in principle, *because* he was the enemy. The idea of principle is an important one as it suggests that behaving honourably in relation to the enemy was linked to a strong sense of what was and was not acceptable to say. Undoubtedly, certain things were deemed improper to speak of:

> *March 26th 1943*
> Katty came at supper time to ask for some loads of manure. She made Mrs Mauger so angry last Saturday as she used the expression 'If we win.' Mrs Mauger was like a turkey cock when she told me about it. With great stateliness and dignity she said, 'I said to Miss Connellan that such an idea had never entered my head and if it had, never, never would it have passed my lips.'

Significantly, there are times when Violet seems to deviate slightly from the neatly cut boundaries of honourable and dishonourable conduct. During the shortage of food, she relents slightly in the way she describes people who work for the Germans:

> *May 9th 1943*
> Mrs Renault is terribly upset about the bread ration.[98] Everybody is, of course, people who work for the Germans will get a double ration of everything. Of course it is a very clever way of getting people to work for them. I can't help thinking in my mind if the boys who are sacrificing their lives for us in the East were to stop and say they could not fight because their food supplies and *their water* had not come up, as I am sure has happened sometimes, where would we all be? The people here are saying they can't work and they don't know what they will do, etc., etc. Certainly the Germans have chosen the surest way to create a panic among the labouring classes.

Although Violet retained great admiration for those who made honourable sacrifices, and there is a sense of disrespect for the panic among Islanders when the circumstances of the

---

[98] On 7 May 1943 there had been a notice in the *Star* announcing that the bread ration for the civilian population was to be halved.

boys in the East was so much worse, she does seem to have understood the power of the incentive in the circumstances, particularly for people such as the labourers who were worse off than herself. She seems also to have understood how food shortages forced some people to participate in underground activities which would not normally have been considered acceptable:

> *December 23rd 1943*
> I went to lunch at Berthelot Street and had lunch with the woman who keeps the barter shop in Collenette boot stores … She said, 'Lots goes on that we know nothing about.' I said, 'Small blame to them, we are all pirates.'

The reference to pirates suggests she was aware that the deprivation imposed by the Occupation had affected their notion of civilised behaviour. This understanding shows a remarkable independence as Violet expressed individual opinions which did not conform to the code of honour.

Other issues in relation to honour are at stake and blur the boundaries still further:

> *April 13th 1943*
> Before I wash up I guiltily hide and lick the vegetable spoons! I was much comforted to find Olive doing exactly the same thing, 'Bless you,' she said, 'We all lick the spoons!' We don't need any vim or rinso now for grease: there isn't any grease. We carefully scrape off any from bowls and put it on a saucer. We eat all the crumbs. We don't lick our plates and that is all we do not do!

While these examples do reflect a form of ironic humour derived from the effect of the Occupation on lifestyle, the shortage of food was causing Violet to behave in a way she would never have dreamt of before. Contextualised in this way, the example suggests that a series of events was beginning to change Islanders' principles, their priority now being to carry on with their lives, not least because there was nothing else they could do. The priority for Violet was having enough to eat. The diaries reveal other occasions when Violet was forced to deviate from her high standards:

> *October 8th 1944*
> James had gone and Cyril had gone up with the milk. I never thought of locking the door. I heard someone in the kitchen, went out to see and there was that detestable soldier who came last Sunday. There was a bucket of apples under the table. He asked for some and I had to give them to him, so now I shan't be able to boast any longer that I have not given the Germans anything, it is *sickening* but I was absolutely alone. He took three large ones, peeled them and put them in his pocket, he kept saying, 'Sehr gut, sticky.' I suppose he did not want his lovely comrades to see he had apples! He asked for matches and milk and I said, nix milk and nix matches. He held out his dirty hand for me to shake but I avoided that and showed him out, and he went away quite peaceably. They are pests.

Clearly, to give this German soldier apples was against her principles, but Violet was more fearful of her personal safety and self-preservation forced her to do something that deviated from her standards. Violet's understanding of the necessity of self-preservation can be seen in her disapproval of acts of outward resistance:

> *January 22nd 1941*
> I was out in the front and Mr Ransson arrived, we chatted for some time and he began shouting about the Germans. I felt horribly inhospitable but I just *could not* ask him in. I can't bear that sort of thing, it is so dangerous and so stupid, so I let him go.

All these examples demonstrate that Violet prioritised self-preservation over honour, despite her socially inherited notion of the importance of honourable conduct, when faced with a situation which threatened her own survival. Throughout the history of the German Occupation of Guernsey there were time when all the ambivalences of the period were forced into focus, and the Liberation of the Islands in May 1945 was a moment when the Islanders, media and, subsequently, historians judged each other's conduct and treated each other accordingly. People who behaved honourably were treated with respect and those who collaborated were ostracised.

It is this enforcement of specific categories that makes the historiography of the Occupation so problematic. But are these categories inadequate? Violet Carey's diary shows that two discourses relating to honour influenced her narrative. The inherited moral code of honour and correct behaviour that seems to have been an inherent part of her character had a strong bearing on the way she dealt with a situation where that honour was jeopardised; in contrast, the shortage of food and hunger, and any situation in which her personal safety was threatened, caused minor deviations from this moral code, and show how circumstances can subtly affect behaviour. Indeed, it is important to bear in mind that Violet was relatively well off financially and so could probably have afforded to pay inflated prices for black market food. Also, she would have had direct access to produce from their farm. The problem of food shortage was much more acute for poorer families and residents in the Town. Considering this, it is possible to see how Islanders who were in a much more precarious situation than Violet may have behaved in a way that was deemed 'dishonourable' after the Occupation.

Looking at the diary in this way demonstrates that the focus on the question of collaboration and the dichotomy of accusation and defence, which has dominated public and historical opinion about the Occupation, does not accurately represent the experiences of the Islanders who lived through it. I would argue that there is a misunderstanding of how the Occupation affected Islanders' concept of time. The acute shortages of food, the uncertainty of the outcome of the war, and the danger that the Germans posed to Islanders caused a change in their sense of futurity. The people of Guernsey were presented with a situation whereby they could not rely on next month, next week or even tomorrow, as they had been used to doing. The main concern was survival, and consequently, at times, even relatively privileged Islanders, such as Violet Carey, were unable to uphold the ideal of honourable conduct, which might affect their future reputation, beyond whatever was immediately necessary.

By looking at the ways Violet's language reflected her attitudes, we have seen that the Occupation caused her to change her notions of correct behaviour. By reversing the process, and looking at how Violet's language reflected her perception of her social environment, it is possible to address the question of the impact of the Occupation on society and on the traditional historical concepts of gender identity and class and racial difference. Major changes were imposed on Violet's life. As I explained earlier, Violet had little to do with domestic duties before the Occupation, but the descriptions of her daily activities show that, as food and fuel shortages became more and more acute, her lifestyle changed. Day-to-day living became more difficult and more time-consuming, and it became necessary for Violet to be more involved with domestic duties. She had to walk to fetch the bread from a depot three times a week. She had to collect rations from town, which often involved standing in a queue for long periods. She also describes how she spent hours doing menial but necessary tasks, such as boiling water and collecting sticks for the fire:

> *January 7th 1941*
> How our lives have altered. No social life at all … One of our most absorbing occupations is hot water. Boiling it, preserving it to make it go as far as possible. Fetching the bread, carrying and fetching the laundry.

> *December 1st 1942*
> We just go on every day doing the same things. I think our lives are bounded now by fire and water. We are always preparing for the fire. The poor men are chopping up endless wood, I am gathering little sticks, drying the ever damp newspapers. Then we have to draw all our water from the rain water tank with a bucket to fill the empty kettles, or from the fresh water well for drinking. All day long and in the twilight or in the dark with a candle in my old horn lantern. And so it goes on.

The fact that it was necessary for women such as Violet to devote more time to housework could suggest the Occupation pushed Island women further into the traditional gender roles of housewife and mother than they had occupied before the war.

Violet also had an awareness of a difference in the way men and women dealt with the Occupation:

> *October 12th 1943*
> The men are getting extra rations of tobacco, they are spending 8s. 6d. on their tobacco this week. Mrs Renault is very indignant because the women get no extras. Poor women, they certainly are having the grimmest time in this Occupation. I think all of them are giving up their food to somebody else.
>
> The men expect and take as a matter of course all the meat and three quarters of the food if they can, but if there are children the mothers are giving up to the children and if there are old people the women are giving up to them and so it goes on. And yet not one woman has committed suicide. I don't know how many men have. Gus Thoumine from Bachmann's has just committed suicide, he could not stand his life any longer. The men say they can't work if they don't have the food. The poor women have to do their work just the same, although conditions have made all women's work four times as hard. Preparing of meals and cooking, standing in queues for hours for a little bit of fish and so on.

> *December 16th 1944*
> The Controlling Committee have practically told the men not to work. It is awfully stupid of them, now the men don't come to work until nearly 10 o'clock and they leave early. How the women are managing to live I simply don't know. They are giving most of their food to the men and children, they are doing all their work, standing in queues, bellowing the fires, chopping wood, gathering sticks and the men take the women's food quite complacently. Talk about guts, the men are puling infants compared to the women. Of course there are exceptions, but very few.

Violet Carey felt the Occupation caused women to regress into a gender role wherein sacrificing themselves for men and children was expected. She is clearly protesting that men allowed women to carry the burden in this way. Interestingly, she also protested against certain characteristics of her female acquaintances:

> *August 31st 1940*
> My temper is very frayed. I like being with men. Mr Bolton said to me, 'It is a shame that this should have happened to this prosperous little Island.' Just that understanding little sentence, that is all, but it was quite enough. And then I go on the tennis field and meet people who say, 'I should like to see Guernsey bombed again and again. It is such fun going into the greenhouses and helping ourselves to tomatoes. How lovely it is getting grapes at 6d. a lb!' I think those pathetic notices outside greenhouse properties, 'Free tomatoes, come in and help yourselves,' are the most poignant of all. And grape growers are selling their grapes for 6d. a pound to get rid of them, so they won't have to let them have the grapes. Grapes for which in normal times they would get 4s. a pound. It is just the life blood of the Island being drained away. And that type of person says, 'This is such an interesting experience.'

By stating 'I like being with men', and advocating the level-headed and rational understanding of the seriousness of the Occupation that she sees in them, Violet is diminishing women who represented an attitude she clearly disapproved of, and setting herself above them. Her portrayal of these differences seems to be related to her approval and identification with attitudes she felt were correct and honourable. She approved of both the women's noble willingness to make sacrifices and the men's rationality. Therefore, whether or not it was intentional, Violet's comments indicate that, in her own opinion at least, there were differences in how men and women dealt with the Occupation.

Born into the de Sausmarez family, and married into the Carey family, Violet inherited 'old wealth'. Both the Careys and the de Sausmarez belonged to the Island elite. Violet's privileged education, her leisured lifestyle and the fact she could afford to employ servants indicate her high social standing. There is evidence in her diaries that she had an awareness of class difference. The following example refers to Violet's sister-in-law, Olive, who had decided to send her ailing mother (Mrs Fisher) to a nursing home where she would receive better care and more food. Rita was Olive's maid.

> *January 26th 1945*
> Mrs Fisher has quite gone back to her girlhood and thinks she is in Durham and Olive is her mother and is quite happy. Rita keeps repeating she would never have sent her mother away. This is a striking example of the difference in environment and way of living of the classes. In our class we have our own bedrooms and we sleep alone. In their class, their mothers would not sleep alone and would never be alone and would get up early and be down sitting by the kitchen fire and peeling potatoes and using their hands all day long. They would not be allowed to stay in bed as long as they could be useful.

Another example shows that Violet saw the labouring classes as unsophisticated:

> *July 16th 1943*
> Poor Ted Ogier has been fined £15 for selling figs above the controlled price. It is so ridiculous to stop the unfortunate growers selling luxury fruit at a fair price. Always there is the whine that it is too dear for the working man. Why should the working man have luxury fruit, strawberries and raspberries, etc., for nothing practically?

However, there were circumstances in which Islanders became more preoccupied with the task of surviving, causing some relationships between members of the different classes to change. Whereas before the Occupation Violet had been in contact with the lower classes, but was in a position of superiority, the fact she now had to queue for rations like all the other Islanders suggests class superiority was no longer so evident. There are examples in the diaries which suggest Violet's attitude altered, if only a little:

> *May 7th 1943*
> Peggy told me about the Belgian beggar. He went to them, she said he was very clean and well spoken and of course said he was very hungry so Peggy gave him *her* potatoes and went without herself, they were just ready for her dinner. He went on to the Durands, said he had had nothing to eat all day and they gave him their food. He went on to the Tukes and they gave him all sorts of things, tins of food and also a suit of clothes. I have made up my mind I *won't* give any food to foreigners. I would rather adopt a Guernsey person, a genuine case and I have adopted old Mrs Baleine who lives in the cottage opposite. We are kindred spirits, we both swear like troopers during this Occupation!

A previous diary entry describing the tribulation that Mrs Baleine's arrival in the parish caused suggests that Violet considered her to be of a lower class:

> *February 7th 1942*
> There is great tribulation in this part of the Parish. Old Mrs Baleine, a terrible old Frenchwoman, has been given one room by George Lucas in the cottage opposite, for which she pays 2s. 6d. a week! The place is not fit for animals to live in! Mrs Renault is frantic at having her for a neighbour. Both Mrs Baleine and Mrs Gallienne wash for the Germans. Mrs Gallienne's husband refuses to live with her because she does so.

While Violet undoubtedly remains aware of the distinctions between herself and Mrs Baleine, she also puts herself on a level with her by claiming they are kindred spirits. This is better understood if it is remembered that Islanders, as well as coping with the invasion of German soldiers, had also to cope with an influx of thousands of foreign workers imported by the Germans to build the coastal fortifications deemed necessary for the Island's protection. This had an important bearing on Islanders' attitudes towards racial difference. Violet showed a mixed attitude of both compassion and distaste towards these foreign workers:

> *December 16th 1941*
> Peggy told us an awful story about one of those French boys of 15 years old. The poor little chap went to the mother of Peggy's maid, he was crying bitterly, he was so cold and his shoes were awful. She gave him a pair of shoes, a boy friend was with him. Some days later the friend went to see her and told her the poor little boy was dead. His mother was dead and they told him they had killed his father and so he tried to hang himself, but didn't before they found him. They thrashed him and when he could, he crept away and drowned himself. These poor French people are given half a pound of bread in the morning and a bowl of weak soup in the evening and that is *all*. They dig up carrots and turnips and eat them raw.

> *October 21st 1943*
> Having sent us the dregs of Europe, the Germans are now bringing over here the dregs of Russia. Men who the Germans say have entered their army to fight Bolshevism and who are real Bolshevists themselves. They are Georgians and the lowest type of humanity. The Germans say they have brought them over here because

> they consider our civilisation is so high, they hope they will learn to be more civilised. Some they have had to send away, they were so out of control. They warn women about them. I think it is awful bringing them over here.

It would appear that the presence of foreign people caused Violet's attitude towards outsiders to intensify. Guernsey had always been an enclosed, insular and safe environment. Violet's own insularity is demonstrated by the fact that, according to the family, she refused to 'know' a person until they had lived in the Island for at least five years. Her family also remember her being liberal with the term 'beastly foreigners'. The presence of both German soldiers and foreign workers must have been a deeply uncomfortable experience and strengthened her attitudes towards distinctions between Islanders and outsiders. The following extract, which describes a journey into Town in a private van with some of the country people from the parish of Torteval, suggests that Violet derived a certain degree of comfort from being in the company of normal Guernsey people, regardless of their position within the Island's class structure:

> *November 27th 1942*
> It was full of cheerful Torteval people and nowhere in the whole wide world are there more cheerful people than the Torteval people when they are driving into Town for the day. They welcomed me hilariously and I sat down, partly on the form in the middle of the van and partly on a sack of potatoes, 'Oh,' I said, 'black market potatoes eh?' This sally wit of mine was received by the man sitting by me with a large grin and a larger wink and he said, 'That is no matter, we say nothing!'
> We jogged comfortably along and passed two foreign gents, they could wave until they were black in the face, there would never be room for the likes of them in the Torteval van and their clothes were accurately described from the tops of their foreign hats to the tips of their foreign toes!
> We picked up two more people and drove in to the cheerful hum of the patois, the one language that has defeated the Gestapo! Some triumph. I do enjoy driving with the country people, they are so cheerful and they all looked very well.

Violet's enjoyment of being with ordinary Islanders is obvious and her comment about the potatoes demonstrates an ability to communicate on a level with them. Returning to Mrs Baleine, I would suggest that Violet derived a similar degree of comfort from finding a similarity in their respective attitudes. However, noting that they both 'swear like troopers during this Occupation' does not signify a change in attitude towards class difference; rather it demonstrates that their shared experience of the distressing circumstances of enemy occupation gave them some common ground.

Other comments demonstrate that Violet retained her awareness of class difference. In her interaction with her maid, Mrs Renault, she continued to distinguish herself from people of a lower class:

> *May 25th 1944*
> Mrs Renault this morning said to me, 'There is an old maid in St Andrews aged 43 and she is going to have a baby by a spaniel and I know it is true Mrs James!' I laughed and said, 'I don't believe it.'
> 'It *is* true, by a foreigner.' I said, 'Oh, you mean a Spaniard!'
> 'Yes,' she said, 'a spaniel,' and nothing could make her call him anything else!

By seeing herself in a position of knowledge, and correcting someone of a lesser education who had misunderstood something, and deriving amusement from the misunderstanding, Violet diminished Mrs Renault. The distinction is subtle, probably subconscious and certainly not derogatory, but shows an inherent class awareness. The extract also suggests that lower class Islanders maintained their sense of class distinction. Mrs Renault referred to Violet as 'Mrs James' and her indignant refusal to be corrected or challenged implies a certain pride and insularity.

Violet's experience of the invasion of both Germans and foreign workers during the Occupation and the consequent comfort she found in Guernsey people clearly posed challenges to her perception of her social environment. However, she retained the attitude towards class difference she had grown up with and held on to a sense of her own social status. The diaries provide evidence that people from all levels of Island society maintained a sense of their status.

However, Violet developed an understanding for those forced to live in a way of which she would previously have disapproved. The serious hardship and deprivation she witnessed among other Islanders and the foreign workers provided glimpses of humanity after the veneer of civilisation was removed. In such circumstances, concepts such as class structure were rendered irrelevant in comparison to the mere struggle for survival. However, these glimpses were only momentary and there is substantial evidence that she maintained both her sense of her social status and attitude towards class relations that she had grown up with. Violet Carey's diaries show that while the Occupation broadened Islanders' experiences of life, it did not entirely undermine the Island's pre-war social framework.

Conclusion

The problem of imposing simplistic categories onto complex periods of history is not confined to the Occupation of the Channel Islands. In *Marianne in Chains* Robert Gildea argues that there are three dominant myths of French behaviour during the Occupation of France which divide people into the categories of the 'good' French, who resisted, the 'bad' French, who collaborated, and the 'poor' French, who suffered intolerably from cold, hunger and fear.[99] Gildea's observations emphasise how the contentious issue of conduct during enemy occupation hinders a true understanding of this aspect of history. He argues that this model is 'very attractive, but too simple to make sense of the diverse and contradictory experiences of ordinary people'.[100] Gildea has attempted to develop historical understanding of the Occupation of France beyond the myths by focusing on the relationships between the French inhabitants and German occupiers in provincial communities. This has enabled him to reassess the complex relationships between the French and the Germans, between Vichy and the French, and among the French themselves, not according to some higher code of 'good' and 'bad' actions that was handed down at liberation, but according to what the community thought was good or bad for it under occupation.[101]

In the same way that Gildea has asserted the need to move beyond mythical representations of the Occupation of France, this analysis of Violet Carey's diaries reveal the importance of deconstructing the persistent discourses of 'correct' and 'incorrect' behaviour that have led to

---

[99] Robert Gildea, *Marianne in Chains: In Search of the German Occupation, 1940-1945* (London, 2002), p.7.
[100] Gildea, *Marianne in Chains*, p.414.
[101] Gildea, *Marianne in Chains*, p.13.

the dominance of the question of culpability within both public and historical representation of the German Occupation of Guernsey. Although there has been some acknowledgement that acts of wrongdoing and collaboration did occur, the circular argument of accusation and defence is still present more than sixty years after Liberation. I would argue that the past cannot be interpreted through the confines of this framework and that an alternative way to further historical understanding of the Occupation is to analyse contemporary testimony which is written in language not structured around the post-Liberation discourse.

However, the methodology I have employed, of identifying the influence of the social and cultural context on a diarist's narrative, demonstrates that historians are at the mercy of the textual sources they choose to use. The point of view put across in a diary is inevitably coloured by the diarist's intentions for writing and by the way that they understand their circumstances. The effectiveness of my approach therefore largely depends on understanding the writer's motives and on his or her ability to incorporate the cultural environment into their narrative. Fortunately, the analysis of Violet Carey's diaries has revealed a woman with an unusual talent for depicting her circumstances in narrative form. Consequently, while her diaries only represent one Islander's experience and are inevitably tainted by the fallibility of their author, they do give an important insight into understanding the impact of the Occupation on society.

During the Occupation Violet was exposed to a level of deprivation she had probably never imagined, as she heard of and witnessed the plight of the foreign workers and of other Islanders. On 20 January 1945 she wrote:

> I heard a pitiful story about two old ladies in the Town who were discovered tearing up their own linoleum with their fingers, trying to make a little fire. They were sitting on the floor and there was no furniture in the room at all as they had burnt it all. They had nothing else to burn.

Yet, although circumstances arose where she related to people of different race or class in a new way, her social and cultural values did not change. Analysis of the content of her daily entries reveals that the most significant effect of the Occupation on Violet Carey was the moments when the veneer of civilisation was stripped away and the privileges of education and wealth lost their value. As shortages became more acute she became more obsessed with food. Life became a primitive matter of survival, even for a privileged, upper-middle-class woman, as is shown by poignant comments such as 'the most important thing in life is "simple food" and the next is warmth'.[102] In this situation issues such as class or racial distinction became irrelevant. Survival itself became the dominant discourse within Island consciousness and the severe shortages of food and fuel which threatened Islanders' survival caused them to live from day to day, not looking much further than the next loaf of bread. Thus their concept of futurity was radically altered as, at times, the immediate problem of survival became more important than the question of reputation and honour.

The dominant discourses evident in Violet Carey's diaries, such as survival, humour and honour, are found too in the tales of heroic endurance dismissed by critics of the Islanders as a cover-up. However, Violet's diaries show that the employment of such linguistic frameworks was not an attempt to disguise fault or scandal. Rather, the discourses reflect the language that Islanders used in order to think about, talk about and cope with a deeply distressing experience. These ways of thinking and talking about the Occupation have persisted in post-Liberation

---

[102] Violet Carey, 7 December 1944.

attempts to come to terms with their experiences and return to normality. Defensive attitudes have naturally arisen wherever Islanders have felt the way they understood their own experiences of the Occupation has not been respected.

Obviously, as Violet herself acknowledged, some Islanders did collaborate in a way that deserved rebuke. While the Occupation caused a shift in normality, and day-to-day circumstances changed, the population of Guernsey was still made up of the same range of human nature as it had been beforehand. There were the 'good' people and the 'bad' people and these people responded to the changes in their situation according to their personalities and specific circumstances. However, the bland and uninformed accusations that Islanders collaborated and fraternised are grossly inappropriate. As Gildea argues in relation to the Occupation of France, the model of 'good' and 'bad' people is too simplistic to encompass the true complexity of Islanders' experiences. Violet Carey's diaries demonstrate that in order to appreciate this complexity further attention must be paid to the language of contemporary testimony that many Islanders who experienced the Occupation have left behind.

The Diaries of Violet Carey, 1940

Book I

June 1940[103]

James and I were sitting peacefully in the dining room when we heard Katty's voice.[104] James groaned aloud. Katty came in and proceeded to tell us all she had done. She seemed to be trying to evacuate the Island. She had hypnotised Mrs Hayes[105] into such activity that she made all arrangements to go by the boat tomorrow, second class because she could not go first class. Katty has also made Dr Robert's dispenser leave him and go back to Dublin by tomorrow's boat. I said, 'What will the girls do?'

'Oh!' says Katty. 'They can go into munition works or go out to Canada or New Zealand.' I gasped and said, 'Miss Vaughan is a trained dispenser, she would be wasted in a munitions factory.'

And then it sounded. The first air raid warning.

We looked at each other. Katty sprang to her feet, clasped her hands on her heart and said dramatically, 'It has come, I knew it would, I have had private information they were going to raid tonight. I was not allowed to tell.' I said, 'We must go out and lie against a hedge.'

We all went outside and, to our eternal shame, left the light on in the dining room with the windows unscreened. It was a beautiful evening, the horrible siren was still howling. Hedley[106] came back at that moment and said, 'The siren is sounding Mrs James!' He was a living argument for drink – we being sober, cold and miserable, he being drunk, warm and happy. I went back and fetched my coat, two rugs and dear Mike[107] and turned out the lamp. At last the siren stopped and it sounded again at 11, the all clear. In the *Star* this evening, they said Pierre de Putron[108] had ordered a preliminary air raid warning to Island personnel about 10pm and cancelled it at 11pm. The primary schools are closed and cinema and hotel dances. We are all very frightened and miserable.

---

[103] Violet seems to have written about the air raid, evacuation and occupation of June 1940 in retrospect. She did include some dates, but they are squashed into the text, which suggests that she added them in at a later date. She resumes daily writing on 4 July. She also wrote more about the air raid and evacuation in June 1941.

[104] Katty Connellan was an Irish lady who lived out on the cliffs in the Forest. She is remembered as being rather eccentric with a very dramatic nature.

[105] Mrs Hayes was a friend of Violet who lived at Le Manoir, in the Forest parish, near to Les Merriennes. Mrs Hayes evacuated to England in June 1940.

[106] Hedley Hamon was the widower of Violet's nanny, Annie. When Annie died, Violet and James had taken him in; he lived with them at Les Merriennes and helped run the farm.

[107] Mike was one of Violet's cats.

[108] Pierre de Putron was a Jurat in the Royal Court and became Air Raid Precautions Commandant. On 18 June, the *Star* reported that 'a preliminary air raid warning was issued from Headquarters to Island Personel about ten o' clock last night'.

Wednesday June 19th

We had a terrible day yesterday. James had to go to Court twice.[109] The English cabinet discussed the position of the Channel Islands this morning. The news came about 4pm. They declared us an Open Town and demilitarized us.[110] At 5pm the order came to evacuate the children. James and I went into Town. I shall never forget it; the Town was humming, queues outside all the banks, the Post Office full. The phone never stopped ringing and people streamed here to ask questions. All the mothers crying but willing to let their children go. It is awful. They took some away at 4am. Boats are coming all day. The children and colleges went today. Evacuations boat came in and took off people.

On Saturday[111] morning at 5am, James burst into my room and said something awful has happened; compulsory evacuation is ordered.[112] Mrs Renault[113] was crying, I got up and went to tell Katty at the Manoir. Mrs Renault said Mr Finey[114] had told the people. 'I believe he has gone off his head,' said Katty. I came back and rang up the police station who said nothing new had been issued and it was voluntary. I rang up Olive.[115] None of us are going. The slogans in the Town were very good: 'Don't go mad. Compulsory evacuation a lie, home is best.'

Tuesday June 25th

The evacuation went on all Sunday and Monday. On Tuesday morning at 6am, my door burst open. I called out, 'I am not going, what do you want?' An astonished voice said, 'It is me.' Baba![116] Oh the joy of seeing her, the darling. She had signed on as the stewardess on the cargo boat and had come for the day. It was too lovely for words.

Michelle told us that the *Worthing* had gone to Le Havre. Anchored out in the bay, she was bombed for thirteen hours. They had nothing to do, it was awful. They sat below with lifebelts on. Then the launches of wounded came out and they methodically unloaded them. Four ships were sunk beside them and they picked up the survivors and also B.E.F. men. Two destroyers were on either side of them shooting A.A. guns the whole time. They got back without a casualty.[117] It was lovely having Baba.

---

[109] The Court passed Ordinances prohibiting use of motor vehicles between 10.30pm and 5am, fixing the prices of goods to the price charged on 15 June 1940 and prohibiting the export of rationed goods. (*Ordinances volume 28*)

[110] According to Cruickshank, after it was decided the Channel Islands should be demilitarised, the fact was not immediately publicised as the British feared the Germans would interpret it as an open invitation to invade. However, this put the Islanders at risk of being attacked and having no defence. The fact of the demilitarisation was eventually published in *The Times* on 29 June 1940 and on the BBC news on 28 June. Both announcements were after the air raid on St Peter Port. (Cruickshank, pp33-4)

[111] This refers to Saturday 22 June.

[112] This must have been a rumour. On 21 June the *Star* published articles encouraging Islanders to stay. This included a letter from the Bailiff, Victor Carey, which emphasised that evacuation was voluntary.

[113] Mrs Renault was Violet's maid and came daily to do most of the housework and some of the cooking. She lived at Les Villets, Forest.

[114] Mr Finey was the rector of the Forest Parish.

[115] Olive de Sausmarez was Violet's sister-in-law. She was the widow of Violet's brother, Teddy. She lived at Pre au Puit, often referred to as the 'bungalow' on King's Road in St Peter Port.

[116] Baba was Violet's nickname for her daughter, Michelle.

[117] The *Worthing* was a hospital ship. It crossed regularly from New Haven to Le Havre and Dieppe and transported soldiers who had been wounded on the front lines back to England.

Saturday June 29th

On Friday June 28th, I went out to lunch with Aggie and Reggie;[118] they were going to England that night. I came home by the six o'clock bus. I hadn't been home very long when we heard the sirens all over the island and the planes, machine guns firing and bombs dropping. They were bombing the tomato lorries and the harbour. We heard the harbour was in mines, etc. The All Clear went about an hour later.[119]

On Saturday, we heard there were twenty-two dead and thirty-six injured. I went to Town and went down the Pollet and along the front. All the windows were blown out. Two sheds were burning but the jetty was all right.

Tomato lorries bombed by Germans in an air raid on St Peter Port, June 1940.

Sunday June 30th

Just after 1pm the sirens went again, we all went into the kitchen. We heard the planes land on the 'drome. I rang up the exchange and they said British planes had driven them off.[120] At 5pm they came back again and occupied the 'drome.[121] The cable with England was cut at 11pm.

---

[118] Aggie and Reggie Sowels lived in Sark, but evacuated to England before the Occupation. Aggie was one of Violet's cousins.
[119] On 28 June the Germans bombed St Peter Port.
[120] This is not strictly true. According to Cruickshank, two of the three British planes that opposed the German ones were shot down. (Cruickshank, p.70)
[121] On 30 June a German plane landed in Guernsey with three planes overhead to cover. They met no opposition on the island but retreated when three British planes attacked. Two of the English planes were shot down. This landing was an enter prise not an order. That evening, a platoon of soldiers was flown into Guernsey and the island officially surrendered to the force which landed. (Cruickshank, pp.70-3)

Air raid damage from German air raid on St Peter Port, June 1940.

July 1940

Wednesday July 3rd

We have to advance the time one hour. We are allowed to listen to our wireless. Attend divine service. We have to be in by 10pm until 6am The Commandant is a Dr Lanz.

It seems like *Gone With The Wind* and I am Scarlett![122]

One old man asked James if you stuck a needle in the same place in one's arm as you did for vaccination for evacuation!

There are 1,200 Germans here and they tear about the roads in lorries and on motor bicycles all day long on the wrong side. The planes fly overheard very low. The letters I wrote on Friday have been returned to me.

I have such attacks of sleepiness, I just have to go and lie down. I fell in my bath on Thursday morning and for days the pain has been dreadful, I wrenched muscles.

Thursday July 4th

Mr Gorvel[123] told James he was working in his field and a young German officer came up to him and patted him on the shoulders and said, 'Don't be frightened old man, we don't fight civilians.' People are much less frightened now and the German soldiers are still polite and do not molest anybody. Some of them say the war will be finished in three weeks time and they will be back in their own country.

Our Orders. [124]

> 1) All inhabitants must be indoors by 11pm and not leave their houses before 6am.
> 2) They will respect the population of Guernsey, but should anyone attempt to cause the least trouble, serious measures will be taken and the Town will be bombed.
> 3) All orders given by the military authority are to be strictly obeyed.

---

[122] Scarlett is the heroine of Margaret Mitchell's *Gone with the Wind*. Her family were southerners during the American Civil War, and their farm was invaded by republicans.

[123] The Gorvels were neighbours who lived at La Roberge, near to Les Merriennes.

[124] These orders were published in the *Star* on 1 July 1940.

4) All spirits must be locked up immediately and no spirits may be obtained or consumed henceforth. This prohibition does not apply to stocks in private houses.
5) No person shall enter the aerodrome at La Villiaze.
6) All rifles, airguns, pistols, revolvers, daggers, sporting guns and all other weapons whatsoever, except souvenirs, must together with all ammunition be delivered at the *Royal Hotel* by 12 noon on July 1st.
7) All British sailors, airmen and soldiers on leave in this island must report at the police station at 9am on Monday July 1st and must then report at the *Royal Hotel*.
8) No boat or vessel of any description can leave the island.
9) No petrol can be sold.
10) Private cars cannot be used.
11) Black out must be observed.

My weight is 11stone, 4lbs.

Thursday July 11th
A beautiful day. I went to fetch the bread in the morning. Katty came to tea.

Mrs Luscombe at the Friquet[125] was at the top of the stairs and looked down and saw a large German standing at her front door. She was very frightened and would not come down, though he repeatedly asked her to do so. At last she thought she had better do so and came down. He said to her, 'Show me your visitors book.' She fetched it and he turned back the pages and pointed to a name and said, 'That was me. You were not afraid of me when I stayed with you then, so don't be afraid of me now.'

Some of their uniforms are green and some are blue-grey. They all wear high leather boots. I have not seen many airmen about, only boy troopers.

Monday July 15th
Girlie[126] was with me last night. Shortly after I put her out planes went over the house. I went into Boy's room and watched them. They were very high and went out at regular intervals. I counted thirty-eight and then there was a short burst of machine gun fire over the house. That was at twenty to four. Lay awake until 4.30, dead silence all the time. Mr Gorvel told James it was not machine guns, they were dropping flares all round the cliffs. It was very frightening. I hear it was a plane trying to get in.

Thursday July 18th
New orders today. Southern coastline forbidden to the public since 10 o' clock last night. Nobody will be allowed within sixty yards of the high water mark from St Martin's Point to Pleimont Point on pain of death. Blackout is now 10.45 instead of 11.15.

Friday July 19th
A lovely day. I slept in the afternoon. Olive[127] came out to tea. She told me that the story is that Victor[128] rang up the Home Office after the raid and asked them why the BBC had only

---
[125] The Friquet was a guesthouse in St Martins.
[126] Girlie was one of Violet's cats.
[127] Olive de Sausmarez was Violet's sister-in-law. She was the widow of Violet's brother Teddy. She lived at Pre au Puit, often referred to as the bungalow on Kings Road in St Peter Port.
[128] Victor Carey was Bailiff of the Island during the Occupation. He was a distant relative of Violet's, being a member of a different branch of the Carey family.

announced that we were an Open Town at 9pm Friday evening and the answer he got was 'That they did not know what the German reactions would be'![129]

Monday July 22nd

There has been a mysterious landing and it becomes curiouser and curiouser. Forty men are supposed to have landed and cut the cable between us and France. The sea became very rough and they could not go back in their rubber boats but had to swim leaving their clothes behind them. The landing was at Petit Port.[130]

Wednesday July 24th

Still pouring with rain. What a rotten month July often is. The hay is down. It is worrying, it rained on St Swithin's day. Another worry is that the milk goes sour so quickly. No planes flew in the night.

I hear that since the landing on Monday night, the Petit Port steps have all been blown up and there is no path down now. They have pulled down all the iron posts with lights on the aerodrome, have smashed the searchlights and removed the big one and put it behind the Carres' farm at St Andrews.

Mr Ransson[131] told us that three came to him at Pleimont and wanted to be billeted on him. They knocked on the door and, when he opened, he called out, 'I thought you were the doctor, I have two grandchildren here down with diptheria and I don't know what to do. Can you help me? Will you come in and see them and will you take them to the hospital for me?' They declined with thanks and he has been left alone ever since!

In this parish one of them asked a man to lend him a bicycle in German and made signs to show what he wanted. No-one could be denser than the Forest men. At last, he threw up his arms and beamed and took him to the aerodrome and said, 'ZOOM Flugplatz'.

There is a young Roman Catholic priest among them, a boy of twenty-three. He celebrates Mass every morning at 8am at St Ives and afterwards goes to a family and has a cup of tea with them. He implores them to build themselves a dugout. They expect the English to bomb us. I can't believe it; it is not logic. They have been told that if the English come, they must give themselves up at once.

Bacon and yeast gave out last Saturday July 20th.

Ted Ogier fell asleep in his chair one evening with the light on and no black out. He was awakened by a thunderous knocking at the door. Two came in and shot the lamp out.

Monday July 29th

At about five o'clock on Saturday the phone went, a strange man said Perdy had died that morning, heart failure. Poor Doris had been down to see her mother, came back and found him in the kitchen. James spent all day with Doris helping her in every possible way. On Sunday James

---

[129] See reference 102.

[130] This probably refers to 'Operation Ambassador'. On 14 July three parties of commandos attempted to make landings on three separate beaches and carry out raids on the German military. These raids were largely unsuccessful: only one party of forty men actually came ashore. They landed at Petit Port and climbed the cliffs. They had been briefed to take any Germans they found as prisoners, but did not encounter any. They did some minor sabotage including destroying some telephone wires. (Cruickshank, p.89)

[131] Mr Rannsson lived in the old coastguard cottage in Torteval.

and I drove over in the van to Le Hurel in the afternoon to see Doris. She was waiting for us in the front. She would not let us see Perdy, she said he had changed so much. Poor poor Doris, I have never seen anyone so gallant and so desolate. The doctor said he died in a heart attack.

Perdy had been doing far too much, digging and bicycling all over the place, and he was so dreadfully worried and unhappy about the separation from his children. Doris thinks he strained his heart the day of the air raid. It is too poignantly sad.

August 1940

Thursday August 1st

Yesterday I had a meeting of the Ladies College Board at 2.30 and so, at five minutes past twelve, I set off on my great adventure of walking to Town. I have bought a little cart to put my parcels in. I walked for one hour and five minutes. I had my little seat and I sat down for ten minutes. I walked on as far as Markie's and went in there for a rest. She gave me a cup of coffee. I went on and arrived punctually at the meeting.

I walked on to Town and had a brainwave on the way. I knew Mr Ware[132] was coming out to us and why shouldn't he bring me as well? So I asked him and he was only too willing.

I met Mary[133] and she and I had a long gossip. Mary told me that the Germans had said the big attack on England will start on Sunday. She said Cliff was having his hair cut and a German under twenty was next to him. This boy said to the barber, 'I die on Monday.' He repeated it three times before the barber took any notice of it. The barber told him not to be so silly and he said, 'I am a parachutist and I go to England on Monday and I die.'

I am absolutely amazed at myself, but I can't help crying over these boys. If only one could send a message to England to spare them, these terrified boys, helpless victims. I hear that no planes stay here at night and no officers! One of these boys, he looked about twenty-three, met a woman with a pram and he looked hard at the baby and he saluted her and asked if he could hold the baby in his arms. She was very startled and rather frightened but said, 'Yes'. He picked it up and held it and said, 'I have a little baby like this, I have never seen it, and I shall never see it for I shall die, I am a parachutist.' It is awful. I can't help thinking if only these boys could meet our boys in the friendly rivalry of games instead of this awful war. They are all loathing the war. We are all victims.

I worry so over Boy. Michelle has a good salary, but Boy only gets 14s. a week. I sent him a parcel, very often of socks, shaving cream, soap, pepsodent and money too, and now I can't send him anything. It is awful. I hear we are not going to be allowed to send postcards, because they will give away addresses, I mean the addresses will give away the positions of factories or airports, etc. and so the British Government won't allow them to be sent.

Poor Mr Collins, the manager of Le Riches,[134] was arrested yesterday and put in prison for alleged injudicious talking. He was acquitted today. All he did was to tell one of his assistants not to try and speak German, but to get the States Interpreter, and one of these loathsome Hungarian girls was spying on him and reported him.[135] There are two Hungarian girls here

---
[132] The butcher that Violet used to get meat supplies.
[133] Mary had been Violet's cook. She was married to a grower, Cliff Cherry.
[134] Le Riches was the local grocery shop.
[135] As a result of this, the States passed a 'Dangerous Talking Bill' against injudicious speech so that Mr Collins could be tried by the Island courts rather than the German courts.

of the lowest class. One of them is at White Gables and when poor Perdy, Doris, James and I were all talking together at Mon Plaisir on the Monday before he died, we discovered she was beside us listening!

This morning Mrs Tourtel[136] and I walked together to the Bourg to get our bread and she told why Mr Timmer[137] was so unpopular; it is not because he is supplying them with vegetables, but because when they arrived on the Sunday, he went up to the aerodrome and met them.

Now a further order has come that we must fill up a form saying how much coal we have in the house. Mrs Renault and Mrs Mauger[138] who have been denying themselves all sorts of things so as to be able to buy a bar of coal every week are absolutely livid about it because, as they say, it will be given to people who go to the pictures every week.

It is a fine day but there is a high wind blowing and poor James is carting hay, he says it is such hard work.

Friday August 2nd

I do feel so sick today, this dreadful nausea, I suppose I am worrying over England. Our poor people over there. I don't know how they can bear it, the awful noise for one thing, let alone the rest of the horrors. We are in a peculiar position here; we are really so comfortable. If the English do bomb us, they won't do anything else, they won't machine gun us and they won't use gas. As Baba says, if you are hit by a bomb you know no more. Of course we are uncomfortably near the aerodrome. I can't believe the English will come here.

Saturday August 3rd

Mrs Renault has just been in and said they have put up a gun on the Corbiere and have been all round these lanes this afternoon. She was funny because she rushed in and said, 'Mrs James, Mrs James, you must not leave the front door open, it is open now and you never know if they will come in!'

James came back about ten and said the Forest Road was pandemonium. He had never seen so many lorries and cars going such a pace. They were full of guns and ammunition. In Town the feeling of rage against Sherwill was universal, and also resentment against Mrs Sherwill.[139] We all say, why should the Sherwills broadcast and send personal messages to their children?[140] Why doesn't he broadcast a short, dignified message? The men say, what does Mrs Sherwill know about these wives, she never has anything to do with them? Saying 'We are all happy and contented'! Does she ever realise what all this means to the Island? If ever any people were an eloquent example of the 'brave old wisdom of endurance,' the Guernsey people are that now. They are going on with their work doggedly and uncomplainingly, outwardly cheerful, resisting nothing, giving in with a dignity that is remarkable. These poor desolate men. Mr Ware told

---

[136] The Tourtels were another family who lived in the Forest.
[137] Mr Timmer was a Dutchman and a grower for exports. He supposedly collaborated outwardly with the Germans during the Occupation.
[138] Mrs Mauger was Violet's charlady. She lived at Les Villets in the Forest.
[139] A.J. Sherwill was the Attorney General and an elected member of the Royal Court. He was elected as President of the Controlling Committee which was set up as a kind of war cabinet just before the Occupation.
[140] The German Commandant allowed Sherwill to record a message to the UK. In this message, he stated that the Island officials were being treated well, that the government was functioning and churches, banks, and shops were open as usual. Sherwill did send a personal message to his own children, but he did not say 'we are all happy and contented'.

me when he drove me home, that he can get through the day all right, he has his work to do, but coming home is too awful; he was devoted to his wife and little girl. His brother-in-law lives with him now, even then he says he doesn't know how he can bear it. He said what gets us down is we hardly see anybody and that is so true. Life is more like a pathetic Christmas Day than ever. When we do meet, we are so glad to see each other and we are so nice to each other. When I go to Town, people speak to me whom I hardly know; they tell me I am so glad I haven't gone.

Bank Holiday Monday August 5th
Today we have ceased to use our boiler for hot water; we heat hot water in a small copper outside, in which we burn rubbish.

Our rationing is now as follows:
Meat – 1s. worth per head.
Butter – 4g. per head per week.
Tea – 3oz.
Sugar – 6oz.
Salt – 1oz.
Alternatively with tea you can have 4oz of coffee or 2oz of cocoa.

Clothes are rationed and we have to register. We can have three articles, i.e. three vests or three pairs of stockings. One pair of shoes and two repaired. We can't buy any more again for months.

Today is foggy and still. The peace around here is almost uncanny; we are always expecting and listening for something.

An aeroplane has flown over being chased furiously by a black backed gull! Won't that gull boast to the other gulls about the enormous bird he chased away!!

James had to rush in to a special meeting of the Court last week to pass a rush ordinance about people who are guilty of injudicious speech. Otherwise they would have been tried by a German military tribunal instead of by the Court.[141]

Wednesday August 7th
James went in to a historic States meeting with Dr Lanz and Dr Maass.[142] The first is the German Commandant and the second is the Chief of Staff, and other officers were there. They raised their arms when they came in and when they went out. Mr Sherwill made a very good speech giving a comprehensive review of all the happenings in the last seven most momentous weeks of our lives.

I did my second trek into Town. I felt just as excited as I used to feel when I was going to Sark in the 7am boat in the 'dear dead days beyond recall'! I started at five minutes to eleven. I don't know why it is *such* an effort because it can't be more than four and a half miles, but it *is* an effort. I packed my baskets onto my little cart and I took my ration of butter, tea and sugar, a bottle of milk, a bottle of water and six duck eggs for Olive. I took also my little steel seat which I saw advertised in the *Daily Mail* years ago, a fisherman's seat, capable of holding weight up

---

[141] It is likely that this was precipitated by the incident where Mr Collins, manager of Le Riches, was arrested for alleged injudicious talking, which Violet recorded on 1 August. The ordinance, the 'Dangerous Talking Bill', meant that Mr Collins could be tried by the Island Court instead of a military tribunal.

[142] This was 'historic' as it was the first meeting of the States since the Occupation had begun.

to a ton. I thought 'that's the seat for V.M.' and bought it. I started off walking leisurely and with a perfectly heavenly feeling that I need not hurry. It was a delightful day, fresh and cool. I decided to walk for thirty-five minutes and then to rest for ten minutes.

I arrived at 1.30, left my little cart at Ware's, went to the bank, then lunch at Le Noury; a horrid lunch (resolution – to take my own lunch next time). When the blasted shops opened, I did my shopping, had tea and fetched my cart at 5pm.

Sunday August 11th
What an exhausting day this has been, the German planes have never ceased to roar overhead until now (4.30pm). When that happens, we know they are expecting English planes and sure enough one flew over at about 2.30 and dropped one bomb. We think it landed on the aerodrome. We don't know how much the 'drome was wrecked on Friday; the barracks are in ruins but not the hangars.

Monday August 12th
A perfectly beautiful August day. Very very hot. The *Star* today says that the Official Statement of the German Commandant concerning the air raids yesterday and Friday is as follows:

> Five German soldiers were killed and four wounded on Friday. Three or four local civilians were slightly wounded.

The Forest Newsagency corroborates that statement:

> A British plane came over yesterday afternoon and dropped a bomb from a high altitude which missed the airport and damaged glass house property in the district.

The BBC said British bombers came over in waves and dropped bombs on our airport. <u>One bomber</u> only came over and dropped five bombs on the airport; he destroyed the men's barracks but did not hurt the hangars.

The British plane flew away down the Talbot Valley and flew very low. All the people came out into the road and cheered themselves hoarse as he flew over them, quite forgetful of the danger from falling shrapnel!

I feel so miserable about the children; they will be worrying dreadfully about us. As we can say of the weather, if it is bad here, it is worse in England; so can we say it of the air raids. A horrible thought – they have to endure that terrible machine gunning.

Wednesday August 14th
There were forty planes on the 'drome this afternoon; they have gone away now (5pm). As the days go by, I am more firmly convinced than ever that England made a very great mistake strategically giving us up. If the Germans land those <u>enormous</u> troop carriers and bombers on the 'drome with the ease they do, the English could have landed their bombers and could have taken off just as well as the Germans do! Their planes come here, rest, refuel, and go off to attack convoys in the Channel.

We have a new Chief of Staff now Dr Maass has gone; he is called Colonel Schumacher.

I think all these ordinary country people are simply grand. They are doing everything according to routine. The hedges have all been cut, the roads are kept clear of weeds. Mrs Brouard has continued to do the flowers in the Forest Church, week by week, having grown them herself and each flower being a perfect specimen.

Germans marching through St Peter Port, August 1940.

Everybody is expecting we shall be bombed again. Our occupation would be quite humorous if it was not so tragic; the English declare us an Open Town and demilitarise us, a direct invitation to the Germans to come and occupy us; the Germans promptly accept the invitation and arrive and take possession, settle down and treat us very well; after forty days, the English try and bomb them out. Why ever let them come in?! It is all beyond my intelligence.

Thursday August 15th
I did my trek into Town today. I had lunch first and started at 12.30. I did not hurry, it was a roasting hot day. I do not wish to complain, but I do think it "ard, dam 'ard' that I have to start my treks in August! Having to carry a parasol does not help matters, but there it is; it is my cross!

Olive and I went on to the tennis field. Everybody is furious with Tetley;[143] he is so thick with the Germans they give him petrol. He is supposed to have lost his job with the Brewery and so is living on his wife's money. Everybody says 'Wait', and the men talk about tar and feathers.

On Friday 9th the Germans had a parade in Jersey. The troops marched through the Town headed by their Air Force band and then gave a concert. In the middle, one of the officers stood up and said, 'Will anybody who can speak German please put up their hands?' Only two or three hands went up, then he said, 'Will those who cannot speak German please put up their hands?' A forest of hands went up and click, click went the cameras and there was loyal Jersey doing 'Heil Hitler' complete!

Monday August 19th
It has rained this morning. James went to a States meeting. I went to Esparanza to take the laundry. After leaving the laundry, I went on to see Mrs Hazell. She was sweeping the yard and

---

[143] J.E.B. Tetley was viewed by many Islanders as being a collaborator as he associated freely with the Germans. (Bell, *Guernsey Occupied but Never Conquered*, p.225)

said she was feeling depressed. She certainly did not show it. Whenever any of us are depressed, and we are together, we always discuss what our feelings would be like when we hear the first phone call! I think of hearing their voices again. And then we discuss the arrival of the boat and what we shall wear. It won't matter in the least whether it is pouring with rain, or brilliant sunshine. Katty has a whole length of pale pink satin to have made up! I can't make up my mind whether I shall be a sweet young thing in blue, or a perfect darling in brown! I think it will be brown because I have a beautiful scarf covered all over with Union Jacks, a bright red handkerchief with a crown on it, an exceedingly vulgar taste red, white and blue brooch, and a pair of gloves with the King and Queen on the fasteners; all these I wore on Coronation Day. I certainly must have my hair shampooed; I don't know if that will make my hair very tidy, but it will smell nice. Mother always said it was all right if one's gloves were smart; mine will be very smart. I always say that well polished shoes are the true hallmark of a well dressed man or woman. I am going to keep a good dab of meltonian cream for my shoes. Mrs Hazell will be faithful to her emerald green for Ireland. We shall be simply suffocated down on the pier because we shall all be there, the entire population of the Island. I love seeing the boat come round the entrance of the harbour; she always looks so graceful. She will be dressed in flags and they will be cheering like mad, and we shall be cheering like mad. And Baba and Boy and Reggie and Aggie will all be on board together!

Tuesday August 20th
I had lunch with Olive and after lunch I went to Bertie and Peggy.[144] Olive said, 'One visitor wanted to be shaved, he could not speak English and by signs he made a pier loafer understand what he wanted, so he dragged the unwilling loafer with him to a barber's shop. The loafer jerked his thumb and said, "E says 'e wants 'is b----y throat cut.' 'Ja! Ja!' says the German, grinning from ear to ear!

Thursday August 22nd
A beautiful day but a very cold wind is blowing. I went down to Passiflora to fetch the bread. I walked back with Mrs Tourtel. We talked about the robberies. She said the Sebires[145] had been robbed and about £20 of wedding presents had been taken and that the visitors had been seen posting parcels after being chased away from two houses. Mrs Tourtel told me they were expecting an air raid tomorrow. She said the British <u>must</u> raid us every eight or nine days to keep our nationality and prevent us becoming a German colony![146] Well, words fail me!

Monday August 26th
The phone rang just now, what an excitement! Our lives are dull now. I only see Mrs Hazell and Katty. As long as I am able to walk into Town, I can see Olive and one or two other people. In the Town itself I don't meet anybody. Our only excitements are the air raids! Apart from the actual danger, our feelings are hideous because all the time one feels, will they get away, will they be hit? And when they have gone we wonder where all that shrapnel that has been wildly flung up into the air will come down. Men say this district is very safe because it is 'under the arch of the guns'. What that means I have not the slightest idea but it sounds all right.

---

[144] Bertie and Peggy Brock were friends of Violet's who lived on Queen's Road in St Peter Port. They moved to the Forest later in the Occupation.
[145] The Sebires were a farming family who lived in the Forest.
[146] This was not true.

In spite of everything, I am glad I did not go away. We are keeping the property safe for the children. It does look so lovely, all the flowers are so pretty and the trees are beautiful.

Thursday August 29th
I saw in the paper that 'In order to stop any support by the civilian population of further English reconnaissance attempts of the occupied British Channel Islands, orders were issued by the Chief Command that Mrs le Masurier and Mrs Michael must be taken over to France at least fifteen kilometres away from the coast, and while there, will have to report daily to the German military authorities.' I am sure neither of those two knew the boys were in the Island; the boys hid down at Vazon and lived for three days on tomatoes and then gave themselves up. This punishment is the usual technique of punishing the next of kin. They were Philip Martel and Desmond Mulholland and they were put ashore here shortly after the Occupation in July and were left. Some say the submarine that brought them was sunk.[147]

Saturday August 31st
We have had a wonderful week of peace from planes. It has been heavenly. And this is the last day of August, the most perfect August we have ever had has drawn to a close. I can't say we have never had such weather before, but never better and not one drop of rain, very little wind and not one soul to enjoy it. No one is allowed to bathe in the south coast bays, no buses to take people to the other bays, no visitors to be taken anyhow. The Germans themselves seem afraid to bathe. As one walks along the roads and lanes, except for the rushing motor cars and lorries, one does not meet anybody. Complete sadness pervades us all, the shadow is over us all. My temper is very frayed. I like being with men. Mr Bolton said to me, 'It is a shame that this should have happened to this prosperous little island.' Just that understanding little sentence, that is all, but it was quite enough. And then I go on the tennis field and meet people who say, 'I should like to see Guernsey bombed again and again. It is such fun going into the greenhouses and helping ourselves to tomatoes. How lovely it is getting grapes at 6d. a lb!' I think those pathetic notices outside greenhouse properties, 'Free tomatoes, come in and help yourselves,' are the most poignant of all. And grape growers are selling their grapes for 6d. a pound to get rid of them, so they won't have to let them have the grapes. Grapes for which in normal times they would get 4s. a pound. It is just the life blood of the Island being drained away. And that type of person says, 'This is such an interesting experience.'

---

[147] Desmond Mulholland and Philip Martel were sent to the Island with orders to meet and guide commandos who were due to arrive on 12 July to carry out a raid on the German military. However, no commandos came; unbeknown to Mulholland and Martel, the raid had been postponed and consequently they were stranded. To begin with they hid on the Island, sheltered by their families. However, aware of the trouble they could cause, they eventually went to Sherwill to say they wanted to give themselves up. Knowing they would probably be shot because they wore civilian clothes and were technically spies, Sherwill found them uniforms. The Germans interrogated them and sent them to France. They were kept there as prisoners of war until the end of the war. Their salvation was probably due to their sticking to the story about landing in uniform and stealing civilian clothes and their genuine ignorance in the face of questions about the actual raid on 14 July. Mrs le Masurier was Martel's half sister. Mrs Michael was Mulholland's mother. They had helped to shelter Mulholland and Martel and could have been convicted of helping spies, which carried a penalty of fifteen years penal servitude. However, they were lucky. They were transferred to mainland France and told to report daily to the German authorities but were sent home in January 1941. As Violet recorded, the Germans announced they had been deported to stop the civilian population supporting further English reconnaissance attempts. (Cruickshank pp.89, 91)

Victor Carey.

Ambrose Sherwill.

September 1940

Tuesday September 3rd

The simplest habits of life are so complicated now. For instance, when I come down in the morning I open the front door and step outside and breathe deeply, then open every window and every door downstairs. Before I have breakfast, I close and lock every door and after breakfast, before I go upstairs, I close every window. If I hear gunfire, I rush all over the house opening every window again! It is very wearying!

Thursday September 5th

Mr Hubert is back from France with the news that agricultural and horticultural seeds have been brought and will be distributed to farmers and growers. Also fairly large quantities of wheat and fodder and certain chemicals. Mr Hubert and Mr R.O. Falla were in France for three weeks. Mr R.O. Falla is still in France arranging transport.[148] I think Mr Hubert and Mr R.O. Falla were heroes to go at all and risk the danger of the boat being sunk by the English.

While we were having breakfast, eight Germans came across the fields from the Gorvel's place, through the yard and past the kitchen window. Mrs Renault said her stomach was turning over and over. Molly,[149] who *never* barks at anything or anybody, nearly went mad with barking; nobody could quieten her and she was all on her nerves for the rest of the day. The Germans were in full kit hung round with different cans and a pack and they were so hot. When I went

---

[148] The Germans allowed representatives from the Islands to go over to France to try and buy supplies for the civilians. The Island had a depot at Granville; goods were obtained by the purchasing committee, and stored there until shipped. Mr George Vaudin became Guernsey's permanent representative in Granville. (Cruickshank, p.123)

[149] Molly was Violet's dog. She was a black spaniel.

for the bread there were several stationed in the lane. I asked one of them if they were doing manoeuvres and he said 'yes'. People were very frightened. Mrs Hazell was stopped going into Town. The rumour was they were expecting marines to land. That was all nonsense; they would not have put on full kit if they were expecting a scrap.

Saturday September 7th
My weight is 10 stone 6 lbs. A lovely day with a good, cool breeze.

A huge fire was caused at St Peters through a bonfire, so now nobody can light a bonfire. Everyone is in a way about it and the court sat privately about it, *but* it is an order! Also no more cream can be made. Cyclists cannot ride two abreast, they must ride one behind the other. It is wonderful how everyone way over fifty has taken to cycling, men and women. Most people have had dreadful falls, but they stick to it.

— Book II —

Friday September 13th
It poured all night and all the morning and blew a gale. Everybody was in the highest spirits because of the rain and the wind. Our conversations were something like this: 'At last the grass will grow; won't this do our garden good; won't they be sea sick; isn't it wonderful; the good old sea; it was our ally at the time of the Armada and it is going to be our ally again; they have missed the bus; the equinoctical gales are beginning; isn't it grand?!'[150]

Tuesday September 17th
The One o' clock News
> Attacks on London, resumed at dusk, were heavier than ever; they lasted six and a half hours. The all clear sounded and, shortly after, the sirens sounded again.
> Another hospital was struck by two bombs and the nurses had to move over a hundred patients. Business houses and residential houses were struck and fires started and some firemen killed.

Thursday September 19th
I was washing my teeth and in the middle of a gargle which might have choked me, when, pop! pop! pop! went a machine gun, apparently outside my window, Mrs Renault yelling below for me; it took all my self control not to go to the window; downstairs I was still holding my glycer Thymoline water! We heard the planes. James, of course, was in the middle of the yard, gazing up, but we saw nothing. Then came bang! bang! bang! the muffled sound of bombs dropping. *No* A.A. gun was fired!

I was taking in some coats and dresses for Miss Hayes to alter. They were all made for twelve stone three and of course looked perfectly awful on ten stone six. I had packed them into a large suitcase and fastened it securely onto my little cart and after lunch I set off. In the middle of the road to Mon Plaisir, I met Jackie Tostevin's father. He eyed my suitcase and then he said, 'Are *you* leaving the Parish Mrs Carey?' And, of course, the enormity of what I appeared to be doing

---

[150] At this stage the Islanders were still expecting the Germans to attempt an invasion of England, using the Channel Islands as a base.

burst upon me in full horror. I thought, well, desperate needs need desperate measures and so I explained to him in a few well chosen words that as I had lost two stone since war began, I was taking some of my clothes to a dressmaker to be altered. The poor man was instantly covered with dreadful confusion and apologised profusely! I said, 'Don't apologise, it is a most natural question to ask.'

I went on. The weather had turned very hot and the sun was shining brightly. When I got to the aerodrome I met Adele,[151] who literally fell off her bicycle and screamed at me, 'Where are you going Mrs James, surely *you* are not leaving the Forest?' I had to explain everything to her.

Tuesday September 24th

Last night the King spoke on the six o'clock news. He did speak well and his voice sounded so strong. Today I say from the bottom of my heart, 'God save the King. God bless the King.'

From the Forest to the Vale those RAF planes dropped leaflets with a message from the King and Queen telling us they have not forgotten us; just a simple message, written in the simplest language, but it has made all the difference; it has wiped away all the bitter feelings that we have been forgotten.

Thursday September 26th

A beautiful day. I passed the Forest Church at twenty-five minutes past eleven. It was such a lovely, cool autumn day that I did not rest at all. I did not meet anybody to talk to and I walked so quickly that I arrived at the Bungalow at a quarter to one.

Olive said that on Tuesday in the Town everybody was one huge beam; the message from the King and Queen was like a tonic.

After tea we went on to the field; the usual crowd were there. People are beginning to be more truculent with them. Mabel Kinnersly[152] found one in her garden. He said the view was so lovely, she said she quite agreed with him, but it was just as lovely the other side of the hedge and would he kindly go there! Another lady had her little dog in her arms and one of them came up and stroked it and asked its name. 'Spitfire,' says she looking him straight in the eye. He went very red and walked away.

They are purifying the libraries very thoroughly; they have taken sixty books out of Boots library. One day Miss Gaudion[153] had just arrived at her shop and she heard a hammering on her door. She leisurely took off her things, hid the till, pulled up her blinds and opened the door. Three of them came in and demanded books. She said she had none. They said, 'You had one in the window last week.'

'I have sold that,' she said.

'You must tell us the name and address of the person you have sold it to.

'A German!' she said. They left her.

Friday September 27th

I had had such a good night that I decided to go to Church at 8.30am I arrived there very early. St Stephen's is so altered; I can't recognise it. There was no one there. I walked around it and memories crowded over me. I went to see the little chapel where Mr Caparne had illustrated

---

[151] Adele Gallienne had been one of Violet's maids.
[152] Mabel Kinnersly was a great friend of Violet's. She was widowed and lived at 'Calais' in St Martins.
[153] Miss Gaudion owned a bookshop in town.

'Oh all ye works of the Lord'. I felt quite sad to find that they had washed all his little pictures out. I quite missed the little fishes which we always looked for. And then, like *The Provincial Lady in Wartime*, I felt I must hurriedly change the subject of my thoughts.

Sunday September 29th

A very cold wind but a fine day. Each Sunday I think, 'Well this last week hasn't been bad.'

There is a very grim notice in the paper. Here it is:

> Notice
>
> It must now be known to a good many local inhabitants that some eight persons recently left the Island in a boat with a view to reaching England.
>
> As a direct result, drastic control of boats has been instituted by the German Authorities, resulting in fishermen in the Northern and Western parts of our Island being unable to follow their vocation and depriving the population of a very large proportion of the fish obtainable. Any further such departures or attempts thereat, can only result in further restrictions.
>
> In other words, any persons who manage to get away do so at the expense of those left behind. In these circumstances, to get away, or attempt to get away is a crime against the local population, quite apart from the fact the German Authorities will deal very severely with persons who are caught making the attempt.
>
> A.J. Sherwill

October 1940

Thursday October 3rd

> 'Scent of smoke in the evening,
> Smell of rain in the night –'
> 'The Recall', R. Kipling

The first line was certainly applicable in the morning when I walked in. I have never seen so many bonfires; all the way in on both sides of the road. I could not understand it until Olive told me we are allowed to light bonfires on Mondays and Thursdays, much to the annoyance of people who do their laundry on Mondays. The natural presumption being that they never wash their clothes!

Victor was going to be allowed to write a letter to the Home Office, telling how we are getting on. A batty spinster who lives in St Martins has written a most insulting letter to the Commandant calling him a German swine and saying she had a leaflet and was not going to give it up and that she was a British subject. The police had to arrest her, which they did, and she was brought before the Commandant. What has happened to her, I don't know. Deported, I hope. Anyhow, with their usual justice, they have stopped all letters going and Victor's as well.

The tea party at the Vallon[154] went off very well. Victor seems to have been priceless. In his soft purring voice he proceeded to tell them about our winters, taking as a premise that last winter was a mild one; he said if it was not raining steadily for twenty-four hours, it was snowing, but neither the rain or the snow was bad compared with the dense, damp fogs which

---

[154] Victor Carey's house.

wrapped themselves round the Island, above the Island and all over the Island like thick cotton wool blankets, completely shutting out all visibility and sound. The only thing that was able to disperse the fog was wind, gales of wind, blowing either from the north, north-east or north-north-east. When they asked tentatively about the sun, he said, 'Oh! We quite forget what the sun looks like, for we never see it until April. And the rheumatism we suffer from in the winter, Mon Dieu! Mein Gott! It has to be endured to be believed!' Victor had tactfully made the most of the only possible subject!

Sunday October 6th
It is pouring with rain. It is very warm.

In the news this morning at 10am they said a little cockney was sweeping up glass and rubble and was watched by a number of people. He lifted up his broom to Heaven and said, 'Hitler's blinking 'ousemaid, that's me!' They gave a description of an air raid shelter in Stepney which has been made very comfortable. The people's motto is 'We take no notice', and they sing:

> I wouldn't leave my little wooden bunk for you,
> I have got one shelter and I don't want two.
> What's a doing there ain't no knowing
> I wouldn't leave my little wooden bunk for you.

On Saturday, a German bomber broke and the pilot baled out and landed in a sewage farm in Kent. A woman gazing up bumped into a lampost; she was the only casualty.

Monday October 7th
A beautiful day, so warm and sunny. Certainly we have had a perfect summer and autumn. On Friday they were taking an armed yacht out of the harbour full of blankets and cigarettes and other essential commodities. By marvellous navigation they managed to knock the pier, and the yacht sank gracefully out of sight. She settled down contentedly in the mud and flatly refuses to move. They don't know what to do about it and *nobody* can help them; it is very strange that in a seafaring community, there is no one able to give any practical advice on the subject. It has been pointed out to them that the flex was salvaged by a firm of their own countrymen plus their allies, the Italians, and so they had better see about it themselves. In the meantime, the yacht is lying snugly in the fairway, making herself a confounded nuisance to everyone.

Wednesday October 9th
In the *Star* this morning, all motor cars of 1939/40 have to be given up to the Germans, also all motorcycles and motor lorries.

There is a lovely south-westerly gale blowing. Our ancient and loyal ally, the sea, is mountains high and every now and then, we have drenching showers of rain. When it pours in the night, we think that as no civilians are allowed out, only they can be getting wet; that is a very happy thought!

James' car and Boys' car will not have to go with this lot. This has been quite a grim week. One of the cows, Snowdrop by name, had a heifer calf. She is a beautiful cow and for years they have been trying to get her into calf. The little heifer is a beautiful little animal. The Germans have ordered all calves born in October to be slaughtered. I put Sir Abraham Laine and Mr Johns[155] on my roll to be honoured for ever and ever in Guernsey; they argued with the Commandant for three hours; the latter wanted to order the murder of all the cattle on the Island. Finally Mr Johns said, 'Well, you will have to give the order yourselves, for I never will do so.'

Saturday October 12th
The most beautiful day of all. As I went for the bread, the larks were singing loudly. There was a white frost this morning. It was lovely, the sun was so hot, and the sky so blue.

Mrs Renault has just come home with the news that a third leaflet was dropped today and on it was written a message to 'everybody living near the aerodrome or near the White Rock to clear out'! Olive was most anxious for me to go there as she said I grumbled so much because I saw nothing and I would see so well at the Bungalow. I would love to, but I don't feel easy being away from home longer than I can help.

Beetle Drives have become very popular in Guernsey. The following letter appeared in the *Star*:

> The Cruelty of Beetle Drives
> Instead of applauding and encouraging these beetle drives and giving space in your paper to, what all decent-minded people will rightly consider a disgraceful undertaking, I think that your duty was to report the matter to the G.S.P.C.A. However, it will now have caught the eye of the authority and I sincerely hope that the matter will be taken up. Such wanton cruelty seems hardly possible in a so-called civilised world. People who indulge in these horrible undertakings are little better than the small boys who tear wings off flies and make the insects race up and down the table. And that the minister of the Church should associate himself with a 'sport' which in my opinion is akin to cock fighting is too dreadful to contemplate. What is Guernsey coming to?

The *Star* says, 'We leave it at that. All you people who are beetle drive fans will appreciate this story. The letter was signed by a very well-known lady of the community.'

Sunday October 13th
5.25pm
I was washing up the tea things and the front doorbell rang. I was alone in the house; James and Hedley had gone to fetch the cows. I opened the door and a good looking young German in a smart *new* uniform was there. He started to walk in and then I suppose he suddenly realised my substantial person was in the way and stopped. He asked for a motor car pump; suiting the action to the word, he said, 'Poomp! Poomp!' and worked his arms and foot up and down. Only a congenital idiot who was both blind and deaf could possibly have misunderstood him. I thought, well I had better be exceedingly stupid, for if I lent him the pump, he would never return it and it would give away the fact that we had a car. I smiled sweetly at him and continued to do so all the time, repeating slowly and perplexedly, 'Nooo! Mr! I do not understand, I am so sorry but I do not understand, I wish I could help you.' He continued to pump vigorously and say 'Poomp! poomp!' and I continued to shake my head slowly and smile sweetly and repeat monotonously, ' No! No! I do not understand.' At last he saluted me and went away.

---

[155] Abraham Laine and Mr Johns were members of the Controlling Committee.

Monday October 14th

After cursing Mr Sherwill up and down, I shall have to put him on my honours list. They wanted to take a thousand men to France. Sherwill told them firmly that we had given in to them in every way, but that we were an Open Town and that they had met with no resistance whatever when they occupied us and that according to International Law they could not deport a single man and he would not allow *one* to go. And that was that.

James went to see Maud[156] and she told him Aunt Edith had told her that a lady was walking down the Grange on Saturday and a German officer stopped her, saluted very politely and said in good English, 'I know I am in the suburbs but could you tell me how I can get to Regent Street?'! These had only just arrived.

They are convinced there are British soldiers hiding in the Island. The new Commandant, 'Bandelow', has published a letter in which he says if British soldiers who are hiding here will report by a certain date, they will be treated as prisoners of war and their relatives will not be punished for hiding them. If they do not give themselves up, and are caught after that date, they will be treated as agents of an enemy power and those hiding them will have to take the consequences.[157]

Colonel Count von Schmettow has been appointed Commandant of the British Channel Islands with headquarters in Jersey.

Sunday October 20th

A very hot, muggy day and drizzling in the morning. There was no service at the Forest Church, the Dean would not allow it.

When the order came out for boats to be given up, Sir Havilland wrote about the derelict boat on the pond at Sausmarez Manor and then forgot all about it! About a fortnight later, one morning he went down into the hall and found it full of soldiers. They had come about the boat and were very curt and solemnly carted it off in a lorry.[158]

Monday October 21st

A perfectly beautiful autumn day, very warm, hot sun, brilliant, blue sky.

The order has come. James has to take his car to St Peter Port on Thursday for the Germans to take away.

I can quite understand people taking to alcohol. I would willingly drink myself into forgetfulness and oblivion.

Thursday October 24th

> Welcome wild North-easter!
> Shame it is to see
> Odes to every zephyr,
> N'er a verse to thee.

---

[156] Maud was James' sister. She suffered from epilepsy and so had a companion, Mabel, who lived with her. They lived in St Peter Port.

[157] This refers to an exchange of letters between Sherwill and Bandelow published in the *Star*. Sherwill thought this would be the best way to make Islanders understand their responsibilities in relation to British soldiers.

[158] In September 1940 eight people had managed to escape from Guernsey in a boat (see entry for 29 September). As a result the Germans had imposed a ban on fishing and ordered that all boats should be handed in. The ban on fishing was later lifted, but restrictions enforced. (Cruickshank, p.122)

> Tired we are of summer
> Tired of gaudy glare,
> Showers, soft and steaming,
> Hot and breathless air.
>
> C. Kingsley

I don't know that I whole-heartedly agree with Mr Charles Kingsley about the north-east wind but I do think I prefer walking in it to that roasting heat. Anyway, I had it dead against me the whole way in to Olive's.

I arrived at Olive's in very good time. After lunch I had a deep, refreshing sleep until 4pm. I went down to see Aunt Edith and Vera. It is so pathetic how pleased everybody is to see one.

We discussed the shop people. I said I was in Le Riches and it made me fair sick to see how three of the *men* there were smarming over the Germans, none of the girls were. Of

Le Riches in town.

course, Cheeseborough[159] was, and two others. One of them was serving a German sailor, and at the end he shook hands with him, hoped he would come back soon and wished him a good voyage! There were six women besides myself, our 'chks' of disapproval could be heard all over the shop!

Vera says there is a society forming over here, calling themselves 'The Black Hand', and they intend to tar and feather all these men, Tetley and Cheeseborough heading the list!

Olive told me that Mrs Sherbrooke was in Creasey's and nobody attended to her for eight minutes and finally a girl languidly asked her what she wanted. She said, 'Mr Creasey please.' He was out, would Mr Beck do?

'Yes.' Mr Beck had to be torn away from talking to some Germans. Mrs Sherbrooke aired her grievances and she ended by saying, 'I'd like to tell you, Mr Beck, that when the visitors have gone, *we* shall still be here. Things will be very different then, as we will not forget.' Mr Beck literally wrung his hands and smarmed and smarmed. He humbly asked if she still wanted Mr Creasey. She said, 'No, not this time.' He turned and was going back to the Germans and she called out, 'But Mr Beck, am I still not going to be attended to?' And, at last, she was served.

Saturday October 26th

Poor James took his car down yesterday to be sold. He does not know what price he has got for it. Mr Ware told me he had taken his down too. They are saying that they are going to take the smaller cars for scrap iron. That is what Mr Sherwill deplores so much, people starting these rumours because he says it puts ideas into their heads.

A week ago on Friday, two more officers were brought here. The order came out that if British officers gave themselves up, they would be treated as prisoners of war and their people would not be punished.[160] These two officers, instead of hiding and waiting to be taken away in a submarine, gave themselves up. In consequence of that promise, ten people are now in prison. The officers were young Nicolle from St Peter's in the Wood and young Symes, whose father is one of the Le Riches managers. Therefore, Mr and Mrs Symes and Mr and Mrs Nicolle are in prison. Mr and Mrs Collins are in prison because Mr Collins employs Mr Symes. Miss Bird and Miss Marriette are both in prison because they are the fiancées of young Nicolle and young Symes and Mr and Mrs Bird are in prison because they are the father and mother of Miss Bird.[161]

November 1940

Friday November 1st   S.W.

A perfectly beautiful day, a mild south-west wind blowing. I was so looking forward to my day in Town. About 9.30am the doorbell rang, this was Tony Walters to say he was working for the States and had been given the day off to go round and warn people that they were going to

---

[159] Herbert Cheeseborough was originally from Yorkshire, lived at Le Panage in St Martins. He was an assistant at Le Riches and was renowned for collaboration.

[160] See entry for 16 October

[161] Hubert Nicolle and James Symes were sent on a reconnaissance trip on 3 September 1940; they had been ordered to gather information about the situation in the Island. Their rendezvous did not appear and they were stranded.
They managed to hide for about six weeks, firstly with their families, and then in the games pavilion at Elizabeth College. They were treated as prisoners of war. As Violet stated, those who helped them, including Sherwill, were also deported, but were released three months later and allowed to return to the Guernsey. (Cruickshank p.99)

all the houses to take men's clothes and silver! Utter consternation on our part. I did not go to Town but came straight home, calling at Markie's on the way, and I only took one hour to walk from the Bungalow to the Forest Church! It is awful.

Sunday November 3rd   S.W.
The gale raged in the night and torrents of rain.
    All those people have been let out of prison. The two boys were here a long time.

> The English will always be fools
> And we shall never be gentlemen.

One of them was supposed to have said that in the last war. And it is true. Those two boys were left here and told they were to take a boat and sail back to England! Anything more criminally casual I can't imagine. Nothing was taken into consideration, the gales or whether they knew anything about a boat or not!
    The atmosphere is so tense and uncomfortable now. Pilot Noyon says some people are going to get a surprise when they come back. He picturesquely says that he is going down to the boat to push the faces of those men who called themselves fishermen and ran away in a boat. They were all growers and the fishermen have had the blame and have not been allowed to go out fishing in consequence.[162]

Monday November 4th   S.W.
It is still blowing a gale but fine. We were getting on with them very well considering, but since these poor boys have been sent over here, everything is changed.

New Orders[163]
By order of the Fuehrer

On or before the fifth day of November 1940, every person who is sheltering a person of the following classes must make the report hereinafter ordered.

1. British subjects not of Guernsey birth with the exception of those who had their permanent residence in the Island before September 1st 1939.
2. British subjects who have come to the Island since the German Occupation.
3. British subjects including natives of the island who had left the island before the German Occupation and who have returned since.
4. Whoever, after November 5th 1940, continues to shelter a British subject of any of the foregoing classes without having made a required report, or who subsequently conceals a British subject of any of the foregoing classes, particularly members of the British Armed Forces, shall be shot.

Thursday November 7th   N.
A beautiful day. I went off in good time and darling Molly followed me and I had to bring her back, and once again I forgot my rucksack! Katty caught me up and walked with me to the Cache. I walked to Carmel and Adele came along. We had a long chat and a man with a delivery van came and offered me and my little cart a lift. He was going to the cricket field! It

---

[162] See reference for entry on 29 September.
[163] These orders were published in the *Star* on 4 November.

was lucky. He was a Mr le Page from the Old Forge Stores. When we got to the cricket field, we sat and chatted for about half an hour. We both agreed that, in spite of everything, we were both thankful we had stayed here. He said such a pretty sentence, I thought, 'that what your fingers had made you cherish', meaning that he had built up his business and could not bear to leave it. He said they made that crossroad where his shop is a rendezvous, sometimes a hundred would meet there and scatter, fully armed and with machine guns.

I had a lovely rest after lunch and the Bridge Club came. They told me the dire news about Mr Sherwill, that he had been under arrest in his own house. For twenty-two hours they would not let him take his clothes off and did not leave him alone for *one single minute* because he knew those boys were here and would not give them away. But they gave him away.[164]

Friday November 8th
Another perfectly beautiful day, cold enough to be bracing and yet a very warm sun. I went to Town in the afternoon. The Town seemed full of officers. I was buying some roller towels and tea towels in Creasey's. Mr Creasey was serving me, and he put my pile on the counter and went to fetch a tea towel they had used in the snack bar to show me how beautifully it had washed. In the meantime two Germans came in and picked up *my* towels and examined them, I immediately became a dear old soul 'Hi,' I cried, 'those are mine.'

'All right Madam,' said the shopman soothingly, and he tactfully led them away to the pile where mine came from. Mr Creasey came back and I said, 'For goodness sake pack my parcel up as quickly as you can,' which he did and I subsided.

I went back to the bungalow to tea. Olive had a tea party, Victor and Mrs Swete[165] were there. Victor told me what *he* thought of the British Government sending these young raw Guernsey boys over here to do a job that they ought to send a trained secret service man to do.[166] He said the awful part is they send them in mufti and so technically they become spies. Victor said after the war he was going over to see the Home Office and Mr Churchill if necessary. I hope he will. They send the boys over here and make quite sure they can't get back!

Saturday November 9th   N.W.
Blowing hard and pouring with rain. I was soaked going for the bread.

It is Grimmer and Grimmer and Grimmer. Poor Mr Sherwill and the Mariette girl have been taken to Paris! The Gestapo are doubled over here. There are 80 German Customs House officials come over to ransack the unoccupied houses. If we make a group of more than three we are tapped on the shoulder and told to move on! All clubs are closed. Only States Committees can meet. There is a rumour the churches will be closed.[167]

---

[164] Sherwill was arrested for helping Nicolle and Symes. He was deported to France along with approximately 23 other relatives and friends who had helped the spies. Sherwill was allowed to return three months later, but was released from his duties as President of the Controlling Committee. (Cruickshank, p.99)

[165] Mrs Swete was Victor Carey's sister-in-law. She came over to be his housekeeper when Victor's wife died.

[166] i.e. reconnaissance – trying to get information to help plan invasion.

[167] There was an order in France that all clubs, etc. should be closed due to risk of resistance. The Channel Islands came under the jurisdiction of the military government in Paris and the German authorities in the Islands insisted on enforcing these orders even though it was not strictly applicable. (Cruickshank, p.162)

Monday November 11th
It is blowing and raining in squalls.

No concerts can be held, no dances. We are not supposed to meet in our houses more than three of us at a time, and not to listen to the wireless in any other house but our own. There are a number of German officers over here now. How safe they must feel, so peaceful and tranquil, no bombs, no night alarms.

Tuesday November 12th   S.W.
An awful night, torrents of rain and a south-westerly gale. I went to fetch the bread with Molly. Kipling has written a pathetic little poem called 'Four Feet Trotting Behind'. I quote it to Molly who is always four legs dancing in front, I tell her that as she is about the only dog left in the Island with a pedigree a mile long, she ought to live up to her ancient lineage. Molly only grins vulgarly and dances on, she says what does it matter, as she does her job well and truly. She comes regularly with the push cart and would come on Thursdays as well to Town if she were allowed. She always goes with the cows and sees they are properly tied up, and would do the same with the bulls if allowed, and there would be fewer regrettable accidents in consequence, and she is a very hard working, responsible dog, and never barks except at them, and that her language is truly Billingsgate.

Thursday November 14th   N.W.
There was a terrific gale in the night, one of the worst we have had for years.

I went to tea at Birnam Court[168] with Victor and Mrs Swete, Mabel was there. I do admire Victor, he is so calm and so dignified and so wise. The position with Sherwill could not have been worse. There was Sherwill doing the job and taking all the praise, Victor taking all the responsibility and any blame. He said that Sherwill had let six weeks go by without consulting him or telling him a thing. He said the Gestapo had found out everything and they questioned all those people to catch them out and they told lies and fell into the trap.

What a curse that boy Nicolle has been to the Island. The bridge club came to Olive's, they were all in the depths of despair over the wireless.[169]

Order[170]

> The favouring of espionage in the Island of Guernsey makes further measures necessary. All wireless receiving sets of the Civil population will be requisitioned until further notice and deposited into a place of safety. In case of non delivery a fine of 30,000 Reich Marks will be imposed or 6 weeks imprisonment.

Poor Victor told me some of his worries, it is perfectly true things are so difficult to guard against. For instance, the British Legion decided to wear their badge always with a view to helping any of these boys who are sent over here. Of course, the Gestapo heard of it and forbade display of any badge. Victor hoped that the British Legion would keep quiet and fade out of the Gestapo memory. Unfortunately November 11th came along too soon and the B.L. asked the Kommandant's permission to lay a wreath on the war memorial. The Kommandant

---

[168] *Birnam Court* was a hotel on Queens Road in St Peter Port.
[169] Wirelesses were confiscated as a reprisal for the landing of British spies in the Island. (Cruickshank, p.99)
[170] This was announced in *La Gazette Officielle* on 14 November.

not only gave permission, but said the German Army would lay a wreath too. Victor was in despair; in spite of the fact of the whole of the Island police guarding that wreath, he saw it being kicked about in Fountain Street! However, the Kommandant went away and the wreath was forgotten to be ordered so the British Legion laid theirs without any fuss or incident.

They took over the *Richmond Hotel* and put 150 men in it. When the 150 left they wanted to put in a fresh lot. When the authorities went to see if everything was all right, they found everything smashed to bits, chairs, tables, doors, windows, etc., and the States had to put it all in order again, and so it goes on.

Sunday November 17th
Katty came to dinner. In pouring rain, in an open lorry, they took Jim's beautiful wireless away with crowds of others. I wonder if we will ever see it again.

Tuesday November 19th
A perfectly beautiful day, warm and sunny. I went for the bread accompanied by Molly. Just beyond the Manoir were about twelve huge soldiers. I thought I would go into the Manoir, and then I changed my mind and went on. They were all across the road but gave me room and then began to tease Molly. 'Boof' they all did to her, and Molly became frantic, barking, growling, trembling all over. I was terrified she would do something and they would shoot her, I hurried on and they formed up and tramped behind me. Oh how I *longed* to point to the sky and say, 'Breetish! 'Ide 'Ide!' I held on to Molly and they tramped by roaring with laughter. I thought what a completely different type they were to the first boys that came over. Everything is altering for the worst. All that involuntary mutual friendly spirit has gone.

James' car is being used by them, it has a large notice 'ZivilFahrbereitschaft' on it.

Wednesday November 20th
Today it is pouring with rain. The misery in the Island now the wireless has been taken away is pretty awful. Rumour has it that the next order will be that all the cats and dogs are to be murdered, and the horror of the young men being deported is always hanging over our heads.

They demand 7,000 lbs of butter a week.

That nice Mr le Page picked me up again last Thursday and we sat and talked, he was very depressed because they are going to have depots for groceries, he says it will ruin him. We both agreed that we had never realised what a prosperous little island this was, and how blessed in every way, and now look at it!

The dark in the mornings is appalling. Sun time I get up at 6am. Breakfast at 7.15am. Dinner at 10am. Tea at 2pm. Supper at 5.30pm. Bed 8pm.

Friday November 22nd
A beautiful day. I did not go out.

> Then doubt not, ye fearful--
> The Eternal is King--
> Up, heart, and be cheerful,
> And lustily sing--
> What chariots, what horses
> Against us shall bide

While the stars in their courses
Do fight on our side?'

'An Astrologers Song', R. Kipling

Tuesday November 26th

James told me *the most awful thing*. When they were thinking of reprisals for those boys being sent over here, they nearly decided to shoot twelve of our leading citizens, but Sherwill talked them out of it.

Thursday November 28th   E.

A beautiful day, very cold. Brilliant sunshine, blue sky and lovely clouds. Last night I saw a number of red flares and searchlights. There seemed to be planes over all night.

I went to the garage and they told me they wanted to bring Boy's car out here. I arrived at the Bungalow at five to one. I had a lovely rest and then I went to tea with Victor again at Birnam Court. Victor told me we are running out of stamps and he has had to devise a stamp. He has done one with the Guernsey arms and he wonders if they will insist on a swastika being put on it. (Another souvenir.)

Victor said the Home Office had the cheek to write and tell him to stick to his post, he said he had no intention of doing anything else and he wrote to French[171] and told him to stick to his, and French on his own authority ordered the evacuation of Alderney. One old farmer there had retired to his garret with his gun loaded, prepared to shoot anybody who disturbed him. He was persuaded to come over to Guernsey. We all fear Alderney will be derelict.

Friday November 29th

Another beautiful day. I went to St Stephen's Church for the half past eight service. It is easier being out at that time (really 6.30am). There were only three people there besides myself.

One old woman who has never paid a wireless licence flatly refuses to give up hers because she says, 'If I give it up how can I hear the news, me?!'

DECEMBER 1940

Tuesday December 10th   W.

A man rang up James, he wanted to know if the Court had passed an ordinance that day that all the dogs were to be destroyed, he had seen it in the Press. I couldn't tell him anything. My heart turned to lead when I thought of the little dancing dog being murdered. However, it is nothing of the sort. They want to bring dogs over from France and Germany and there are no muzzles in the Island and no leather to make them, so we have to keep all dogs on the lead for three months for fear of rabies. Bad enough. Any dog without a lead will be shot by the Germans, or arrested by the police.

Our letters are being returned to us. They have never left the Island.

Monday December 16th

A lovely day, much warmer. While I was getting up in the dark I heard a car drive up into the yard. I thought they are coming after James! But it was Ware fetching the calf. It is sickening, all calves born before January have to be killed, it is our third heifer calf they have taken.

---

[171] Mr F.G. French was the Judge (chief administrator) of Alderney.

Girlie and I were sitting peacefully in my room. I was doing sums and suddenly, without any warning, Bang! Bang! Boomp! Boomp! Boomp! Guns and bombs. Girlie and I sank gracefully to the floor and stayed there. The house shook. It was over in three minutes I suppose. Downstairs I went and found that James and the men had not only *seen* the English plane, but had *seen* the bombs dropping on the aerodrome, and I had seen *nothing*! But I had heard the beautiful engines.

Mrs Renault has just been to say (3pm) that one Guernseyman has been killed and three wounded and several Germans wounded and that the new hangar is smashed to bits. The men were playing cards under the hangar. The lunch hour has been changed, it was from one to two, and now it is 12.30 to 1.30pm. The Guernseymen tried to run off the aerodrome and the officers wouldn't let them. The plane flew slowly away from the aerodrome, and passed right over this house, but I did not see it, because I was reclining on the floor of my bedroom! Just one plane and three bombs dropped so accurately that they have destroyed the work of months. The men on the aerodrome were told to go home as quickly as possible, because the British would come again tonight! I don't think they will, the plane has done the job.

The hangar was only finished on Saturday, photographed on Sunday, and completely demolished on Monday! It was only big enough for one aeroplane. They are going to build eleven hangars like that. It was beautifully camouflaged as a greenhouse and the Germans were boasting that the English would have to be extremely clever to locate it. Well, apparently that boy with his exquisite marksmanship *was* extremely clever! The Officers were screaming with fright and hanging on to the Guernseymen in abject terror. I suppose the gun crews were in that condition too because they forgot to fire until the plane was well away. She seemed to start machine gunning from the aerodrome. Guernseymen say that long after she had gone, they met them coming, crouching, doubled up against the hedges, creeping along and deathly pale.

The men say my field is a wonderful sight with the camouflaged guns and huts and there are pails of a black fluid with which they can detect the approach of planes. I do hope they will go away in such a hurry, they will leave all that behind and I shall claim it as lovely souvenirs.

Tuesday December 17th
Such a lovely day and not very cold. I went to see Katty on my way to fetch the bread. She said she hid in the cupboard under the stairs. She made me very cross, because she said she had no sympathy for the Guernseymen who were killed and wounded because they had no business to be working for the Germans for higher wages, that *she knew* they were getting higher wages. They are *not* getting higher wages, they are paid £1 10s. a week and 8s. if they are married, just the same as any other employee by the States, and they are driven up at the point of the bayonet. I don't know what will happen after this. While we were arguing, bang! bang! bang! went the machine guns. I was *not* going to be shut up in that blinking Manoir in the dark with all the shutters shut, so I departed hastily and went on to fetch the bread. The machine guns were going off all the time but there wasn't a sound of a plane, so I was sure they were practising. In fact I am beginning to think their technique is to fire before the plane arrives and after its departure!

Thursday December 19th   S.W.
It poured with rain in the night but it was only drizzling a little when I started off to Town and it stopped altogether when I arrived and then a downpour came.

Victor told Olive a good story. The Germans suddenly decided they would make a house-to-house collection of leaflets,[172] so a policeman and a German were detailed to collect them. They began to plod methodically down one street and the German decided it was much too slow, so he suggested he would take one street and the bobby should take another. The bobby agreed with alacrity and off the German went. The next house the bobby knocked at was opened by the man of the house. 'Have you any leaflets?' says the bobby. 'Oh *no*,' says the man. 'Haven't seen no blinking leaflets.'

'Haven't you, old chap?' says the bobby, pulling two out of his pocket. 'Well, here are two for you!'

Friday December 20th   E.
It poured in the night but it was fine all day. I went to Town in the morning. There is now a new noise in the Town. On all sides you hear the her! hur! her! hur! her! hur! of panting dogs straining at their leashes and see exhausted owners leaning against anything they can find. It is awful!

Tuesday December 24th   N.E.
In the afternoon I went with the laundry. When I came home, I found Mrs Renault was in a state of wild excitement. It said in the *Star* we were to have our wireless back, the postman had told her. I said I would not believe it until the wireless was back; the *Star* had reported we were to change the time and had to contradict itself the next day. And where was the *Star* anyway, of course it had not come; whenever there is anything extra important the *Star* fails to make an appearance. I fumed and swore and suddenly, like a hurricane, James appeared. 'Where are the wireless receipts, yes we can fetch them, I am going now with the cart, the *Star* was kept back until 3 o'clock to print the news!' Wonder upon wonder, I found the receipt AT ONCE! I wonder why they have given us them back?

Two Germans came here this morning looking for chickens to roast. James told them our game fowl were certainly not fit for roasting, which happened to be true. They start with being survival of the fittest and go on from muscular strength to muscular strength. They always remind me of that music hall ditty:

> Oh that cock must have crowed
> When they built the tower of Babel
> Fed by Cain and Abel
> Reared in Noah's stable.
> All the shots that were fired on the field of Waterloo
> Could not have penetrated
> That intensely elongated
> Double breasted
> Iron chested
> Cock a doodle doo!

THE WIRELESS IS BACK IN THE DINING ROOM AND I HAVE HEARD THE 7 O'CLOCK NEWS.

---

[172] This refers to leaflets dropped by the RAF with information about England.

Wednesday Christmas Day

A fine day but cloudy and not so cold. A heifer is sick so Lainé is coming to see it. James has gone to the Câtel church. There is no service in the Forest. I am longing for the day to be over. I rang up Olive and she said the prisoners connected with that dreadful Nicolle boy are being released.

I listened to a service on the wireless. We heard the news. All quiet on both sides.

I said to Mrs Renault, 'I won't wish you a happy Christmas, I can't.' And so she said, 'No, I can't wish you one either.'

'But,' I said, 'I wish you a happy Christmas in `41.' And we both drank to that in Spanish wine.

Friday December 27th   N.W.

I went to Peggy and Bertie. Peggy had just got back, she told me a very interesting story. She said she had seen Doris and Doris told her she had had a chat with the chauffeur who drove the adjutant about. There was some heavy bombardment heard this morning and this chauffeur asked the adjutant about it and he said he had heard it too and he went on and said that 'Every bomb that is dropped on France shortens our stay here.' The chauffeur tried to draw him out and he went on, 'I consider that our position here is most precarious and I shan't be surprised if we are all gone by February.' He might of course been trying to catch the chauffeur out, *or* he might have been stating a perfectly genuine opinion!

Saturday December 28th

I did not go to Town, I went to see Markie instead, she was very pleased to see me and told me a good story. We were talking about the camouflaged hangar and she said she had heard they had made a wooden hangar in France at St Malo and put a wooden plane in it as camouflage and the RAF had found out about it and had dropped wooden bombs on it with a message that it was not worth a real bomb!

Olive and I confessed to each other our secret conviction that being without the wireless had added zest to our lives! We both looked at each other, rather horrified, and then explained ourselves. We discovered that we had only been told *good news* which always bucked us up *enormously*! Olive said she would go to Town and meet people and whisper, 'Have you heard any news?' and quite openly they would pull out of their pockets a typewritten slip of paper. I think if we had had a different type of Kommandant we would *all* have been in prison! Maud had the news brought to her twice a day and she used to write it out for James and then we heard so many joyous rumours which gave us such thrills. Anyhow, if the wireless is taken away again, we shan't feel the bottom has dropped out of everything, like we did. I am told it has cost the Island a thousand pounds taking away and restoring the wireless!

The poor postmen spent all Christmas Day and Boxing Day returning them, if they hadn't had to do that, they would have spent Christmas Day quietly at home for the first time in their lives as postmen!

Monday December 30th   S.W.

Dear Molly flatly refuses to be led by anybody but me, she just sits down. The reason is psychological. Having come to the lamentable conclusion that I have gone quite mad, Molly thinks it is *her* duty to lead me and the little cart to fetch the bread, and so bravely and

Mabel Kinnersly.

Ethel Hazell.

conscientiously fulfils her duty and we are both satisfied. I am as long as she wags her tail all the time and she is always pleased when she is seeing a job well done by doing it herself.

On Saturday there were some people talking very indiscreetly about the Germans in Le Noury at lunch time and a man who was there handed a note to the girl in the pay desk to give to them, and in it he said he was a member of the Gestapo and they would hear from the Gestapo shortly!

They had all the pork in the Island for their Christmas dinners. Four hundred had dinners and four hundred will have dinners on New Years Day with champagne and wine and spirits galore, all at the expense of the States.

Tuesday December 31st
Pouring with rain. James went to Town and I had lunch and tea with Katty. I spent a very pleasant afternoon and I was quite comfortable until I suddenly realised I had come out without my identity card! Ugh! Cold shudders ran up and down my spine! If I am caught, I decided I would say 'Kommen mit mir,' and I would tap my forehead at intervals until I had got them safely within my own gates and then I would hand them over to James and rush up and get my card and put it in my pocket and come down and be a 'dear old soul'. However, mercifully, none of these precautions were needed because I did not meet a soul going home.

The rain did not cease all day, it poured all the night before.

Maud had copied out the message sent to the Channel Islands on Christmas Day. This was it:

> 'We remember the people in the Channel Islands: the people very dear to our hearts.
> We wish them a happy Christmas, but a still happier New Year.'

And so (this year) has come to an end, one of the very loveliest years Nature has ever bestowed on us, in vivid contrast to the hideous conditions imposed upon us by man.

Never have we had such a perfect tomato crop, or such a good potato crop, free of disease. The grapes likewise and the flowers. All the crops have been good.

James and Violet Carey, late 1940.

The Diaries of Violet Carey, 1941

January 1941

Saturday January 4th   N.E.

A black north-east wind blowing colder than ever. My fingers ache intolerably.

When we could not have our wireless, one couple hid theirs in a large pouffe and the Germans searched their house. There was a gramophone on a table and they asked to play and were graciously given permission, and the lady of the house sat on the pouffe the whole time and they never found it.

The prisoners have arrived: Mr Sherwill and Tommy Mansell, etc.[173] Mr Sherwill can't be Procureur,[174] the Germans won't have anything to do with him at all. James met one of the prisoners who told him about their *awful* experiences. They were away sixty days and never changed their clothes or had a bath. They were alone in cells 6 ft by 5 ft and only went out two days with guards. The French wardens were as good to them as they could be. The fathers of the two boys were told one day that the boys were to be shot, two days after a reprieve, two days after they were shot and so on. This torture went on for the whole sixty days. At last on December 22nd poor *poor* Mr Symes could not stand it any more, his nerve gave way completely and he opened a vein in his arm and committed suicide. Two days after, the real reprieve and the real release of the prisoners came. It is too tragic, he was such a *nice* man and had one of the sweetest smiles I have ever seen.

Tuesday January 7th   N.E.

The sky is full of snow and it is sleeting. James had to go to Court today at 11.30am. I have not been out today. It is so dark in the house we have had to use the electric light all day, we are lucky to have it. How our lives have altered. No social life at all. If the telephone rings, it is a moment of tense excitement and expectancy, wondering for whom it has rung, generally it is James. When we were first occupied, I had the idea of ringing up all my friends periodically to have a cosy chat with them, but, alas, the Gestapo have squashed all those ideas. One of our most absorbing occupations is hot water. Boiling it, preserving it, to make it go as far as possible. Fetching the bread, carrying and fetching the laundry. Except for ourselves, we do not meet a soul on the roads going and coming and we know all the houses that are empty. It is a weird, silent world, the silence broken only by the roar of their planes in the air and the roar of their cars on the road.

---

[173] These prisoners were the Islanders who had been deported for helping the two commandos, Nicolle and Symes, who had landed on the island to spy. (See entry and footnote for 26 October 1940.)

[174] Mr Sherwill had been the Procureur (Attorney-General) and President of the Controlling Committee before this incident. However, following his return from prison in France, the Germans did not permit him to perform any duty having public character. (Bell, *Commando*, p.49)

Inspector Sculpher[175] told James of an interesting conversation he had with the German head of police here. The German could simply not understand or get over the fact that people here came to Court when summoned, without being fetched by an armed guard. He said, 'But how do you make them come?'

'Oh,' said Sculpher, 'they receive a summons and they come!'

'Yes, but *how* do you *make* them come?'

'We don't have to *make* them come, they come,' said Sculpher rather helplessly. Then Sculpher went on and said to him, 'Anyhow, we treat our prisoners quite differently before trial. You treat yours as if they had been convicted of the most awful crimes, we treat ours as if they were innocent until proven guilty.'

'But how do you make them speak or tell the truth?' asked the German.

'Oh, we don't have to make them speak. They speak all right,' said Sculpher. The German went away, shaking his head.

In the market last Saturday, a German asked a woman who sold eggs if she had any and she said 'No.' After he had gone, she whispered to a friend of hers who was standing by, 'I have plenty at home, I will let you have a dozen.' Some minutes later the German came back, tapped her on the shoulder and told her to come with him. Outside there was a car with an officer in it, who told her to get in and take them to her home, on pain of death if she refused. She was to give them all her eggs and, of course, she did, and they brought her back to the market. She thought hard how they had found it out, and then she remembered noticing a quiet, little, strange woman who had been standing near her at the time, and who had disappeared. One of the Gestapo.

Sunday January 12th   S.E.
The air raid has sent a great number of the Guernsey people into the asylum who would never have gone there otherwise. I wonder if they will ever realise all the misery they have caused innocent people. The extraordinary thing about it all is they have the most enormous admiration for the British people and regard the young airmen as gods. They say to the people here, 'We can be friends, why can't our governments agree?' One of the sentries outside Government House was a gardener and he made friends with the Springfield gardener and one day he said to him, 'I don't want to kill you, you don't want to kill me, *he* gets all the praise and we die.'!

Tuesday January 14th   S.W.
A fine day and warmer. I went for the bread and left the front door unlocked for the postman. I came back about 12 to find Mrs Renault on the verge of a nervous breakdown and James in a hurricane of rage against Timmer! A German had come in by the front door and walked all over the house downstairs and was shouting. Mrs Renault was outside and came in and found him in the kitchen. He asked for 'Miss Michelle Carey'. Mrs Renault was just able to call James and show the German outside. He wanted to know when she had been in Germany. James explained that she had been in Austria not Germany and had never been in Berlin. The German was in plain clothes and was a member of the Gestapo. James said he was very nice and said himself it was all red tape. He wanted to know when Michelle left school, the dates of her visits to Vienna, the dates of her time in St George's Hospital and where she is now. I

---

[175] Inspector Sculpher was the Chief of Police in Guernsey.

said I thought the Bauers[176] were enquiring after her through the International Red Cross and James said the chap had suggested that too! James did not get a single date right, he kept saying that I would know, etc. It is an extraordinary thing, I haven't been for the bread myself for three weeks, I haven't left the front door unlocked for months and this should happen when I do both things. I *always* seem to miss everything. As a matter of fact, finding the door unlocked probably put him in a good temper. He wanted to know if she had evacuated. James was in a temper with Timmer because he brought the German here and hid himself in the lane. He is a fool not to know that he would be seen.

Wednesday January 22nd   S.W.
A beautiful day. No wind and bright sunshine and warm.
   I was out in the front and Mr Rannsson arrived, we chatted for some time and he began shouting about the Germans. I felt horribly inhospitable but I just *could not* ask him in. I can't bear that sort of thing, it is so dangerous and so stupid, so I let him go.

Thursday January 23rd
I had a lovely walk in, for a long time I have not seen so many cars rushing about. I hear some very grand officers have come over today and that is the cause of all the commotion.
   After tea I went to see Peggy and Bertie. Peggy told us the worst story I have heard yet. A woman at St Peters was looking out at her front garden and she discovered a young German standing in it. He was standing quite still, suddenly he shot himself and fell dead. Feeling sick and dizzy, she didn't know what to do, but she didn't have to decide because in a minute her garden was full of Germans, and they buried him there!

Saturday January 25th
The unrest among them here is getting worse and worse. Some have told the F.N.A.[177] they want to be taken prisoner and to stay here and work for the States. Doris said, 'One day this week, there were two Germans looking at a vegetable stall in the market and a young German was standing behind them eating something out of paper bag. When he had finished, he blew out the paper bag and popped it. Without looking to see where the bang came from, the other two dived down the steps into the air raid shelter followed by roars of laughter from the whole market!

Thursday January 30th
Countess Blucher and her sister were at Olive's when I came back. She is very concerned because they are always wandering around Havilland Hall. They were there today, one was a very important looking officer. They don't come to the house and ask to see her, they just nose around. I wonder if they want to put a gun there. Once, two of them did ask for her. In course of conversation, they asked permission to smoke, and offered the Countess and Princess Radziwill cigarettes. The Princess cannot or won't speak German and she has a very sweet, placid face. She said she tried to convey as eloquently as she could by her expression that she was an inveterate smoker, but would sooner endure the fires of Hell than smoke a German cigarette!!

---

[176] After finishing school and before going to train as a nurse, Michelle had stayed as a paying guest with the Bauer family in Austria.
[177] According to Michelle Nixon F.N.A. stands for 'Forest Newsagency'. I have been unable to identify who or what this was. The local shop was called Luff & Co. at the time.

Seven months ago today they arrived. I don't know what it seems like. Aeons and aeons of time. A year ago today Boy arrived on sick leave. I never thought he wouldn't be able to come again.

February 1941

Thursday February 6th   S.E.
I went out of an icy cold house into the balmy atmosphere of spring. I stood outside the front door and I breathed deeply at 6.30am suntime. It certainly has taken a European war and a German Occupation to have Violet Mary up and dressed at 6.30am! It became a *lovely* day. I had a beautiful walk in. Young Brehaut caught me up and walked with me. He told me when they first came to Milestones, his mother was dreadfully upset and was crying bitterly and the Germans patted her on the shoulder and said, 'Don't cry. We shall only be here for three weeks, we have conquered France in a fortnight and all the other countries and England is such a tiny little Island, our governments will come to an agreement and we shall all be home by Christmas!' He said those Germans were very clean and carried up all the china for Mrs Brehaut to put away in a top room. They went away, and others came and now the house is in a terrible state. He said that there were pantechnicons[178] on the pier with the names 'Weymouth' and 'Southampton' on them, and they took them away to Germany to pretend they had landed in Weymouth and Southampton. He said a friend of his told him a German with a map of England had stopped him and asked how he could get to Liverpool, and when he had made the German understand he could not get to Liverpool, the German tore the map in shreds and cursed something 'orrible!

Friday February 7th   S.E.
It poured in torrents all night and there was a thick fog in the morning. I went to Town. In the fish market I met an old biddy who I have met now three times, she plants herself firmly in front of me, she wears an old macintosh and an ancient hat and she says, 'Cor, what a to do, eh?' I say heartily, 'Yes indeed.' Then she turns away to go and says, 'They say we shall be on the rocks next week, but I don't believe it, eh? Cor!' I say even more heartily, 'No, of course, not more do I!' and we part until next time!

Thursday February 13th   S.W.
The Bridge Club came. I went to tea with Victor. There was no one there but myself. He told me that Dr Brosch is worried to death over us, the civil population, they expect a great attack from the RAF. How extraordinary it is that our enemies should be so concerned about us because of our own air force! Dr Brosch has ordered a thousand men to train to deal with incendiary bombs, etc. And all we are feeling is, 'Why don't they come? How I wish they would come.' They were photographing over the aerodrome earlier in the week, so we can expect them any day now.

Thursday February 20th   N.W.
I was afraid I would not be able to go today. It was snowing hard at 9am but by 11am it was quite fine and to my surprise not very cold, so off I went. I had a beautiful walk. I met Mabel Kinnersly at the corner of Mount Row. She was very upset because Mrs Sherbrooke, Peter and

---

[178] Furniture vans.

Bet[179] were all under arrest in their own house. They had not been allowed out for two days, with Herr Geiss, one of the Gestapo with them all the time. They had two maids, Guernsey girls, aged fifteen and sixteen and they had been caught signalling out of an upper window. The house is in the Gravees. The girls had been taken to prison, one was kept in prison and the other sent back and made to go out to be a decoy.

I saw Peggy Brock in the evening, she had been doing Mrs Sherbrooke's shopping for her. Peggy said Mabel talked too much which is quite true. I had tea with Victor and he said the same thing, he knew about it and was very disturbed. We never know where these sorts of things will lead to.

Friday February 28th   S.W.

I have heard the astonishing sequel to the Kinnersly and Sherbrooke episode. One of the girls called Doris Guille, aged 17, did it all for a joke! She began it weeks ago when she threw an anonymous letter in a German officer's car, saying that 'Mrs Sherbrooke was a secret agent and a British spy'. They searched her room and found a photograph of her sitting on a German's knee with her arms around his neck. She seems a bit dotty and they say she has seen too many films. She broke down under a German examination and confessed everything. They are still detaining her. The other girl is completely innocent.

March 1941

Monday March 3rd   S.W.

A fine day, but cold and showery. I have had no Red Cross letter today. We all live for the post. Our peak hour is about 1pm. The postman came but only with a notice of a dairy meeting. I was told that there were bags and bags and bags of letters in Guernsey, they are delivered 2,000 at a time and until those are answered and despatched back, they won't deliver any.

There are any amount of helpers at Elizabeth College, it really is the only place where anybody can do war work. Some canteens have been opened and have been shut again. St Sampsons have some wonderful communal kitchens for workmen whose wives have gone away. Miss Ross told me she helped at one, they not only feed the men but they darn their socks and clothes and wash them. They have soup kitchens at the Câtel.

Bread is to be rationed, the order is in the paper today. Six pounds, 2½ oz a week, per head. That is just about what we take.

Thursday March 6th   N.W.

Not at all a nice day, but I was able to walk to Olive's. Olive had three tables of Bridge, the usual people. I had tea with them and then I went to see Aunt Edith and Vera. Vera told me that the 'Black Hand' had three down on the list. She said with much relish, they are all going to be thrown into the harbour with bricks round their necks so they won't come up again!

The two girls are still in prison.[180] The innocent one was taken to Jersey. The guilty one is at Fort George. She did lead them a dance. When they ordered her to go for a walk, she *did* go for a walk, miles! And then stood completely still for twenty minutes in the teeth of the N.E. wind and they had to stand completely still too! In the same wind! For three nights they sat up

---

[179] Peter and Bet Kinnersly were Mabel Kinnersly's son and daughter-in-law.
[180] This refers to the incident Violet wrote about on 20 and 28 February 1940.

in Mrs Sherbrooke's house and signalled wildly, but in vain. They left a boy to watch all night in the house and he slept soundly and the girl he was supposed to be watching rushed down and woke him up to be in time to open the door to the officer. Anything more comic opera can't be imagined!

The stock phrase in the Island now is, 'The Germans take a very serious view of the mattter.'

On Monday night the Brocks were kept awake by the Germans halting *everybody* and banging around the bushes looking for something or somebody. The latest thing they are taking a very serious view over is a derelict moth aeroplane that has been found in a garage. About eight or ten years ago Noel built a moth plane. I can remember all the excitement about it, he tried it out at Vazon, it rose about 100 feet and crashed, and never rose again! Young Kenneth Bell is in charge of this garage, and found this plane and reported it. 'The Germans took a very serious view of the matter' and were quite convinced it was kept there for someone to fly to England, they tried to start up the engine and the engine started at once! If the devil wasn't in that, I don't know who was. The serious view of the Germans became an absolute panic! They have taken the unfortunate Kenneth Bell to France.

Thursday March 13th   S.E.
A perfectly beautiful day. No wind, blue sky, and sunshine. I had a very pleasant walk in.

Olive told me a good story, it happened today. A German was in a shop in Town and he put down a half crown to pay for what he had bought and he said, 'This is your King's head and he has gone to America.'

'Oh,' said the shopman. 'Then why do you take the trouble to bomb Buckingham Palace if the King is not there?' The German was so annoyed he bounced out of the shop leaving his change behind him.

I went to tea with Victor. He was very cheerful. He said he had had a very quiet week with no undue alarms. Victor told me what he noticed about the Germans here is they are all permeated with fear. They are terrified of each other, of all of us. He said if he has to write to them about anything, they never answer back in writing, always verbally, and also, when he is talking to them, even if they can speak English perfectly, they always speak German with an interpreter.

Friday March 14th   S.E.
Another beautiful day. I went to Town. I managed to get 1 lb of raisins at Plummer.[181] The queue reached round to Berthelot Street. The queue outside Pommier and Collins[182] is now nearly as big. I had lunch at Berthelot Street. The spies were there again drinking Spanish wine! That stamped them as foreigners at once!

I went up to the Bungalow to tea with Mrs Fisher and Olive. Ware fetched me at 5.30 and driving out told me the awful news about James' car. At 8.30am this morning, Ware saw a car driving down the Chêne Hill at 40 miles an hour. A bus came out of the St Andrews road and hit the car at the back. The car turned over and over four times. It was driven by a German interpreter and a Swiss girl was with him. The girl was badly hurt, the man only had a cut hand. This is the second bad smash the man has had. The car was smashed to smithereens, number 1403, poor James' car.

---

[181] Tea shop in the Arcade.
[182] A delicatessen shop.

Olive de Sausmarez. *Emily Fisher.*

Saturday March 15th   S.E.

Another lovely day. Doris came out to tea and I gave her ormers for tea! We did have a lovely meal, and we felt so completely replete, the first time for months! It has been the most wonderful tide and the ormers are so huge, real grandfathers who have retained their youth because they are so beautifully tender.

Doris told me that the First Lord of the Admiralty had made the most heartening speech last night on the seven o'clock news. A wonderful speech in which he said that once the flood of American help started to come, the end of the war will come very quickly.

Tuesday March 18th   E.

A nasty, cold, east windy, morning. Dry.

The little dancing dog and I went for the bread. Molly danced the whole way there and back because she was the off the lead. The order was not renewed on Saturday. The weather improved and was beautiful in the afternoon. Molly and I took the laundry and then we went off to Dingle for hen's eggs and to the Gorvel's for duck eggs. Only Mr Gorvel was there. How that poor man has changed, he has shrunk to half his size, he looks awful. The lack of food is hitting men who have to do hard work terribly. James says they feel it most when they have to lift anything.

The BBC announced the casualties: on Merseyside, 500 dead and 500 wounded. On Clydeside, 500 dead and 800 wounded, just like that, and immediately talked about the East.

Wednesday March 19th   E.

Notice[183]

On account of an act of sabotage, I order in agreement with the Island Commandant the following:

1. The curfew for the civil population is from 9pm to 7am.
2. The States of Guernsey have to report daily in writing to the Inselkommandantur starting on March 19th 1941 until 12 noon, 60 men, 18-45 years of age, who are used in accordance with the Island Commandant's order for performing guard tasks during night time.
3. I especially draw attention to the most severe penalties for acts of sabotage. (Death sentence)

Signed: The Field Commandant Schumacher Colonel

Monday March 24th   S.E.

I went to the aeroplane vineries this morning for beans. Molly galloped the whole way there and back. Olive and I were saying to each other how the children would say to us, 'What did you do in the Occupation mummy?'

'I filled hot water bottles,' said Olive, poor dear, she certainly does, day and night, for her mother. I shall say, 'I walked miles!'

Thursday March 27th   S.E.

New Moon

A lovely morning. I had a very pleasant walk in. Olive told me about the turmoil in Queen's Road. They had all been in an uproar because they had been told the whole road was to be evacuated. Bertie Brock and several others went to see the Kommandantur and he was very nice to them and he said they would not require any more houses at present.

They are in Beechwood, Belmont, Sausmarez Lodge, and Feckenham House and Petit Marche. The Chauncey's have had to leave Mount Durand and have gone into Mrs Sidgewick's house in King's Road. The Germans went to see Rozel and Winnie Harvey's house. Winnie's gardener put them off, so they never went inside at all. He told them, shaking his head all the time, that it was in a *terrible* state of repair and *no* conveniences whatsoever. Winnie having literally spent hundreds on it! This turning people out at twenty-four hours notice is awful. These seem much more aggressive and typically German.

Monday March 31st   S.W.

An ominous law was passed on March 21st. Conferring power on the President of the States of Guernsey to require any male person who shall have attained the age of eighteen to perform the duties that may be assigned to him by the said President or by any person or persons acting under his authority.[184]

---

[183] This was copied from the *Star*, 19 March 1941. The *Star* also reported that someone had 'deliberately and maliciously cut a telephone wire in the neighbourhood of the airport.' The Germans responded with the punishment that the five parishes nearest the airport had to provide men for guard duty.

[184] This law was passed following acts of sabotage by Guernseymen. The Germans had punished the Islanders by demanding that men perform guard tasks, and this law made such guard duty legal.

And whereas the said 'Projet de Loi' having received the sanction of the British Civil Lieutenant Governor was submitted to the German Feldkommandant who thereupon accorded his approval thereby?![185]

April 1941

Friday April 4th   S.W.
A lovely day. It rained in the night. I went to Town.

Victor was talking to me about the King's speech at the time of evacuation. It was sent over and Victor was told to read it in public, not before 2.30pm, on Thursday June 27th and on no account was it to be published. Victor thought they gave him those orders so as to give them time to send it to the Foreign Office, who would tell a neutral embassy to let the Germans know we were demilitarised and an Open Town. They didn't.

This is the King's speech:

> Home Office, June 24th 1940.
> I am commanded by the King to transmit to you a message from His Majesty for communication to the people of Guernsey in such a manner as may seem to you advisable having regard to the interests of National security.
> signed John Anderson
>
> The King's Message
> For strategic reasons it has been found necessary to withdraw the armed forces from the Channel Islands. I deeply regret this necessity and I wish to assure my people in the Islands that, in taking this decision, my Government have not been unmindful of their position, it is in their interest that the step should be taken in present circumstances. The long association of the Islands with the Crown, and the loyal service the people of the Islands have rendered to my ancestors and myself are guarantees that the link between us will remain unbroken, and I know that my people in the Islands will look for peace with the same confidence that I do to the day when the resolute fortitude with which we face our present difficulties will reap the reward of victory.

Doris asked me if I knew about the speech because people were criticising Victor and saying he had suppressed it. After he had told me, I went to the Greffe and copied it out.

The Germans are always at the Greffe, they *cannot* understand why there are no Jews here!

Wednesday April 9th   N.E.
Still north-east wind. I went for vegetables. They had beautiful celery and lettuces. It is strange to walk along the silent, deserted lanes and roads. I always used to say that the Sark gulls and larks sang just that much better than the Guernsey ones. I don't think so now. It is because of the silence in Sark, and now that we have that silence here, the birds have the same atmosphere to sing in.

---

[185] A Projet de Loi is a draft of a law which would normally be sanctioned by the Privy Council, but this was obviously not possible during the Occupation. Violet's exclamation probably reflects the fact that the law had been sanctioned by the Feldkommandant.

Saturday April 12th   N.E.
Same old wind. This is a blackthorn winter.[186]

The German authorities have sent the civilians here one egg each for Easter. What an incomprehensible nation they are, that is a very kind gesture. And yet at the word of command, they would machine gun and massacre every one of us.

Thursday April 17th   N.W.
A perfectly lovely day. I had a beautiful walk in. I took my tea for the first time. This morning Mrs Renault called to me to come quick and I came quick! There were four RAF flying high up overhead making the most lovely sky writing. It looked like an 'E' to me, but other people said they wrote 'OK' and didn't the Jerries get into a stew!

Prince von Oettingen called on the Countess Blucher, he knew a number of her people and was able to tell her that her estates in Czechoslovakia were intact and that her nephew was looking after them. When he was going, he asked if he could call again. She said, 'No, when peace was declared and happier times come again she would welcome him warmly but, until then, she could not receive him.' I do *like* her dignified attitude. So different from some of the people who accept cigarettes and cigarette coupons from them.

Thursday April 24th   N.E.
A black, bitter, biting north-east wind blowing, and I had to walk to the Bungalow in it. It was *awful*. I went through the lanes.

I met Lyon Falkener[187] and he said they were trying to cook out of doors and it was miserable, it would be! I told him we were managing quite comfortably on a small wood fire in the study, we could use two small saucepans and we are three people and they are only two. He did look ill. It is dreadful how ill and white all these men look.

Saturday April 26th   N.E.
Still the same old wind, but we must not grumble at it because it is a foul wind for England and they are assembling here to go to England. It looks as if our staunch allies, the wind and the waves, are once more going to play their part in helping us. Oh! *Why* don't the RAF bomb our aerodrome to pieces? How we *long* for them to come and do it, even the people who have greenhouses near the aerodrome say they don't mind what happens to them if only the RAF would come. Poor Richard, whose greenhouse was smashed, said to me, 'Never mind, that was a grand lad who did it.'

Those two girls who hoaxed the Germans have been tried in Jersey, one has got seven months imprisonment and the other five months.[188]

Monday April 28th   N.E.
A beautiful day. No wind. All the young green looks so lovely. The birds are singing so beautifully.

The order today is that men are to have 11oz of meat a week and women 9oz a week.

---

[186] A country saying for when there is a very cold spell and the blackthorn is in flower.
[187] Lyon was the husband of Ethel and father of Margery.
[188] This refers to an incident recorded on 27 and 28 February 1941.

I have just listened to the 7pm news and a despatch on a record from a BBC war correspondent in a battle against the Italians in Abyssinia. We could hear the shells falling and he described them as close ones, and that he and the van were covered in mud. We, sitting in armchairs, gazing out at the peaceful pageant of Nature in the Spring! That is what makes our lives so unreal and horrible, knowing what is taking place in England, while we are defended by the enemy themselves. As I walked along some weeks back, the beautiful yellow of the unpicked daffodils in the fields literally hurt my eyes.

May 1941

Thursday May 8th
Olive told me a delightful story. A Mr O'Keafe here had occasion to visit the German authorities, the officer said to him, 'Who do you think will win?'

'The English of course,' he replied. The officer puffed and blew and then said, 'The war will be over in three weeks time.'

'Don't you think you are rather flattering us?' replied Mr O'Keafe.

The queues for fish have grown longer and longer. One fishwoman is horribly rude to everybody, she exasperated one woman in the queue so much that the woman picked up a piece of fish and slapped her face hard with it! The people were giving 12s. 6d. and even 25s. for crabs.

Tuesday May 13th
Fish are to be rationed, the riotous queues in the fishmarket have made it necessary. We are ordered to fetch our fish ration cards from the Ladies College.

> Order – Fish Rationing
> The word 'Fish' used in this Order means wet fish, lobsters, crawfish, crabs and spider crabs which have been caught by means of the use of a boat. One Rationing card to be issued per household. When there are two respective purchasers, the one whose card shows the longest interval since purchasing fish shall be served first.

The Essentials Committee is authorised from time to time by notice to fix the maximum amount of fish that may be obtained by any person at any time. At present each entire household is allowed to have 1 lb of fish per week.

We had a limpet pie today and very good it was. The limpets were boiled for two hours, they come out of their shells quite easily and then have to be bearded. We used some of the liquor they were boiled in with peas and carrots and potatoes and mixed it all together and baked it in the oven.

Thursday May 15th
I always say it is remarkable that when one is busy and occupied, one *can* forget the Germans are here, it is strange but too true and then one is brought up with a sickening jolt, as I was this afternoon, when I saw a German in the garage examining Boy's car. He had a book with the numbers of all the cars left in the Island.

I wish I had seen some of the 'disgraceful scenes in the fish market' the papers talk about! But I haven't seen one. This poem was in the *Star* today:

The Charge of the Fish Brigade
Half a step, half a step, half a step onward
Into an open space trod the few hundred.
Forward, the lucky few, but for the fish they knew
Lined on the stall to view
Watched the few hundred.

Forward the Fish Brigade, was there a man dismayed?
Not tho' the faithful knew someone had blundered.
Theirs not to make reply, theirs not to reason why
Theirs but to try and buy with but a chance they know
Stood the few hundred.

Curses to right of them, Curses to left of them
Curses in front of them, volley'd and thundered.
Stormed at by seller's shout, boldly they stuck it out
Heedless of raucous voice. Waiting for piece of choice
Gazed the few hundred.

Pushed by a basket there, squeezed to a pancake there
Froze with a ghastly stare, charged like an army while
All the queue wondered.
Smothered with rancid smoke that made you fairly choke
Sarnians stood hopeful.
But when the smoke did clear folk knew with great despair
No fish was there to share.
Hopeless few hundred.

Moans to the right of them, moans to the left of them
And moans behind them, volley'd and thundered.
Stormed at with shout and yell, while hopes to zero fell
They, who had fought so well
Come thro' with laboured breath. Crushed near to point of death
All that was left of them
Battered few hundred.

When can their glory fade? O! The mistake they made.

THEY HAD NOT ORDERED
Honour the charge they made
Honour the Fish Brigade
Hopeless few hundred.

Anonymous

Friday May 16th
A beautiful day. I made up my mind to catch the bus at the Bourg at 9.30a.m. Pheeeeew, what a commotion! If I were catching the boat to England, there could not have been more upheaval. I arranged my basket and my bag the night before. We had breakfast much earlier, and I thought I had allowed ample time for that, and discovered to my dismay that I take twice as long to eat this war bread made of bran and potatoes, so I could only eat very little for breakfast. Then

darling Molly had to be shut up in the stable, and I could hear her indignant protests all along the lane! At last I started on my great adventure and arrived at the Bourg at twenty past nine. Two buses were waiting there, I got into the first and had reason to be thankful that firstly country people know all about one's affairs, and secondly that they volubly put one right if one is wrong. There was only one woman in the bus, who, with the amazing correct power of deduction that country people have, concluded that I did not want to go to town via St Martins and the Fort road, but via Victoria road, so she told me this bus was going by the former route and the other one was going my route. I was grateful to her, because I was going to the Ladies College and Elizabeth College. It was lovely to sit in the bus in the cheerful atmosphere created by country people out for the day. There were about a dozen of us in the bus.

At the top of the Grange I got out, and we parted with mutual expressions of respect. Carrying both my baskets I made my way to the Ladies College. It was about twenty minutes to ten, and there was quite a long queue waiting already. Everybody was very cheerful and I listened to them. How these women get through their work is a perfect marvel. One said she took her little boy to school twice and fetched him twice; they were all very bitter about the fish and eggs, one said she had a baby who she considered required at least three eggs a week, and didn't the other think so?

'Yes,' said the other, 'Of course they ought to have at least three eggs a week, don't I know it, there's nothing you'll teach me about bringing up children, I have had two sets of twins and three other children besides.' I gazed at her with awe and admiration. A very nice looking woman was standing beside me and we chatted for some time, and then she said to me, 'I was at your wedding Miss de Sausmarez! I remember it as if it was yesterday'! At last the doors opened at five past ten, and I wondered why they hadn't at half past nine, and why people whose work was sedentary always started so late. When we got into the Hall, I thought the procedure was excellent. One by one we stopped at a table with a girl behind it, who directed us to put the ration book with the name of the Householder on top and proceed to the lady on the right who would deal with it and then give us our fish ration card.

Saturday May 17th
Another lovely day. I went to the potato depot to get new potatoes, I was told I had to take 25lbs at 2d. a lb. Why?! I didn't mind because I had my cart. What woman can carry 25lbs far? Really not only are we suffering from Occupancy, but from Bureaucracy as well, and which is the worst?! How can the poor people pay out 4s. 2d. at once from their wages?

Doris came to tea, she looks much better. How we wish we could see *Punch* and the newspaper just now, also I would like the music hall songs. I don't think anybody who hasn't been actually in the Island at this time can even understand our feelings, or realise how completely we are cut off. If they did they would keep on sending us messages, Oh how I *ache* with longing to hear from the children. It is sixteen months since Jim went back and nearly a year since Michelle went back.

Sunday May 18th
A lovely day, with a nip in the air, I did not go out. James went to the Câtel Church in the evening. Katty came to lunch. She brought the dire news that the Aeroplane Vineries Depot was closing and all the vegetables were being distributed to the different shops in town. It *is* annoying but only fair. When they have nothing else to sell, they will keep open and keep their

Forest Church.

employees on by selling vegetables. Liptons are doing it already. Collins the meat shop are starting next week. I do think it is splendid the way the Island is carrying on. Never have the hedges been cut so well. In spite of the poor deserted closed Forest Church, the churchyard is beautifully kept. I think these rationing cards and rationed clothing cards are excellent, through the rationing the shops have been kept open all the winter and employees kept on. Of course it is most annoying the shops closing at four, and especially for country people, and we have sworn good and hard about it, but I know it is really all for the best. Our administration have done remarkably well. Mr Falla and Mr Vaudin[189] have managed to buy a great many essential commodities from France.

A man came to see James to try and get James to help him, of course James couldn't help him. He had got drunk last night at the Caves de Bordeaux and he had brought a bottle of spirits through a German soldier, he had it in his pocket and went out, met a policeman who snatched the bottle out of his pocket, and he knocked the policeman down! So of course he is for it. James said to him, 'What can I do to help you? You were in the wrong, and what I *can't* understand is how you men can accept favours from the German soldiers, and you fought in the last war too!' I *was* so glad James said that. The man said, 'They all give the German soldiers 1s. and they get the spirits for us.' The Guernseymen are not allowed to buy spirits. It is not only poor workmen who accept favours from the German soldiers, quite decent people accept cigarette coupons from them, even though their own men are away fighting. It is annoying.

Tuesday May 20th

The food question is getting more acute. I don't believe they make any difference in England between women and men. Here they do, the women's ration is smaller than the men's for meat and bread. As a matter of course, the men expect the women to give up all their meat ration

---

[189] Agents representing Guernsey in Granville on the Purchasing Commission.

to the men, and as a matter of course the women give it up, even though they are working just as hard, if not harder than the men. The women also give up their rations to old people and children if they are living with them, the women are expected to do so, that they have to keep up their strength, too, seems to be quite overlooked. A communal kitchen has been opened in St Peter Port, but only for men. One has been opened in St Martins for women and men. That the women have to walk much more now and stand for hours in those exhausting queues does not count at all. It is an extraordinary point of view, because the women have worked as hard as the men in the greenhouses always. The men are all complaining they can't work hard because of the lack of food, in spite of their shortened hours 8.30am to 5.30pm. The women work longer hours and harder than ever.

Wednesday May 21st

We are all going to be photographed for our identity cards.[190] Guernsey's great camera census begins on Monday. It will be the most colossal job of its kind ever undertaken in this Island. The whole of the adult population have to be photographed and the work will take the best part of two months to complete. Three copies of each person has to be taken, one for themselves, one for the registration form in possession of the Constables of the Parish, and one to be filed with the same forms in the custody of the Registrar-General of Identification. There are over 22,000 civilians over fourteen years of age in the Island so 66,000 photographs will have to be taken. A delivery van has been converted into a travelling dark-room which will be used to change each spool of film.

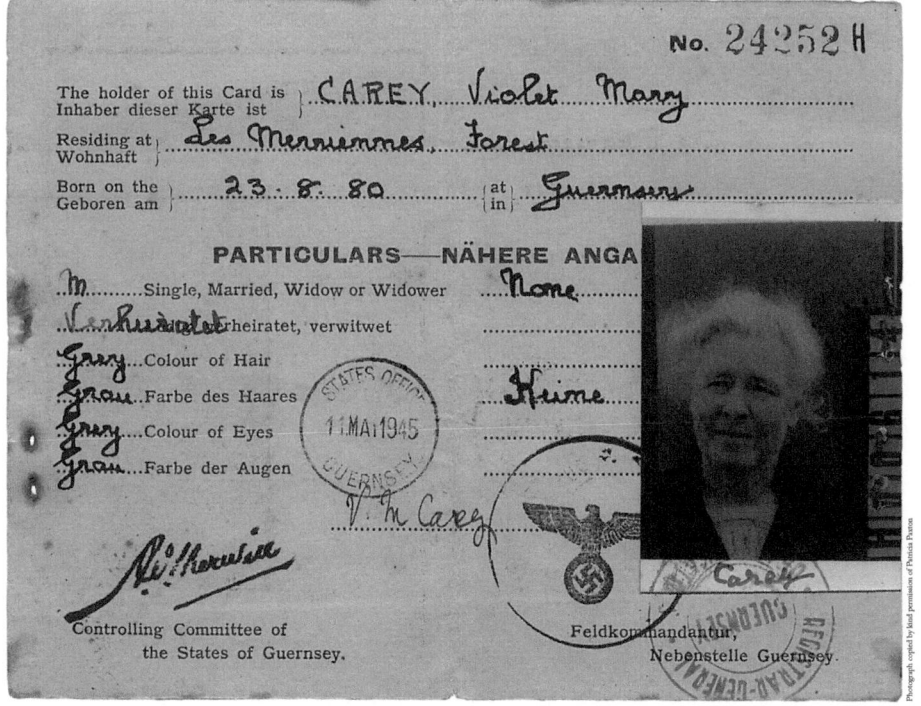

Violet Carey's identity card.

---

[190] This was announced in the *Star*, 21 May 1941.

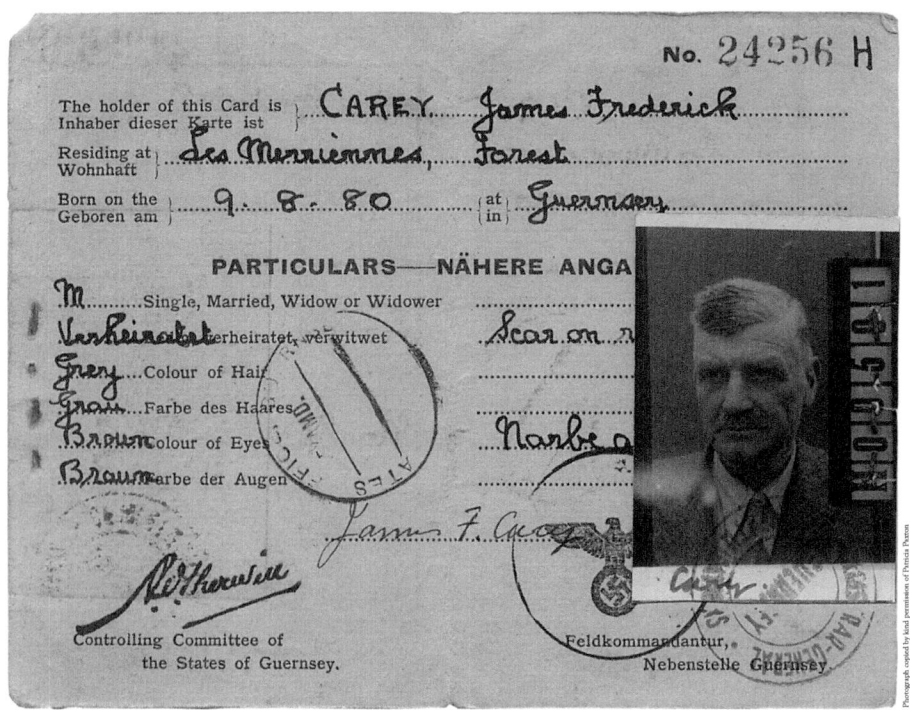

James Carey's identity card.

Friday May 30th

S.W. wind. A lovely warm day. In the morning I met Violet and we went to the vegetable depot together. I could have as many peas as I liked, only 2lbs of carrots (6 carrots), nothing else. No lettuces. I met Mr Bolton on his way back from being photographed, he said the apparatus was like the guillotine, but he was done very quickly. Several people stopped me and advised me to go then, because no one was there! I could not make them understand that I wanted to go when plenty of people were there, to have a pleasant chat, and an agreeable gossip. I went about half past two. Mrs Mauger accompanied me, we met a good many people coming away. We had to take our hats off, and stand behind a frame and were snapped immediately.

I met Mrs Hazell whose hair was very well brushed, and she said she wished she had put on her earrings, and she wanted to wear a sardonic expression, but she did not know what a sardonic expression looked like!

Saturday May 31st

It was very foggy in the morning. I went to the potato depot. I met Mrs Elias de La Rue, as soon as she was within speaking distance she said, 'As I saw you coming along Mrs Carey, I said to myself, Auch, but 'asn't Mrs Carey gone thin!'

'Yes,' I answered cheerfully, 'I have lost two stone and feel all the better for it!'

'Oh well,' says Mrs Elias, 'As long as you are 'ealthy is all that matters.'

When I was going to be photographed Mrs Walter Renault caught me up. 'CO'O'O'OR,' she said, 'Haven't you gone thin Mrs Carey, I was looking at your back as I was coming along, and I said to myself, *that* is not Mrs Carey's back surely!' I answered her the same as I did Mrs Elias. 'Oh well,' she said, 'as long as you feel well, that is the main thing. I suppose the truth is we all ate too much, that is what we did!' I agreed heartily with her, and said, 'Wouldn't I like a pound of chocolates!'

'Oh,' she said, 'Don't I long for some chocolate.'

The other day I met Norah de La Rue, and we stopped and 'Gosh,' said Norah, 'We met you coming around the corner the other day, and we said to each other, 'But, hasn't Mrs Carey gone thin,' etc., etc., etc. So apparently it is 'Fore and Aft and Zideways'!

June 1941

Tuesday June 10th
Gay Brock came to tea. She was very cheerful. She told me more about the way those girls hoaxed the Gestapo. They rang them up from a public 'phone and said they had seen a parachutist drop on Lihou. A hundred soldiers with fixed bayonets, loaded revolvers and drawn swords went out on motor bicycles, in buses and motor cars to catch him! Then another time they rang them up and said there was a boat load of British officers coming in at Vazon. The guard was turned out at Springfield. The whole load of three thousand were made to stand at arms all over the island while the fourth thousand marched out to Vazon to round them up! After that all public telephones were shut up. It is a beautiful story.[191]

The laundries cease to function through lack of soap next week.

Wednesday June 11th
A finer day. No rain. Blue sky and sunshine in the morning but cloudy in the afternoon. Still cold. The May blossom is not quite out yet. The Laburnum all over the Island is beautiful. The rabbits are beginning to be an awful pest, eating up all the young crops. Some of our innocent administrators suggested to the German authorities that they should have friendly shooting parties on the cliff to shoot the rabbits down, Guernseymen and Germans together. The German authorities nearly passed out with horror at the idea of being near a Guernseyman with a gun, so the idea has been abandoned.

We heard on the BBC today that the Germans bombed a hospital in Crete which was full of New Zealand wounded. Parachutists descended and took the hospital. They made all the New Zealand walking wounded march smartly in front of them, if they did not march quickly enough they said they would shoot them, they shot nine and killed two. On the nine o'clock news they told us that they made twelve New Zealand soldiers march in front with their arms held up in the air and they made the other wounded lie on their faces in an orange grove for hours. The fundamental difference between them and our fighting men is they do those kinds of things, bomb and machine gun women, children, hospital ships and hospitals, and our men won't. How can we be friends with them?

Sunday June 15th
Michelle's 27th birthday.

Very few Red Cross messages are coming now. If only people in England could realise our utter feeling of desolation they would all send us one every month. Unless one has experienced it personally, no one can imagine what it is like to be under German occupation. Prisoners, completely in their power.

---

[191] See entries for 20 and 28 February.

Friday June 20th

Never shall I forget these days. June 19th, 20th, 21st and 22nd 1940. On the 19th the Douzaine and Constables after 6pm went methodically round the Parish asking people to register themselves and their children, far into the night they were doing it. The mothers and children were not allowed to assemble at the school on the Bourg because of the fear of air raids, so they had to assemble at the *Gouffre Hotel*. Four times they assembled there before the children were taken down to the pier early in the morning on Friday June 21st. To the astonishment of the Douzaine nearly everybody registered themselves and their children. Then came that dreadful Saturday June 22nd. Mr Finey went off his head, and all the night before he was knocking up the people telling them to go, saying the men would be shot and dreadful things would happen to the women. At 5am on Saturday morning James burst into my room, followed by Mrs Renault sobbing, they told me general evacuation had been ordered. I went over to Katty and told her, and she said at once, 'Has Mr Finey gone off his head?' and she was right. I rang up Olive and told her and she was very upset, and then I rang up the Police Station, and found there was absolutely no truth in the report at all. I said I had had a very good night and I was blowed if I was going away. It went all round the Parish that I had said I had had a very good breakfast and I was blowed if I was going away. A great many said as long as I stayed in the Parish, they would stay and they still say it.

Never shall I forget the sight of High Street those days, the run in the banks. There were no more evacuation boats after Sunday. The poor Bailiff and Crown Officers were on the trunk line to the Home Office night and day. The Home Office sent an order to Victor to stick to his post. Victor sent the order to Judge French in Alderney to stick to his post, but that craven ordered general evacuation of Alderney and fled to England.

I thrill with pride and admiration for the way the essential services carried on, the way the clerks in the banks worked day and night, so that they were able to send away in time all their ledgers and books, all securities, in fact all papers of value, leaving only petty cash in the banks, and working short handed, because all English clerks in the banks and Post Office and shops were evacuated. Our administration deserves the highest praise. Also the Country Douzaines and people who methodically worked day and night, liberating and feeding deserted animals, milking deserted cows. The way people left their houses was terrible. Meals cooking in the ovens, frying pans on the fire, the lights on, dogs and cats shut up in the houses. Unwashed crockery. The people who cleared them all up were heroes.

On Friday June 21st the following letter appeared in the *Star*:

> To The People of Guernsey
>
> In these grave and anxious times, I strongly exhort one and all to remain calm and avoid panic. It behoves us to behave as true and loyal men and women of Guernsey and to apply ourselves to our duties with that quiet determination which has always characterised all islanders. I, therefore, implore you not to be alarmed by reason of the precautionary steps which the authorities are taking.
>
> Let us remember that evacuation is voluntary, there is no compulsion.
>
> Beyond teachers, children of school age and under with Mothers or other relatives in charge, as well as men of military age, it is impracticable for others to hope to be evacuated.
>
> Victor G. Carey, Lieutenant Governor and Bailiff, June 20th 1940

High Street.

Owing to His Excellency the Lieut. Governor being called from the Island, the Bailiff was yesterday sworn in by Jurat A. Drake (Lieut. Bailiff) as Lieut. Governor in so far as civil duties only appertain.

On Saturday June 22nd an emergency meeting of the States was called. A Controlling Committee was created and Mr Sherwill was made President. Jurat Leale made a very good speech. He said they had 'to set up machinery to evacuate a large slice of the population and that 72 hours later 10,000 people had been evacuated and he asked to pay a tribute to the work of Mr Guillemette, who had practically spent the whole of the last two days at the end of the telephone and with him a band of workers who had just worked and worked and worked till they literally could work no more. He also said the Home Office definitely stated we evacuate at our own expense.'

Monday June 30th

A year ago today the Germans occupied Guernsey. No mention was made on the wireless about us. Is it policy? Or callous neglect? We always listen in to the European broadcast now, it is so much more interesting than any other broadcast and the announcer has such a nice intelligent voice, so unlike those dead voices. One of them announced the following the other day, all in one breath, 'Nine-enemy-aircraft-have-been-brought-down-today-three-of-ours-are-missing-there-is-going-to-be-an allowance-of-sugar-for-jam-issued-soon.'

We drove down to the coast and round, we had our tea by the roadside. There are heaps of new signposts all over the Island, we noticed one at Vazon was decorated all over with 'V's! 'V' is a sign the French are using, they make it as they pass each other, with their fingers, and tap it out in morse on the tables in restaurants. 'V' for 'Victoire'.

A year has gone by, a year nearer Victory. Our administrators a year ago were faced with the two grisly spectres: 'unemployment' and 'lack of food'. There has been *no* unemployment and *no* lack of food.[192] They have done magnificently. They have grown in the greenhouses the most beautiful vegetables and potatoes, all cheap and plentiful for us. We have got through the winter far better than we ever dared to hope.

July 1941

Saturday July 5th

Another boiling hot day. Molly and I fetched the bread. We are to be allowed no more flour. The boat which is covered with 'Food for Guernsey' in huge letters all over it, brings the tiniest cargo for us and is packed with munitions and guns! No Red Cross letters are coming.

The new excitement over here is the letter 'V'. Their signboards have been covered with it, especially in the Câtel and on the coast. On one board in St Martins someone has written, 'Long live General de Gaulle'. The following notice appeared in the paper today:

> Warning[193]
>
> I have been informed that the letter 'V' has appeared written in public places in the Island, that this matter is regarded very seriously by the German authorities, and that the person or persons who have done this are breaking a military order and rendering themselves liable to severe punishment.
>
> Moreover, should the culprit not be discovered, the population may be penalised in the same way as in the case of acts of sabotage.

---

[192] In a recent study of the Occupation, Dr Knowles Smith records that unemployment was a problem: 'Unemployment in the early days, due to the sudden contraction of the potato and tomato business, meant that Islands' Labour Departments had an enormous problem with which to deal. They tackled it with many new schemes, such as road widening, tree felling and some textile and clog making work, but still there remained large numbers of unemployed.' She claims that this was one of the reasons that many Islanders worked for the Germans. (*Changing Face of the Channel Islands Occupation*, p.63)

[193] Published in *La Gazette Officielle*, Saturday 5 July. At the beginning of July 1941, islanders responded to a radio appeal from Britain to put up 'V for Victory' signs as part of the general resistance campaign in Europe, although the appeal had not been directed to the Islands on the grounds that organised resistance was not feasible. (Cruickshank, pp.160-1)

The culprit or culprits must be discovered within 72 hours of the publication of this warning. May I warn my fellow Islanders against committing these foolish acts, which accomplish nothing, but merely bring grave consequences in their train.

signed Victor S. Carey
Lieutenant Governor and Bailiff

In Jersey they have had their wireless taken away, curfew at 7pm and in the streets where the 'V's are, all the people have been fined £1 per head. One poor old lady of 76 at Albecq had some 'V's put on the noticeboard affixed to her wall. The officers went in and were horrible to her and made her wash the 'V's off, and told her she was responsible for them, and she has been quite ill on it.

Tuesday July 15th   S.W.
St Swithins Day
An enormous German lorry trailing a big gun behind it came blundering down our lane and knocked out a stone weighing quite half a ton from our wall at the corner. Why the whole wall did not collapse, I don't know. The men have put it back. We have no peace. Lorries and cars pass all day long and turn to the Corbiere. They are avoiding the main roads now and going in all the lanes, for shelter as they expect to be bombed any time. How we long and long and listen for those dear lads to come. If they could only listen to 'Auntie Vi' who would tell them to come, not just occasionally, but at least three or four nights running. It would send these people running away as quickly as the boats would take them, these hoarders who are eating up all our food, turning people out of their houses. We are so miserable and desperate, to be bombed by the British would be a relief, even the people whose greenhouses have been destroyed say only, 'They are grand lads.'

They have been practising firing their big guns today, they fire at the ruins on Lihou and never hit them and we say, 'Good! another shell wasted!'

Wednesday July 16th   S.W.
A beautiful cool day. I went for the laundry for the last time, and I went in to see Mrs Hazell on my way back. She has had her seventh message from Moiya dated May 7th. 'You lucky devil,' I said.

'Oh, do you think I am lucky Mrs Carey? I suppose I am,' she said. I have not had one direct message from the children.

Mrs Renault tells me all of the parish are worrying very much because I am so thin! It is very sweet of them and I told her to assure them that I feel very well and much more comfortable. Mrs Hazell showed me her Guernsey made wireless. She says that all those little Shippham ninepenny bottles are filled only with sea water, about a hundred of them. If that is true, again I say, staunch old ally the sea!

Friday July 25th
It rained in the night. Olive went down at 8am to get fish. She got a nice piece of conger. I went to see Miss Ross to ask her advice about my hands, they are just awful, so scaley. She advised me to try and get some calcium, but of course, I couldn't. I was advised to paint them with an evil smelling tar mixture.

There is some trouble over 'V's. Some people at St Martins have painted 'E' before the German 'V' and, for a reprisal, all people living within 1,000 metres of the *Beaulieu Hotel* where this was done have to give up their wireless. The Germans have painted their 'V's over two branches of broom leaves like the leaves on our pennies to show they have had a victory over Guernsey. In Jersey they have fined the island £3,000 and taken all the wirelesses away and made every individual pay a 5s. fine in the street where the 'V' is.

Poor Monsieur de Guilleborn was talking to a man called Le Page and spoke of the 'V's and made a 'V' in blue pencil on Le Page's saddle to show him what he meant. He tried to rub it out and couldn't. He thought Le Page would wash it out but, instead of that, Le Page went straight to the German authorities and showed his saddle to them and the poor Frenchman was tried by a military tribunal and has been taken to France.

Saturday July 26th
In the *Gazette Officielle* the following notice appeared on Wednesday and Thursday July 9th and 10th:

Reward of £25[194]

A reward of £25 will be given to the person who first gives to the Inspector of Police information leading to the conviction of anyone (not already discovered) for the offence of marking on any gate or wall or other place whatsoever visible to the public the letter 'V' or other sign, or any word or words calculated to offend the German authorities or soldiers.

Victor G. Carey, Bailiff

The squealers are all squealing that Victor signed himself 'Lieutenant Governor, Bailiff' and that he had no right to sign himself the former, and would get into great trouble because he had no right to offer £25 for the apprehension of a subject of King George VI, stating he himself was a subject of the King.[195] He didn't.

Notice on Friday July 25th[196]

It has come to my notice that the signs 'V' and 'EV' have been drawn in black at certain points along the Forest Road in the neighbourhood of the Beaulieu Hotel, on walls and on the roadway and on a signboard of the German army. This matter is regarded very seriously and as an act of sabotage by the German authorities. As the person or persons responsible for such acts have not given themselves up to the authorities, the people in the vicinity of this district must be held responsible for these acts. It is ordered by the FeldKommandantur that the wireless receiving sets of all persons living within a radius of 1,000 metres from the *Beaulieu Hotel* shall be surrendered not later than 6pm on the 26th July.

Victor G. Carey, Bailiff

Also two St Martins men must stand sentry from 10pm to 6am at the besmeared street number signboards and at two more signboards.

---

[194] As stated, this notice was in *La Gazette Officielle* on 9 and 10 July 1941.
[195] That is incorrect. On 20 June 1940 the Island's Lieutenant-Governor left because Guernsey had been demilitarised. The Bailiff was sworn in as Lieutenant-Governor that day in accordance with instructions from the British government. (Hocart, *An Island Assembly*, p117) This had also been announced in the *Star* on 21 June 1940.
[196] As stated, this notice was in *La Gazette Officielle* on 25 July 1941.

German Propaganda
'V' – German Victories on all Fronts.[197]

> The whole of Europe is impressed by the unique propaganda campaign which all believe is the symbol of the uniting of hundreds of millions of people with the German people.
> This unity has been expressed by the letter 'V', the initial of the word 'Viktoria' (victory). The sign of the certainty of the German victory in the struggle for Europe; also as the sign which can only be attributed to those whose colours have never borne a retreat, but only victories.
> Paris and the French provincial towns have also taken up the 'V' campaign. The 'V' is not only to be found on the Eiffel tower, but also on the most famous buildings a large illuminated 'V' is displayed, and flags bearing a large 'V' are to be seen everywhere. All cars have the letter 'V' painted on them and everybody in France is wearing a brooch with the letter 'V'.
> 'V' is the sign worn and displayed with the German confidence of a German victory on all fronts.

And the German word for victory is 'Cieg [*sic*]'. Curiouser and curiouser.

I don't see much to admire in the people who scribble 'EV's when they are quite sure no one has seen them and then allow the parish to be penalised. Many people think that these 'EV' scribblers are very careful *not* to do it in their own parish. The exception is poor Mons de Guilleborn who has been so severely punished, and who said at his trial, 'Punish me, but don't penalise the Island.' I admire him *enormously*.

Poor Victor, for days he was afraid the parents of the children who had scribbled 'V's would be sent to France. As a matter of fact, the Kommandant was sweet to the children who confessed. He made them all go and see him and he told them they were very naughty little children and they must not do it again and gave them chocolates.

Victor told me that the great difficulty is the people are quite human, but every single little misdemeanour or trouble has to be reported to Berlin and it is what Berlin decides that is the final word. If they are satisfied with the measures taken by the Command here, well and good, but they can order any punishment, even 'death', for anything.

August 1941

Saturday August 2nd
A beautiful day. James went to Town after lunch. Doris came out. She told me two remarkable stories. A woman told her that she noticed a group of women she knew talking in the most friendly way to a German soldier. The woman was so surprised because she knew the other women and did not think they would have been friendly and she was so curious that she joined the group. Her amazement was increased by discovering the German soldier was talking in fluent patois! After he had gone, she asked about him and they said they had known him for years. He settled here years ago and married a Guernsey girl. In 1938 he went to Germany on a visit and was not allowed to leave. He has been sent here now and finds his wife and children have been evacuated to England.

---

[197] Violet has copied this from an article in the *Star*, 23 July 1941.

The second story is gruesome. A man was watching some Germans drilling in his field. He was watching from his house. The officer drilling them was in a furious temper and was cursing them the whole time. When he had dismissed them they rushed on him and killed him with their bayonets and buried him in a trench nearby! Presently another officer came with some other Germans and they all talked together and gesticulated and then all went off together, presumably to look for the missing officer.

Doris showed me a copy of the leaflet that was supposed to have been dropped at the Vale. Like me, Doris does not believe in leaflets unless she sees them herself.

From the RAF
Cheer up! Coming to liberate you shortly, before 1941 is out.
RAF coming. Take cover.

Wednesday August 6th   N.W.
The Germans are still breaking into the houses occupied and unoccupied in the Forest and doing senseless damage. Their own police are working zealously to catch them and some have been caught and forced to return the things they have stolen. No Red Cross message for me from anybody. The postman says he has one or two for the Forest people every day now.

Friday August 8th
It poured and poured with rain in the night and was still pouring with rain this morning.

I went to Town fairly late in the morning, it had cleared up. I had lunch at the Berthelot Street restaurant with Bobbie Seabrooke and tea with Gay Brock. I had my usual chat with Miss Gaudion. She said she had an officer in last week who told her she must learn German. She asked him, 'Why?'

'Because we are winning the war madame,' he replied.

'Oh no you are not,' she said, 'and, what is more, it will be much better for you if we win the war, for we shall give you freedom of speech and freedom. You come back here after peace is declared and I shall still be here and you will tell me I was right.'

'Ah Madame, will you then be glad to see me?' he said. 'Oh yes,' she said, 'after peace is declared.' He came in again on Wednesday, but he was so down-hearted and morose that she did not say anything to him. It *is* pathetic, how they respond to the smallest atom of kindness, the soldiers offer people cigarettes, butter, milk and bread.

Book III

Saturday August 16th   S.W.
A fine day but a very cold wind. Molly and I fetched the bread.

I had tea with Mrs Milburne yesterday. She told me that their horse was tethered in front of their house and she saw a German soldier go up and pat it, so she went out to him. He said in English, 'I want that horse.' She said, 'You can't have it'. He looked very nasty and he said, 'I will have it.' She said, 'Show me your permit, your papers.' He said, 'I haven't got one.'

'Be off then,' she said, 'or I will ring up the Kommandant'. And he went. But she is very nervous that he will come back again.

Berthelot Street Restaurant.

Everybody was out, Hedley had left the back door open. I was in the dining room and I heard Molly raising Cain, so I went out and sure enough there were two Germans at the back door. They were reading my notice, 'Kein Durchgang'. They wanted milk, I was so thankful I had the sentences the Countess Blucher gave me.

> 'We have no milk, we send all our milk to the States Dairy.' – 'Wir haben keine Milch. Wir mussen unsere milch an die States Dairy abliefern.'
> 'We do not make butter.' – 'Wir machen keine Butter.'
> 'We have no eggs. There is no food for the fowls so they do not lay.' – 'Wir haben keine Eier. Die Huhner bekommen kein Futter, deshalb legen sie nicht.'

One of them was quite nice but the other was horrid. They went off. People say they come like that and ask for milk or ask to telephone so as to get into the house to look around and to take things such as chairs and tables.

Sunday August 17th

A fine day but still very cold. Katty came to lunch.

We are hearing about the 'Battle of Guernsey'. Several of the Germans have said it. That there was a battle here when they took us and three thousand people were killed altogether. It was a four days battle and so the Germans say they are not going to give this place up and that is why they are bringing all the big guns over here. They say they know it is true because it was in all their papers. Last year we heard they were showing a film to themselves of the 'Occupying of Guernsey' but none of us were allowed to see it. We suppose they exhibit all the devastation of their air raid as part of the battle. Well, so it was, their bombs and machine gun bullets versus our tomatoes!

Friday August 22nd

It rained most of the morning, but cleared up in the afternoon. I sent a message to Baba via Mrs Mauger. 'Jurat and Mrs Carey are quite well and longing for news of you and Master Jim. The farm and Hedley and Molly are all right.'

I saw Miss Gaudion who told me her German officer had told her that in the German broadcast of Lord Duparc's message they said that 'we were very happy under Nazi rule'. 'Damned lies!' he said. He had listened to the English broadcast.

She also told me the true story about Monsieur de Guillebon. It was Smith who reported him to the German authorities, not Le Page. The Gestapo went to Le Page and demanded to see his bicycle saddle, where the half obliterated 'V' showed, and asked him if Mons. de G. had done that, and Le Page said he had done it just to show him what he meant, and they made Le Page sign on a paper and, on that, gave poor Mons. de G. that savage sentence to satisfy Berlin. And that is their method, justice does not come into it at all. They must find a victim, punish him, send a report to Berlin and if Berlin is satisfied, all is well, if not, they are for it and we have reprisals.

Monday August 25th   Grey day

It poured and poured and poured with rain all night long and in the morning there was a thick fog and it has been dark and heavy all day. The news has been very good today.

Our ration of meat is 6oz per head per week. No tea or coffee of any kind, but we are having 3oz of salt instead of 2oz. I can't think why we have not had that amount of salt all the time because we are making it on the Island from the sea. We dry it thoroughly and crush it in a pestle and mortar and it is beautiful salt. We are allowed half a pint per head a day of separated milk. A quarter lb of butter each a week. One egg a fortnight for three people. Three oz per head of sugar a week. One lb pot of jam a month. I now eat one slice of bread and marmalade for breakfast. Potatoes, lettuce and tomatoes for lunch. Two slices of bread and butter and tomatoes or jam or honey for tea. Soup and three or four potatoes for supper. At present we are having real tea.

On Friday we were told that the gas would give out in ten days but now some gas coal has come and it will last for six weeks.

Tuesday August 26th

There is an order in the paper ordering us to declare our wireless sets today.

Le Riche brought the groceries today. Once a fortnight the van comes with a dear old horse. The driver and the horse both have their lunch here. Mrs Gorvel's and Mrs le Tissier's orders are left here. There was considerable heartburning today between Mrs le Tissier and Mrs Renault because Mrs Gorvel had a pot of jam. They both examined the pot of jam minutely and diagnosed marmalade. Mrs le Tissier announced firmly that she was going in tomorrow to demand her ration of jam even if it was only 2oz. Mrs Renault proceeded to shatter my peace of mind to pound me into promising I would go and demand my ration of jam on Friday.

Sunday August 31st
A beautiful day, a real summer day. Katty rushed in while we were having breakfast to fetch her bread. She was very excited, she said the Wyses had sent for her to help them because Mrs Wyse was stricken down with the universal plague. I said, tell her to chew and suck and swallow young blackberry leaves, it is a certain cure in 24 hours, but Katty would have none of it. No, she had her own remedies which cured you in a few days. I protested that 24 hours was only one day. She waved all my protests aside and rushed off on her bike telling the hens and the cats in the yard all about her remedies!

What a queer life we in this Parish are leading, no church or chapel on Sundays. We just go on day after day the same. When I go out I meet the same half dozen people every day at the same spot. We all have our routine which does not vary. If I did not go in to Olive every week, I should certainly go quite mad. All the same I think this is a very blessed little Island. For all our difficulties we seem to find a remedy in the Island, this last, the blackberry leaves for the plague. We are making our own salt, wine, vinegar and bean flour. The people now are gathering the Carrageen Moss down at L'Ancresse and Perelle and making puddings of it.

I think what is keeping us in health more than anything is the enforced rest we all have, the curfew keeping us indoors at night, the rationing of light, we are all in bed at half past nine sun time. Dr Aikman always said one hours sleep before midnight is worth two after midnight.

SEPTEMBER 1941

Monday September 1st
The fatal day has arrived. The day Mr Churchill told us to be on our tiptoes with efficiency and expectation. Poor Mrs Renault, she gets so depressed when she hears on the wireless a call for more women workers. 'Oh,' she says, 'wouldn't I like to be working in England, I would work with such a good heart, we can do nothing here.' So many of the women are feeling that way ,and the men too. The men look much worse than the women, although the women are having far less food. Mrs Renault gives all the eggs she can get to her husband and all her meat.

About 7pm the phone went and I answered it and the policeman said, 'Mrs Carey, you must be at the Grange Lodge at 9am tomorrow morning.'

'Heavens,' I thought, 'it must be when the devil drives.' So I said I would be there.

I had supper first and I started to walk at a quarter to nine. I met Mrs Hazell at the top of the lane and she walked with me as far as Timmers where we saw a van unloading. 'Oh,' said Mrs Hazell, 'that is Mr de Garis from the Vilette, I am sure he will give you a lift.' He was only too pleased to have someone to talk to on his long drive. He took me to the top of the Carmel. It *was* such a help. He told me he had delivered 300 marrows to Timmer. He said people were very down on Timmer and said he was hand in glove with the Germans. He didn't believe it, that Timmer was *terrified* of them. He told me that there were some Germans on his field and one of them was in great distress, crying bitterly. He asked him what was the matter, the German could talk English and answered that he had just had the news that his father, mother and four children had all been killed in an air raid and he did not know where his wife was. War is beastly.

I arrived at Olive's about 10pm. I met a good many Germans when I was walking down Carmel. I did not feel in the least afraid of them.

Tuesday September 2nd
A beautiful day and really hot. I was at the Grange Lodge on the stroke of nine. Three other people were there. We sat in the hall and waited and chatted and watched all the people going in and out, they seemed very busy. At last a young man with a foreign accent asked us what we wanted, we told him and he told us to go up to 'room 5, Lieutenant Bloel'. The two women went up first and they were a long time and then at last my turn came. Lieutenant Bloel was middle-aged. I sat down and he proceeded to ask me questions. Was I Irish? Had I any relations in Ireland? The date of my birth? Was my health good? Was my home all right? Were my material circumstances satisfactory? I answered all his questions and then he said there must be a mistake because I had not relatives in Ireland. 'Oh no it wasn't,' I said, 'I have a great friend in Ireland, a friend of over thirty years standing, and I knew it was she who was enquiring after me, and I said, 'We are allowed to send messages to friends as well as relatives through the Red Cross, so couldn't I send a message to this friend, Mrs Bernard?' So he said, 'I will do my best for you, but I cannot promise the letter will arrive. You can write four pages and bring it to me, and I repeat, I will do my best to send it.' Their methods are quite beyond my simple comprehension. He did not tell me the name of the enquirer, I had to supply that and he did not tell me the date.

I heard that there will be no meat this week and we are going to be cut down a quarter of a lb of bread a week per head.

The Martels have lent us an electric oven. It is lovely. Gerald Guilbert fixed it up today. With that and our own turpie we are very well off.

Friday September 5th
A lovely day, a warm summer day. Olive went down to the fish market before breakfast and came back triumphant with beautiful mackerel. I went down to Grange Lodge with my letter for Mrs Bernard, which it took me ages to write on Wednesday. Lieutenant Bloel was very stiff when I asked him the date of Mrs Bernard's enquiry. He said the enquiry came from the German authorities in Paris! I said 'Oh,' and no more. I wonder if my letter will go.

Saturday September 6th
I have discovered that I should go to Grange Lodge every Monday to get a permit to sleep out every Thursday! I should walk to Town on Monday, returning the same night to get the permit! I don't think!

Monday September 8th   N.E.
Violet came to tea at about 6.30pm. We heard the sound of planes and machine gunning and bombs dropping. It is extraordinary how difficult it is to locate sound. I thought they were attacking a ship between Jersey and here and not on the Island at all. Violet thought it was in the west and James thought it was in the east. James said there were a great many planes and

they dropped a number of bombs, he thinks at Pleinmont. Anyhow, those dear lads have been over us and our visitors won't sleep tonight. Chee! Chee! Chee! Why should they have such peace and quiet when our poor people in England don't?

Tuesday September 9th
We are all walking on air. Gone is that awful dreary desolate feeling of being completely forgotten. Everyone has a tale to tell. The people at Pleinmont had a lovely view. They say there were fifty British planes and they flew so low you could hit the wings with a potato!

There are so many rumours about yesterday I am going to write them down.

1st rumour: That a ship was sunk off Alderney.
2nd rumour: That a ship was sunk of St Martins Point.
3rd rumour: That a ship was sunk in the Harbour.
4th rumour: That barges full of troops were sunk outside the Harbour and the men were machine gunned in the water. *A foul lie.*
5th rumour: That the town was machine gunned. Another foul lie.
6th rumour: That no Guernsey lorry driver was allowed on the pier today. The lorries were stopped at the barrier and Germans took them and filled them and brought them back to the barrier. No Guernsey ambulance was allowed on the pier either.
7th rumour: That a gun crew were killed at L'Ancresse in the night.
8th rumour: That a ship was sunk off Sark.

Truth
1. I saw a Red Cross plane fly over our house, I heard it in the aerodrome and I saw it fly away later.
2. Our meat went to Jersey by mistake and now it has arrived here safely, also the oil tanker.
3. The RAF came yesterday and last night and we are not forgotten!

Monday September 15th
No British planes came today. Since the raid last Monday the following orders have come out:[198]

1. It is prohibited to leave any house during the alarm or during the continuance of any recognisable action.
2. All civilians outside must quickly enter the nearest house or air raid shelter.
3. All vehicles must go to the nearest shelter.
4. Listening to wireless broadcasts during an alarm or action is forbidden.
5. Everyone who believes in disregarding these orders renders himself or herself liable to severest punishment.

And we will all rush out to see what we can see and to cheer the planes just the same.

Friday September 19th   N.E.
A fine day but bitter wind. I went down to Town early. Mr Ware told me he could drive me as far as St Margaret's Lodge. A great relief.

I had a chat with Aunt Edith and Nelly Welch. Poor poor Nelly, she looks terribly ill, she is far worse than any of us. She is like a skeleton, a dreadful colour and she has no appetite.

---

[198] Published in *La Gazette Officielle*, 11 September 1941.

A number of men and women look dreadfully ill and they are so thin. I think everybody is so gallantly cheerful and hopeful.

I had my tea at the Bungalow and Mr Ware came for me at a quarter to five. He told me an English plane was over earlier in the afternoon. The Germans were giving a lecture to a number of recruits at the Guet at Cobo and the English plane flew very low and machine gunned and killed a good many. A butcher brought the news to town, he had been on his round to Cobo. There is no doubt about it, news travels faster by word of mouth than by any other way. We *never* use the telephone and no news is published in the papers and yet we hear everything so quickly.

Friday September 26th
A lovely day. I went to St Stephen's Church. I haven't seen that comic member of the Gestapo lately. I used to follow him all over the Town. He gave me such joy. He was a huge man and he used to wear real comic cuts or music hall clothes. I have never seen such exaggerated plus-fours as he wore, with a very new Guernsey. All the Gestapo seemed to wear plus-fours of different sizes and shapes. If they wanted to listen to us, they would make a devious stage-like course for us, then stand beside us and gaze hard into an empty shop window or up at a window. By then we were quite ready for them and anybody who knew another language such as Hindustani or Malay would talk it. People like myself would lower our voices and say, 'Do you think it is going to rain?'

'*No*, but the wind will blow.' People who could talk Guernsey French were absolutely safe, because the Germans themselves say they *cannot* understand it. I don't think there are many members of the Gestapo here now.

Saturday September 27th
A lovely day and very warm. Molly and I fetched the bread and we went to see Katty who was very upset because while she was out on Thursday some German soldiers had used a ladder to climb into her bedroom and had taken all her blankets. From off her bed! It is no use, one cannot leave a house empty. The Germans watch the houses and know exactly who goes in and out. I think that is why they are always coming here and asking for milk and eggs, just to find out if the house is empty.

Doris came to tea and brought a horrible rumour. That they are going to take to France all men and boys, from the age of 14 to 45, who have been born in England, as a reprisal for the treatment of Germans in Iran. It is awful if it is true.

Sunday September 28th
There was a muffled knocking at the back door just now. I thought it was Germans, but when I opened the door a Guernseyman was there who said to me in a sepulchral voice, 'Is Jurat Carey in? Ingrouille speaking.' I called James who went out and came back and slipped by me with two packets of cigarettes in his hand. Ho! ho! I thought, with my acquired countryman's power of deduction, secret barter! I was right, a possible hundredweight of wheat from the threshing!

Tuesday September 30th
Another beautiful day. James had to go to Court for the Jurat election. He met Olive in Town who said she had heard the order for the deporting of men from here had been cancelled. James told me that it hadn't, the German Command here hope it will be, they are really upset

about it. It is a reprisal because fifty Germans have been sent to Russia. It is extraordinary they should take it out on us when we have made no opposition whatever, but it is not *so* extraordinary when one analyses everything. We are such suitable victims for Berlin to pounce upon, completely helpless, nothing to sabotage, no factories, no railways, no weapons, just prisoners in a camp surrounded by a natural barrier, the sea. Oh, we are eminently suitable! They wanted the Controlling Committee to pick out the men, but they flatly refuse to have anything to do with it. They say they won't take any men in key positions or any farm workers. They want 1,100 from here and 1,100 from Jersey. If they are married they will allow their wives to go with them. If they can't get enough English-born ones, they will take men whose wives have left them. Where are they going to take them? It is awful.[199]

October 1941

Thursday October 2nd

A perfect day. Bright sunshine, no wind and warm, but not too warm. I had a lovely walk and I arrived at a quarter past one.

I heard only one piece of news. That the authorities at Elizabeth College had said the scheme for taking the men away from here had been abandoned.

Tuesday October 14th

It is very sad the potato crops and the apple crops are so poor this year. Sugar is so scarce. The hardest thing of all for the farmers who have no electric light or gas in their houses is that they are only allowed one short candle per head per week for the stables and the houses. Poor Violet is in despair, and everybody else. They don't know how they are going to get through the winter months. No one dares to leave their house to spend the night with other people for fear of it being broken into at night.

The page in the *Star* of bartering is getting longer. One person is offering 30s. for a lb of tea!

Thursday October 16th   S.W.

Another beautiful day with a strong south-west wind blowing. I took all my food and walked slowly in to Olive's. I was dreadfully tired when I got there.

Everybody is terribly upset over the evictions. Nobody feels safe. They are swarming into St Martins now. They have taken the *Queen's Hotel* in spite of strong protest and in spite of being told that 300 civilians feed at the communual kitchen every night. They say they must have it to feed their troops and they have kept all the boilers. They have taken literally a hundred or more small houses and cottages, giving the people only a few hours to clear out, sometimes allowing them to take everything, sometimes not allowing them to take a thing. Rumour has it they are going to take Sausmarez Manor for a hospital because there is central heating, but there is no electric light. They have taken the *Douvre*[200] for a hospital. They have gone into more houses in Mount Row and Kings Road.

---

[199] The Controlling Committee's minutes for 26 September 1941 state, 'The President said it was possible that 1,200 males between the ages of 18 and 45 years would be sent from the Island by the German Authorities. After considerable discussion it was resolved that it should be pointed out to the German Authorities that if all men engaged in agriculture and horticulture were exempted, too great a burden would be placed on other classes, and a suggestion made that exemption should commence at age 25. With regard to differentiating between married and single men, it was resolved not to offer any opinion, but to point out that, in view of the fact that the wives of many of the men had evacuated, the particulars given in the list which had been prepared of men between the ages of 18 and 45 could not be used as a guide.'

[200] Hotel in St Martins.

Sunday October 19th   S.W.

I was weighed on Friday. I now weigh ten stone. I was twelve stone three before the Occupation.

Booty Ozanne was very funny at bridge the other day. She was playing with Olive and Vera and Maud Drake. Booty looked at Vera and, in a voice of sincere admiration, said, 'What a blessing it is to see a double chin nowadays!' Vera didn't know whether to be pleased or annoyed. Booty and Olive always muffle up their necks in scarves; they 'can't bear seeing scraggy necks', says Olive severely to me. I maintain I have *not* a scraggy neck, but a firm chin and a well defined jawbone, denoting the innate strength of my character and the perfect oval of my face! Katty is always telling me what a beautiful figure she has now, so I am going to tell people what a beautiful face I have!

Friday October 31st

There is a great scarcity of potatoes. They have been having 45 tons a week. That is stopped. 2,000 tons of potatoes are coming from Germany. In spite of the shortage, they mined a man's field the other day, although he begged them to give him two days to lift his crop. They would not do so.

November 1941

Thursday November 6th   S.W.

I had a lovely walk in. I was so hot I fair perspired! and revelled in it! Katty caught me up and walked with me, she told me that that Mrs Brouard who was found dead in her bed yesterday died from evictions. She was an invalid and 84. She was evicted from Victoria Road. She went to live with the Nicholsons at St Martins. They were evicted. They moved into another house at St Martins and were threatened with evictions again and she died.

Olive thought of a lovely name for them, 'the Banderlog' out of Kipling's book. They are just like them. I shall call them that for ever more.[201]

Friday November 7th

Another beautiful day. Olive told me another lovely story, overheard in Collivet.[202] A German soldier was buying a silver ring in there and an officer came in. They both saluted each other and the officer lifted his hand. The soldier didn't. When the officer had bought what he wanted, they saluted each other again and the officer again lifted his hand and the soldier didn't. After the officer had gone, the soldier said to Collivet in English, 'All b----y nonsense.'

Saturday November 8th   S.W.

Another beautiful day, but there was a white frost this morning. Everybody is gathering acorns to make coffee with. I have an idea acorn coffee is not good for us, so I won't touch it. Daisy Kane told me it stained the cups something awful, so what must our insides be like?

Tuesday November 11th   S.E.

The 23rd Armistice day anniversary.

Katty arrived about seven with a message from Kathrine:

---

[201] The monkey people in Kipling's *Jungle Book* who were despised by the pack. Kipling spelt it 'Bandar-log'.
[202] A small jeweller's shop.

No. 72/311. Sent on 23 June 1941 from Kathrine Harper.
Municipal Buildings, Grimsby, England.
Have you received Mother's letter telling that Michelle abroad and your James married. We are all well. Write us news. Harper. (Sister).

Well! Well! Well! Darling Boy, I do hope he is happy, that is all that matters. I am sure he has chosen a nice girl. Oh it is tantalising to hear so little. And my darling Baba abroad. I wonder if she is on a hospital ship in the Mediteranean? Or in Egypt? If only Kathrine could have told me. I was aching and longing for news. By jove! When I *do* get it, it is some news.

Friday November 14th
The potato shortage is becoming very acute, they are only allowed five lbs per head a week. The people have to queue up to get permits from the Market Constable.
There was a sinister order in the paper yesterday:

> Notice[203]
> All persons now residing in Guernsey, whose chief domicile was outside the Island before the 1st July 1940 are requested to present themselves, not later than November 15th 1941, at the Registry (Greffe Office), Royal Court House, St Peter Port.
>
> This order particularly applied to those persons who on the above mentioned date, only intended to stay in the island temporarily, for instance, those who were here on holiday, for reasons of recuperation, visiting friends or relatives, or those who soujourned here more or less regularly at certain intervals and who might even own a house or property in Guernsey.
>
> Failure to comply with this order will render the offender liable to punishment in accordance with the 'Order concerning declarations and restriction as to place of residence' of November 9th.

There is a new gas restriction. Consumption of gas for any purpose whatever is permitted only during the following hours:

1. From 7.30am to 2.30pm.
2. From 5pm to 9pm.

People are going to bed at 8.30pm! This restriction is to stop Germans burning gas fires all night! It is against them and not the civil population.

Wednesday November 19th
There is another important notice today.[204]

> Persons whose domicile was outside this Island before July 1st 1940 and who have reported at the Greffe Office, Royal Court House, are requested to furnish that office with the following additional particulars not later than Wednesday November 19th 1941.
>
> A. Nationality   B. Date of arrival in the Island.   C. Date of birth.

---

[203] *La Gazette Officielle*, 13 November 1941.
[204] *La Gazette Officielle*, 19 November 1941.

Thursday November 27th   S.E.

Another beautiful day. I had a lovely walk in. Everybody is talking about these poor French people who have been brought over here. Mrs Scott found a little boy of twelve crying bitterly in the Pollet. He was so hungry, so she took him into Tills and fed him. About a fortnight ago they put a notice in the paper that no French money was current over here and then brought these people over with French money only. It does look like reprisals. They picked boys off the street and coming out of school. The Pommiers are being absolute angels, taking their French money and giving them money in exchange.

December 1941

Wednesday December 3rd

Another quiet night without incident. When one realises the gigantic front we are fighting on, we know we are only one atom, still we do like to be remembered, if they would send only one plane once a week, how it would cheer us.

I have just read *The Crystal Box* by Mary Butts and in it she writes the following, which I think all parents and guardians should have printed and framed and hung up in a prominent place in their houses to prevent them making some cruel mistakes again:

> After the War, we, the Young, found ourselves on the farther side of that gulf, angry with the fires of hell and unspeakable sacrifices, the generation before me understood as little as it had shared. We were wounded over and over again, once the war *was* over, when we found that so few of our parents had their arms open to the wild young things it had spared. All of us had worked hard; most of us were half dead for want of being cared for, for want of understanding, we were too wary, too disillusioned, too tired to *ask* for, yet consumed with secret longing of our need. If it had been offered – but how many parents out of ten thousand, with quietness, with love-in-reserve, said, 'This was our coming-of-age gift to you. If you've been bad, you've been brave; if you've been tiresome, you are tired out. Whatever you've done – and some of you have done supremely well – it is you who have suffered most. Whatever we have done and suffered, we cannot have suffered what has been done to you. Come home for a little to be cared for and let us see if we can find a way to save such children as we have left.' How many of them said that?

Mrs Renault told me the woman next door has had her clothes stolen off the line, silk underwear. She washes for the Germans and they are always at the house, one walked into Mrs Renault's kitchen. We certainly must keep our doors locked.

Saturday December 6th N.W.

Another quiet night and fine day. I am dreadfully upset. While I was fetching the bread, two little French boys, aged fifteen, came and asked for some coffee and that cruel Mrs Mauger refused to give them any. She said, 'I did not know what to do,' the d----d fool. I said, 'I thought you would have known my character better than that.' I was angry, the bad luck that I should be away just then.

Monday December 8th   N.W.

Another quiet night. A fine day but very cold.

Japan has declared war on America and Great Britain. Canada has declared war on Japan. Japan has occupied Shanghai. Japan declared war on America yesterday. President Roosevelt made a splendid speech which we heard, actually from America, as clearly as if he was speaking in the room. The applause was deafening. The wireless is too wonderful I think. Mr Churchill made a speech at 9pm. He sounded very tired. Now it is indeed 'The World War'.

―――――― Book IV ――――――

Sunday December 14th   S.W.

Pouring with rain. Katty came to lunch. James went to the Câtel Church. It is a strange thing. The Church is our only public air raid shelter in the parish and yet the authorities consider it too dangerous to hold services in the Church.

Monday December 15th   S.W.

Another December is coming to a close. I am making no Christmas preparations. I have no materials for Christmas pudding. The gallant shops are making their windows pathetically Christmassy with frost and holly and crackers.

Tuesday December 16th   S.W.

It poured in the night, torrents of rain. In the news they told us the casualties after the attack of the Japanese on Pearl Harbour[205] while negotiations were going on and war not declared. 360 planes attacked the American ships there, also submarines. They killed 4,000 American sailors and sunk a battleship, three destroyers, a minesweeper and aircraft carrier.

I asked Gay to come this afternoon and Peggy rang up and said she could come. I had a nice fire in the study, it was lovely having them. Gay brought her tea, but Peggy came after tea. Peggy told me that Mabel Kinnersly found an officer had billeted himself in her house when she got home last Friday!

Peggy told us an awful story about one of those French boys of fifteen years old. The poor little chap went to the mother of Peggy's maid, he was crying bitterly, he was so cold and his shoes were awful. She gave him a pair of shoes, a boy friend was with him. Some days later the friend went to see her and told her the poor little boy was dead. His mother was dead and they told him they had killed his father and so he tried to hang himself, but didn't before they found him. They thrashed him and, when he could, he crept away and drowned himself. These poor French people are given half a lb of bread in the morning and a bowl of weak soup in the evening and that is *all*. They dig up carrots and turnips and eat them raw.

Thursday December 18th   S.W.

A beautiful day with a heavy frost. I started off as early as I could and walked briskly. The gorse is out in places and the birds are singing. I arrived at Mabel Frere's at half past twelve. We had a nice

---

[205] Pearl Harbour (Hawaii): Sunday 7 December 1941, 366 Japanese bombers and fighters struck at the American warships lying at their moorings, 15 ships were sunk and 4 damaged. Also struck were Pearl Harbour's airfields and 188 American aircraft were destroyed and 2,330 Americans left dead or dying. (Martin Gilbert, *The Second World War*, p.272)

chat. She thinks exactly as I did about our unpreparedness and sacrifice of youth. We both loathe the way the BBC announce complacently that we are always fighting at tremendous odds.

James rang up to say *three* Red Cross messages had come. He gave me the numbers.

Friday December 19th

Two years ago today Jim left to join up.

A fine day. I went to Town to get my messages and at last, at long last, I have heard where Michelle is, in Nigeria! It is a *lovely* Christmas present to hear she is in a safe place. What a one Baba is, here have I been, fearing she was on a hospital ship in the Mediterranean and she is far away in Africa.

If people *only* knew what it meant to us to get these messages, I am sure they would send them oftener.

The Town is so gallant. They have put all the Christmas decorations they can in the shops. I hated being in the Town all the same, one could not help contrasting peace-time Christmas! I could not wish anybody a 'Happy Christmas'.

Thursday December 25th   N.W.

Our second Christmas Day under Nazi rule. May 1942 be a happier one. Still we have our wireless, which is a great thing to be thankful for.

There are no services in the Forest Church, which is considered to be safe enough as an air raid shelter when an air raid is going on but too dangerous to hold services when nothing is happening!

It is a lovely day, no wind.

James went to the Câtel Church this morning. At ten minutes to one on the Forces wavelength there was a Channel Islands broadcast. At 3.30 in the overseas news, Mr Churchill and Mr Roosevelt spoke and at four the King spoke and 'God Save the King' was played. Before that we heard the bells of Bethlehem. The speeches were very good. Between Mr Churchill's and Mr Roosevelt's speech we heard we had captured Ben Gazi. After the speeches I thought again how magnificently we are led.

James and I had chicken, broccoli, roast potatoes and a treacle pudding for dinner. For one day in the year I am not hungry, I feel like the Hounslow bus on a wet day, full up inside! It is a lovely feeling not to be hungry.

Saturday December 27th

Mr Hartley Jackson[206] is livid with rage. The *Star* asked him to write a Christmas message and he did, a very nice one. In the middle of the message came this paragraph: 'What of the present? The recognition that Christ was born into the world to save the world and bring peace on earth is the need of Britain and her Jewish and Bolshevik allies'! He went to see the editor and was told the German censor had inserted that paragraph. He went to see him and he agreed to withdraw the paragraph, so he went back to tell the editor and the editor had allowed the article to be printed. It is rotten.[207]

---

[206] Vicar of St Stephen's Church.
[207] Frank Falla, a journalist for the *Star*, had asked the Reverend Hartley Jackson to write a Christmas message to the people of the Island. He wrote that 'the recognition that Christ was born into the world to save the world and bring peace on earth is the need of the world.' This was altered by the German censor to the words quoted by Violet, and, despite Falla's attempts to get the article deleted, it was printed. (Frank Falla, *The Silent War*, pp.36-7)

The Diaries of Violet Carey, 1942

January 1942

New Year's Day
January 1st
I think they must have been drunk last night. They were firing their revolvers and letting off rockets on the aerodrome. This afternoon they have had a band playing on the aerodrome.

There were three notices in the paper yesterday.

> Notice
> With immediate effect, the cutting or removal by other means of trees or shrubs is forbidden in the Channel Islands.

Katty says Dr Brosch is appalled at the way the trees are cut down and he says the climate will be ruined and it will take a hundred years of tree growing to put it right. And *look* how they have ruined the Island! And propose to go on ruining it. I wonder if they will bring us coal? As it is we have practically no fire at all. I am quite used to sitting wrapped up in a rug every day. If it wasn't for the pain in my hands I would be quite comfortable.

Saturday January 3rd
I was wakened up in the night by the sound of dull explosions. Later on an English plane rushed over from the east to the west and was machine gunned at Pleinmont. We haven't heard of any casualties. The men have picked up three nasty pieces of shrapnel round the house. James said two fell where he was standing outside last night. I call that a warning, I shan't go out again!

I met Mrs Sebire. We both beamed at each other. No one could be closer to the guns than she is. I should think she was well under their arch! 'Well,' she said, 'that was to show them they don't own us, we still belong to England.' I heartily agreed and I said, 'Doesn't it cheer us up to hear those beautiful engines?'

'Indeed it does,' she said, 'And you can never mistake them, they are so different.' We parted in the highest spirits.

Mrs Mauger told us a horrid thing happened on New Years Eve. The Germans were letting off fireworks in the Town and people were watching them. A man aged 42, called Fisher, was watching, his daughters had gone with the Germans and he hadn't liked it and had remonstrated with them. He turned his back to walk into his house and he was shot in the back and died.

Thursday January 8th
A German officer has said we are the next most fortified place after Brest.

Molly and I fetched the bread. I waited until after tea and then I walked to the Bungalow. Olive told me that Alioner Walters has had a visitor, a corporal, for a long time in her annexe. She hasn't had any more to do with him than she can help. On Christmas Day a knock came at her door and she opened it and there was her visitor with a parcel done up in gay paper and he begged her to take it as a Christmas present. She felt very embarrassed and asked him to come in. She opened the parcel, it contained a lovely box of liqueur chocolates, a box of gingerbread biscuits and a box of chocolate biscuits and a packet of Turkish cigarettes and a gilded fir cone. At the bottom of the parcel were two picture postcards of a beautiful hotel in Coblenz and written on it was his hope that Monsieur and Madame would come and stay in his hotel as honoured guests after the war was over. Alioner said she felt a lump come up in her throat and she wanted to cry. He told her he owned the hotel and was just pining to go home.

Monday January 12th   N.E.
Bitter north-east wind and freezing hard. It is wonderful how we are managing without a fire. I look very fetching in a pale blue balaclava helmet and gaiters edged with blue. I wrap myself up in a green plaid rug and wear grey woollen mittens, I am quite warm. We light our rationed wood fire in the evening.

Violet phoned that poor Hedley was very ill. I am afraid he won't get over it. Poor old Hedley, he has been with us 28 years. He was quite well on Thursday, only weak still, and he collapsed on Friday. It is his heart. Frank went for the doctor. He couldn't come today because he hadn't enough petrol. He won't see Hedley until Wednesday. These are the conditions we are living under.

Thursday January 15th   S.E.
The poor Countess Blucher had a dreadful time last weekend. She was playing bridge at Olive's and about 7pm the maid rang up to say the Germans were there. She rushed back, and so they were, and they told her she probably would have to leave and they went away. Among them was a very young officer, he came back having pretended he had left his gloves in her drawing room. He came into the room and whispered to her, 'Don't be depressed, they are saying it is not at all suitable,' and he rushed away. She thinks they are playing cat and mouse with her like this because her sons are serving against them. The Military take no notice of the Civilian Kommandant's orders at all.

Wednesday January 21st
Last evening a car drove up into the yard. It did give me such a fright but it was only Mr de Garis to see James. Our nerves are in such a bad state, it is awful when we hear footsteps or a car stopping. The Germans were measuring round the boiler pit today. What for?

I went to see Hedley in the morning. He is very weak. Violet told me the farmers were getting very depressed over their land, never knowing when a field will be seized and ruined. 'V' may stand for 'victory', but it certainly stands for 'vermin'.

Wednesday January 28th   S.W.

There were torrents of rain in the night and it is bitterly cold today and blowing hard. We have three *Star*s a week now and three *Evening Press*, owing to shortage of paper. Such thin little papers, they are posted easily through the letter box.

Saturday January 31st

Molly and I fetched the bread. A gallant little lark was singing in the sky. James has discovered that his Brouard and Catholic fields have been marked out, he doesn't know what for, but hopes the schemes have been abandoned. Also they have been taking his carrots wholesale.

At eight o'clock tonight, Violet rang up to tell us poor old Hedley had just died. He had been unconscious all day and had quietly passed away. They were so thankful he had died before curfew (10pm) because they could have got no one to help them. Poor old Hedley, I do miss him dreadfully.

February 1942

Sunday February 1st   N.W.

It poured with rain. Katty came to lunch. In the afternoon Frank came to look for Hedley's papers. He told us things were getting very grim in the Island. Dr Cambridge had told him that one case of dementia had been admitted to the asylum, caused by starvation, and another case, a big man, had been taken to the Emergency Hospital. He was so emaciated, and when they weighed him he weighed only 6 stone 9 lbs! Dr Cambridge implored Frank to tell all the farmers to feed their cows as much as possible to keep up the milk supply as milk is worth its weight in gold now.

Working men are giving 25s. for a rabbit and 15s. for a hen and offering £3 for a lb of tobacco and 35s. for a lb of tea!

Wednesday February 4th

There have been several cases of black market here. The men were sent over to be tried by a Military Tribunal in Jersey. During the period of September to December 1941, four men purchased in Guernsey four pigs, fifteen cows and two young heifers without permit, and, after slaughtering them, sold the meat. They were found guilty and were sentenced as follows: the first, twelve months imprisonment and a fine of 3,000 Reichsmarks (1 Reichsmark is 2s. 1d.); the second, eight months imprisonment and a fine of 2,000 Reichsmarks; third, six months imprisonment and a fine of 1,400 Reichsmarks; fourth, five months imprisonment and a fine of 1,200 Reichsmarks.

We may run people in for the black market over here, but if there was no black market in France we would starve. All our food is bought from the French black market.

Saturday February 7th   N.E.

More hail. Snow. Sleet and wind! Molly and I fetched the bread.

There is great tribulation in this part of the Parish. Old Mrs Baleine, a terrible old Frenchwoman, has been given one room by George Lucas in the cottage opposite, for which she pays 2s. 6d. a week! The place is not fit for animals to live in! Mrs Renault is frantic at having her for a neighbour. Both Mrs Baleine and Mrs Gallienne wash for the Germans. Mrs Gallienne's husband refuses to live with her because she does so.

Sunday February 8th   N.E.
We are certainly up against primitive things. We are thankful when we have our backs to the wind, we are filled with a glow of satisfaction when we get the fires to burn. As Kipling would say, 'That is another story.' I had been trying to get the fire of wood to burn, it only gave a dull glow. James came in and said forcibly, 'Why, you have let the fire go out.' Considering I had knelt before the fire like an appealing and humble devotee and had blown and blown and blown with the bellows for hours and hours and hours, my silence was more eloquent than words. The next night he knelt before a similar sulky fire and blew and blew and blew and he said, 'It is extraordinary how this elmwood won't burn!' Once more my silence was more eloquent than words!

Saturday February 14th
Doris came to tea. Poor Doris, she says once she is free, she is off to England, and hopes never to see Guernsey again. I think it is so sad. I feel I want to hug my poor gallant little Guernsey to me, and never leave her.

They are now bringing over here the dregs of Europe. They are supposed to have brought over 2,000 foul Communists, Spaniards and all sorts, and fouler women. The town was full of them.

Sunday February 15th
Olive told me the Countess had told her that the Prince von Oettingen was full of admiration for the dignified way in which the Guernsey people had behaved. He would do all in his power to help the civil population.

Mr Churchill spoke at 10 o'clock. He told us Singapore had fallen. He did speak well. His restraint and generosity are so wonderful. Never has he said, 'I told you so.' He begged the British people to be as united as the Russians were in disaster, not to criticise but to pull together. It was a very comforting speech.

Monday February 16th
Violet came and we walked all my stores up to Michelle's room. Every night, last thing, I walk the bread, butter and silver upstairs and every morning I walk them down again! What a life. The poor Tostevins have had three geese stolen, each worth £5. They were locked up too.

Thursday February 26th
One of the Sarres from Torteval was ordered by the Germans to drive round Mrs de Guerin's new corner, he did and a car coming out of Kings Road crashed into him, there were officers in the car. Young Sarre was tried by a German tribunal, given a month's imprisonment and fined £100, although he was absolutely in the right.

One of the Frenchmen went to a house in Doyle Road and asked for food. The daughter of the house opened the door, was afraid of him and ran to fetch her mother in from the garden. When they came in, they found the Frenchman had gone, and also their dinner which was in the oven!

James took some wheat to Violet to be ground after tea, so I did not go until rather late. I did not have a bad walk in because there was very little wind. Olive had quite a number of stories to tell me. One of them was about the Countess Blucher's beautiful golden retriever called Tarzan. The maid was feeding Tarzan and he slopped his food onto the floor and the maid idiotically snatched the dish from him. All dogs are hungry now and he snapped at her and made a terrible deep gash in her hand which bled profusely. They rang up Dr Sutcliffe and he was out, and they could not get any other doctor so they sent over to the German doctor at the Vauquiedor. He sent back he could not come to them and asked for the maid to go to him, and sent an orderly to help her to walk if she was feeling faint. The Countess took her over and he gave her an injection and bound up her hand and sent her to bed for three days. She was quite all right at the end of the three days. The extraordinary thing is that he told the Countess he had specialised in dog bites and had cured many people of them!

Friday February 27th   Variable
At last the wind is shifting. A fine day. I went to the Ladies College to give up poor Hedley's fish card. When I got there I could not find the right room, so I asked a man who was passing if he could tell me where it was. He turned around and he was Peter Kinnersly, who promptly hugged me most affectionately. It is so heartening to be kissed by a boy!

He told me a delightful story about his son Charles, aged 2½. He had a German officer come to see if he could billet someone on them and asked how many rooms they had. Peter said one sitting room and two bedrooms. The officers pointed to a second sitting room and asked what that was. 'Oh that is my son's playroom.'

'Oh,' said the officer, 'You only want one bedroom.'

'Oh no,' says Peter, 'my son sleeps in the other, I could not have him in our bedroom at his age,' in a shocked voice. 'Zo,' says the officer, 'and yet he needs a playroom at his age?' Before Peter could invent anything else, the door burst open and in barged Charles on his little tricycle, shouting at the top of his voice, 'Daddy, Daddy, don't you speak to nasty old German!' Peter burst out laughing and, marvellous to relate, so did the officer. He patted Charles on the head and went away and Peter has not had anyone billeted on him.

March 1942

Tuesday March 3rd   S.E.
In the evening a German soldier came. He wanted everything, offered an unlimited amount of cigarettes for onions, onion seed, eggs and butter. I said 'nix' for everything. None of us will ever forget the word 'nix', either the German soldiers or us. It means 'no go', 'no', 'nothing doing', in fact every negative possible.

Wool is to be released this week. That has been a scandal. The girls were buying the wool and knitting comforts for the German soldiers and making them pay enormous prices. One girl brought £20 of wool from Warry and Warry actually let her have the wool. Now they are trying to ration the wool.

Timmer is to have all the greenhouses within two miles of his place, 30,000 feet of glass. The Germans are appalled at the budget. They are unable to understand that the Island's prosperity came from the export and visitor trade.

The men who have been working the greenhouses have been playing a dirty game, all of them foremen as well. They have drawn their wages every Friday and have hardly worked at all, saying sanctimoniously they would not work for the Germans, quite forgetting they were not working for the civilians as well and that is why there is this appalling shortage of food.

The farmers are bitter and furious because they have been working from 6am to 10pm to keep the milk and butter yield up. The greenhouse hands start at 10am till 12 noon, 1pm till 5pm and slacked and stole all they could. *Now*, all those greenhouses Timmer has taken over will be for the Germans only. People are allowed to keep their own if they work for the Germans. No man up to 35 is allowed to work in the greenhouses. He must work on the harbour, at the airport or at St Andrew's brickfield and there is always the grim fear they will take the men away. It is awful.

Friday March 6th   N.E.
Another bitterly cold day, gloomy, heavy and dull. In the evening I rang up Olive for a chat. She told me that five policemen had been run in for stealing from a German store in the Pollet, and that Sculpher[208] had been in gaol for one day and one night and was suspended and Langmead put in his place. What fools, what d----d fools.

Saturday March 7th   N.E.
Another bitterly cold day, but fine. Molly and I fetched the bread.
    Mr Ware brought the meat and told us three more policemen had been arrested including Harper. The German police had been watching them since before Christmas and have now pounced. What curious methods they have. Fancy not arresting them when they discovered them for the first time. They found a lot of German butter and tins of tomatoes in the chimney in one policeman's house. Some of the billeted German soldiers have said they might be shot.

Monday March 9th   S.W.
Violet came in the afternoon.
    Everybody is furious with those policemen playing into German hands like that. The Germans are hoping for an excuse to take complete control of the Island. We don't know what will happen now.
    Our wireless faded away at 2pm and has been completely silent ever since.
    Violet came in the afternoon. Poor Violet does worry so much, she thinks out worries that no one else thinks out. Her latest idea is that we shall all be literally in rags when we go down to meet the boat! Such an idea would never have occurred to me! I said if we are then we shall vie with each other who is the most ragged and the ones who are tidy will feel quite out of it! That theory didn't seem to comfort her at all.

Tuesday March 10th
What a dreary business life is now. All the news we have of our people is months old. We rarely telephone to each other. We do not go to each other's houses. We only meet by chance. We just go on day by day, trying to make the fire burn, blowing with bellows, eating the same food day after day and very lucky to have potatoes. So many people haven't any. One of the farmers here had two sacks of potatoes, a cwt in each sack. A man came and asked him to sell them to him and to name any price. 'Well,' said the farmer, meaning a joke, 'what do you say to £5 a cwt?' The man produced a pocket book, took out £10 and handed it to him, took up the sacks and went off with them, leaving the farmer with his mouth wide open!

---

[208] Inspector Sculpher was the Island's Chief of Police.

The Pollet.

Thursday March 12th   S.W.

A beautiful day. The gulls were making such a noise this morning and all the birds were singing so beautifully. Molly and I fetched the bread.

In the evening I walked in. It was a lovely evening. In Carmel, I met Peggy. She told me twelve policemen were arrested now. They were the black market, they had been selling the stuff. They stole tins of butter and tins of tomatoes, one policeman is supposed to have enough tins hidden up his chimney to last him two years.

Saturday March 14th   S.E.

Olive told me the Symons have two visitors, one of them is a musical student, so he and Mrs Symons have much in common. He told her he hated the war, hated fighting against the English, because he had spent some years in England and made good friends.

About 7 o'clock a German soldier came here, he was walking into the house, I just stopped him in time, and also he noticed my notice 'Kein Durchgang' and pointed to it and looked at me. 'Ja! Ja!' I said firmly. He asked for eggs, just behind me there was one on the table. I stood in front of it and for the first time regretted my vanished two stone! I said, 'Nein, no eggs'. Of course about nineteen fowls and two noble cocks marched proudly into view and the twentieth fowl was proudly proclaiming her existence by laying an egg. He held on to his belt with one hand while pointing with his thumb over his shoulder at the hens and roared with laughter and said, 'But Madame, all hens no eggs' in a mixture of French and German, I couldn't help laughing but I said firmly, 'Nein! Nein! Nix! Nix! Keine eggs.' He went off still laughing.

Monday March 16th   S.W.

There was a thick fog when I came down but after all that it was only half past six am! It cleared up afterwards and it was a lovely morning. They tell me we have sunk two ships in the Channel.

It is an extraordinary thing that although people have their wireless, they can hardly tell you any news! I suppose nobody's memory can retain any news very long. It is so depressing having no wireless.

This afternoon I was sitting darning my beloved French stockings, when James came into the dining room with such a nice man to repair the wireless, young Nicolle from St Andrews. He was very chatty and we both held the same opinions on several points which made us warm towards each other. He said he had no patience with the men who are now wishing they had gone away. 'Every man could have gone away if he had wanted to,' he said firmly and I heartily agreed. He said, 'I am ashamed I did not go. I sent my wife and child away, but I stayed behind to look after four properties and what has happened? I got turned out of my own house at one hour's notice. I was not allowed to take anything except a few clothes and I have since been turned out of every house, four times altogether and now they are going to pull down my mother-in-law's house because it is too near the aerodrome. I might just as well have gone, but I don't blame anybody but myself.' I did admire him for speaking like that.

Tuesday March 17th   S.W.
New moon 0.50am.

A thick fog. Molly and I fetched the bread. In the afternoon I strapped the wireless firmly onto my push cart and Molly and I started in a thick fog and drizzle to take it to young Nicolle at St Andrews. He said it really had been out of order for a long time, mainly due to the fluctuations in the cable caused by the terrific pressure the Germans make through using so much electricity.

I saw all the devastation at the Vauxbelets and Rosenheim. Three huge fields at the Vauxbelets are full of enormous huts. 120 sleep in them: Spaniards, French, Belgians, Dutch, Japanese, Chinese, all mixed up together, with no windows open and a stove in each hut. They have a hut for the women who have come over to cook for the men. They have been given sacks filled with hay to sleep on, no other bedding, so they never take off their clothes, wet or dry. Rosenheim is completely ruined, the lawns are torn up and they are making a tunnel there. The field opposite the church is also completely ruined, filled with huts and a broad granite road running through it.

Wednesday March 18th
Gay Brock came out. It was lovely having her. She said she had ridden round St Saviours and saw all the devastation they had done there, it has to be seen to be believed. They have taken all his fields away from one farmer, destroyed all the hedges, he fears he will never have his land again, because he doesn't know where his boundaries are. There were hundreds of foreign workmen working and dozens of cement mixers and in one field they were building a huge cement arena, having excavated a pit for it first, and that is the place for the enormous gun, in the middle of St Saviours parish. One farmer told Gay another reason why the land is ruined is because they are mixing up all the soils, earth, clay, cement, granite.

Gay told me their maid saw two German soldiers go into a field, draw up the pegs of two heifers and started walking away with them, she saw three men rush out of a nearby house and they made the Germans give up the heifers.

Thursday March 19th   S.W.

I did not go to Town today. The scandal about the greenhouses is terrible, people are starving now and the greenhouses are empty. Victor gave the whole of the Vallon over to the Glasshouse Control Board and they haven't planted a thing there, and to think the potato board only allowed the farmers to plant five perch of potatoes each! Why? This year they are imploring them to plant ad lib, when they haven't got the seed!

Friday March 20th   S.W.

Everybody is planning beautiful meals! Olive is always dreaming of lovely food but somehow my desires are still humble. I am so thankful I have no craving for sugar or sweets or chocolates. Mrs Hazell and Katty say they are mad with longing sometimes for sugar and Mrs Renault longs for chocolate. Mary and Violet are like me and so when we are free they are coming to tea with me and on the table will be four crusty two pound loaves of fresh white bread, and four pounds of golden Guernsey butter and a pot of real tea, made with four teaspoonsful, one for each of us and one for the teapot. Mary has promised she will cut me thin slices of butter and bread and then Mary, Violet, Molly and me will munch silently and contentedly, and every now and then we shall drink a cup of *real* tea, and Mary will say, 'Will you have some more bread and butter Mrs James?' and I shall say, 'Yes please Mary,' and Violet will say, 'Do, because I cut bread very badly,' and we shall munch away until the two pound loaves are finished!

Thursday March 26th   N.E.

The Countess' maid is quite well again.[209] She saw the German doctor every other day. She had chloroform and any number of injections and he dressed it every other day for weeks. The Countess offered to pay him and he refused to be paid. He said, 'Madame, the Guernsey people have suffered so much. Allow me to do my best to relieve the suffering of one of them.' It is pathetic these springs of friendliness and kindness that keep welling up between them and us all the time. It leaves me speechless with amazement that they should support such a cause.

Sunday March 29th   N.E.

The King has ordered today shall be a day of prayer. I wonder what the prayers will be like? Will they continue to tell the Almighty what to do? Or will we at last acknowledge we are a stiff necked generation and acknowledge we are miserable sinners? I always think our Lord showed his keen sense of humour when he likened us to sheep, the silliest animals in the world.

Monday March 30th   S.W.

Mary and Violet came in the afternoon. We had a fire. I haven't had one all week. Mary said the broccoli had all been stolen. She told us some people near her had had an officer billeted on them, they had been very friendly with him, and he had sat with them in the evenings and had had meals with them. When he left to go away he said, 'Goodbye,' and told them the only regret he had was that he would not be here to see the Guernsey people starving!

---

[209] The Countess' maid was bitten by a dog. See entry for 26 February 1942.

April 1942

Good Friday, April 3rd   S.W.

Darling old Pegs came to see me about half past five. She has more startling news about the police. Apparently it has taken a European war and a German Occupation to discover that this corruption has been going on since 1935! They have been systematically robbing Bucktrout and Colonel Randall. The latter has missed vintage port for years. He was asked to go to the Grange Lodge, taken into a room filled with cases and cases of wine, and asked to identify any of his. He did easily. At Bucktrout's, one of the men left a door open for the police to get in. One week, Chilcott could only supply his customers with a quarter of their ration because the meat had been stolen, the police again. The Germans have applied the third degree to the police. Some of them are terribly bruised.

Saturday April 4th   S.W.

A fine day. Molly and I went for our bread.

There is an offer in the paper of £1 for a quarter lb of tea. The food shortage is more acute than ever. There is no meat for next week. The country people are very bitter against the townspeople and authorities. Everybody was ordered to plant vegetables, even to dig up their lawns, but the order was not enforced. The townspeople would neither plant any vegetables, or buy them by the cwt, but continued to buy 1d. worth of carrots and 2d. worth of parsnips and the Germans had them all! Now the townspeople are swearing at the country people for not growing more.

Doris came in the afternoon. She told me a sordid story. A German soldier was going on leave. The day he was going, he received a parcel from his wife, a plump, trussed, uncooked chicken. He gave it to three friends and told them to eat it. When he came back from leave, he reported to his officer to put him under arrest because he had found out that his wife had been unfaithful to him and he had shot her and her lover! The officer said to him, 'Who sent you that chicken?'

'My wife,' he replied. 'Well,' said the officer, 'your friends are dead, the chicken was heavily poisoned.' What a story! Doris and I whispered in unison, 'Five accounted for!'

Thursday April 9th

I had a lovely walk in. There were very few soldiers. One incident happened along the Forest Road. There were three soldiers on the path, two of them were sitting in the hedge and the third was on the path. As I approached and was just close to the one standing on the path, a Guernsey boy rode by and shouted to him, 'Get out of the way of the lady! Manners!' and rode on, they called out to him, 'Kommen Sie' and he came back so I waited to see what they were going to do. He stopped and all three shouted at him in German, which neither he nor I understood, but they didn't touch him and at last let him go on, as he rode by me he called out to me, 'They wouldn't get out of the way Madam, I couldn't stand that,' Dear plucky boy, but as a matter of fact I think the soldier would have got off the path, because they always do.

Sunday April 12th   S.W.

People in the Town are still amazingly optimistic that we will be free this year and that Germany will be finished. The Germans themselves say Germany won't go through another winter. We daren't think of going through another winter ourselves.

Wednesday April 15th   N.E.
Boy's 26th birthday. New moon 3.33pm.

James heard that a man was trying to buy potatoes from a stall in the market, two lbs. The other man was willing to serve him, there was a German officer standing by, so the purchaser said, 'Do you think you had better serve me as I am not registered with you?' and pointed to the German soldier. 'Oh, don't mind him,' said the stallholder, 'he doesn't understand, it will be all right.' The officer said in a very American voice, 'That's right, don't mind me, go ahead,' and burst out laughing. He told them that he had been born and brought up in America and had gone over to Germany to see his grandparents and had been forced to stay and fight, his mother was American, his father German.

I wonder what Boy has done today?

Thursday April 16th   N.E.
A lovely day but icy cold wind. Molly and I fetched the bread.

I went in to see Katty. She told me that somebody broke into the cottage at Fontenelles where Ilsa keeps her sheep and goats. The next night, Ilsa had the sheep in the Fontenelles itself! She said she couldn't do it again, the smell was so awful! Dr Brosch was furious and has arranged for a police patrol for that district. Ilsa said to him, 'Now you know what Guernsey people are suffering.'

Seven swallows were seen yesterday. That is very early for swallows.

Friday April 17th   N.E.
The wind is still north-east and it is cloudy today. It cleared up and I set off without dear Molly to fetch my wireless. The desolation at Rosenheim must be seen to be believed. The whole of the garden and lawns are a desolate clayey dump of rusty nails and wood. The field opposite is an encampment and the field is ruined. I noticed very few soldiers, but there are hundreds of the foreigners. They are *awful*.

The wireless was ready. I went to Violet's for tea and got home about half past six and James and I heard the news at 9pm after a whole month without it.

Saturday April 18th   N.E.
Berlin has declared Guernsey bankrupt, this little Island that was so prosperous up to June 30th 1940. Kind Germany is going to help us, but she must have some security, so she has decided to take all landed property belonging to those who evacuated and who are declared 'enemy nationals'. All who have charge of landed property belonging to enemy nationals have to make declarations in duplicate before April 30th.

Sunday April 19th   N.E.
Still north-east wind. A beautiful day otherwise. I saw the new moon last night.

Katty came to lunch. We listened to the news at one o'clock. What a joy to have the wireless again and the news at one o'clock. It makes all the difference.

Poor James was walking two cows with colic up and down for nearly two hours, they had eaten too much clover with dew on it.

In the news they told us there was an appeal from the food ministry not to waste bread, that too much bread was found in dustbins! Words fail me! Exclamations fail me! Swear words fail me! An appeal! Not an order! Don't the authorities *know* that a huge majority of the proletariat will *not* eat anything but fresh bread, will *not* eat the heels of loaves?! The poorer they are, the more snobbish they are on the subject. It makes *us* nearly burst with impatience and rage, when we think of our poor people here literally starving, our poor men weak from want of bread and meat. I think that is what they miss more than anything, when they had two large slices of meat cut right across the sirloin and unlimited bread at every meal. Now they have two mouthfuls of meat and carefully cut slices of limited bread, and when there are children both parents are giving up their bread.

There are now eighty cases in the Emergency Hospital of 'Occupational Malnutrition'. The Germans object to that name, but the doctors firmly use it. In fact there was a rumour that Doctors Cambridge and Sutcliffe were in prison for using it, but that is not true.

Monday April 20th   N.E.
A beautiful day, how awful it is to think that all this lovely sunshine cannot bring any prosperity to Guernsey.

Violet came to tea. She told us the decent clean Frenchmen at the Vauxbelets were going round the farms begging the people to allow them to sleep, they would pay anything, they can't endure the appalling conditions in the huts provided for them.

There is a rumour that Dick Gibson has been turned out of his house for saying people were dying of 'Occupational Malnutrition'. Three of the doctors, Gibson, Bernard Collings and Cambridge, asked the German doctors to come and see three patients in the Emergency Hospital. The German doctors hummed and hawed and finally said they would come in a day or two, and the doctors said, 'Our patients will be dead before then.' So the German doctors, very unwillingly, agreed to meet our doctors at the hospital at eleven o'clock the next morning. Our doctors were there, but no German doctors arrived and ours had to go off to their patients. As soon as they had gone, the German doctors arrived and the Matron showed them the emaciated corpses, for all three patients were dead. The German doctors did not say anything.

Our doctors want them to appeal to the Red Cross to send us food. The German doctors dare not say we are starving because they are afraid of Berlin. They have been forbidden to even hint that we are in any but the most satisfactory condition. The High Command were ordering everybody to plant foodstuffs everywhere.

Saturday April 25th   N.E.
The police trial is over. It began on Wednesday and was described in the *Evening Press* as 'one of the most amazing trials ever to be recorded in the history of Guernsey'. Instigated by the German military authorities, two thirds of the personnel of the Guernsey Police Force were arraigned before a German Tribunal to answer charges of the most serious nature of larceny on a grand scale. Civilian supplies were robbed as far back as 1939. There are eighteen police officers involved and four civilians. They stole from five stores under the charge of the German Army authorities or the Todt Organisation and also local stores and shops. The alleged robberies will be made the subject of special enquiry by the Royal Court.

On Friday the trial was ended. There was no defence. They had stolen sausages, bones, 50lbs of meat, 50lbs of lard, 10lbs of dripping, boxes and boxes of tins of butter, grain and tins and tins of meat, six pounds of butter in each tin.[210]

Opinions are very much divided and are very interesting. A number of people are very much impressed (as they were meant to be!) by the dignity and fairness of the Judges, and their

---

[210] This was reported in the *Star*, 25 April 1942.

patience. I *say* it was jolly good propaganda, and I would like an account of the third degree before I commend German mercy and fairness.

Monday April 27th   N.E.
Pouring with beautiful rain. On Wednesday at 6pm and 9pm the Channel Islands were mentioned. Lord Portsea asked if anything could be done about the Channel Islands, Jersey and Guernsey, if food could be sent through the Red Cross, either by plane or ship? The answer he received was that '*It was impossible to send food to the few remaining people there.*'

30,000 in Jersey! 23,000 here!

We know that if food was sent to us, we would not benefit by it, but why make a statement like that which is absolutely incorrect.

We are very worried because they are going to ration electricity.

May 1942

Saturday May 2nd   N.E.
Still north-east wind but much warmer. I did not meet a single human being when Molly and I went for the bread. I did not meet one car or lorry or van going, it was extraordinary.

Katty told me a young German doctor, aged 25, had been murdered in Sark by a jealous husband. Mrs Mauger told us he had been murdered in Alderney by soldiers!

We have been pestered today. Two this morning wanting eggs. A third wanting a bicycle. A fourth wanting milk. He was a nuisance. He asked for James and I said he was in bed with a bad ankle. I showed him the Countess' sentences. Fortunately Raymond was there and kept telling him nix. He tried to push his way into the house, but I stood stolid in the doorway, with darling Molly growling behind me and we just faced each other for I don't know how long. At last he went off and then another came wanting lettuces.

Mr Ware brought us our meat, and said the murder had been committed in Sark by soldiers, a young doctor, Mr Ware said with great relish, they had either bashed his head in, or shot him, or stabbed him, he didn't know which.

Sunday May 3rd   N.E.
Molly barked furiously last night about 1.30am. James came down on his hands and knees, and I came down too, but all was quiet. After that I did not sleep at all.

The Prince von Oettingen has left us. We are all very sorry because he did his utmost for the civilian population. He could not have been kinder or more considerate.

Friday May 8th   S.W.
I went to Miss Ross today, she is very encouraging about my feet, she says I will soon need no supports, if I go on losing weight like I am doing. She told me that a doctor had told her there have been no cases of appendicitis for a long time, she said when she was training after the last war, her hospital was filled with appendix cases. *We* must be careful when we are free again!

Woolworth is being supplied from the Printemps in Paris for the German soldiers only.

I walked up to Markie from Town. I arrived at about half past three. Markie gave me *real tea*! Oh what bliss! I spent a pleasant afternoon with her. She told me that Victor had had a special official letter telling him he was held responsible for the behaviour of the people in Guernsey and that if any sabotage happened, he would be taken to France as a hostage. It is horrible for Victor.

Bobbie told me that Cissie would only see the German soldiers who were billeted on them in the kitchen, she would not allow them to go anywhere else. I do admire Cissie for that. She did not accept anything from them.

Nelly Welch is selling all her jewellery and buying rabbits and fowls and having them kept for her in the cold storage against starvation.

Sunday May 10th   S.W.

Mr Churchill made a magnificent speech at nine o'clock this morning and he told us to cheer up, a thing he has never said before. Generally he repeated his first speech, that all he had to offer was 'toil and iron, blood and sweat,' and in one speech he said he saw 'a glimmer of light'. How I love his cleverness and dexterity in his speech when he said 'he was so glad to see the workers in Trafalguar Square clamouring for action, and not whining for peace'. I am sure that is a sincere feeling. Oh! he was heartening.

Monday May 11th   S.E.

James and I had a terrible fright. Two Germans came about half past eight and asked how many people lived in the house. We had to say only two!

Thursday May 21st

Walking in I noticed the 'V' sign everywhere, but whether Dame Nature writes it herself I don't know. Bent brambles, hay stalks and thorns were all over the paths.

There are a good many spider crabs in the market now. Olive said she was waiting at Mrs Lucas' stall for some fish, when Mrs Lucas suddenly said to her, go to Mrs Tuck's stall, she has just had some spider crabs, Olive went over and was the third in the queue with about six people behind her. Mrs Tuck looked coldly at them and said, 'I am not going to serve you until I have had my dinner.' They waited standing first on one foot and then on another while Mrs Tuck drank her tea and munched bread and butter with her toothless jaws, a crony joined her, and they had a good gossip, she went across to another crony and had another good gossip, she came back and languidly handed out spider crabs one by one! She has gone on to Olive's black list. We all have our own black list of the shopkeepers who have been horrid to us and whom we will never go near in peace time!

Friday May 22nd

I paid Victor a visit in his chambers. He was so pleased to see me, I was quite touched. I told him I had been longing to come and see him and now I brought him his tobacco from James. I thought he was looking very well considering all he has to bear. He was quite cheerful except for one thing. He told me that he is convinced that Berlin does not want us to be well treated and always removes the men who behave decently to us. For instance, the Prince von Oettingen has been removed. His successor has not been appointed yet. The Prince was a gentleman. Victor is very afraid that kind little Dr Brosch will be removed.

Wednesday May 27th

In last night's paper was the following notice:

> Forest Church not to reopen
>
> The Dean of Guernsey regrets that after consultation with the appropriate authorities he is unable to sanction the reopening of the Forest Church at present. He would, however, be grateful if some householder in the parish might offer a room which might be licensed by him for a monthly communion service and possibly other services.

I was sure the Dean would have his way. With my experience of different Committees, the Dictators on them always get their own way. Katty may offer the Manoir, surrounded by huts full of ammunition, a much more dangerous locality than the Church. I wonder how many people will go to be ministered to by that craven poltroon, Finey? I can't see the church being kept closed if Mr McCartney, Guille, Waterbury or Froisaard or Kilshaw were our clergyman.

Thursday May 28th   S.W.
Poor poor Katty came in just now, utterly distraught. They have taken her cabin completely away, and smashed all her shrubs and flowers. Wanton destruction all over her brake. It is too awful and pitiful. They came with a lorry and took it away, so it was official.[211]

Friday May 29th   S.W.
A dreadful thing has happened. The day before yesterday, or rather the night I suppose, two Guernseymen and two Frenchmen escaped in a boat. We don't know if they have been caught or not.

JUNE 1942

Monday June 1st
A glorious first of June. Well it certainly is glorious as far as the weather is concerned. It is the most beautiful warm day. James will be gone all day. The Royal Court's police trial takes place today beginning at 10am.

Tuesday June 2nd
Another perfect day, very warm. Molly and I went for the bread.
   Addressing all the policemen, the Bailiff said:

> You have brought shame and humiliation to every single soul in the Island, from the Royal Court downwards. When you were sworn in by the Royal Court, we reposed in you our honour and trusted that you would justify the confidence we placed in you. And how have you repaid this?
>   Clothed in the uniform of Policemen, you have abused your privileges, such as being allowed out after curfew, and have pillaged our property, stolen, thieved and gone on in this terrible way. I am filled with shame. It is revolting to think how you have abused your position.
>   I cannot imagine what all the foreigners in the Island – brought up, as they are, to look upon the British Policemen as an example to the world – think of you. I have nothing further to say except how much I regret having to speak to you in this way.[212]

Friday June 5th
I went to Town fairly early and I went to Le Noury. Nellie Welch goes to Le Noury every Friday at 11am and sits there until 12 noon and has a chat with everybody. I think it is such a good idea, I am going to do it myself henceforth! Everybody is so convinced that we are going

---

[211] Katty had lived in a cabin on the cliffs but since the Occupation she had been living at Le Manoir and looking after it for its owner who had evacuated.
[212] This article was published in the *Star*, 2 June 1942 and was headed 'BAILIFF DENOUNCES POLICEMEN'.

to be free soon that they were discussing going away. Nellie said she ought to be allowed to go before anybody to see an oculist to prevent her going blind. We all agreed with her and said all the people who needed medical attention should be the first to go. Mrs Burnett has been causing great amusement because she says *she* ought to be one of the first to go because she was caught here. Everybody hoots at that because we all know that she refused to go at the last minute and her husband had to send her clothes back to her. Nellie says she is going to fly. I said I have heard the States are not going to allow any passenger boats to come for six months, only cargo boats. The first boat will bring diesel oil and food boats will come. No passengers to come until the food situation is normal.

Mabel Frere had heard that a submarine had taken twelve men off the Hanois lighthouse. That one of the sailors was an ex-policeman from here who had joined up at the beginning of the war. He telephoned from the lighthouse to our police saying who he was, told them the submarine had taken the twelve prisoners and advised them to notify the Germans so they could send more men to the lighthouse! A lovely story.

Nelly told us the Germans have been to look at her bungalow. She is living in one of their flats. Mr Welch was out, so Nelly received them in her bedroom, she being in bed. She told them they were welcome to the bungalow, that she had left it because *their* guns had rendered it unsafe. She would not dare live in it, and it was crowded with furniture because they had ordered people to empty the attics. They replied, 'Madame, we will not trouble you any further.'

There are such a lot of barter shops now.

I had quite a thrill when I noticed in some of the shops little red, white and blue bouquets and also the 'V' sign. I also saw several girls in red, white and blue dresses and had a greater thrill when I realised that subconsciously I was wearing a red hat and a blue and white cotton frock!

Coming home the heat was terrible. When I got back I found James in the depth of gloom over the electric rationing. I said 'Everybody expects us to be free next month so why worry!'

Saturday June 6th
About a week ago, the Germans heard there was a British destroyer outside. They nearly went mad with terror. All the cinemas were closed and they were rushing all over the Island. They thought the invasion here had begun.

I can't get over the thrilling optimism there is all over the Island. One secret I hug to myself is that, if it has not been further tampered with, the trunk line to England can be made to operate in twenty minutes time. I don't believe it has been touched because they all seem to live in watertight compartments and never tell each other *anything*!

Mrs Mauger told me her weight, 10 stone 1lb. She has lost 5 stone 11½lbs!

The prevailing topic of conversation here now is 'Feet'! It quite takes the place of the weather and is certainly the one touch of nature that makes us all akin. We notice each other limping and ask tenderly after each other's feet. Many people have stopped me and asked after mine. I must limp unconsciously. I had a chat with Mrs Jones in the Arcade on the subject. She said hers had been so bad in the winter with frostbite, she thought she would lose a toe. Dr Gibson told her he had cut off nine toes from nine people! Everybody is getting better now the warm weather has come. It certainly has been cruelly hot today.

Monday June 8th   N.E.
A lovely day with a nice breeze. The news is wonderful. Violet came to tea.

The paper arrived. Alas! We have all been so bucked and excited that we overlooked the fact that we are still helpless prisoners and in the paper is the order:

> Notice
> By superior orders, the wireless receiving sets of the civil population of the Channel Islands are to be requisitioned and placed under the custody of the Feldkommandantur. Sets used by subjects of the Reich and of countries allied to Germany are excepted. Contravention of this order will be punished by imprisonment up to six weeks and a fine of 30,000 RM: 60,000 shillings and 30 pence.[213]

One rumour is that this is because of the warnings the BBC are giving to people in occupied countries to take cover and telling the French in particular of the imminence of an attack.

Another rumour is that the German Civil Authorities here have had another rap over the knuckles for being too kind to us. Anyhow, we have to hand over our wireless by 8pm on Wednesday 10th.

Violet told me that they were awakened by the most awful din this morning between 4 and 5am. They looked out of their window and saw they were surrounded by tanks. Frank dressed and went out to put his frightened heifers into a place of safety and, having done that, he came out of the stable and had to stand by and watch one enormous tank come through his beautiful field of wheat, go over his crop of parsnips that he had finished weeding the night before, go over his crop of potatoes, go out of his gateway, carrying the posts away, go into the yard of the Carré's farm opposite and crush flat a fowlhouse and go on its devastating way. He had to go and quiet his cows who were nearly mad with fright.

Tuesday June 9th
It is much cooler today, quite fresh in fact. Just after breakfast two soldiers came and asked all kinds of impertinent questions, how many people lived in the house, was the land cultivated, how many horses and cows we kept, etc., etc. Katty came in to hear the news at 1 pm and said they had been to every house and that she had inside information and knew they were given that to do to keep them employed. These visits leave me absolutely sick with apprehension. I can't sleep at all now.

In the paper tonight, there is the following notice:

> Radio Set Collections
> Regarding the collection of radio sets throughout the Island, readers will understand that the calling in is not in any way a punishment imposed on the civilian population, but for purely military reasons.[214]

The Germans are only allowed to listen to their own broadcasts and they must tune in low, so as not to irritate the civilian population. This notice is probably put in by kind Dr Brosch to tell us he <u>had</u> to give the order.

---

[213] This is part of an article published in *La Gazette Officielle* in *Guernsey Evening Press* on 8 June 1942.
[214] *The Star*, 9 June 1942.

There is also another order asking us to answer all these questions these men ask us who keep calling on us. They certainly seem anxious to placate the civil population.

Of course, what we are afraid of is how much wilful damage they will do before they leave?

Thursday June 11th   N.E.
The order about the wireless is only for the Channel Islands.

James heard a horrid story. Some Frenchmen were brought here eight months ago. They were told that when they had been here six months they would have leave. They asked for their leave and were told they could not have it. They refused to work. They were in St Sampsons. They were taken to St Saviours, crowded into huts there, given no food or drink for forty-eight hours, made to stand up all the time, and when they fell from exhaustion were beaten with rubber whips. This story is true and not a rumour.

Molly and I fetched the bread. It is blowing hard and so cold, but although I had no gloves my hands kept warm, what a relief it is to have them warm and not to suffer from that awful pain in them I suffered in the winter.

Some people say they don't like the bread, but I like it very much. There were two schools of thought in the nursery when I was young: one was 'Leave a piece for Mr Manners!'; the other was 'Now let me see a nice clean plate'. We in Guernsey now all belong to the second school of thought. We don't leave one crumb of bread or one drop of gravy on our plates. I find the crusts of my toast rather hard, so I break it up and keep it to put in my soup at night. One day Olive came to tea, I was breaking my crusts off and laying them aside rather dreamily, when Olive swooped upon them and said, 'My goodness, you are not going to throw away all those crusts are you?' and before my paralysed brain could make a protest she had eaten the lot! A most regrettable incident.

I am now using the third hole in Damaris' belt and the sixth hole in my own belt! I always laugh to myself when I think how I acquired that belt. I was having tea with Daisy and she showed me a very smart leather guide's belt. She said she had ordered it for Mrs Bell, who had given her measurements, and Daisy had sent them up and this belt had arrived and when Mrs Bell had tried it on it was much too big. 'Good gracious Daisy!' she said, 'when you ordered my belt, did you think I was a battleship?' I had always longed for a strong leather belt, so I said, 'Daisy, I expect I can be that battleship' and, sure enough, I could do it up in the first hole! But now I have become a destroyer!

Monday June 15th
Michelle's 28th birthday. It is quite cold today, very unlike the boiling hot day on which she was born.

Violet came to tea, and we talked of the days that are no more, of the lovely parties we used to have today, and how Michelle's birthday party was *always* fine. Poor Violet was very down about missing these years of her boy's young life. It *is* hard.

After supper when James was in the garden I heard a shout in the kitchen and I went out and there was a German soldier standing there, he wanted milk. He was the most polite soldier who has been here, and he actually believed me when I said we had no milk and showed him my sentences! He was so courteous, I asked him if he was a German or an Austrian, he said 'German', and then clicked his heels and saluted me and said 'Wiedersehen' and went.

Wednesday June 17th   N.W.
Still cold but fine. The German soldiers are very jubilant, they say they have conquered the whole of Libya! That is the kind of news we shall hear all the time now.

Saturday June 20th
A beautiful day. Molly and I fetched the bread.

Peggy came to see me after tea. We do feel alike. She said she can't sleep now, like myself. If she wakes up, in a minute she is wide awake, and listening, listening for our planes and can't get to sleep again. Also like me, she can't read, all we read is dope, we can't concentrate on any book. We all find stairs trying and have no energy. I have given in and I lie down directly after dinner and I sleep for hours. I take my sleep when it comes. I never go out anywhere in the afternoon, except once a fortnight when I go to Town. Peggy was saying won't it be too wonderful to be able to make engagements and leave our houses with the doors unlocked and the windows open, to be able to go out and breathe the night air after 9pm sun time, and 11pm this time, and not be afraid of being shot or dragged off there and then to prison. We both agreed that we did not know what we should do if we did not *know* that all this misery is only temporary.

I told her what I'd heard about Libya. That we were only using Libya to keep the Germans put there, that we wanted Tobruk. We did not want to extend our lines of communication, but we had to defend Egypt. It made me understand the situation much better, I think it is so *hard* on our brave men out there that they appear always to be retreating, and are therefore criticised. I simply can't *stand* hearing any criticism about anybody, especially of our own States, when I know what I know and yet cannot say a word.

Monday June 22nd
Violet was telling me how sleepy she and Frank always were now, the moment they sit down to rest, they go off to sleep. James does too. I frankly give in and retire to bed every day after lunch and have a good sleep. I can't sleep at night, so I take sleep when it comes to me! The doctors say it is lack of sugar that makes us do this.

Violet told me Frank is Procureur of the poor at St Andrews and has to give poor relief to sixteen families. One man, who is ill and can't work and has a wife and four children to support, brought his grocery book, 27s. a week and he wanted a pair of child's shoes, 18s. 9d. a pair. The uppers were very good, the soles made of brown paper and they wore out in a fortnight.

Workman's trousers, 15s. a pair to workmen, 30s. a pair to young farmers, worth about 8s. 6d. a pair.

The 'Star Help the Children Fund' is a splendid fund, it gives these poor children any extras there are for them, it has reached over £1,000 now.

I must say, the way our charities are kept up is wonderful. The Local Blind Association and the Nursing Association are both very well off and all the others as well. All these plays and concerts have made splendid contributions to our charities.

Everything is being kept up to date so well. All the hedges have been cut and trimmed, the grass at the sides of the roads and lanes is dug up. The weather is so beautiful and the flowers and the young green and the birds are singing so sweetly, and yet it all seems such a mockery when one thinks that our salvation will come through the sacrifice of young lives. It is awful.

Book V

Tuesday June 23rd

I never thought I'd use this book for my diary. It is Katty's birthday, '60 years a Queen!' She had such a pleasant birthday party, Mrs Hazell, Miss Lois Marquand and Mrs Wyse and myself. She gave us such a lovely tea. Real tea to begin with. We brought our own bread and butter, she provided jam, we had carragean shape and rhubarb and strawberries, cream and sugar (!), and seed cake. She had saved up seeds for it and real flour and especially two rations of sugar and her ration of butter. She took it to Mrs Raven in Kings Road to make it for her. She had to bicycle in to fetch it today. When she fetched it Mrs Raven handed her a packet of sugar and said she had only used half, she really could not bring herself to use two rations of sugar in one cake! Poor Katty, who wanted to give us a really sweet cake for once! And, as she says, she can save her sugar because she does not take any in her tea. It is strange how people will so seldom do exactly what one wants them to do. The cake was very good anyhow.

Tuesday June 30th

Two years ago today we were occupied. Another beautiful day. They are hard at work haymaking. We had a quiet night, not a single plane flew over, and none flew over today.

We heard that my Torteval field is completely ruined with guns and huts.

This morning one of the German police came here and asked an indignant James if he was stealing his own potatoes! James denied the accusation with such warmth. The German was very conciliatory and asked if many Germans came here and all sorts of questions. James thought they are trying to stop the wholesale robbery of potatoes that is going on.

July 1942

Wednesday July 1st

Six months of this year has gone and we are now in our third year of Occupation. It is very depressing. Of course, hearing no news is awful. On the front page of the *Star* they say there was a terrible raid on the west and south-west of England, thousands of incendiary bombs were dropped and many casualties, and so on and so on.

Victor has put an impassioned appeal in the paper for people to grow more vegetables. Why, oh why didn't they make us grow more potatoes and still more potatoes? It is no use *asking* people to dig up their lawns and flower beds, they *won't* unless they are made to.

Some people still obstinately persist in saying potatoes are fattening! I have lived on potatoes and soup for the whole of the occupation and I am steadily losing weight.

Saturday July 4th   S.E.

A decidedly cold wind but a fine day. Molly and I fetched the bread.

Mrs Mauger had heard all sorts of wild rumours, her daughter told her Mr Churchill had resigned! Of course that was not true, I don't believe any bad news now, only good news! The Germans would never spread good news and nobody is likely to make up good news, and so when we do hear good news, it will be true.

Thursday July 9th
The Frenchman came again today for food. He went to a good many houses in the parish yesterday. I think he is being decidedly clever, nobody refuses him and he doesn't have to work.

Saturday July 11th
A lovely day. Molly did not come with me to fetch the bread.
 Mrs Mauger asked me if a Frenchman had come here asking for food? I said 'Yes, three times.' She said she had been warned about him by somebody in St Andrews, that he was a professional beggar, he told a glib story. Certainly I thought he was a beggar, I also thought, 'poor beggar', I quite believe he is hungry. However Mrs Mauger said, with her eyes flashing, she had settled him, she had told him she would ring up the Kommandant about him. He had been to Mrs Duffy and poor old Mrs Baleine and taken her bread. I had my suspicions confirmed when I gave him a plate of potatoes and he left two pieces! None of us leave a crumb of anything, we are all too hungry.
 Mrs Carre of the Blicqs has been goodness itself to the Frenchmen at the Vauxbelets. Some of them came to say 'goodbye' to her and she gave them a regular lecture. She said to them, 'You are all very young, and you did not know anything about this place when you agreed to work for the Germans, but now you do know that your work here is ruining the Island and us and we are your allies, and is it fair of you to come and devastate our Island like you're all doing? I want you to tell the French people about us and prevent them voluntarily coming here, of course those who are forced to come can't help themselves.' I am so glad she did and I am sure it will do a lot of good.

Monday July 13th
Violet came to tea. I think Violet is so lucky in Frank, nothing disturbs his calm faith that we will be free soon. He won't hear a word of criticism against Mr Churchill or the government. He is quite sure they know what they are doing and that they know best. It doesn't matter how awful the rumours are, Frank brushes them all aside and goes tranquilly on with his business. Violet says she thinks he deserves the V.C.

Tuesday July 14th W.
A fine day but a cool breeze.
 I have just read *Letters to a Friend* by Winifred Holtby. They are very interesting. On March 20th 1924 she went to a meeting at which Winston Churchill was speaking. She describes him as follows: 'Churchill I found quite detestable as anything but a humourous evening entertainer. I loved him for that. He is so unbelievably like his cartoons. He really and truly wore the overcoat with astrakhan collar and cuff in which Punch draws him laboriously supporting the weight of his former liberal self. He really and truly points an accusatory finger at the crowd and cries in sepulchral tones, "I say that if another war is fought, civilisation will perish." (Laughter) (A sweeping gesture) "A man laughs." (Out goes the finger) "That man dares to laugh. He dares to think the destruction of civilisation a matter of humour." (Rocking chairs and hoots of laughter from the gallery – in which I joined.)'
 And *that* was the popular feeling in England about defence in 1924! And Churchill has been so generous, he has never once said, 'I told you so.' Probably none of those people who were there, and who would be about fifteen years older when war was declared, were young

enough to join the Air Force or even to fight at all, and yet they had the power in their hands to render defenceless the young lives they called upon to be sacrificed in their defence in this war, and were able to laugh and hoot at the one man in England who had enough vision to forsee the terrible fate of youth. It is *so awful* to think of it.

Friday July 24th   W.

A foggy stuffy day. It did not clear at all. The hot plate is a definite sucess as far as cooking goes but oh, the dust and dirt! Worse than a kitchen range. For a few months I have lived in Fairyland with an electric cooker, shining aluminium saucepans and kettles and now back to the blackest of saucepans and kettles, eternal dirty hands and smudgy face!

Saturday July 25th   W.

We hear rumours all the time. The latest is that the British have warned ships they sail at their peril on the sea from the coast of France to the Baltic. What about our food ships?

Sunday July 26th

Still a foggy, drizzly, stuffy day! Katty came to lunch. She did not tell us any news.

A German soldier who is billeted on some people and can speak English has implored the people he is with to tell the Guernsey people not to shout the news to each other in the High Street, he said the soldiers were ordered to arrest anybody who did so, and he doesn't want to hurt the Guernsey people and yet he and the other soldiers are liable to be punished if they don't report people.

Some people *are* so stupid, they *will* tell news on the phone although we have been constantly warned the Gestapo are listening in.

What a life ours is now, so dreary, no wireless, no messages, we dare not speak. I have to hide this book all the time, in case anyone came in and took it. When I go upstairs I have to shut all the windows and lock all the doors. We are all getting so irritable with each other, and we are all so tired.

Poor Mrs Renault came in last night in a terrible way, the Germans are digging up their potatoes, main crop as well as earlies, so she and her husband are digging them all up today. Freddie Torode has had three perch of his main crop dug up. One of James' cows was milked this morning, a gallon of milk taken.

August 1942

Sunday August 2nd

Mr Sherwill is Attorney-General again. He has been allowed to come back to the Bar.[215]

James had a fracas with a German officer on Friday evening. The Germans had been practising throwing grenades over the cliff from our field which is full of potatoes, and they had trampled it all over. They were returning and passed James and Molly. Molly was loose. One of the officers stopped and pointed at Molly and said he was going to shoot her. James immediately took the war into the enemy's country and said, 'What are you doing all over *my* land, your men have been trampling on my potatoes all day and I am going to report you to the Kommandantur!' The two officers hastily departed.

---

[215] In January 1941 the Germans had removed Sherwill from public office following his involvement with two spies. See entry and footnotes for 4 January 1941.

Bank Holiday Monday August 3rd

There is a nasty notice in the paper today.

> NOTICE
>
> As from August 1941, all inhabitants of the Channel Islands who are held in custody for any reason by the German Authorities, whether in the Channel Islands or in France, are liable to the Death Penalty if attacks of sabotage are made against the Occupying Power in the Occupied Territory.
>
> In addition, I declare that henceforth I reserve to myself to nominate certain members of any parish, who will be liable to the death penalty, in the event of any attacks against communications as, for instance, harbours, cranes, bridges, cables or wires, if these are made with the assistance or with the knowledge of the inhabitants of the Parish concerned.
>
> In their own interest I call upon the population for an increased activity and watchfulness in combating all suspicious elements and to co-operate in the discovery of the guilty persons.
>
> Espionage = the death penalty
> Sabotage = the death penalty
> High Treason = the death penalty or penal servitude for life.
>
> The population of the island are once more reminded that in accordance with the German Military Law, and in agreement with the Hague Convention, the above are the penalties.
>
> Der Feldkommandant, gez. Knackfuss, Oberst.[216]

Tuesday August 4th

A fine day, very hot. Molly and I fetched the bread. I felt dreadfully tired, and so slept heavily until tea time. I can't do without my rest in the afternoon.

I have two slices of toast and butter for breakfast. I break off all the crust and put it in my soup for supper. I am sure if I only had two slices of *bread* and butter for breakfast, I would not be satisfied.

Wednesday August 5th

This morning I went to see Katty's cabin. It was a beautiful day and so hot with that lovely blue haze on the cliffs. I did not meet a soul. The sea and the cliffs and the Moie Point were all so beautiful. It is awful to feel that all those beautiful cliffs are filled with ghastly mines. And then I came to the abomination of desolation of what was 'The Cabin'. Poor poor Katty. Every bit gone. The garden left a tangle of roses and other bushes.

Thursday August 6th

Olive rang me up to tell me she had had a message from Damaris and in it she said, 'Jim met his wife in Guernsey in 1939. That she was charming and had some money and that Michelle liked her very much.' Most satisfactory.

Oh what depths or rather heights of joy those azure envelopes give us, we walk in air after receiving them.

---

[216] *La Gazette Officielle, Guernsey Evening Press*, 3 August 1942.

Monday August 10th

Frank was moving his cows on the Hougue and an officer was drilling some men up there. The officer took one man and shook him violently, kicked him hard and made him march five paces, turn round and march back again and repeated the process again and again and the man stood it and the others looked on with stolid faces.

Wednesday August 19th

Raining but warm, James heard a plane at 6am this morning. It poured all the morning. After lunch, as usual I sat in the study listening! listening! for the postman and sure enough he came. A message to James from Michelle.

> Sent on June 2nd 1942 from
> Red X B 20. Warwick House, St James, London, SW1.
> Engaged to marry Geoffrey Stanley. Hope to join him down south. Difficulties present. Owing transport. You will both love him. Loving kisses. Michelle.

What a lovely message. I have looked up her letters about him and in every one she says how nice he is and what a good time he gave her on the 'Worthing'. I tried to ring up Olive and was told no one could phone because there was an air raid! 'An air raid,' I gasped, listening to the steady patter of the rain and all the other peaceful country sounds but not a sound of a plane. 'Yes,' the girl said, 'it is a practice and may go on for hours and no one can phone!'

I am certain something has happened on this day the 19th of August. The Germans are humming like a hive of bees. Rushing about.

1.30pm

There is something up. James has just come in to say there are sentries in the fields dressed up in camouflaged macintoshes and branches of trees on their heads, and the machine guns in the different fields are manned, it looks as if the Germans were standing to arms. It is a foul day, thick fog and pouring with rain.

2pm

Mrs Renault has just come in to say a leaflet has been dropped telling us that if more than three English planes appear overhead we must take cover. It is exciting. I am thankful darling Michelle's letter has got through, bless her. I keep trying to phone but can get no answer. It is exasperating. I haven't wanted to phone to anybody for ages, and now I want to phone to everybody I can't.

4pm

Mr Gorvel has just come to say Timmer has the jitters as badly as the Germans, he is all of a tremble! I am so excited I don't know what to do. What with Michelle's message and the feeling something is happening.

8pm

Freddie Torode came and told us Timmer was beside himself with fear. James and I have had supper, both full of suppressed excitement! He has just come back from the heifers and says there are sentries all along the roads! I don't for one moment think anything will happen here at all, but it is too lovely to think they are all standing at arms in the rain and will be all night, che! che! che!, with branches on their heads walking about like 'Birnam beeches going to Dunsinane' and, by the by, why do we give the Germans credit for being the inventors of camouflage, didn't Shakespeare invent it first?

Anyhow, with their thoroughness, they have cut off the phone and it is 'ard, damn 'ard'. I can't phone Michelle's delightful news to anybody! I expect we shall be cut off for days, but the people are so decent, the way they run in and tell us every scrap. James used that word I haven't dared to think of even, 'free', at supper. Perhaps within a month, says he.

Thursday August 20th

A beautiful day. A gun thundered past at about 1 am. There were no planes and otherwise the night was quiet. Mrs Renault said Mrs Mauger went to Town yesterday and came back and said the town was seething with excitement. Sentries everywhere. Rumours flying.

1. That two large boats were waiting to take *all* the Germans away.
2. That we were all going to England.

Facts

All the foreigners were sent back to their camps and confined in them. All the telephone girls were sent home. The sentries have branches of firs on their heads still.

I have made up my mind to go Town this evening, or burst if I could not phone! However, I tried at 1 pm and, oh joy, heard the girl's voice.

Friday August 21st

Pouring with rain. I am glad I have not gone to Town. In the paper they said there was a 'Fiasco of British landing on France'. A large scale landing of English, American, Canadian and de Gaulle forces landed near Dieppe on Tuesday August 18th. 1500 prisoners were taken, among whom were sixty Canadian officers. The forces which landed were everywhere annihilated and 28 tanks were destroyed. Three destroyers. two torpedo boats and two transports were sunk through artillery fire, and four transports and five cruisers and 83 planes through aerial fire. I wonder![217]

The curfew here was altered without warning from 11pm to 5am to 10pm to 6.30am which is awful for the farmers. However, we hug ourselves and say the more restrictions we have, the better the news.

All the excitement has died down. It was extraordinary how soon one felt there was something up on Wednesday, even in the house one felt it.

Saturday August 22nd

A nice morning after the rain. Mrs Mauger had an exciting day in Town on Wednesday. She was in Town about 11 o'clock. The excitement was intense, everybody whispering to everybody else and giving themselves away unfortunately, for the Germans asked the people how they had heard the news so soon about the landing on Dieppe when they themselves had heard it much later. The Guernsey people heard it at 10am and the Germans heard it at 11am. The Town was packed with Frenchmen, they had all been sent away from their work. She said the Town was like a holiday.

Sunday August 23rd

Mrs Renault and I have a set dialogue.
   I say, 'Men don't talk Mrs Renault.'
   She says, 'Men, they haven't time.'

---

[217] The *Star*, 20 August 1942: 'Fiasco of British Landing in France: Churchill's wild venture at Stalin's dictation.'

James gave me a practical illustration. At 6pm he went up to fetch the milk cans from Mr de Lisle's farm at the top of the lane. I prepared supper, and to my huge satisfaction, I managed to get a roaring fire in the hot plate, and I had supper ready at 7pm. Boiling hot soup, hot stew and hot vegetables. No James. 7.30pm I locked up the house and closed all the windows and dressed and was going to look for him when I discovered a game fowl pullet in the conservatory. I could not persuade it to go out and finally it landed in a shallow box of seeds that were worth their weight in gold, seeds that are quite unobtainable! I stood motionless and looked at the bird and the bird stood motionless and looked at me. Molly came round the door quietly and, being a perfect lady, went out quietly. At last the bird stepped daintily out of the seed box without upsetting it, I breathed again , the bird went out, I locked the door, and Molly and I started on our search, to find James in the gateway chatting. This was twenty minutes to eight. At last he came in and had supper, he *said* there were a lot of farmers up there and they were discussing *ploughing*! I wonder.

Tuesday August 25th
Molly and I went for the bread.
    Gay said the Germans said the Guernsey people did nothing but laugh over the raid on Wednesday and so in the next raid we are all going to be confined to our houses for 48 hours. Bertie said it was quite true, everybody was laughing in the Town and especially outside Elizabeth College, to see the officers running in and out like so many ants. Outside the *Beaulieu Hotel* they had six lorries with a machine gun on each, standing there all day. They did have the wind up properly.

Thursday August 27th
Raymond the cowman has just come in to tell us that curfew will be 9pm next week and that they are going to take our telephones away! They are so furious with us for laughing last Wednesday.

Friday August 28th
A beautiful day. I can really wear a summer hat.
    Peggy told me that she was in the Grange on Wednesday during all the excitement (*how* I envy her). She said she had never seen such a sight in her life. Such an exhibition of mass hysteria, they were running in all directions and screaming and shouting. She said she was standing by the road sweeper and she caught his eyes and they both roared with laughter together and all the Guernsey people were shouting with laughter all down the Grange. The soldiers had fixed bayonets. There were barricades all over the town.
    I met Gouliot at last, I don't believe I have seen him this year. I asked him when he thought the war would end. 'In about four years,' said he, cheerfully. I groaned. 'Well,' he said, 'We shall never give in, and we can't beat the Germans yet.' Such common sense but so depressing.

Sunday August 30th
It is curious and interesting to take note of the completely different schools of thought the English and the Germans have about Guernsey. The English considered us of no naval or military importance and therefore declared us an Open Town and left us undefended.

The Germans consider us of such importance they are going to make us the most fortified place in Europe! They are convinced that when the second front is opened, the English and Americans are coming to capture us. Alas, we are convinced that they are going to do nothing of the sort.

Monday August 31st
Violet came to tea. She and James were talking about potatoes. The Potato Board has ordered James to supply them with three ton six cwt of potatoes. He can't, the Germans have spoilt his crop. Violet said they had ordered Frank to supply them with far more than he has. Frank has asked the Potato Board to come and see what the tanks have done to *his* potato crop. These are all German orders, they want to take our crops.

Clifford Gorvel came over to fetch his tobacco ration and said Churchill had made a speech, in which he had said 'the Channel Islands would be relieved soon.'! I wonder! And I wonder what he really did say.

September 1942

Thursday September 3rd   S.W.
Molly and I fetched the bread. I met Mr Clem Brouard outside the house. I haven't seen him for over a year! He looked very well, I thought, one of the few men who looks well. He said all his family were well. The Brouards have five visitors in their house, they have had them a long time, they are 'surveyors'. They won't allow the Brouards to use their own wireless, when they go out they take parts away with them. They were going to Jersey for a holiday and wanted to take the wireless with them, Mrs Brouard firmly said, 'No', she would take it to the States Depot. So they locked it up in a cupboard and pasted a swastika over the keyhole.

They asked Mrs Brouard to fry some potatoes for them, they gave her a big tin of butter and a rich piece of pork to fry with the potatoes and they made her use all the butter and watched her the whole time, they weren't going to give her any chance to take any potatoes.

The ordinary soldiers are much nicer about the wireless, in several places they allow civilians to listen in when they are out.

Friday September 4th
Not too fine a day. I got up at half past seven and made my breakfast, coffee and two slices of toast. All the morning I had been feeling more and more excited and when I sat down to breakfast, I could not eat it. I choked with excitement. I could not have been more worked up and excited if I were going to take the first boat to England, or the first plane! And I was only going to take the Civil Transport bus to Town which left L'Eree at 9.15am. The buses began last week, they are driven by charcoal. The weather cleared and I went up in plenty time, in fact if dear Molly hadn't delayed me I should have been able to catch the bus going down to L'Eree. I was disappointed because I am longing to do that journey and see everything.

I waited a long time for the bus. It was not full when it came, but we picked up people all the way. I got out at Mount Row and went to the Bungalow to change my hat. The day was beautiful at last and I could go down to Town without a macintosh.

I arrived at Le Nourys soon after eleven to find them all there. I had met Maud on the way down, and as usual at the top of her voice she asked me if I knew any news? I politely called her an ass and told her how everybody said how dangerous she was! And she didn't mind a bit and only laughed! Everybody was full of beans, and talking about the wonderful convoy that has just got through without attack. Twenty-five miles long and three miles broad going to an unknown destination.

They were talking about the buses. Poor Lady Ozanne went out to the Emerency Hospital, and had to walk all the way home because the Germans commandeered the last bus for themselves, and Dot Williams had to walk home from Grande Rocque and carry her old dog for most of the way. The Germans want the buses to bring them in to the pictures. I don't think we shall have the buses long, the Germans say they won't allow us to have them if they are not full, but most people won't go out to the country to be stranded. The sickening thing is they don't use their lorries, the lorries return to Town empty.

Saturday September 5th

The plague has taken a new and terrifying form. One is suddenly taken ill with violent pains, people faint and run high temperatures. The doctors don't know what to do, they called it para typhoid at first but it isn't para typhoid. After a few days people recover and are terribly weak. They think it is the bread which is made of bean flour, pollard and bran. They tell us to bake it for half an hour, and it certainly is very good after it has been baked. There is enough so called flour in the Island to last us till Christmas and heaps and heaps of coal.

Violet told us of two farmers, one had 1,000 onions dug up and the other 500. Everybody is picking their apples, they will all be stolen if we don't.

Sunday September 6th

A really beautiful autumn day. The day of prayer here, though I believe the King ordered September 3rd to be the national day of prayer, the third anniversary of the war.

The Sebire girl is leaving old Madame Sairey. They can't find anyone else. People say nobody will want to employ foreign maids again, but I think they will have to. Domestic service has become so farcical in this Island. The hours now are 9am to 12 noon. Very often that means 10 past 9 they come and they leave at 10 minutes to 12 and they demand £1 a week for that. If they come in the afternoon it is from 2pm till 10 to 5pm. No evening work whatever. No living in. The men come about 8.30am or later and leave at 6pm or before. The other day James managed to get two boys to come and cut the oats, it was a fine day, but the Germans were shooting in the next field, so Bill the man told the boys to go home because his nerves could not stand the Germans shooting. Of course James knew nothing of this till the evening. And so it goes on. The Germans say they brought all this foreign labour over here because the Guernsey people would not work. I am afraid it is not all patriotism.

Saturday September 12th

Another beautiful day, boiling hot. Molly and I fetched the bread. James went to Court but came back for lunch.

Mrs Mauger informed me the Channel Islands were the key of the world, and that after the war the Americans would take possession of us! She is full of excitement and does not expect to sleep tonight and is quite convinced there will be tremendous dog fights over the Island very soon, and that we shall be in the thick of the invasion.

There is one thing no German's savage irritable brain can stand and that is a shut gate or door. All over the Island can be seen evidence of this idiosyncrasy. The Young's poor back gates are sagging drunkenly, the Mainguy's back door is smashed. Having smashed the gates they proceed to smash the stone pillars or gateposts. They have been asked why they do it, and the answer they give is, 'I do not know.' It nearly makes me cry to see the Youngs' poor car in the yard, absolutely savaged. Why didn't the States sell it for our food?

I have just read Priestley's *English Journey*. It is very grim about the unemployment. He says the unemployed feed on bread, magarine and tea. We have neither wheaten bread, margarine nor tea! But we are eating plenty of fresh vegetables and tomatoes now and fruit.

Sunday September 13th
Raymond told us a British plane flew over the White Tower at Pleinmont and machine gunned it. The plane flew so low, none of the guns could touch it. A British plane flew over the Town church about 5pm. Everybody was cheering it and the German police were trying to push the people into the shelters, and fining them a mark for cheering it. Oh!! *What* a souvenir to have! The receipt for a mark's fine for cheering an RAF plane. I *wish* those darlings would come over on the Fridays *I* am in Town, but they *never* do. I have not seen *one* British plane yet, not *even* in the distance. It is hard luck.

Town Church.

Tuesday September 15th
I was going to the Manoir to pick up sticks and I saw two men talking. They stopped me and said, 'Have you heard the awful news Mrs Carey?' I said, 'No.' They said, 'The order is in the paper that all British born people in the Island are going to be evacuated to Germany.' I felt stunned. Did it mean everybody? It is too awful. I came home and waited and waited for the paper. At last the paper came:

Order

By order of higher authorities the following British subjects will be evacuated and transferred to Germany.

A. Persons who have their permanent residence not on the Channel Islands, for instance those who have been caught here by the outbreak of the war.

B. All those men not born on the island and 16 to 70 years of age, together with their families.

Detailed instructions will be given by the Feldkommandantur 515

Der Feldkommandant, Knackfuss[218]

It is too frightful for words. It means nearly all the clergymen and all the doctors except Dr Bisson and nearly all my friends. I have great hopes that the Civil Command here will make representations, all that will take time. This is a reprisal for the Dieppe raid. Are these rehearsal raids any use?[219]

Wednesday September 16th

I have hardly slept all night thinking about this awful order. We have heard that it is a reprisal for the bombing of Germany from one of the soldiers. He was told that they bombed England. 'Yes,' he said, 'but when we send nine planes over now you send a thousand.' He spoke as if a thousand planes went over very frequently now, he also said that if it goes on there will be a revolution in Germany.

James went to Town. He came back with the news that 8,000 will have to go. The Bailiff is fighting hard to keep the men in key positions. They say there will be a medical examination. The Germans and the Controlling Committee had a meeting and John Leale told them exactly what he thought of them and what the world thought of them. He could not have spoken more strongly or more plainly. Whatever he has done in the past, he certainly stood up for the people at this meeting.

A fishing boat escaped last night with three men in it.

I rang up Nellie, her husband answered the phone, poor Nellie is prostrate. I rang up Peggy Brock, they will have to go if the Bailiff fails to keep them, because Bertie was born in England. It is all so awful.

Four hundred have already gone from Jersey and they say they want our people to be gone by Sunday. It is all reprisals and revenge.

Thursday September 17th

I have hardly slept at all. They say the fishing boat has been caught.

The numbers vary all the time. Some say 8,000, others 4,000, and so on. They now say they are going to have a drastic comb out of people in key positions here. Sick people will have to

---

[218] *La Gazette Officielle*, 15 September 1942.

[219] It was not a reprisal for the Dieppe raids, but rather a reprisal for the British interning Germans working in Iran in 1941. Hitler had ordered that the British-born Channel Islanders were to be used as hostages so that he had bargaining power for the German citizens in Iran. However, the order was not carried out immediately. In September 1942 proposals were made about an exchange of seriously wounded prisoners of war and the Swiss government suggested including Channel Island residents who wanted to go to Britain. It became apparent to Hitler that the deportations had never happened. The order was re-issued and carried out as a matter of principle even though the Iran Germans had long been forgotten. A total of 1,846 British born Islanders were deported on 26 and 28 September 1942. They were interned at Biberach, Würzach and Laufen. (Cruickshank pp.216-19)

prove 65 per cent disability. The first boats are going on Monday, and Dr Rose and Dr Sutcliffe are going on them. The only doctor to be left here is Dr Wilson who is over age, even Dr Bisson was born in England.

We have heard that they have planned this in the Spring because of the shortage of food. They certainly have been working at the Greffe the whole year and made the most minute enquiries about the birthplace of all the Court in the Spring. Oh it is hell, hell, hell. To think of all those clean, decent, kindly Guernsey people taken away like that.

Friday September 18th
Not a very fine morning. I haven't slept at all. I got up earlier and had my breakfast and caught the 9.15am bus to Town. I felt I must see them all once again. We arrived in Town at five minutes past ten. It was quite fine. I met Peggy who told me she had slept better last night. Mrs O'Donnell joined us, she is convinced they will be rescued.

I went to see Victor. He was so glad to see me. Poor Victor, what a burden he has to bear. He told me two facts:

> 1. That the German administration here had made a list of men in key positions for exemption.
> 2. That he was with them two hours explaining to them that real Guernsey people were born all over the world. Apparently, in a year, perhaps two Germans are born out of Germany. They had no idea such a thing was possible as for Guernsey people to be born out of Guernsey. They agreed to make a list of genuine Guernsey people for exemption.[220]

Like me Victor was <u>bitterly</u> disappointed in the Dieppe raid. He had heard we lost 3000 men, dead, wounded and prisoners. I know it would double my misery if Boy was killed in a rehearsal raid.

Victor told me he had tried his hardest to make them reduce the age limit to 60, but they told him it was orders from Berlin, and therefore impossible to do anything. He said they were very sympathetic and helpful as far as they could be.

The Town seemed to be completely empty. I went on to Le Noury. Nelly had been to Lucas House for medical examination. She doesn't know if she is exempt or not but thinks she is, they won't separate husbands and wives, if one is exempt, the other is. Mr Frere was at Lucas House waiting to be examined. Nelly said all her neighbours had been so kind offering help, such practical help, one has given them two rooms in their cottage to store things, another has offered to do any sewing, another washing and so on. She said they all said the same things: 'Fancy them sending you and Mr Welch away, and you both *so old*'!

The fishermen who escaped have not been captured, but their boat has been found overturned, we think they are drowned.

That nice Mr Ridge was at Le Noury's. He was so calm and so helpful. Oh! They are all so great and courageous. I want to cry all the time and I can't. Several gallant boys and girls were married at the Greffe so as not to be separated.

---

[220] Island Archives: Correspondance with German Authorities, G/1-5 contains two letters from Victor Carey requesting exemption for Colonel Brousson, one of Victor's confidential secretaries, and H. Carey Brock, the Receiver-General. The Bailiff's files may have additional information but these are closed documents.

Saturday September 19th
There is a rumour that the BBC has told the Germans they have twenty days more to make up their minds to end the war. Oh! How I *loathe* the BBC. They announce all these things in their complacent voices, stir up the hornets' nest, have no power to destroy it, and we, poor, helpless people, become the victims. After the twenty days they are going to attack on a second front. Why, why, why tell the enemy the plans? It is just like ringing the bell to tell the runners in a race to run their hardest. The BBC has done us an untold harm. Then they give us those sickly broadcasts about 'our beautiful cliffs and glorious bays'. *We* know what has happened to our beautiful cliffs and glorious bays, they don't. When they had our children in the studio singing songs, would they announce the names of those children to the anxious listening parents? Oh no. I think we would have done much better if there had been *no* wireless.

There are all sorts of rumours where our people are going to. Some say the Black Forest. Others to a place on the Swiss frontier. Some say they will be in the train four days, others say two days. On the notices served to them it is written they are going to a concentration camp with no liberty.

Our people are wonderful, all the orginisation they have accomplished in such a short time. Every man, woman and child will receive a two pound loaf of bread, half a pound of biscuits, a tin of paste, a tin of sardines, quarter of a pound of cheese and a quarter of a pound of butter. Every child under three will receive a half a pound of rusks. The men will get a substantial allowance of tobacco and cigarettes and everbody will be provided with a basket. These foodstuffs are for the journey. Other arrangements are in hand to serve all evacuees with refreshments before they depart. This is all given by the States. Bureaus are open night and day to sew for the people and to repair their shoes.

Black Monday September 21st
Pouring with rain, the wind has gone down. I rang up Gay to ask about Peggy and Bertie, and they have not been told to go yet, so they won't have to go today. The Forest people have to meet near the Church at 12 noon, but no one can go to see them off. I don't think they want us, none of us could bear it.

Katty came in to say she had been down to the Gaumont to see people off. They were wonderful and were singing 'There will always be an England' as they went off. About five hundred have gone, four people from the Forest.

It cleared up for a bit and rained again this afternoon. Violet came, she had seen one of the papers and she said there was nothing on it about a concentration camp or no liberty. Just directions that they can take. They were told to take a knife, fork, spoon, cup and bowl. A blanket. A suitcase. And they can have a trunk sent after them.

They fetched Mr McCartney from the Communion Table to go for a medical examination, and at the evening service he announced that he had been exempted, but had not yet received his exemption paper. He is so ill and he looks worse than anybody.

It is blowing harder than ever and raining hard. They say the sea is raging outside.

Tuesday September 22nd   S.W.
An awful night. I don't expect many people slept thinking of our poor people on the sea. We heard first thing this morning that the ship was still in the harbour. What a relief.

They had another medical examination at the Gaumont and there have been a good many more exemptions. The Pommiers had two field kitchens down on the pier and were distributing soup and ham sandwiches and a hard boiled egg for each person.

I feel I can't eat anything, everything chokes me. I was lying down and Mrs Mauger arrived, bursting with excitement. She told us all the civil transport buses had been commandeered to take the people home and that there were two British battleships lying outside. Oh, can it be true? Anyhow, our staunch old ally, the sea has again come to our help. She said all the women and children slept at the *Royal* and the men on board. She said, they were not going at all. The dairyman said they had to be on board again at half past three. What can one believe? Is England at last strong enough to help us?

Wednesday September 23rd
Oh, what a week! We never know what is going to happen next, good or bad.

Katty had seen the McCleods and they had told her how grim it was on the boats. One was a coal barge with no accommodation, the other was a ship wth benches and tables, nothing else, no Red X ship. That was all a rumour. He said they finally arrived on the pier between three and four and were not allowed on the boat until seven. They waited in that new waiting room the Germans have built by the Weighbridge. He said he could not speak too highly of the kindness they received from everybody, including the German soldiers and sailors.

There is no doubt that this is a reprisal for the bombing of the towns in Germany. People say it is a sign of weakness, their deporting helpless people. I feel it is a sign of weakness us bombing helpless women and children as we can't beat the men yet. There is a German soldier who has been billeted with the same people for over a year. He loathes Nazism and the war; the people said to him, 'What do you think will happen after you are beaten?' He answered, 'When you have beaten us, you will have to fight Russia, the war will not end.' It is all so dreadful.

I have been fearing the worst all day, and no one has been to tell me anything. The wind is terrible and the sea is mountainous high and it is the highest tide we have ever known. James has been to a States meeting, he came back at half past five and said they have *not* gone, they have 24 hours more notice.

It was Stroobant who ran the Commissariat on the Pier, not Mrs Pommier, she helped. They were given real mutton stew. Stroobant stayed up all night cutting ham sandwiches although he was going himself. The meals were wonderful, provided by our Essential Commodities Committee and run by the junior officials.

On the coal barge there was no sanitation whatever and Dr Sutcliffe insisted on buckets being provided. The people were on board the boats all night and were allowed off at 11am yesterday.

Stroobant had a farewell party last night and when they were leaving they sang 'God Save the King' as loud as they could.

Thursday September 24th
The soldier billeted on the McCleods was whistling all over the house on Monday morning. They thought he was being horrid, suddenly he sidled into the room where they were, went up to Mr McCleod and offered a packet of soup squares, crept out of the room and started whistling loudly again. They think he was afraid he was being spied upon. And that is what they are like, all in deadly fear of each other.

A butcher died on board, and a poor woman with a three-week-old baby nearly died, the doctor insisted on her being put ashore. Dr Maglasham had a terrible attack of angina. The Guernsey Red Cross were magnificent, working night and day. How great everybody was. Several people formed themselves into committees to try and deal with the difficulties.

Doris rang me up just now (3.30pm). I could tell she wanted to talk and then thought she had better not and our conversation became as follows: 'Hello Vi, are you all right?'

'Yes thanks, are you?'

'Yes thanks, is James all right?'

'Quite thanks, how is your mother?'

'Oh, she is very well, thanks, hope we shall meet soon.'

'So do I.'

'Well I must say goodbye now.'

'Au Revoir.'

'Bye bye.' It is not much use phoning.

I left at half past seven. I stopped at Markie's and had a chat. She told me two stories. One of the people on the coal barge had set an alarm clock and it went off. Suddenly pandemonium among the Germans on guard and roars of laughter from the Guernsey people. The Germans thought it was an air raid alarm. I arrived at about half past nine.

Friday September 25th

I went to see Aunt Edith before I went to Town. I arrived at Le Noury's soon after eleven. Nelly told us of their interview with the German doctor. The German doctor said 'Strip', examined him and said 'Gut'. Mr Welch said he had a bubble of asthma, he said 'Gut' to Nelly too and their hearts sank and then they were told they were exempt. Nelly thinks he wants to exempt people. The Princess Radziwill who was acting as an interpreter said the same, he exempted all pregnant women and women with little babies. Apparently so many people did *not* know of the medical examination and so did not try and so they have had to go. The Germans would not allow it to be announced in the paper. It is heartbreaking.[221]

I waited outside the Star Office until a quarter past two, because I wanted to subscribe to the Bailiff's Fund. When they were open they told me I had to go to the National Provincial Bank. When I got there, of course, it was full. I had to wait ages. The Bailiff opened a fund to help 'all our dear friends who were to be evacuated' and in two days over a thousand pounds was subscribed.

We heard they were supposed to leave the Island at 7pm.

Saturday September 26th

A much quieter night. We hear they left at 1am, so they have really gone in spite of all our hopes. How the Guernsey people have worked to help them. Young Gordon Kennedy sat up all night making haversacks out of deckchair seats for the poor people.

Tuesday September 29th

In the afternoon Mabel Kinnersly came and brought her tea and later Peggy Brock arrived. We had a lovely gossip. Mabel said her 'billet' has just come back from St Malo and saw our

---

[221] Ken Tough, article in CIOS Review 20, p.63: 'In an obvious change of policy the Germans allowed no newspaper publicity on this occasion, although rumours of impending action were rife.'

people. He said they were given a hot meal when they arrived. They were put into second class carriages and each was allowed two seats and if troops were put in the train, they would have to stand. There is an idea they have gone to a Winter Sports camp at Freiburg with very good hotels. Dr Brosch was heard to say that they would all be in England in six weeks time, that they had been taken for repatriation. When the buses left a woman in St Martins leaned out of a window in a house on the route and waved a Union Jack until the buses were out of sight.

October 1942

Friday October 2nd
A beautiful hot day. I saw in the paper last night that A, B, C & D had to send their monthly messages before Saturday, so I went into town today by the bus. We arrived in town at 10am. I did all my shopping which was not much and went to Le Noury soon after eleven. Peggy said Bertie had had a chat with a policeman who was on duty on the Pier during the Sunday evacuation. He said some of the scenes were priceless, so funny, that the Germans themselves could not help laughing. One man who was slightly tight sang 'Auld Lang Syne' right through over and over again. Three or four other men kept seeing people in the other boat's queue they wished to say goodbye to and would go over and kiss them heartily, they went again and again. The policeman said the best of all were two old soldiers who came to the gangway carrying two kit bags, there was a German soldier standing by the gangway. They dropped their kit bags at his feet or on his feet and showed him by eloquent pantomime that he was to carry them on board for them. He meekly stooped down, picked the two bags up, shouldered them and staggered across the gangway, followed by the two swaggering soldiers!

Mr Hartley Jackson had eight suitcases, one so heavy it took two men to carry it. Mickey Kinnersly was in charge of the babies, she looked around for a cabin for them, found a nice large one, and settled the mothers and babies in it. Suddenly the door opened and the Captain came in. 'Doch,' he said, which means 'Well I'm blowed' or words to that effect, and he went outside again and let them keep it.

Some men brought down golf sticks and tennis racquets. A man gave a letter to a German officer who was coming to Guernsey, and he gave the letter to Victor. In it he said that they had had a very comfortable journey and soldiers carried all their luggage for them. They were only six in each compartment and only travelled by day, they had had a hot meal on arrival. It was lovely hearing all this.

Sunday October 4th
Such a grey day. Thick fog early and heavy, close and grey all day. Katty came to lunch.

Our days are so strange. I get up at 6am, breakfast at a quarter past 7am, lunch at 10am, tea at 1.30pm, supper 5pm, bed at 8pm sun time! Ten hours rest anyway, if not sleep, and rest from 12 noon until 1pm. We nearly all of us are living the same life, I think it is all that rest that keeps us well, both men and women.

Monday October 5th
What a day! What a day! Thrills! Thrills! Thrills! At half past eight this morning Raymond arrived with the news that Sark had been invaded by the British, that they had taken 200

prisoners and wounded five civilians.[222] The news had come from a German who had driven in a bus to the Grange. The bus was not allowed to pass Grange Lodge and Grange Lodge was surrounded with sentries with fixed bayonets. It is wonderful how Torteval always hears the news first. James went into Town for the Chief Pleas and heard that the British had landed on Sark on Saturday night and killed three Germans and taken two prisoners. Raymond heard they had landed on Sunday in the small hours of the morning.[223]

Violet and Mary came out, one from Town and the other from St Andrews, and neither had heard a word, so I had the great pleasure of telling them. Mrs Renault said the Germans were patrolling around the Gouffre and the Moye all night.

Thursday October 8th
Curfew 9pm.
It rained all day. Molly and I fetched the bread in deluges of rain. It cleared up for me to go to Town.

Olive told me about the poor Skeltons. She had played bridge with them in Sark, she said they were charming and Mrs Skelton was so young and pretty, he paid for the nurse in Sark and took a great interest in everything connected with Sark. When the order for evacuation came, he said he could not face a concentration camp and to see his wife tortured, and they made the suicide pact. They took poison, but she hadn't enough. He died and she was out on the Common, too weak to move in torrents of rain for over 24 hours. Everybody thought she must get pneumonia, but she hasn't and she is going to recover.

Friday October 9th
I went to Le Noury's. They were all talking about these new evictions. All one side of Sausmarez Street, which means poor old Mr Willie Ozanne, aged 93, has to move, also General de Lisle, and they are not allowed to take their furniture. Nearly all the Grange, the Fort Road, Rouge Huis. A General has been over and said the soldiers were too scattered and must be in blocks. They looked at Mrs Robinson's house and asked if it was cold, '*Very*,' replied Mrs Robinson, and she shivered violently the whole time they were there! The interpreter whispered to her that they did not consider her house suitable.

Our poor little gallant town is completely empty now. Le Riches bill is now 3s. 8d. for a fortnight! My butcher's bill is 4s. 6d. for the week. There is nothing to buy. I change my books and that is all I do.

───────── Book VI ─────────

Saturday October 10th   S.W.
This morning Molly was sitting under the kitchen table and suddenly she growled and made a fuss and a man passed with a cow. Mrs Mauger and I both told her how surprised we were that she should make a mistake, poor Molly looked so self conscious and miserable and then Mrs Mauger exclaimed, 'There is a soldier out there!' We both told Molly how clever she

---

[222] This was 'Operation Basalt'. Twelve British men landed and climbed up the Hog's Back on 3 October 1942. They were told by a widow that Germans were billeted at *Dixcart Hotel*, and that they were polite and respectful and that islanders regretted the Channel Islands had not been mentioned in the King's Christmas message. They were also given a newspaper with information about the deportations. They killed two Germans, took another prisoner and took him back to England. The raid led to further deportations in February 1943. (Cruickskank, p.240)

[223] The *Star*, 8 October 1942: 'British attack and bind German troops in Sark. Immediate reprisals for disgraceful episode.'

Boarded shop.

was, it is remarkable because the windows and all the doors were shut. Mrs Mauger said Mrs Hazell's cow goes nearly mad with fright when they pass her in the road. That is much more understandable, a self respecting aristocratic Guernsey cow, who is probably a connoisseur of smells, objecting to the odour she meets!

Sunday October 11th   S.W.
A knock came on the door about 2 o'clock. I went. It was one of the foreigners, very dark and well dressed. He said he was hungry. I fetched him some potatoes and tomatoes. I can't describe

the look of scorn and loathing he gave to me, I suppose he expected to be invited in to partake of a six course dinner. I said furiously, 'Well, if you can't eat those you are not hungry.' We looked at each other with mutual dislike and fortunately Raymond came. The foreigner caught sight of apples, so he wanted them and said he could pay for them. He wanted 4lbs. I weighed out 4lbs of Mrs Lucas' apples and he produced a handful of money and at last I got rid of him. I am not lucky in the foreigners who call here, other people seem to get such nice ones whom it is a pleasure to help. Jim always used to laugh at me when I talked of 'beastly foreigners'! I know no word adequate to describe them now!

Tuesday October 13th
Darling old Pegs arrived about five. What a difference it makes when someone comes to cheer us up. Peggy had a good deal of 'swen' to tell us.

A poor man from Sark was brought over from Sark under armed arrest, we presume he helped the English in their raid. They landed at Dixcart and went over the Hog's Back. The Germans woke up Miss Duckett and Miss Page at Dixcart at 4am. They asked the officer if anything had happened. 'Plenty is happening,' he replied grimly! It has upset them.

Peggy and I said we were longing for the day when we should see British soldiers, sailors and marines marching down the High Street. We will stand side by side, hand in hand, and we shall be cheering and sobbing at the same time. What we can't visualise now, is their smartness after seeing such sloppiness for three years. I shall walk in in the middle of the night if necessary.

Sunday October 18th
A drizzly day. Katty came to lunch.

There is a tremendous wave of optimism over the whole Island and in contrast the front page of the newspaper is most interesting. We have always said we must conclude the contrary. The optimism is also caused by the depression of the soldiers.

On Thursday October 15th 1942 the following headlines appeared in the *Star*:

> 'Winter scarcity will expose Churchill's bluff'
> 'Two British Transports sunk off Africa'
> 'In four days 12 boats have been destroyed, 8 more ships. Thus the enemy have lost during the last four days another 18 ships with a total of 143,000 gross registered tons between Newfoundland and the Cape of Good Hope due to action of German submarines.'

Evening Press, Friday October 16th 1942:

> 'The Ubiquitous U-boat. Germany controls the waters of the world.'
> 'E-boats strike deep into British waters'
> '8,000 tons of shipping sunk off Channel coast'

The *Star*, Saturday October 17th 1942:

> 'U-boats throttling the sea routes of Britain'
> 'If convoys cannot get through the war is lost'
> 'More Soviet Forces trapped and annihilated'
> 'Germans seize great works at Stalingrad'

Churchill said in Edinburgh, 'We have reached a dark and serious moment in this war.'

And so we know! And yet how curious it is that their own soldiers are so depressed and say, 'Germany is finished and England has won the war'!

Thursday October 22nd
In the paper they denied that our people had gone to forced labour, they said they had gone to an internment camp. I do *hope* that is true.

I had a lovely walk in with the south-west wind behind me. I left at 6.30pm and arrived at about ten minutes to eight.

The Germans are still in a fever over the Sark raid. No communication is allowed between Sark and Guernsey now. The fishing boats have only just been allowed to go out.

Friday October 23rd
I went to Le Noury's at 11.20am, they were all there. They had the most amazing story to tell about Mrs Sherbrooke. In the flat above her lives a German Naval officer, a man about 60, she had never spoken to him. One day this week he sent his servant to ask her if he could come and see her, she said, 'Yes,' and wondered what on earth he wanted to see her for. He came, she said if he hadn't been an enemy she would have described him as a charming man. He saluted and said, 'I have just come back from Paris, this parcel is for you. Ask me no questions and don't tell anybody,' saluted and departed. She opened the parcel and it contained a perfect photograph of her husband in uniform, a lovely photograph of her youngest son, who is 15, at school. She can't get over it and has told everybody and shown the photographs to everybody.

I met Mabel Kinnersly who gave me my 'Kings Head'. She knows a mysterious boy who cuts out the King's head in an English shilling and also cuts out a beautiful 'V' under the King's head and mounts a pin on it. He does it with a fretsaw. It is lovely, I wear my marquisite crown and G.R. on top of it. We have to provide the shilling and pay him a mark. We all wear them under our coats. Mabel Kinnersly wears hers openly, but it is rather silly because if the Gestapo spot it they will take it from her.

On my way home I met Peggy. We walked together the whole way to the Chene. Peggy told me that the BBC had asked the people in England not to mind because there was going to be a restriction on the sale of eclairs and cake would be 1s. 6d. a lb and also there would not be so many iced cakes! Words failed us.

I arrived home at twenty past eight and it was pitch dark.

Saturday October 24th   S.W.
Mrs Mauger told me a mysterious story. The postman brought a woman a letter and told her there was 5d. to pay because her letter was unstamped. At first she refused to pay it and then said she would open the letter and see if it was worth 5d. The postman said she could and she did. It was a long letter from her son in England!! How did it get here?

Mrs Mauger told me of a family who has a soldier billeted on them and with whom they have become very friendly. They have a little girl with whom he is very friendly. He was stroking her hair one day and he said, 'If Hitler ordered me to shoot this little girl I would shoot her.' I am glad to say they had the spunk to turn him out of their room and to have nothing more to do with him.

Sunday October 25th   S.W.
A fine day and warm. Katty did not come to lunch because of her cold, she stayed in bed.

Yesterday, Mrs Hazell, Peggy and I were talking about our feelings when we were free, we all agreed that the greatest thing of all will be to be able to talk all the time without looking over our shoulders to see who is listening to us. We feel that that is a thing we will *never* be able to make people understand. *No one* can understand that *awful* feeling of being spied upon unless they have experienced it themselves. There is so much we feel our people will never understand. I wonder if I shall ever be able to laugh again? Peggy said Bertie and she heard a child laughing, they both started at the sound and Bertie exclaimed, 'My God, did you hear that? A child laughing! I don't know when I last heard a child laugh.' There are only nine children left in the Forest!

Monday October 26th
Violet came and we turned out my linen cupboard. Soon after four a tornado arose. It poured torrents of rain and the trees bent double with the fury of the wind. I have never known a worse storm. It lasted until 6pm and then became as calm as possible. James came in soaked and frozen, he was out in the field milking.

Violet told me such a sad story. A Mrs le Page lived near them, her two little girls, aged ten and seven went away to England with the school. The shock of the evacuation made her blind. Doctor Sutcliffe told her that when her children returned she would recover her sight, it was her nerves that were affected. Later on she couldn't walk properly, she staggered all the time. Last week she developed excruciating pain in her head, and particularly in her eyes, she was taken to the Town Hospital and she screamed so much, they removed her to the Mental Hospital, she was there two days and died.

November 1942

Monday November 2nd
Change of time. One hour back.

We are now one hour ahead of suntime and exactly the same time as England. I had a lovely snooze this morning and it was nice to have breakfast without electric light. It certainly suits the household and I should think all farms and it is much better for the cows to go out an hour later, it won't be so cold. Of course suntime would suit them best of all.

Violet came to tea and we prepared James' study for the sweep. Violet told us how awful this new time is for them. It is now dark at 6 o'clock. They are only allowed one candle each a week, including the stables, and they have no other light. They dare not light their candles too early, they dare not have fires yet because they have so little fuel. It sounds awful and too miserable for words. When they had that extra hour of daylight in the evening, it shortened the evening, and they could go to bed at a reasonable hour. It will get worse and worse as the days get shorter.

Thursday November 5th   N.W.
I left at a quarter past five. It had rained all day, but it had stopped when I left. I arrived at about twenty to seven. It was very dark, the worst bit was Ville au Roi. I met so many prams on the path and shadowy bicycles kept passing me. I took my supper with me. I was very interested

walking along in the gathering darkness at the number of bicycles and prams I met with large sacks on them. I imagine black market potatoes.

Friday November 6th

A fine day. I went to Town and met Gouliot on the market steps. Gouliot was grinning from ear to ear. Instead of our usual greetings about the state of appetites, Gouliot said, 'Hello Vi, heard the news? I am walking on air, it is too wonderful. The first big victory we have had. I have got today's nine o'clock news, I will let you read it, come along to the Guille Allez,' (this was 11am) and Gouliot strode on with me literally running behind him. He leapt up the Guille Allez stairs six at a time, me panting after him, and in the Library slipped a paper into my hand. I took a large book and sat down in one of the windows and read it. O … .h the thrill of it, I longed to copy it, but did not dare, I memorised as much as I could and this is it:

> General Montgomery's Order of the Day, 'The Germans are in our power. I call upon every man to fight to the end of his endurance.' The response was supreme. The Germans ran away so fast and we following them did not know where we were. We could not even begin to count the prisoners.[224]

After that I walked on air to Le Noury's. They were all there and I listened to all *they* had to say, and then I said my little piece of authentic nine o'clock news. I did enjoy myself. I kept looking round for Gestapo. There was one girl in the far corner of whom I was suspicious, she smiled at me and Nellie said in a loud voice, 'It is all right, she is smiling,' and the girl apologised, but said she could not help listening, so we invited her to listen. How thrilled we all were.

When I went to the market, I stood and listened, it was exactly as if the markets were filled with birds. A lovely sound. All the Frenchmen were whistling their loudest. Mr Ware told me they were rounding them up out of the Town yesterday. They always strike when the news is good!

Friday November 13th

It rained all yesterday afternoon and all night. I went to Town by bus. There were black heavy clouds all day, it looked like snow and it was much colder. I had to wait a long time for the bus and when it came it was packed full.

We arrived in Town at 10.30am. I did my jobs and hurried to le Noury's and found them all there, full of swen and enthusiasm and spirits.

They are still panic stricken over the raid on Sark and have actually taken poor Frances Pittard prisoner and brought her over here. They wouldn't let her pack a suitcase even. They won't let any of us see her or take her anything. Poor Frances, just because she was living at the Jaspellerie. They are trying to make out she helped the raiding party. The Dame writes they are questioning her over and over again.[225]

Monday November 16th

A lovely day and not at all cold. I heard a blackbird whistling for a few minutes. I had such a shock after lunch. I took all the rest of the day to recover from it. I was preparing supper

---

[224] General Bernard Montgomery's British tank force broke through German and Italian defences at El Alamein (Egypt) in early November 1942. This marked the point where Germany went on the defensive. (Merriman, John, *A History of Modern Europe* (London, 1996), p.1272)

[225] This refers to an attempted landing in Sark on 3 October 1942. See entry and footnote for 5 October 1942.

just after lunch and a sharp knock came on the back door, I thought it was Germans. When I opened it, a man stood there and said he had come to read the electric light meter. On my way to the larder I picked up the dish of potatoes and took them with me and went in front of the man, stepped into the larder and placed the dish on the topmost shelf and my eye caught the ----[226] hanging there. I literally froze with horror. Fortunately he was not on top of my heels and I turned and said, 'Will you speak to Mr Carey first, he wants to speak to you?' I stood firmly in the doorway. He said, 'Let me read the meter first.' (The meter is in the larder.) I said, 'No, just speak to Mr Carey before he has his sleep,' and I stepped out of the larder and shut the door firmly, and took him to the study and said to James in a loud firm voice, 'Here is the electric light man, you want to speak to him, don't you?' Fortunately James understood me and I shut them in together and rushed to the larder, clasped the B.M. to my bosom, it was literally B., and ran upstairs with it. I felt like saying 'Pheeeeew' all day.

Violet came to tea and we did some jobs together. Her brother-in-law had dinner with his mother on Friday. When he returned to his empty house, he found it had been broken into and all his food taken, his week's rations and everything, some eggs he had and butter he had made and they had tried on two new suits he had, but had left them.

Tuesday November 17th

A lovely day but much colder. Molly and I fetched the bread. I have always longed to be out when our planes pass over and I had my wish granted today. When we were in the lane near Passiflora, I heard planes distinctly and then bang! bang! crack! crack! went the guns for a few minutes. Mrs Tourtel was fetching her bread and we had a nice chat coming home.

One of the German soldiers at Pleinmont has said, Hitler is like a man at the top of a ladder, he can't go any higher and the English are at the bottom of the ladder, waiting for him. This soldier thinks he will lose his entire army in Africa. This soldier is longing for the British to invade this Island and take him prisoner.

There was a peculiar notice in the paper last night and tonight:

Notice

It has been discovered that foreign labourers are begging from the civil population.

As these foreigners are receiving sufficient food, there is no reason for the civil population to give further food out of fear or on compassionate grounds. Furthermore the public are warned not to come into close contact with these foreign labourers. Patrols will see that this order is carried out. Infractions will be severely punished.

Knackfuss[227]

They *are* frightened.

Thursday November 19th

A still, cold day. I left at half past four, it was absolutely still, no wind, dry, heavy clouds and cold. I did not speak to a soul the whole way in and felt terribly depressed. We are all longing for Christmas to be over. I can't help thinking of the times I bought things for the children's stockings, how I *loved* those Christmasses and anyhow I have always loved Christmas.

---

[226] The word written here is illegible.
[227] *La Gazette Officielle*, the *Star*, 17 November 1942.

The reason for that notice in the papers about us and the foreigners is 'disease'. Some say there are several cases of typhus among them.

We heard an extraordinary thing, one of the soldiers in the AA battery on the Corbiere is called George Falla. He said his father was in the army of occupation after the last war, died, and left him and his mother in Germany. The Guernsey boys asked him how he could fight against us when he was Guernsey. He said he had been made to serve and would be shot if he didn't.

Saturday November 21st   N.W.
Another cold, still day. Molly and I fetched the bread. James went to town. The clouds became blacker and blacker but we only had one small shower.

They have been surveying our field above the greenhouse. They are going to lay a cable through it. They have run one through my field near Cavendish Vineries and, looking up the field, the trench they have dug looks a perfect V.

There has been news of our evacuees besides messages. An Irishman has been sent back to Jersey in ill health and he has made a report. He said they were all in an internment camp. They were not made to work and they could go out with guards. From the St Malo quayside, the party from the boats were led to a train awaiting them. Half went to southern Germany and half went to western Germany. The rations issued at home before they left lasted some of the evacuees nearly a fortnight. The camp comprised about fifteen huts, capable of holding eighty to a hundred people. Each hut was divided into cubicles. Curfew was at 10pm. The fathers took the older boys with them leaving the younger children with their mothers. The huts were centrally heated and had electric light. The beds were covered with straw mattresses and had sheets and blankets. The evacuees evolved a camp administration and fifty men formed a police force. There were ten German soldiers acting as interpreters and there were six women interpreters. Dances were being held three nights a week, whist drives twice a week, a concert once a week. Church services twice a Sunday. A statement has been made that the rations are better than they were in Jersey.

We have heard they are worse off in Jersey than we are here.

Monday November 23rd
We are having a cold November. People are suffering terribly, there is so little fuel available. People are suffering from heart attacks from the cold and from lack of sugar. We all dread the winter and long for the muggy warm, foggy, wet weather we used to have now.

Wednesday November 25th   N.E.
A dull, grey day. It is trying to rain and I don't think it is so cold. The field is full of foreigners and a huge lorry has just driven up (10am) and knocked down the wall and we can do nothing and say nothing.

We have been ordered to report if we discover anybody stealing from us. Do we report, not if we know it. One farmer reported some soldiers had stolen his potatoes, he saw them, he reported it, he was fined ten marks for not detaining them. Another man did detain a soldier forcibly and was sent to prison for six months for touching the sacred person of a German soldier. Another man told the owners he saw soldiers stealing their onions, he was fined ten marks for interfering!

Friday November 27th
Not too bad a day, rather raw but not raining. I left here to catch the bus at twenty minutes past nine and I waited and I waited at Mon Plaisir until five minutes to ten.

At five minutes to ten Mrs George Lucas came out of Mon Plaisir, she said, 'I would have brought you a cup of coffee if I had known you were there,' which was very sweet of her. I said, 'I think I must have missed the bus.' She said, 'Why don't you come in the van with us, Mr Sarre's van from L'Eree?' While we were talking the bus arrived packed out and the van was just behind it, so I waited for the van. It was a covered van with seats on both sides and a bench down the middle. It was full of cheerful Torteval people and nowhere in the whole wide world are there more cheerful people than the Torteval people when they are driving into Town for the day. They welcomed me hilariously and I sat down partly on the form in the middle of the van and partly on a sack of potatoes, 'Oh,' I said, 'black market potatoes, eh?' This sally wit of mine was received by the man sitting by me with a large grin and a larger wink and he said, 'That is no matter, we say nothing!'

We jogged comfortably along and passed two foreign gents, they could wave until they were black in the face, there would never be room for the likes of them in the Torteval van and their clothes were accurately described from the tops of their foreign hats to the tips of their foreign toes!

We picked up two more people and drove in to the cheerful hum of the patois, the one language that has defeated the Gestapo! Some triumph. I do enjoy driving with the country people, they are so cheerful and they all looked very well.

We arrived in Town at half past ten and I did all my jobs and reached Le Noury's at ten past eleven. Nellie was there sitting on a parcel which she called 'pure gold'. It was actually two pounds of sugar which she had purchased in the black market for £1 a lb!! Tea is now £6 a lb!

I came home by the 2.30 bus. In the evening, when I was getting my water, I heard a step and I stiffened and glared and found Mr Gorvel glaring at me! I realised our amazing situation, that now we *never* expect the step of a friend. However. Nous Verrons.

December 1942

Tuesday December 1st
The first day of the last month of this year, only three more weeks, come Friday, to Christmas. *How* we are all longing for Christmas Day to be over, I shan't send *one* card.

We just go on every day doing the same things. I think our lives are bounded now by fire and water. We are always preparing for the fire. The poor men are chopping up endless wood, I am gathering little sticks, drying the ever damp newspapers. Then we have to draw all our water from the rain water tank with a bucket to fill the ever empty kettles, or from the fresh water well for drinking. All day long and in the twilight or in the dark with a candle in my old horn lantern. And so it goes on.

It has been a beautiful day today and not too cold. Molly and I fetched the bread. Mr Crousaz doesn't believe any good news, only bad. I think he sees no hope for anybody.

Wednesday December 2nd
Gay rang up and said she could come out. It was lovely having her. I had a glorious fire because the coalman came today! Gay and I discussed our health. We agreed we were both very well, and Gay is wonderful because she has just had a major operation. One noticeable fact is that

people don't have the colds they used to have and we think that is because we are all living in a much colder atmosphere and because we don't crowd together in the cinemas, etc. Dr Aikman always said, live in a cold house, dress warmly and generate your own heat. I heard a doctor give lectures on the wireless and he said, as far as I could make out, to create a hardy people, they must be uncomfortable, very cold and underfed! Oh dear! Oh dear! Must we refrain from eating all the lovely meals we have decided we shall have when we return to civilisation? Anyhow I can walk steadily for two hours without a rest.

Saturday December 5th
We had a dreadful shock today. A nasty letter from the Electric Light company telling us that we are exceeding our electricity ration, and during the period of September quarter we used 367 units of our ration. This must cease immediately otherwise the electricity to our premises will be cut off immediately. Our ration for the September quarter was 30 units!

Olive exceeded hers and went to see Mr Bartlett about it. He told her the Germans were tightening up everything. They themselves burn it night and day. Our ration from December to next March is 85 units. Once more the farmers are muttering and complaining with a righteous cause, but will one of them go and state their case? *No!* The farmers have no more allowance than anybody else. Others don't get up till 8 or 9. The farmer is expected to be up at 6 and use light in his stable, also other people can stay in their beds in the dark, the farmer has to do his stables at night and possibly sit up with a calving cow. We have no more allowance than the Renaults or the Maugers who don't need the light like we do.

Sunday December 6th   S.E.
A fine day and a soft wind. Katty came to lunch. After she had gone, I thought James was upstairs and there was a persistent knocking at the back door. Three foreigners. I peeped and hid, I think they knocked for half an hour and at last went away, they did not try to come in although the door was unlocked. James wasn't in at all, he was down at the Big Glie chasing heifers! I was glad I did not know I was alone in the house.

Everybody is plagued with rats. I heard an amazing story, a man at St Peters saw two rats, one lying on its back and clasping an egg on its tummy and another rat dragging it along by its tail! I did not believe the story. James says at Wellingore Hall they had a glass case with two stuffed rats doing exactly the same thing.[228]

Poor old 'piggles' is going to be killed soon and James is going to be able to keep half. He is quite excited at the thought of having pork and bacon. At first they said he could only keep a quarter but they are letting him keep half. One farmer cut his pig exactly in half and kept the hams and the tail half, giving the butcher the head half! How I laughed when Mr Ware told me about it, he was so angry. I thought, the poor old farmer had got his own back for once!

Friday December 11th   S.W.
Blowing almost a gale but fine. I went to Town in the Torteval van. It was not so full. My chatty farmer was on the bus and we had a most interesting talk. He told me with many chuckles of delight that a boat was sunk by the RAF off Jersey a week or so ago and it contained all the chocolate and tobacco for the troops here for Christmas. A Gerry had told him.

---

[228] Wellingore Hall was a school in Lincolnshire where James had received part of his education.

We were going along quite peacefully. We came to the Cornu, and I thought the woman opposite me was having a fit; she screamed in Guernsey French, got very red in the face and flung herself flat on the floor and pulled feverishly at a sack that was underneath the seat. I asked, 'Whatever is the matter?' The van had stopped by then, my friend pointed to the road and I saw it was strewn with limpets. They hadn't come out of the woman's sack, but out of a sack that was tied underneath the van, belonging to no one in the van, so we were all very complacent about the limpets. It is wonderful that there is one limpet left on the rocks when one sees the mountains of them for sale in the fish market every Friday.

Monday December 14th   S.W.
King George's 47th birthday.

Another fine warm day. Torteval has arrived with a horrid rumour that Berlin is not satisfied with the number of people evacuated from here to Germany. I am sure it is because that blasted BBC won't keep silent about it. People say here it is our people in England want to know about us? I am perfectly certain that our people in England would understand that silence is the best policy as far as we are concerned. If they knew what it was like to be in the complete power of the Banderlog.

A very good subject for our discussion group would be 'Is the wireless a help or a hindrance in the war?' I know we would all say, don't allow any broadcasting in the war. It is only a danger.

Tuesday December 15th   S.W.
A lovely day, brilliant sunshine. Molly and I fetched the bread. Mr Crousaz actually told me something, bad of course! We have lost fifteen million tons of shipping in the whole war. To think of all those men drowned, the finest type of man, it is heart breaking.

I went to Mrs Hazell's party for Mrs Mauger's school. The three children were there and also Mrs Fricker with her little girl aged twenty months, called Moiya, and Ernie Mauger's wife with her little girl called Betty, aged sixteen months. Both babies get two pints of full cream milk a day (all the babies do) and foods and they certainly looked very well and fat. They were such good babies. They certainly wanted to look inside every cupboard, but that was only natural, we all want to do that!

Sunday December 20th   S.W.
Katty came to lunch. Katty must have had a busy day that Saturday she told us she had banged into the tar boiler. She told Gay Brock she had walked into barbed wire entanglements in the dark on that same Saturday. She could not get free. So she found she had a box of matches with her and burnt the paper wrapping around her rations and called for help and the German soldiers came running to help her and picked up her parcels and disentangled her. She told Mrs Brown-Clarke and Mrs Raven that she had walked into a minefield and she found she had a box of matches, etc., etc! Then she told someone else she found herself among the big guns after she had lit her flares, etc., etc., etc! So, I repeat, she must have had a busy day.

I am taking vitamin B. The chemists have it now. My nails are so bad and so is my hair. It is horrible. Everybody who has been to the doctor for every complaint is told they lack vitamin B. I haven't been to any doctor, but to Mr Cumber the chemist who says you can never have too much vitamin B.

There are no hairpins to be bought now and clever people are using ordinary nails to keep their hair up!

Tuesday December 22nd   S.W.
The men are having extra tobacco and cigarettes for Christmas. Eighty cigarettes extra and a quarter lb of tobacco over the holiday period from December 21st to January 4th 1943. Everybody is having 2oz extra of butter, 3oz extra sugar, 3oz extra salt. The *Star* fund is giving the children 5lbs of potatoes, 1s. of vegetables, 11oz of sugar, 6oz of butter, 1s. of jam, 4d. of sweets.

Wednesday December 23rd   S.E.
Three years ago today Michelle arrived home for Christmas.
 A beautiful day. I got up bright and early and went up to Mon Plaisir to catch the bus. We jogged slowly into Town. We arrived at a quarter past ten to my surprise.
 I saw Florrie McCrea standing on the Court steps. She was very breathless because she had climbed all the way up to the Police Court looking for the Greffe. She proceeded to chasten me. She said, 'I did not know you have got so thin.' I said, 'Oh! I am very well indeed.'
 'Oh,' she said, 'I suppose you can walk *now*'! I said indignantly, 'I could always walk.'
 'Oh, you must feel so much more comfortable now,' said Florrie, more grim than ever. Poor Florrie, I tactfully refrained commenting on her appearance. She and Ruth look the worst of all of us. Now my really *kind* friends address me as follows: 'Hullo Vi, how *slim* you have got, it is *so* becoming, you look at least ten years younger.' *That* is what I call tact and, of course, absolute truth!
 It was a beautiful day, the sun was so hot and bright. But none of us are in good spirits, the news of our poor evacuees is so bad. They are starving and we can't help them. Messages keep coming through wishing they were dead. It is *awful*.

Thursday December 24th   S.E.
Christmas Eve.
Darling old Peggy came to see me this afternoon. She had been to see Victor this morning. He was terribly upset. He had had a message from the camp commandant of our people in Germany asking him to send any food he could to help our people because they were starving. Victor was in the greatest distress, because he had the hopeless feeling that any food he sent would never reach them. Our helplessness is too awful.
 James came home with the rumour that the German Civil Authorities have received over 100 anonymous letters from people in Guernsey telling them of hidden wireless, and that they have said they must take notice and that is why the notice about the wireless has appeared in the paper. The Gadarene swine. Oh! I do hope somebody will find out who sent the letters. James heard it on very good authority it is nothing more than a rumour. Torteval told me that all the trouble about the hidden wireless is due to the girls that go with the soldiers and that the authorities are forbidding any intercourse whatever between civilians and soldiers. They don't want the soldiers to hear any news.
 Ilsa asked the authorities to extend the curfew tonight and tomorrow night. They said it was impossible because they expected the British and Americans to invade us these two nights! They *really* think that, it is *amazing*. James said when he was riding home in the dark he had never seen so many sentries and they kept flashing torches on him.

Friday December 25th   S.E.

At last Christmas Day is over. Poor desolate, neglected little Forest, with no church and no communion service. Mr Finey won't even come out and give us a service in someone's house and he is allowed to do as he likes. I could manage to get back in time from a service at the Forest Church, but I can't from any other church, and we daren't leave this place with no one here.

Saturday December 26th   S.E.

A beautiful day but distinctly colder. Molly and I fetched the bread. Mr Crousaz was at his gloomiest. I think he reads and swallows whole every word of the front page of the papers. Any bad news he believes implicitly. I am quite sure than when peace is declared and I fetch the bread and say to him, 'Well, Mr Crousaz, what do you think about peace being declared?' he will reply, 'I have heard a rumour about it but I don't believe it.'

Thursday December 31st

Olive said the Procureur had asked people to deny this foul rumour that is all over the Island that the Bailiff has been forced to sign a paper for the young men of military age to be taken away and for the young girls to be taken to work in munition factories. I believe the Germans start these rumours themselves to make us miserable.

The Germans are receiving anonymous letters complaining against the Controlling Committee at Hirzel House. The Gestapo were always going there, and finally they asked why they came and they told them about the anonymous letters. I never thought we had such Gadarene swine in the Island. In consequence of one anonymous letter, an officer and men went to search a house for a wireless. The woman said they had no wireless. The officer went into her sitting room, threw himself into an armchair, and made her stay with him while the men searched the house. At the end they searched the room where the officer was but found nothing.

And so we have come to the end of another year under Nazi rule. They are hourly expecting an invasion by British and American troops. We are convinced that no such invasion will take place. We are also convinced they could have held this Island with a civil administration. They need not have left a single soldier or gun or tank here. They need not have built one air raid shelter, one dug out, one gun emplacement. They could have left the Island exactly as they found it. What a testimonial we could have given them if they had let the Island alone and not destroyed anything. Instead of that, we fully understand the meaning of that realistic phrase 'the abomination of desolation' in some parts of the Island.

I would like to know exactly how many lives have been lost, how many ships, how many guns, equipment, ammunition and tanks have been lost defending this Island against what? Nothing. This little atom of the British Empire, the acreage of the Duke of Northumberland's estate. One English estate!

The Diaries of Violet Carey, 1943

January 1943

Tuesday January 5th   N.E.
A fine day and colder. Molly and I went for the bread. When we came back the temperature had changed and it was much milder. In the afternoon I went to Violet for tea. It was lovely walking there, like a Spring day.

At tea we were talking about the anonymous letters and Frank said a young clerk who had to do with Grange Lodge told him they received about five anonymous letters a day denouncing Guernsey people. The German Authorities said, 'We are not your enemies, it is your own people who are your enemies.'

There is a pantomime, *Dick Whittington*, being acted at the Central Hall. Raymond went to it on Saturday and he told us they sang German songs in it!

I came home soon after six and it was quite light. The days are lengthening. How we notice the daylight now, it is so precious. Violet and I told each other how economical we thought we were and how extravagant we really were! We were discussing fire and water as usual, sometimes a kettle takes two hours to boil! And we have to go puff puff puff with the bellows.

James is definitely getting fatter again. I am so glad. We have been living very well lately.

Thursday January 7th
A beautiful day, so mild and sunny. Molly and I fetched the bread. I had tea early and meant to start at 4pm. Fortunately I was delayed and I was in my bedroom dressing at a quarter past four when the guns went off, a terrific barrage. I rushed to the window and there I saw, flying over the Bigard, three British planes! I saw them, very large. They were flying very slowly down towards the sea. The banderlog were screaming at them with their guns and they flew, graceful as swans, sublime in their insolent contempt, black puffs of smoke from shells, and tracer bullets bursting up in the sky far above them, and far from them and after they had gone. With glee, I watched the shells bursting in the west, oh what a glorious moment. It was bliss without alloy.

I started on my long walk and met Mr Tourtel near the Heaumes. 'I saw them! I saw them!' I said before he could say anything, he only heard the barrage. How we beamed at each other and we all agreed it was the loudest barrage we had ever heard.

Olive had a lovely fire. She told me a good story. When the black market first started, Mabel Frere asked to be directed to it. She thought it was a building.[229]

Saturday January 9th   S.E.
A bitter bitter cold wind, it is cold today. Molly and I fetched the bread. I gave Katty some veganin to take to poor Flora Durand, who is doubled up with pain. The doctor can do nothing for her, he says it is the cold. It is hard, they can't operate for appendicitis, because her appendix has so many adhesions, they can't get at it.

Thursday January 14th   N.
It poured in torrents all night and it was very cold today, a bitter north wind is blowing. I wore my rubber boots and thickest coat to fetch the bread and I was beautifully warm. Molly deserted me today, she could not bear the wind. Mr Crousaz for the first time was cheerful.

It was quite fine when I fetched the supper, the moon was beautiful. Just after I finished outside, it hailed and it rained, so I was very lucky. It seems like an impossible dream to remember the time when we just turned on a tap and hot water gushed forth ad lib! Now I have to put on rubber boots and go across the yard, fetch a kettle, empty that kettle, fill it again from a bucket drawn up from the tank outside the back door, carry it across the yard, carrying a dim lantern with a smoky candle in it, put the lantern down to open the door, if unskilfully the wind blows the door to, hits the lantern, out it goes. I grope in the mud for it swearing hard and so on ad infinitum.

Tuesday January 19th   S.W.
A fine dull morning, very mild and the birds are singing so beautifully, poor darlings, they really think Spring has arrived. Molly and I fetched the bread.

There were *not* German songs in the pantomime, they were Scotch songs and Torteval did not know the difference![230]

Saturday January 23rd   N.W.
A beautiful day and the birds are still singing. Do they know winter is passed or are they living in a fool's paradise?

Molly and I fetched the bread. Mr Crousaz very cheerful. Coming back I met Mr Ridge, who depressed me more than ever because he doesn't think for a moment we shall be free until peace is declared.

The Germans are trying to make us teach German in the primary schools. Jurat Roussel had to go and see them about it. They asked him why we are so unfriendly, that the Jersey people were much more friendly to them than we are. He replied, 'You are our enemy and look how you have ruined our Island.' They agreed with him about the Island. That is where it seems so hopeless to even have any real contact with them. They are all in separate watertight compartments and have no agreement with each other. The Military Administration ruin the Island, the Civil Administration have no say in the matter.

---

[229] This was either a common mistake or there has been some confusion about who exactly said this, as the story has been attributed to many people!

[230] See 5 January 1943.

Tuesday January 26th   S.W.
Mabel Kinnersly came out to tea. She told me to warn James not to have his hair cut at a hairdressers. The doctors are warning men about that because of typhus. The foreigners go to the hairdressers and leave lice and fleas there and that is the danger. First of all one has a rash with typhus, then for three days very high fever, and then a coma and if one can't be wakened from the coma, one dies.

She told me Peggy and Bertie were expecting someone to tea on Sunday and left their front door unlocked, they heard someone in the hall and Bertie went to see, thinking it was their guest, and he found two Frenchmen standing in there. They bolted out of the front door before Bertie could get at them.

One soldier has just come back from leave. He went to Hamburg. He said he never wanted to go on leave again. Hamburg was a heap of ashes. Lots of them don't want to go on leave now. One here was talking about the RAF. He said they only bomb military targets, but of course civilians were killed.

Wednesday January 27th   S.W.
Mabel Kinnersly amused me very much, she said everybody was so irritable now, one dare not speak to them. I said which is best, to be like me and never see or speak to any outside person from weekend to weekend at least for a fortnight and then I go in and meet people at our club (anyway I am delighted to see them and overjoyed if anyone comes out to see me), or to see people every day and get sick of each other? We are all at breaking point with strain. We just feel we cannot bear it one day longer. Mrs Hazell thinks we won't be able to bear the stupendous relief either when it comes. I don't agree with her, we shall all feel so young and strong when the mental torture is removed.

Mabel also told me that she and Peggy were discussing my *lovely complexion*! and wondered what cream I used. Mabel told them she had known me for years and wouldn't mind betting I used no cream at all, only cold water! I said, 'You are quite correct. I have never put cream or powder on my face and I am always washing it in either warm or cold water, not hot water.' Mrs Bernard once had a marvellous face cleansing cream which you rubbed on your face and it made the dirt roll out of the pores in lumps. She tried it on my face and she could not get any dirt out at all, there wasn't any! I am writing this now so that when I make my century, in case I make my century, in case I am not here in material form my family can tell the Press Representatives my recipe for a lovely complexion! I was frightfully bucked to think they think there is something lovely about me!

Thursday January 28th   S.W.
We had the following communication which came by post to James.

> Nebenstelle, Guernsey
> der Feldkommandantur 515
>
> By order of the Commander in Chief of the Channel Islands, General Mueller, you have to report yourself and your family members for a medical examination at the Regal Cinema on Friday January 29th by 5pm.[231]

---

[231] More Islanders were deported in February 1943 as a reprisal for a commando raid on Sark (see 5 October 1942). (Cruickshank, p.219)

It is all Freemasons, ex-officers and criminals. It seems to be all the execution, five Jurats, the Bailiff, doctors, clergymen, lawyers, constables, the sheriff and so on and so on. Hundreds of farmers (the Freemasons). They have no age limit. One old man of 87 is being brought from the Emergency Hospital on a stretcher.

James and I are just stunned.

Of course I did not sleep at all. I lay in bed and shivered and shivered. I thought how thankful I am the children are away.

I rang up Violet before and she offered to come and help and they had plenty of room, they would take anything. Dear little Violet, what a brick she is. I thought I would pack up the silver, china and glass and blankets and plate and linen and all our clothes and send them down to Frank and Violet. And I sent the family pictures and chairs to Maud and that was all we could do. It really was not much good thinking at all.

Friday January 29th

I went in by the two o'clock bus and went to Olive's to leave my basket as I was staying the night. Maud Drake received me and she said at once, 'Don't be worried. We don't believe it is an evacuation at all.'

James arrived about half past four and at five minutes to five we went to the Regal. There was no crowd, just a few people. First of all we had to show our identity cards and they had a good look at us. Then we were given a paper with our name and number on it and we had to join the queue. There were about a dozen men and only one woman. A tall young officer about seven feet high asked me if I would like a chair and brought me one and then he came up again and said I would not be kept waiting long. Very soon he took me into a room, a huge officer was sitting down and there was another one, also another woman came in. The tall young officer questioned me, 'Have you any complaints?' I said 'No.'

'Are you under a doctor?' I said, 'No.'

'Are you quite well?' I said, 'Yes.' The big officer said, 'Gut,' and that was all. The tall officer led me out and I sat down on my chair again. Presently he came to me again and asked me if I wanted anything. I said I was waiting for my husband. 'Does he know you are here, can I fetch him for you?' I thanked him and said my husband knew where I was. Very soon James was ready too.

I went to see Aunt Edith again, and Vera and she were in. Vera pointed out that the order was only a local one, it did not come from Berlin. The last evacuation, they said for 'evacuation to Germany'. We none of us thought of that.

Saturday January 30th   S.W.

I got up early to catch the 9 o'clock bus.

James went to Court and I fetched the bread with Molly. The wind was terrific. At the Crousaz's gate I was completely lifted off my feet and blown against the wall. The Crousazes were going to the Regal today and the Bailiff. They say the first on the exemption list are farmers and growers and then doctors. We hear that everything is postponed in Jersey for a month. It is all so worrying. They are adepts at mental torture. They say they can't understand us, we are so unfriendly and arrogant and then we laugh so much, which of course is quite true, we all do. I am beginning to think it is a mistake to laugh at people who are possessed with fear. I wish now the Freemasons had talked to them when they had the chance and explained that British Masonry was not political like the Foreign Masonry, that it was only a charitable philanthropic society.

February 1943

Wednesday February 3rd   N.W.
12 noon.
James has just rung up to say he has been told he is exempted. I can't describe my feelings. He said he could not say more on the phone, but will tell me tonight when he gets back.

Mr Ernest de Garis rang up to tell me James was exempt. I feel so sick all the time although the relief is enormous. But how hideous it is to think they are taking others. James came home very tired, the only thing he has heard for certain is that there are very few exemptions.

Friday February 5th   S.W.
Everybody is talking about the people who are being evacuated. It is all just *too* awful. So many men and women were crying piteously. Peggy and I saw poor Mrs Tourtel, she was crying bitterly because she is torn between her mother and her husband. All doctors, chemists, dentists are exempt. What have we done in Guernsey to have so much misery thrust upon us?

Nan-Nan rushed at me, she was sobbing, 'You are not going?' I said, 'No, no, we are exempt.' Mary too could hardly speak, she was so upset.

Saturday February 6th   S.W.
General Mueller is the Commander in Chief of the Channel Islands.

James came home about 7pm. He was quite overwhelmed by all the different people who had stopped him and told him they were so glad he was exempted. He said the misery and sorrow in the Town is too awful. Poor, poor helpless little Guernsey.

The present orders are they must be at the Gaumont on Tuesday at 3pm to go down to the White Rock to board the boat.

Friday February 12th   S.W.
A misty rain falling and no wind. I had to wait a long time at Mon Plaisir. At last the bus came and as usual it was full, as usual they continued to pick people up until they were standing on the outer step. We arrived in Town at twenty past ten.

I went to Le Noury at eleven. Several people were notified only this morning to go today. They can't make any arrangements. It is just *awful*. Everybody was so sad today. A man with three children was notified only this morning from Vazon. A woman who was going to have an operation was told she could have the operation quite well in Germany and was made to go.

I had a long wait on the pier for the bus. It was full going out but no one was standing. As we passed the Weighbridge we saw all our poor people standing in a queue in the drizzle waiting to go on the White Rock. It is so heartbreaking, nothing helps Guernsey. Mrs Fuzzey and her helpers worked all the morning cutting up vegetables for the meal they were served on the White Rock.

Saturday February 13th   N.W.
146 people have gone away, among them sixteen children. James went to Court. He brought the news that the men and women have been separated, the men taken to Germany, the women left in France. It is too awful.

Rumour has it they are sending out 500 more notices of evacuation, non-commissioned officers and boys of military age. Where will it end?

Sunday February 28th

Peggy told me that last Sunday she was alone in the house after tea and was sitting in her drawing room. Every door was locked. Bertie was at Mr Bolton's. Suddenly she heard footsteps in the hall and men's voices. She thought Bertie had brought Mr Bolton back with him. She opened the door and she heard the lavatory door shut with a terrific bang and men's voices again. It flashed on her that they were thieves, so she rushed to the front door and called out to the Jehans to come and help her. They came as quickly as they could and opened the lavatory door which was not locked and saw two foreigners running away as hard as they could. They had got in at that small window and thought the house was empty. That is the second time foreigners have got into their house.

I heard a *horrible* story the other day. The OT[232] have a prison camp in a quarry here. A man was at the top of a telephone post repairing a wire and he could look down into this quarry. He heard fearful screams coming from the quarry and he looked down and saw the OT rolling a naked foreigner back and forth on a large table covered with barbed wire. The man felt so sick, he had to come down without finishing his work. He could do nothing.

March 1943

Monday March 1st   N.E.

Another beautiful day. March has certainly come in like a lamb.

Violet came to tea, she was so happy, she had received a lovely photograph of her two boys from a prisoner of war. It was a snapshot taken on a wall by the sea. They look so well grown and well dressed and happy. The youngest, David, has changed a lot, but the eldest, Roy, hasn't changed at all, except that he is much bigger. She also had a lovely message from her brother-in-law about them, so she was happy.

Tuesday March 9th   N.E.

James went to inspect the milk depots today in the dairy van. He went to Cobo. He said I wouldn't know it. They have taken all the slipways away and blocked up the entrances. A railway is running there and they have taken the road away! He heard they are making artisans register with the intention of taking them away to work on the Continent. They will only leave agricultural and horticultural labourers here. Everything makes one cold with fear. I feel physically sick all the time. We certainly understand those sentences, 'cold with fear', 'possessed with fear', 'beside themselves with fear'.

A quotation from Virgil's *Aeneid*, written in 19BC, was published in the *Star*:

> Rumour
>
> Off at once speeds rumour through the great cities. Rumour, a cursed thing than which no other flies so fast; her nimbleness gives her strength and she runs into the air and stalks along the ground and hides her head amid the clouds. She it was whom earth, her mother, stung by the anger of the Gods, brought forth, her last offspring as a sister to Coeus and Enceladus, swift of foot and untiring of wing. A monster, hideous and huge, who was for every feather of her body a watchful eye beneath – most strange to tell – for every eye a tongue, for every tongue a busy mouth and

---

[232] OT stands for Organisation Todt, the German organisation which imported foreign workers to the Island to work on the fortification programme.

ears to attend. By night she flies, hissing in the darkness, midway beneath earth and sky; by day she sits sentinel on top of some tall pile or lofty tower and makes great cities afraid; as apt to cling to what is false and distorted as to proclaim the truth.

'"Rumours are a cursed thing!" Well might Guernsey still repeat in these latter days. This Island suffers from nothing so much as malicious tongues, false statements and sheer inventions. AD43 is no better than 19BC. Bitterly we know it.'

Thursday March 11th   N.E.
A fine day but damp and the weather seems on the change. Molly and I fetched the bread. It cleared up again in the afternoon but drizzled in the evening.

I am suffering from swelled head. My head could not be more swollen. I could not be more proud of anything than I am of the way I can light a fire with very little real kindling wood, no coal and only one piece of paper. Stick by stick and puff by puff I make that burn and cook supper on it in the study. I collect all the little twigs myself and dry them myself. Nobody helps me, they would only steal my twigs if I gave them the chance! I hide all my twigs! And as I have said before I am bursting with pride.

The Guernsey spies are paid a weekly wage and are given £5 for everybody they denounce.

Thursday March 18th   N.E.
A white frost and a lovely day. The birds are singing so beautifully. Molly and I fetched the bread. Mr Crousaz told me the bread was made of Guernsey wheat only. Nothing was mixed with it. He said dolefully, 'It isn't any good, we must have hard Canadian or American wheat to mix with our wheat to make good bread. Wheat must be grown on a Continent to be any good. Wheat grown on an Island is never any good.'

I had a beautiful walk into Town. The birds and the gulls were more beautiful than ever. I only saw Nan-Nan to speak to. She had her little cart and had been to fetch vegetables. She was talking about these foul Guernsey spies. They are paid £2 a week and £5 for everybody they denounce.

I arrived at the Bungalow at a quarter past six and was met by Mrs Fisher, whom I am sure ought not have been out in that bitter wind. Poor Olive has lumbago. Maud and I payed poker patience.

Friday March 19th   N.E.
I arrived at Le Noury about eleven. They were all there. Nelly said she and her husband always leave their house by different doors, so as to make people think one of them is always in the house, the things we have to do!

Nelly told me a lovely story. She went to see an old woman and she was told the old woman was in bed, 'Oh,' says Nelly, 'Is she ill?'

'Oh no, Ma'am,' was the reply, 'she is only tired of bellowing.'

'Good gracious,' said Nelly, 'she must be in terrible pain, what is the matter with her?'

'She is not in any pain at all, she is tired of blowing the bellows for the turpie' was the answer! I think my sequel to that story is even funnier. I was chuckling over it to myself and longing to repeat it to somebody and I met Mrs Frossard and told her the story. Instead of roaring with laughter, Mrs Frossard said very indignantly, 'Did Mrs Welch say that happened to her? That is *my* story, but there were *two* old ladies and they said they had gone to bed for a week because they were tired of bellowing!' I always say, 'Fate has such a tremendous sense of humour,' Mrs Frossard being the *only* person I met to tell the story except Mary.

I went to see Victor. He told me about the *awful* time our first evacuees had in September. They were not expected and nothing was prepared for them at all. They were put in a camp that Poles had been in before. The condition of the camp was indescribable, no sanitation and nothing to clean the camp with. They were there for six weeks, men, women and children. They were starved and the children, our little Guernsey children, picked over the garbage to try and find some food. Then they were taken to Biberac and the Red Cross parcels began to arrive.

I asked Victor about our church and he said he had had a finger in the pie because he had asked different heads of departments about reopening it and they were all against it being reopened, especially St John's Ambulance, and so it is still closed. Victor asked Mr Finey if there was a house he could hold a service in and Finey emphatically said, '*No*.' Finey is having a lovely holiday. Of course he could hold services in a house.

Monday March 22nd

A beautiful day but a cold wind. I had a lovely reply from Iris.[233]

Violet came to tea. She told me the Germans were knocking down the hedge in her brother-in-law's field on the Hogue. Edward Martel was watching them, so a soldier said to him, 'You do not like us knocking down your hedge. This year we are knocking down your hedge because we are ordered to do so. Next year we shall build them up again because the British will order us to do so!'

A girl of seventeen has given birth to German triplets in the Town hospital. One man was talking to a German officer about the German babies here and the officer replied, 'Oh that is nothing, half my men have British blood in them.' Some time ago I noticed such a number of red haired soldiers here and I innocently remarked I thought Germans were always fair or dark, but not sandy or red haired. The answer I received was, 'There were a great many Scottish soldiers in the army of the Occupation of the Rhine!'

The evacuees are being fed so well that they are sending parcels home to their people here. A prisoner of war sent a parcel of very valuable medical supplies to one of the doctors here.

There was a letter in the paper on Saturday from Mr Sherwill:

> Arrived on Tuesday Feb 16th. First three hours of journey beastly; then good. Travelled comfortably, ample food. Left women and children and most elderly men in France (Compiegne). Received Red Cross parcel, tea and 50 cigs. Tuesday. With rations and parcels, amazingly well fed. Camp excellently organised. Weather and scenery magnificent. Hardships of first evacuees a thing of the past. No one need worry about any internee in this camp.

Friday March 26th   S.E.

A dull grey day, it rained in the night. The birds are all singing so beautifully.

People are using sun tan oil to fry with now. They say it is a great success.

---

[233] Iris was Violet's daughter-in-law.

Katty came at supper time to ask for some loads of manure. She made Mrs Mauger so angry last Saturday as she used the expression 'If we win.' Mrs Mauger was like a turkey cock when she told me about it. With great stateliness and dignity she said, 'I said to Miss Connellan that such an idea had never entered my head and if it had, never, never would it have passed my lips.'

Wednesday March 31st
Blowing a gale. Dull but no rain. March is certainly going out like a lion.

When I was washing up the supper things, I looked out of the window and a pig rushed down the avenue! I yelled to James but it was too late and Mr Piggy disappeared. Poor James had such a chase. Finally he found it, happily digging in Mr Tourtel's garden and after a lot of trouble got it back into the sty. In the meantime, the other one hid in the garage. Anyhow, I managed to push him into the sty. I had no idea a pig could run so fast. I have always thought it a very humorous sight watching <u>other</u> people catching a pig, but I don't think it at all humorous when Mr and Mrs James Carey have to do it at the age of 62!

April 1943

Friday April 2nd   S.W.
A beautiful day. I went to Mrs Carey with my dress. She is altering all my things so nicely.

I arrived at Le Noury at about a quarter past eleven. They were all in the highest spirits. I hear the French tyres for bicycles that are being sold here have Vs spaced all round the outer tyre and inside is written in French, 'Stop in France, OK.'

We were talking about the clerks that are working for the Germans.[234] The Germans are making absolute pets of them, telling them not to work too hard, paying them enormous wages and giving them rations of bread, butter and sugar, and they have inoculated them (against what?) and made them sign three papers written only in German so they don't understand what they have signed. I don't like it. I think it is very sinister.

Saturday April 3rd   S.E.
Another beautiful day, but the wind is cold. Molly and I fetched the bread. James went to Town all day.

I am dead tired. I don't know if it is the Spring languor but I feel more tired every fortnight after my long walk. The doctors have promised us that we shall get strong again when we get enough food. I do hope we shall. Today my left leg has been giving under me all day and it is so painful. Also the black spots in front of my eyes are worse. However I think every ache and ill will disappear when we are free.

All of us complain of our memories now. We find the only thing we can do is do a thing when we think of it. For instance, if I am having my dinner and think of fetching water from the well, I must swallow my mouthful and go and fetch the water at once, and so on. If I am making my bed upstairs and remember I must fill the pepper pots, I must immediately leave

---

[234] Some Islanders did work for the Germans. Knowles Smith states that up to three quarters of the civilian population worked for them directly or indirectly. She suggests that one reason was the high unemployment caused by the collapse of the tomato industry at the beginning of the Occupation. The Germans also ordered many Islanders to do compulsory work and refusal would have been punished by imprisonment. Knowles Smith claims that the Germans offered higher wages, but points out they forbade the Island Authorities paying more. (Knowles Smith, *The Changing Face of the Channel Islands Occupation*, pp.59-64)

off making my bed and rush down and fill the pepper pots, and probably when I am fetching the supper from the hot plate I shall remember to finish making my bed and I must rush up and do it. Probably Molly, who never forgets anything, will swallow the supper! And so it goes on.

One thing we are revelling in is the light. Oh! It is a joy not to have to carry a lantern about with us in the evening.

Monday April 5th   S.W.

Another boiling hot day. We had no fire last night and won't have one tonight. No hot water bottles either. What a joy it is not to have to boil kettles last thing.

Violet came to tea. She had had no messages. We looked through Baba's clothes and I can now wear a very smart light grey coat she has. It is an old one, I look extremely nice in it. I long to send her a message telling her I can wear her clothes! Of course I won't, I shall meet her wearing them! It is comical to think, at the age of 62, I can wear Michelle's clothes.

Wednesday April 7th

A bitter bitter wind. Molly and I picked up sticks at the Manoir. I have put on all my winter clothes and we had hot water bottles last night. I had a lovely fire in the afternoon because Peggy came to tea.

Peggy told me a story that has come from German sources. Goering thought London was razed to the ground by his Luftwaffe and wanted to see for himself, so he went in a plane to London. They passed over a town which was flattened and he rubbed his hands and said, 'Gut! Gut! My Luftwaffe has done well indeed.' The pilot got very red and said, 'I am sorry your Excellency, we have half an hour more to go, that town is Wilhelmshaven!'

Peggy and I were talking about the Fish Market and what a complete black market it is. You can only get fish by bribing the fishwomen. One man amused himself by watching the fishwomen in the Fish Market and he saw one woman go out of the market with a big parcel of fish. He followed her. She went down Fountain Street to the Town Church. She met a man who laid four of his fingers beside his cheek and she nodded at him, so the other man followed her back to the fish market and saw him served with four fish, without having his card stamped, and he saw another man given a huge parcel of fish and his card not stamped.

Saturday April 10th   N.W.

A beautiful day but still cold.

Mrs Mauger brought a horrible story. A grower in the Talbot Valley was having his greenhouse robbed, so he decided to stop in it and watch. His friends advised him not to stay alone. He said he was a match for any foreigner. A Frenchman came to the greenhouse and they had a fight and the Frenchman blinded him in one eye with a fork and hit him and stunned him with a sabot.

She also told me another story. That some soldiers have died from eating chocolate poisoned with arsenic and that *we* were going to have that chocolate at Easter and it had been condemned. Also that some thousands of tins of tunny fish, each tin pierced, was sent for us and those have been condemned too.

It is astonishing with what passive fatalism these soldiers accept their fate. One of them said, 'If I stay here I shall be killed. If I go to France I shall be killed. If I go to Russia I shall be killed. What am I to do with my money?' And another pulled out a packet of notes in the Post Office and tried to make the girl accept them because he said they were no use to him, he was going to Russia and he would soon be dead. She said she had never seen him before and she didn't want his money and, of course, did not accept it.

Tuesday April 13th   N.W.
A perfectly beautiful day with such a hot sun. Nearly up to 60 in my bedroom.

Molly and I fetched the bread. Katty came to fetch hers. She said a soldier threw a packet of chocolate to Barbara Gorvel. She caught it and took it home and her mother ate most of it and was dreadfully sick. Luckily nothing worse. Ilsa had a huge packet of it and she ate one or two pieces and was dreadfully sick. Ilsa said it had marzipan in the middle and the marzipan was very bitter. I don't think that chocolate was meant for us, we only have plain chocolate. It is very alarming.

Katty was in despair. She said the Guernsey boys have been ordered to tidy up the Manoir and they are cutting down all her shrubs and digging up all her bulbs and making the place so bare.

I now have to go out of the lower door and walk all the way up the avenue to the hot plate. We keep the other door locked because of thieves and we dare not leave a lower window open anywhere, the simplest thing takes so long to do now. Before I wash up I guiltily hide and lick the vegetable spoons! I was much comforted to find Olive doing exactly the same thing, 'Bless you,' she said, 'We all lick the spoons!' We don't need any vin or rinso now for grease: there isn't any grease. We carefully scrape off any from bowls and put it on a saucer. We eat all the crumbs. We don't lick our plates and that is all we do not do!

Wednesday April 14th   N.W.
Gay Brock came unexpectedly to tea. I was so glad to see her. Poor Mildred Brock has lost her strength and she was one of the strongest women in Guernsey. It is a shame. Of course none of us have any strength. The Emergency Hospital is full of elderly women who have never had to work in their lives and don't know how to prepare food, and also they have not got the fuel and they are literally dying of starvation. It is just awful.

Prices of underwear. Ladies knickers, two sizes, £1 8s. 9d. per pair. Ladies vests, two sizes, £1 3s. 9d. each (sales tax extra). Gents underpants, two sizes, £3 a pair. Gents vests, three sizes. £2 10s. 0d. each. Quality about 3s. 6d., normal times, or 2s. 11d.

Saturday April 17th   S.W.
Another roasting day. This is a heatwave, the thermometer is nearly 70 in my bedroom. Katty has raised a storm in the Gorvel family. I met Selina, who told me the boys came home furious with Barbara for accepting chocolate from the Germans, and the poor child never did. The only person who took it as a joke was Mrs Gorvel herself. Katty came for her bread and I told her. I thought anyway this is a lesson to *me* never to repeat anything Katty tells me.

Sunday April 18th   S.W.
Another lovely day, but not so hot. Katty came to lunch. Our conversation was too comic. Evidently we had *both* made good resolutions to be careful, so we talked about the weather and cauliflowers and birds and food and we were dull!

Wednesday April 28th   S.W.

James went to Town today to get his workman's boots. At last he had received the order. They made an old man from Grande Rocques come to Town three times before he was given his boots. Cyril Gorvel has got his at last, both he and James have been waiting the whole of the winter for them.

May 1943

Friday May 7th

It rained last evening. It is fine again today.

Peggy told me there has been sabotage with the cable they have been laying all over the island. They were going to have a grand ceremony testing it and they did test it and nothing happened. They have discovered that the people who laid the cable have destroyed it in parts with acid and it is completely useless! They will have to do it all over again. We don't know what it is for.

Peggy told me about the Belgian beggar. He went to them, she said he was very clean and well spoken and of course said he was very hungry so Peggy gave him *her* potatoes and went without herself, they were just ready for her dinner. He went on to the Durands, said he had had nothing to eat all day and they gave him their food. He went on to the Tukes and they gave him all sorts of things, tins of food and also a suit of clothes. I have made up my mind I *won't* give any food to foreigners. I would rather adopt a Guernsey person, a genuine case, and I have adopted old Mrs Baleine who lives in the cottage opposite. We are kindred spirits, we both swear like troopers during this Occupation!

6pm: James has just come in with the rumour that our bread is to be reduced next week to 3½lb a week for women and 4½ lb a week for men! The doctors have been fighting it as hard as they can, but Berlin says we must be the same as other occupied countries. I am sure it is a savage reprisal. They have chosen 'starvation spring' for the time to start it instead of starting it in the winter when there were plenty of roots, or waiting until the potato crop was in. James keeps saying the *men* won't be able to work, but doesn't seem to think a bit about the women.

The order is in the paper tonight:

> Manual workers male, over 21, 4lbs 12oz a week.
> Manual workers female, over 21, 4lbs 4oz a week.
> Other adults, over 21, 3lbs 12oz a week.
>
> The bread ration of the rest of the population unchanged.
> Signed: A.J. Laine and Genhmigt Fuer der Feld etc. Gez, Dr Casper O.K.V.R.[235]

Peggy and I mournfully agreed with each other England is a substantial fortress with the doors securely locked and poor little helpless forlorn Guernsey is outside at the mercy of any evil wind that blows.

Sunday May 9th   S.W.

The same foul cold wind and squalls of hail. I don't remember when we had such a cold May. The temperature in my room is 50, the same as it has been all the winter.

---

[235] *La Gazette Officielle, Guernsey Evening Press,* 7 May 1943: 'BREAD RATIONING'.

Mrs Renault is terribly upset about the bread ration. Everybody is of course. People who work for the Germans will get a double ration of everything. Of course it is a very clever way of getting people to work for them. I can't help thinking in my mind if the boys who are sacrificing their lives for us in the East were to stop and say they could not fight because their food supplies and *their water* had not come up, as I am sure has happened sometimes, where would we all be? The people here are saying they can't work and they don't know what they will do, etc., etc. Certainly the Germans have chosen the surest way to create a panic among the labouring classes.

Katty came to lunch. It is so awkward. I shall have to tell her we can't have her any longer. O … h never, never, never will I ask anybody to come regularly again. It is such a mistake. Everybody who has done it says the same.

Tuesday May 18th   N.E.
Another lovely day. Molly and I fetched the bread. Mr Crousaz was in excellent spirits.

I fainted in the night. It was horrid. I fell with such a bang and had to recover myself all in the dark, because planes were passing. That is the second time I have fainted in the night. I feel dreadfully shaky today, I am glad I am not going to Town this week.

We are rationing ourselves with potatoes now. We tried a lb a head for the day yesterday but James found that was not enough, so we are trying two lbs a head per day. The right ration is five lbs a head a week per person! If only the authorities had done their job properly and insisted on everybody who had ground in Town planting it with potatoes, we all would have plenty.

The women in the fish queues on Saturday firmly refused to buy spider crabs if they had to give up coupons for them. It was a successful women's revolt against bureaucracy, the authorities had to give in and a good job too, when they have hundreds and hundreds of spider crabs to get rid of, crabs that would not keep.

Curfew is to be from 11pm to 5am, beginning on Thursday.

Friday May 21st   S.E.
When James went to the greenhouse this morning he found half his crop had been dug up in the night. We had the police out, but they can do nothing because if the soldiers are caught stealing potatoes, the civilians must not touch them.

The market stall holders have a new black market of their own. To get away from the controlled prices, they hide the vegetables and fish under their stalls and only sell them for exorbitant prices. It is called 'under the counter' prices. They are quite open about it. They say 'yes', they have the stuff under the counter and will sell it for their own price.

Thursday May 27th   S.W.
Another thick fog, a heavy, dull day and it is drizzling.

It cleared up in the afternoon and I left here at a quarter to four. I had a lovely walk. I met Gouliot in Mount Row. I haven't seen him this year. 'Are you hungry?' says he.

'Ravenous,' says I. He said he had been all over the Island looking over the fortifications. He said they are wonderful from a military point of view, prepared for every contingency. They have a railway from St Sampsons to Pleinmont, he counted sixteen engines. He said the work they have done is marvellous.

Saturday May 29th   S.W.

A roasting hot day. Molly and I fetched the bread. James' new boots leak like a sieve.

I went to look for the post today and found *four* azure envelopes. I nearly fainted with joy. One from Michelle to James (at last), at long last. Sent on January 29th 1943: 'Arrived home. Decided against marrying. Well and enjoying life. But worrying and missing you. Charlotte Carey good to me. Back work soon. All love. Michelle.'

When her much longed message does come, it is *sure* to be a bombshell! But perhaps she only means she won't marry during the war, which is very sensible and not that she has broken off the engagement. Anyhow, the joy of having a message from her and Jim is indescribable. I feel a different being.

Katty came to fetch her bread. She was talking in a loud voice in the yard and the Rhode Island Red cock was beside her. Every time she spoke loudly, he crowed loudly, he *was* going to be cock in his own yard. It was too funny for words. Katty had to stop talking. She was completely defeated.

June 1943

Saturday June 5th   S.W.

Still very cold and a thick fog. I heard a lark today. The wind has completely dropped.

All the messages people are receiving sent in February are very cheerful and many of them speak of 'reunion shortly'. It is heartening. Last year I personally had no hope of being freed. I made up my mind we would have to go through the winter, although many people disagreed with me and I hoped they were right. This year I certainly dread the idea of going through another winter. I don't think the English would blockade us so effectively as they are doing now if they did not feel confident they could relieve us. We understand they think we have sufficient food for two months.

I don't know about the fruit, but the potatoes have not suffered at all from that cold spell and gale.

There was a very good letter in the *Evening Press* on Friday from a man or a woman who signed themselves 'Sarnian':

> I think there are many things to be thankful for. We have not been subject to dangerous air raids. We have enough to eat. Our children have plenty of full cream milk, we have good milk, though separated, the best of butter, fresh fish in small quantities, shell fish, and soon, tomatoes, potatoes and fresh vegetables every day. The grousers complain because they are denied meat sometimes and many other goods which really they are better without. Since the Occupation the general health of the Island, I believe, is far better, no epidemics and that is a great deal to be thankful for. Even those who used to drink too freely are looking far better now the supply is so limited. Patience instead of grousing is what is required and all will come right.[236]

I like the cheery optimism of that letter, but unfortunately all is not so lovely in the garden as the letter suggests, because there is the grizzly fact that some of our poor poor people are slowly dying of starvation or 'malnutrition', their condition being so miserable all the time and there is literally no food in the Island containing the vitamins that they need. It is so *awful*.

---

[236] *Guernsey Evening Press*, Friday 4 June 1943.

Monday June 7th
Rumour says they have been told in England they cannot have cream on their cakes any more! Violet and I roared with laughter. After nearly four years of war, what a terrible deprivation. Also that they are going to be rationed to have *only* 12lbs of bread per person every week! There is a horrible rumour that our 3¾ lbs of bread per head is going to be further reduced. *Are* they trying to starve us slowly to death?

Tuesday June 15th   S.W.
Michelle's 29th birthday.
A drizzly foggy day. Molly and I fetched the bread. In the afternoon, in a macintosh, I went to Violet for tea. A tremendous shower came when I was at Favonirs, so I lay back in the hedge and did not get wet at all. I met Violet at 'Weekes', the shoemaker, unfortunately he could not repair my rubber boots. After that shower it was quite fine.

At tea, after drinking a cupful, I felt decidedly refreshed, I said, 'Violet what have you given me to drink?' wondering if it was carrot tea or a blend of acorn coffee, carrot tea and bramble tea. I knew it couldn't be, it was too delicious.

'Why, real tea of course,' says Violet, 'to drink Baba's health and wish her a speedy return!' No wonder it was so good. Violet says she has some left still, £6 a lb!

After supper, Cyril came with the news that two heifers were missing from the Glie. James rushed off and I visualised him plunging about in a minefield. A thunderous knock came on the door, I thought it was a German, but it wasn't, it was Freddie Torode to say the heifers were tied in Mr Robilliard's field. I always say there is always some kind man in the Parish who will help one. I told him James was on the Glie, so he told me not to worry, he would bike down and tell him, which he did.

Thursday June 24th   Midsummer Day
A beautiful day. Molly and I fetched the bread. Mr Crousaz had some beautiful greenhouse parsnips to sell, the price is ridiculous, 2½d. a lb. I don't know what the Food Control are about, they make us pay 4d. a lb for cabbage which has no nourishment in it and the parsnip, which is a useful vegetable, they only make us pay 2½d. Poor Mr Crousaz said he had put them in in November and here is June and he has had to wait all this time for his crop and that is all he is allowed to charge. It is short sighted because the growers will only grow the profitable vegetables and will not grow the useful ones.

I started for Town at 4pm and arrived at half past five.

Friday June 25th
Another beautiful day. I went to St Stephen's Church. I arrived at Le Noury at 11.15. They were all there. They told me the meanest story I think I have heard. A greengrocer called Bell was asked by a woman if he had any strawberries to sell. He hadn't and she appeared to be so disappointed that he said he had one lb which he had bought for himself and he had given a huge price for them and she could have them if she would pay the price. She took them. She was a policeman's wife, she went and reported him and he was fined heavily.

Nelly told us an amusing story. A woman told her she and her sister went for a bicycle ride yesterday through the lanes. They took their tea with them and had it in a field of uncut hay. They sat themselves against the hedge and their bicycles. Several German soldiers rode into the field and followed their invariable custom of riding through the hay, as they passed these people, one of the horses trod on one of the bicycles. The woman who owned the bicycle called the officer the most appalling names and swore horribly at him. The officers rode away and after a few minutes one came back alone and rode right round the field, stopped in front of the women, saluted and in the most perfect English, apologised for his horse having trod on the bicycle and hoped it was not damaged.

I asked Mr le Mesurier at the bank if the Germans had taken anything. He said they hadn't taken a thing out of the bank. They have given people certificates for share certificates and bearer bonds. He said they couldn't do anything with the share certificates, it was just to upset people. They also wanted sovereigns.

Tuesday June 29th   S.E.
Another lovely day. Molly and I fetched the bread. Poor little dancing dog, she dances along quite merrily there and back, but after that she just lies down like a dead dog. Cyril says, 'Poor Molly is always tired now.' Her food is just vegetables, first of all potatoes, then carrots and now parsnips and very lucky we are to have vegetables to give her.

July 1943

Friday July 2nd   S.E.
Another fine day with cold wind. Out of the wind the weather is oppressive.

James says they have put iron girders all over two of Mr Heaume's beautiful fields to prevent gliders landing. I don't think there is one thing left undone in the fortifications of this poor little Island. I can't understand how all this inexhaustible supply of heavy material has been allowed to come here, mainly brought on barges: enormous machinery, lorries, buses, girders, railway engines, enormous guns.

In the paper tonight there is a picture of one of the guns in the Cotils and under the picture was written 'Broadcasting at 2.30 yesterday afternoon from Bremen, the news announcer made it known that there was now three years since the German forces arrived and took possession of the Channel Islands, in which were numbered strong fortresses in these outposts of Great Britain. The Channel Islands were now bristling with weapons against any form of attack: Guernsey especially being strengthened in the matter of the power of gun fire, and joining with the continent in showing resistance to any invasion from the Atlantic. Indeed the power of German gunfire in Guernsey had been put to the test on occasion, when British vessels, apparently attempting to effect a landing, were met by the fire of heavy guns. Guernsey's capital, (St Peter Port) still contained 17,000 persons, the remainder having fled. The German troops were guarding to prevent any recapture of the Island.'[237]

Marvellous news and we none of us know anything about it!

Monday July 5th   S.W.
A doubtful day and coldish wind.

Violet came to tea and brought my shoes back. I think our craftsmen are too wonderful. These shoes of mine were so bad when I took them the first time that I apologised for taking them! This time I took them as a forlorn hope. They are beautifully repaired with old motor tyre! I have only one other pair of indoor slippers, so I must wear them. I should like to give them to Guille Allez museum to be put in a glass case to show how clever our people were in this Occupation.

---

[237] *Guernsey Evening Press*, Friday 2 July 1943.

Wednesday July 14th   S.W.
A beautiful day. A real summer's day. The birds are singing so beautifully. I banged salt and shelled peas most of the morning. James went to a dairy meeting. He heard today, to our astonishment, that there were still 18,000 troops in the Island and the highest number we have had is 60,000. I had no idea we had so many. The Germans have insisted on taking blood tests of all the girls working in the dairy, to the fury of the girls.

Violet and I were discussing clothes pegs! I have only seven left after three years. I said gloomily, 'I suppose I will have to tie my clothes on to the line with string.' Violet said more gloomily, 'I haven't any string!' However, I can let her have some. It is extraordinary how we have managed to make substitutes. The Gorvel boys are the most inventive. They have made a beautiful press to press out sugar beet and a wonderful contraption with an old bicycle frame to grind wheat.

Friday July 16th   S.W.
A thick fog, but it cleared up and it is a lovely day. One of the pigs is ill with eryspeus. A great many pigs have it from wrong feeding.

Violet and Mary came out. Mary hasn't been here for over six months. We discussed whether we could bear to go through all this again. That splendid little Mary said in spite of losing all her furniture and her house being destroyed, she is glad she did not go away. I am glad I did not go away, but I wonder very much if I could go through this again, except one would know what to expect. Violet says she couldn't. It is this awful separation from the children, those three wasted years.

Poor Ted Ogier has been fined £15 for selling figs above the controlled price. It is so ridiculous to stop the unfortunate growers selling luxury fruit at a fair price. Always there is the whine that it is too dear for the working man. Why should the working man have luxury fruit, strawberries and raspberries, etc. for nothing practically.

Tuesday July 20th
A dull heavy day. Molly and I fetched the bread.

Even the birds are not getting a balanced diet, why I can't think. For some time I have noticed as I walk along birds, thrushes and sparrows letting me get quite close, in fact we both stand still and look at each other. At first I thought they were young birds and could not fly properly until they flew all right. Then I thought they were showing remarkable intelligence and discernment in recognising my beautiful character, the same traits that are usually attributed to the character of St Francis of Assisi. In the paper last night they write about 'the casualties in the feathered world':

> Birds have become tamer of late, this being especially noticeable to cyclists. Sparrows and thrushes in particular cheekily remain stationary in front of oncoming traffic, only hopping out of the way at the last minute. Apparently many have left it too late and have paid the supreme penalty, as many are often seen to be lying dead on the roadside, having been struck or run over. In recent weeks these casualties have been on the increase; no fewer than five being noted on a stretch from two to three miles last week.

It is a curious thing. I don't see any difference in their food supply. Poor little birds.[238]

---

[238] *Guernsey Evening Press*, Monday 19 July 1943.

Thursday July 22nd   N.E.

A foggy, drizzling morning. Molly and I fetched the bread. It cleared up slowly and I had no rain going into Town. It was grey and dull and depressing. I left at 4pm. By the Bourg chapel I met a company of soldiers singing. They were singing better than usual and marching better than usual. I stopped to let them go by and, as they passed me, one boy gave me such a friendly smile and I smiled back. He had such a jolly face. As I walked on I thought I won't glower at these poor helpless boys any more. They are just as helpless as we are and they are going to their death because they only route march them before they take them away. I walked on feeling quite warmed by that boy's smile and I wondered if he felt likewise from my smile.

Sunday July 25th

A fine day. The cows were nearly milked dry last night. Instead of sending twenty pots of milk (ten gallons) to the Dairy this morning, James could only send four pots (two gallons). About forty pots were stolen last week. James and Mr Gorvel think it is Guernsey people stealing milk for the black market. If it were soldiers they would not milk exactly so many pots. There is a very big black market for milk and butter, one can get all the butter one wants for 35s. a pound.

Thursday July 29th   S.E.

I am very proud of myself the way I can tell the time by the light. I have no watch or clock. They can't mend any watches or clocks now. I don't make any mistakes.

Gay Brock came out to tea. She said Mildred was much better, she was going to stay a month at Blancheland. Dr Gibson said that some of us manage to withstand starvation better than others. Poor Mildred is one of the worst cases, she is starving for lack of sugar and fats. Poor Gay had such a pain in her back form oedema and when she stood up to go she could hardly stand and had great difficulty in picking up her handbag with her fingers. We are all the same, sometimes I can't hold anything.

August 1943

Monday August 2nd   S.W.

It is much colder today and cloudy.

Six O.T.s tried to set the Town on fire on Saturday night! They have just come back from Hamburg and they say the devastation from air raids there is awful and for a reprisal they decided to burn our Town down. They had spread sawdust in one of the shops and poured petrol over it, but fortunately were caught.

There are all kinds of rumours about our food. That we are going to have more cooking fat, more sugar and salt and *more coal*! That we need desperately. The rumour going about is that the British Red Cross has said if they don't give us more food German prisoners will have their rations docked.

Another affliction we have caused by oedema is we can't swallow. Besides being struck comical in our legs, shoulders and arms, we are struck comical in our throats. Quite suddenly we find we can't swallow anything, food, drink or even saliva and there we are grimacing horribly and trying in vain to swallow. The only thing to do is *not* to try, but to wait until the spasm has passed.

Such a lot of their planes have flown over today screaming and whistling.

Wednesday August 4th   S.W.
Another beautiful day. In last night's paper, on the front page, we were told: 'July lost Britain and USA 1½ million tons of shipping, lost in the Mediterranean. The British Mercantile Marines has had to bear the greater proportion of losses. The Yankee's policy is to lose as little as possible in the war effort and to take the lead in merchant tonnage when the struggle is over.'[239]

It is an extraordinary thing that never is a German plane shot down. Never is a military objective damaged. Never is a German soldier killed. Only hospitals, churches, residential parts and shops are hit. Only women and children and the sick and wounded are killed by the RAF.

The Germans have brought over French cattle here, they are on the airport. With the cattle they have brought over the gadfly. This pest has never been seen in Guernsey before. When James was made President of the Farmers Association, a professor wrote to him from England, asking him the reason why the gadfly could not live in the Channel Islands? Of course, James did not know. Perhaps the climate kills it.

Thursday August 5th   S.W.
A dull morning but it did not rain, a strong wind blowing. I left here at ten minutes to four. I was glad the wind was behind me.

There are three reports about the O.T.s who tried to set the town on fire.
1. That the O.T.s are in prison.
2. That they are deported.
3. That they have been shot.

A German officer has said, so rumour says, that if his wife and children are killed in Hamburg he will shoot five Guernsey women! A General visited us last Sunday and said, 'Guernsey was a disgrace to Germany, a blot on her Escutcheon.' That was after he had seen all the devastation they have done here.

Friday August 6th
Not a nice morning and quite cold. I went to St Stephen's Church.

Nelly Welch is very ill. She can't keep anything down. She has been like that for over a week. The doctor can't help her. It is awful the condition we have all got into. I did miss her at Le Noury's.

I met Mabel Kinnersly literally spitting with rage. She had ridden down Market Street which is and has always been one way traffic *up* Market Street and a German policeman popped out from behind Chilcott's van and fined her one mark!

I had lunch at Berthelot Street with Mrs Moorhouse. She was very interesting. She told me that Hitler took a tremendous interest in these Islands and that when the second evacuation was ordered Knackfuss telephoned to Hitler himself asking him to countermand the order and Hitler wouldn't. He has given commands to hold these Islands at all costs because they are the only British possession the Germans hold. I always thought that myself.

Sometimes it comes over one the extraordinary things we do as a matter of course now. I calmly open my little bundle of crusts in the Restaurant and put them in my soup! Others bring their slices of bread.

Peggy and I are both quite sure that when we are free the first thing we will do will be to weep bitterly. We are both feeling the same about that, so when it happens I am going straight

---
[239] The *Star*, Tuesday 3 August 1943.

to Peggy, well supplied with huge handkerchiefs and we are going to sit together in comfort and enjoy a really good cry together. And then we hope we shall recover our self control.

Tuesday August 10th

It has been a miserable day, fog and drizzle all day and cold. James has gone out with Mr de Garis in a car, looking at calves, selecting those to preserve.

There is a rumour they are going to take bicycles from everybody living within two miles of Town. There is also a rumour we are going to have more bread because the flour isn't keeping. Another rumour that tonnes of macaroni has gone bad. We don't know if it is German orders forbidding the food to be released that causes the food to go bad.

The Guernseymen working at Timmers say they cannot understand it but now the Germans working there call them 'Komerade' and can't do enough for them!

This is my seventh diary. I now sleep on six diaries! I don't know where I am going to find the eighth.

Friday August 13th

Another miserable day. What a wretched August we are having. James went to see Maud and to a meeting. Mary and Violet came out to tea.

The reason why we are having more bread is that we have 900 tons of flour perishing and being destroyed by rats. We are going to have a big ration of macaroni for the same reason.

We were discussing the prices of things, and the reason why they are so outrageous is because we buy everything in the black market in France. We have to.

Monday August 16th

Another beautiful day. Brilliant sunshine. Blue sky, no wind. Cyril brought the news that three men and one wife escaped on Saturday in a motor boat. Their parents have been arrested. Mrs Renault heard two wives had escaped and another man whose wife died some time ago and he has a little girl in England and he was just mad to see her again.

Tuesday August 17th   S.E.

Another beautiful day. Mrs Renault brought the news that it has been heard on the German wireless that the boat was picked up forty miles from England. There were two women on board.

On Thursday last in the afternoon, there was a solar halo, a brilliant circle of prismatic colours around the sun. Also a fine display of shooting stars about 11pm.

Wednesday August 18th   S.E.

Another roasting day. There are more rumours about the boat that escaped. One man worked for the O.T.s so he will have a good deal to tell. They went in one of the biggest and best motor boats with plenty of petrol, she went about eight knots per hour, the same speed as the *Courier*, and they left on the best tide of the year, it carried them twenty miles.

It has been a boiling hot, exhausting day.

Thursday August 19th

Another roasting day. Molly and I fetched the bread. Mr Crousaz told me everybody in Town is very angry with those men for going. Their poor people have been put in prison, but have been let out again. Nobody is allowed to bathe anywhere or go on any beach and the fishermen have to deposit £20 before they are allowed out.

I had a very hot walk and arrived at a quarter to six. I saw Maud Drake. She had been to the Vallon this afternoon. She said Victor was not worried about reprisals over that boat escaping. He doesn't think they will do any more. A fisherman whose wife and children are in England can never go fishing again. The bathing places are closed and the order is that no civilian can set foot on any beach. The humorous part about it is that the RAF have dropped leaflets asking the civilians to keep away from the coast and the beaches and now the Germans have obligingly made it an order!

Friday August 20th
A doubtful morning. I went to church. Poor Maud has had to join the no stocking brigade. We do hope stockings will be put in the Red Cross parcels coming to us. I have worn out two of mother's half cotton half silk stockings, one pair of Michelle's school stockings, one pair of my girlhood stockings and one pair of evening stockings. I still have some more to go on with.

I arrived at Le Noury in good time. They were all talking about the boat. Fourteen people are supposed to have gone, including two expert Belgian engineers who know *everything* about the defences of the island.

Saturday August 21st
What an awful night I had with 'occupational' and fever. I was shivering, my teeth were chattering and then I was in a bath of perspiration and so it went on all night. I looked too awful in the morning. I could not fetch the bread. I could not do anything and I was bad again tonight but with no fever.

Thursday August 26th   S.W.
I believe I have found a cure for Occupational. I have given up supper altogether. First of all the soup and potatoes, but I was just as bad when I ate rice pudding and when I drank milk only, so now I make tea my last meal and I really believe that has done the trick. Last night, for the first night since 2½ years, I was well. Certainly no one has been worse than I have been because I have never stopped.

Saturday August 28th   S.W.
A cold, grey day. Molly and I fetched the bread.

There is a good wireless story going about. A man heard they were going to search his house for the wireless. When they came they found him sitting on a box covered with a cloth, holding his head in his hands. They told him they were going to search for his wireless. He was groaning. He said he had a stomachache and diarrhoea and he was much too sick to go with them and they could go where they liked. They searched and did not find it and came back and were most sympathetic with him and he thanked them and they went away.

They are searching public houses for black market goods and they are searching lorries. One German policeman asked a lorry driver to give him a lift up a hill. He sat by the lorry driver and told him he was sick of searching for black market goods.

I feel as if I would love to get drunk today! I do feel so exhausted. Poor Mr Bolton says all of us who are over sixty will never be the same again. It is such a dreary thought. I say having real tea again will make all the difference. I try to imagine myself going to Committee meetings and having stalls at bazaars and I simply could not do anything like that now. I have no strength whatever.

September 1943

Thursday September 2nd   N.W.

A lovely morning. Blue sky. Sunshine and cool. Molly and I fetched the bread. I started for Town at ten minutes to four. I went to see Markie and we had a nice gossip. I arrived at the bungalow about seven.

Everybody is very upset about Nelly Welch. She is so very very ill from acute starvation. She is so weak now, she falls down when she gets out of bed. Nelly was one of those people who maintain they *cannot* eat vegetables and so Nelly has not eaten vegetables, and she is such a strong domineering personality her poor husband cannot make her do anything. Although she has sold all her jewellery and other things and bought all those rabbits and chickens and put them in cold storage, she would *not* eat them, she was so convinced we were going to be worse off than we are and besieged and she was keeping them for when the bad time came. She has lived on strong tea, limited bread and butter and potatoes and has not had enough food for over two years and *now* she cannot keep anything down but is sick all the time, and the doctor says it is one form acute starvation takes. She is so ill she has no wish to live.

Peter Kinnersly told Markie a strange story. One of his tame Germans who has left the Island came back for a few days holiday. He told Peter he loved Guernsey so much he hoped to come often for a holiday here. He said he had been on leave at Hamburg, he had on a new uniform and all new clothes, there was a terrific raid and he was in a shelter and was all right. When the raid was over he got up to go and felt very queer. He stood up and all his clothes dropped off him in brown powder and he was completely naked. The result of a new kind of bomb which disintegrates everything!

Friday September 3rd

The fourth anniversary of the declaration of war and we are now entering into our fourth year of captivity. I went to St Stephen's at 8.30am. There was quite a big congregation.

I was in good time for Le Noury. Everybody was all in very good spirits. I had lunch at Berthelot Street. I met Mrs Swete, she is so frail and shaky now.

I went to see Victor. He is very concerned at the idea of us having to go through another winter because he says there is no doubt about it, we are all in a low state of health. I suggest hope will buoy us all up. After all we have lived on hope all the time. The first summer we were quite sure 'our friends and visitors' would be gone by Christmas. In January 1941 we expected great things in the spring, summer and autumn and so on and so on. Now we can say the three worst years are behind us and we have learnt how to take care of ourselves and save our fuel, etc.

The most extraordinary thing now is the Germans themselves are saying the war will end soon. A fisherman went to Grange Lodge for a permit to fish, he never expected to get it, but to his surprise he was given it at once and the officer said to him, 'Very shortly you will be able to go where you like in your boats without any permits!'

Sunday September 5th

Pouring with rain. Planes flew over last night and, my word, there was a fierce barrage. I went to the window and I thought *all* the shrapnel was coming in! It was like a shower of hail all over the house and in the front and in the meadow. I retreated very quickly.

Poor Mr Dingle has got into trouble. A matron of one of the German hospitals came to him and wanted to buy a pig. He only had his sow which he did not want to sell. However, she persuaded him and offered him pounds and pounds of macaroni and sugar as well as money and he accepted and actually allowed her to take the sow away without paying him at the same time! He was ordered to Grange Lodge and bullied and shouted at and accused of dealing with the black market: 'You think yourself very clever, don't you?' He answered, 'Clever? I think I have been very silly. I have received nothing and I have lost my sow!' They shouted at him more than ever and he doesn't know what is going to happen to him. He had much better be like James, who *shouts* at them when they come asking for anything: 'You milk my cows, you dig up my potatoes, you steal my apples, you destroy my land, I won't sell you a thing, get out!' and Molly barks in chorus!

Poor Harold Fuzzey is in prison for three months and has been fined £60. The Germans went to see his car and a Guernsey swine was with them. He discovered a second car and pointed it out and Harold Fuzzey had never notified it. He said to the swine, 'Fancy giving away a countryman like that.'

'Oh,' the man answered, 'I am working for them, they pay me £3 10s. a week and I would only get £2 10s. if I worked for a Guernseyman.' I hope Harold Fuzzey knows who he is.

Monday September 6th   N.W.
A lovely day but much cooler.

All of us make it a point of honour now not to ask the meaning of our remarks. For instance, I said to Olive, 'I will publish your letter for you', she quite understood I meant 'post your letter', and refrained from comment. If we understand each other we say nothing, it is so comfortable. If people point out my mistakes, I reply blandly that I am making up a cryptic Red Cross message!

Friday September 10th
Another fine day and very close. Mary and Violet came in the afternoon.

My latest theme for discussion is: what shall *I* do the first day we are free and the following days? Everybody but myself has a bicycle and they will all jump on their bikes and go here, there and everywhere but I shall have to walk everywhere. I don't know whether I shall walk in and stay at Olive's and go down to meet the first boat or to be on the spot to meet the first plane? Olive says she won't dare to leave the house in case anyone phones from England, but I think private phones will not be allowed to come through until all the official phoning is done. What a day of days it will be, the first free day. We will be able to talk without looking over our shoulders all the time, phone without fear. I have just read *Peculiar Treasure* by Edna Ferber. I wanted to tell Olive about it, but I dared not mention it on the phone because they would take it and burn it.

Wednesday September 15th   S.W.
Curfew tonight 10pm till 6am.

A lovely day. James went to a States meeting. All the morning the enemy have been skirmishing round the place with their steel helmets covered in leaves. They all had their guns with them and were popping them off at intervals. Molly, with every drop of her Irish blood at boiling point and running freely from the tip of her tail to the tip of her nose and back again, was barking furiously at them and I had great difficulty in getting her to coming in out of harm's way. I was terrified until I had her safely inside after Mrs Renault told me the gruesome story of the Watson's dog. The enemy were skirmishing round the Watson's place and the dog was barking at them and one of them shot and wounded it. They seized the dog and proceeded to bury it alive. Mrs Watson rushed out, a tornado of fury, and made them shoot the poor dog humanely and then bury the dead dog properly.

Skirmishing is only playing hide and seek very badly. The children and I could have taught them how to play it much better. Fortunately all our apples are picked.

Monday September 20th   N.W.
Violet said how difficult it is to patch men's working clothes now. She looks after Frank's and her brother-in-law's. The stuff for patching is rotten now and so are the clothes. Boots are beyond mending now. The situation is desperate. James has worn out his and Boy's coats. What the men are going to do for working clothes I simply don't know. They all look very nice when they go to Town because they have not worn their good suits very much. If we are not freed soon I don't know what is going to happen, Many people now wear no stockings and so we go from bad to worse.

Friday September 24th
A perfect day. Hot, sunny and no wind. Mary and Violet came out to tea. Mary told me a lovely story about the doctors. Five of them drove out to Grande Rocque. Dressed in singlets and shorts they marched past the sentry singing a German song lustily. They had a lovely bathe, formed up again and marched past the sentry again singing more loudly than ever. The sentry took no notice of them and let them go by.

I had such a good rest this afternoon and pleasant dreams and woke up to the sound of those awful boots! The two sounds we hear frequently now are the sound of those boots and the sound of poor bicycles screaming for oil.

All the cows were milked last night. Thirteen pots taken and eight pots taken the other night.

Saturday September 25th   N.E.
A showery day and much colder. James went to Town. Molly and I fetched the bread.

About one o'clock a car drove up. Mrs Mauger called out, 'Here is a car full of Germans.' I am sure my heart stopped beating and I went cold all over. They drove up into the field and then disappeared. Mrs Mauger went out and looked for them but could not find them anywhere. At 2pm the car drove away. Mrs Mauger said they were soldiers and not officers. I think they went to examine the mysterious cable in Mr Gorvel's field. I felt so sick for the rest of the day.

Mrs Mauger and I say good bye to each other in the following manner: 'Well goodbye Mrs James. Another week nearer Victory.'

'Well goodbye Mrs Mauger. Another week nearer Freedom.'

Monday September 27th   N.E.
I am now suffering from occupational dottiness. James was out in the evening, I fetched my water and I said firmly to myself, 'I must *not* lock the door,' and was only brought to my senses later by an indignant James shouting outside my window to be let in. I place things so I fall over them to remind myself either to carry them up or downstairs. I fall over them all right, swear hard and leave them where they are!

October 1943

Saturday October 2nd   S.W.

A dull day. Molly and I fetched the bread. It cleared up in the afternoon and was beautiful. Mrs Mauger was full of lurid stories, chiefly about the maternity ward in the Emergency Hospital. It was no use my shutting the dining room door after she had finished one story, she came in with one spoon which she put into the sideboard drawer and then went back to the kitchen and settled herself comfortably to leisurely wash the kitchen floor and discourse pleasantly at the same time. I settled myself with my knitting and proceeded to listen pleasantly. Slop! Slop! Slop! went the water and then, 'Ave you 'eard, Mrs James, that those ships have not been scuttled at all? It is the Germans that 'ave put that story about, what for I don't know.' I hadn't heard, I agreed there was no sense in it. Swish went the cloth and then, 'Ave you 'eard Mrs James about the black baby at the Emergency Hospital? Yes, a black baby 'as been born there, the father is a German and the girl's father will give £1,000 to anybody that will adopt the baby!' I exclaimed in horror, that I didn't believe it. 'Yes, it was true,' and she knew who the girl was. A pause and Mrs Mauger washed a little more of the kitchen, then she began again, 'Of course you 'ave 'eard that the doctors have told one woman she is going to have triplets and another woman that she is going to 'ave four babies and they 'ave examined another woman with the x-rays and they 'ave seen six 'ands and only two 'eads!' I was reduced to convulsive silence. 'And this infant diarrhoea is awful. I am going to tell Ernie tonight to stop Gladys going there, she always wears a woollen dress and wool catches the germs quicker than anything and there she will bring it back to my grandchild Betty. I must tell Ernie, you see the mothers won't nurse their babies, that's what it is, they should be made to I say.' Mrs Mauger told me the constable had come to her on Thursday and told her the Germans were going to fire round her way on Friday and she stayed in her house at her own risk. She stayed.

Sunday October 3rd   S.W.

A beautiful day. I never woke until nine o'clock, I don't know why. Mrs Renault told me she had had to play hide and seek with the sentries to get here on Friday. There was a sentry in front of her house and she dodged behind him and hid behind a hedge till his back was turned and there was a sentry in front of the Gorvels and in the front here. She crept behind the hedges through the fields and at last arrived here.

There has been such a row about stockings that the Controlling Committee are going to issue some more. There was a notice in the paper that stockings would be issued one day last week, 10s. a pair, rayon.[240] Enormous queues queued up the High Street at all the shops before they opened. When the shops opened, the shop people told the queues the stockings were all sold to orders already. Creasey and Falla were exceptions, they had taken no orders. Some people were able to have three pairs. One shop had the audacity to put up a notice, 'Stockings sold out yesterday,' the day before they were released. Of course it is really all black market. The people who take the shop people things, milk and eggs, etc., have the preference. However, there is going to be more control in the future.

---

[240] *La Gazette Officielle*, the *Star*, 28 September 1943, 'Ladies stockings: Limited quantity will be on sale from Wednesday 29th September 1943'.

Monday October 4th   S.W.

We have put our clocks back an hour today, so we are the same time as England. A link!

A fine day. James went to Chief Pleas. Violet came to tea and brought a pot of the most lovely sloe and apple jelly. It is delicious. Violet told me all about the babies in the maternity hospital. Her sister-in-law has just had a baby there and it nearly died of the diarrhoea. Fortunately, a friend of the mother's offered to nurse the baby and saved its life. She is nursing her own child and can nurse this baby as well which is very wonderful because only three mothers can nurse their babies out of the 21 mothers there. The doctors say it is due to the lack of food. It is a shame to say they *won't* nurse their babies, they can't. The babies of the nursing mothers are all right. The illness is caused by the babies being given milk from a cow that has just calved.

Violet says there is a black baby there, an Algerian father, and rumour has it the girl's father has offered £2,000 to anybody who will take the baby. Also, the woman who is going to have triplets has had a little girl and twins during the Occupation, so if the triplets live she will have had six children in less than four years. So Violet has corroborated Mrs Mauger's statements more or less!

James came in with a tale that the mother of the black baby says 'An Alsatian chased her across the fields and the baby is the result!'

Mrs Renault went for a walk to the Gouffre yesterday and went into the *Gouffre Hotel*. She said it is too awful how they have wrecked it. Everything smashed, looking glasses, tables, chairs, sideboards, floors, everything. There is nothing left, everything ruined.

Tuesday October 5th   S.W.

A lovely day and so warm. Molly and I fetched the bread. Only robins seem to be singing now.

The cows were milked again last night, they were outside.

I was feeling very depressed and dear old Peggy arrived. Peggy very often arrives just when I am feeling most depressed. She had the most amazing thrilling news to tell me. May Sherwill had had a message from her husband[241] and this was in the letter: 'Will be with you for sure in March or April. We know more than you do. Send me a Union Jack immediately and ask no questions. If we can't communicate for a while, don't worry!' Now what *does* he mean? Peggy told me Mrs Nicolle had written to her son, a prisoner of war, and sent him her spectacles prescription because she has broken her spectacles and asked him to send the prescription to her occulist in London, to send him the new spectacles and for him to send them to her. Her son has written and said he would do that, *but* it would take at least four months and that *she* would be able to send to London herself before that. Those two letters came from an internee and a prisoner of war. It is heartening because, as Peggy truly says, they would not be so cruel knowing our circumstances so well, as to send letters like that if they did not know what they were talking about. But how desolate and completely cut off we are. Peggy and I wondered if our people will ever realise what it means and what mental torture we go through.

James found two soldiers wandering about our field at the back just before curfew, they asked him a lot of questions in German which he could not understand and he said to them, 'Ha, sucks to you, you are looking for my cows and you don't know where they are,' and they did not understand him.

---

[241] May Sherwill's husband was Ambrose Sherwill, who had been deported to Germany in February 1943.

Friday October 8th   S.W.

It is fine today but still no sun and heavy clouds and atmosphere. Robins were singing but no other birds.

James is going to Town to get a pair of boots. The procedure is as follows. James wrote his name down on a form some months ago. He received a notice telling him he can't get a pair of boots before October 9th. He has to go to the Ladies' College to try on the boots and if he is lucky the boots will be sent down to Beghins and he will be able to go and buy them today and bring them home, or he will be told to go another day to Beghins to get them. That procedure applies to everything, shirts, vests, etc. Nobody can get anything for their men. Of course coupons have to be given up. A grower has written a letter protesting about the way this procedure wastes a day's work and suggesting that the clerks at the College should serve the workspeople either before 8.30am or after 5.30pm, out of working hours in other words. My word, I think those clerks would pass out if they were expected to work before 10am and after 5pm, although the men who keep them from starvation work from 6am to 11pm!! It is extraordinary but true.

── Book VIII ──

Saturday October 9th   S.W.

I am now sleeping on seven diaries and I never thought I should have to start the eighth! This is positively the last book I have to use up as a diary. Will I have to manufacture a ninth I wonder?

It is a beautiful day. So hot. I settled down in the dining room with my knitting in the afternoon and Mrs Mauger proceeded to wash the kitchen floor and to give me all the gossip. Slop, slop, slop went the water and swish, swish went the water and then I knew she was settling back on her heel and then she began. 'Mrs James, 'ave you 'eard about the party for the man arrested for making "V" signs?' I said, 'Yes, what had she heard?'

'When they were questioned at Grange Lodge, the Germans there said, "You enjoyed yourselves singing 'God Save the King' and 'Rule Britannia'," and they turned back the men's lapels and said, "Oh, you are not wearing your V brooches, I suppose they are on your working clothes! Go home and you will know your punishment in a fortnight's time!" A Gestapo said to Stroobant, "I 'eard you singing hang up your dirty washing on the Siegfried Line and all your other songs, and I will tell you why, because I was there!"' One of the girls was a nurse at the Town Hospital, and she said she was on night duty so they let her go, all the others were sent to prison for the night and they have all been told they will know their punishment in a fortnight's time.

Nearly everybody is full of hope we shall be freed by Christmas.

Monday October 11th   S.W.

A gloomy, sombre morning. It is not cold but so dark. I am reminded all the morning of Kipling's poem, 'Boots! Boots! Boots!'[242] I don't know how many soldiers have passed today.

'Will ye no come back again. Will ye no come back again? Better loved ye canna be. Will ye no come back again.'

---

[242] Kipling, *Boots*: 'We're foot-slog-slog-slog-sloggin' over Africa-
    Foot-foot-foot-foot-sloggin' over Africa-
    (Boots-boots-boots-boots-movin' up and down again!)
    There's no discharge in the war!'

Tuesday October 12th   S.W.
Another dull gloomy warm sombre day. Molly and I fetched the bread.

Mrs Renault is very excited because she has heard we *are* going to have Red Cross parcels. We shall have to pay 4s. 6d. each for them. I do hope she is right. The men are getting extra rations of tobacco, they are spending 8s. 6d. on their tobacco this week. Mrs Renault is very indignant because the women get no extras. Poor women, they certainly are having the grimmest time in this Occupation. I think all of them are giving up their food to somebody else. The men expect and take as a matter of course all the meat and three quarters of the food if they can, but if there are children the mothers are giving up to the children and if there are old people the women are giving up to them and so it goes on. And yet not one woman has committed suicide. I don't know how many men have. The men say they can't work if they don't have the food. The poor women have to do their work just the same, although conditions have made all women's work four times as hard. Preparing of meals and cooking, standing in queues for hours for a little bit of fish, and so on.

The children are having an allowance of chocolate for three months, but it is very poor stuff.

One of the saddest things in this Occupation, there is no allowance made of our *own* authorities for the old people. The children have extra sugar and milk and jam and bread, etc. The Miss Gardners have started a fund to help the 'Aged Poor'. The fund can help them to pay for their rations and buy wood and fuel for them, but nothing else.

Wednesday October 13th   S.W.
Another dull sombre cloudy day without a grain of sun. Mrs Renault brought the dire news that poor Mr Dingle has to go to prison for three weeks and has had his motor licence taken away. They have kept him waiting since July in their cat and mouse tigerish way. Poor man, he has lost his pig and received nothing but punishment in payment. What a lesson to teach us to have nothing whatsoever to do with them.[243] Still, we all say hopefully and cheerfully, it won't be long now. There is a good deal of unrest among their men here, they are dreading being sent to Russia and longing for the English to come and take this Island.

Thursday October 14th   S.W.
I left here at ten minutes to three and had a lovely walk. Thrushes and blackbirds were singing. There was no wind and it was so warm and sunny. I wore Baba's grey coat and felt very smart. I walked through the lanes to the Falkeners. They were so pleased to see me. I haven't seen Ethel for over a year. Old Lyon came in to tea and apologised for his ragged coat and darned trousers, every man's working clothes are the same. He showed me his darns with justifiable pride, for he had darned them himself and they were beautiful darns. He told me he had patched his stockings because they were past darning and had made stocking legs into sleeves for his cardigan. He must be very neat handed. Ethel does everything herself and has no maid at all. Lyon says he has never had such good cooking and doesn't want to make a change and have maids again.

I left about six and at the Caches I met Peggy and Bertie returning home. I asked Peggy if she was going to Le Noury's tomorrow. I said, 'You know, Peggy, don't think me an awful coward but I am afraid to go.' Peggy said, 'Oh, I am so glad you said that, I am afraid to go too and I hadn't the moral courage to say so. It is too dangerous, you never know where the Gestapo

---

[243] See entry for 5 September 1943.

are and those people are so terribly indiscreet.' I quite agreed. We parted and as I walked along I felt awfully disappointed because I did enjoy those mornings so much, but so many more people come now and talk in such loud voices, as Peggy says, it has become quite out of hand. I am very sad about it. I arrived about seven.

May Sherwill has *not* sent a Union Jack.[244] Victor advised her not to. A message has come from someone else asking for yards and yards of red, white and blue ribbon from Biberach.

Friday October 15th   S.W.

A beautiful day and so hot. I went to St Stephen's. I did not go to Le Noury. Maud said there was a tremendous crowd there. I am very sorry not to go there.

I met Aunt Edith who looked very tired. We are all showing the strain now. I went to Miss Ross. She told me it is pitiful to see children's feet now, a baby of 22 months was brought to her with septic nails. She says it is the *awful* shoes provided for the poor children now, hard wooden soles and misshapen uppers. She advises the mothers to let them go barefoot as the lesser evil. It is *awful*.

Thursday October 21st   S.W.

A fine day and very warm. I have a horrible cold and feel a worm and no man. Molly and I fetched the bread.

Having sent us the dregs of Europe, the Germans are now bringing over here the dregs of Russia. Men who the Germans say have entered their army to fight Bolshevism and who are real Bolshevists themselves. They are Georgians and the lowest type of humanity. The Germans say they have brought them over here because they consider our civilisation is so high, they hope they will learn to be more civilised. Some they have had to send away, they were so out of control. They warn women about them. I think it is awful bringing them over here.

Katty told me a story about Mrs de Garis of the Villette nursing home. Mrs de Garis was in her nurse's uniform one day and she came out of her dining room into the hall and found four or five German officers in the hall, they smiled and bowed and leered at her and she asked them what they wanted. 'Isn't this the brothel?' they said! She was absolutely staggered and furious of course and said 'Certainly not, this is a nursing home.' Quite unabashed, they bowed and apologised and went out. What a nation. How can we *ever* have real contact with people like that.

Saturday October 23rd   S.W.

A fine morning and very fresh. Molly and I fetched the bread. Katty came over this evening in an awful state. She is beside herself, she expects to be turned out. She says she has heard from a German source that they are going to bring those awful Russian Georgians into this district. It is so frightening for all of us. She isn't certain. Once more, a war on our nerves. She also has heard that at a big conference in Germany, Hitler wondered if they had better go on with the war with Russia because the carnage is so *awful*, the roads are completely blocked. Can that be true? Is it the end? She had also heard two of these Georgians had been shot, she heard they are sex mad.

Tuesday October 26th   S.W.

Another beautiful day, so hot and sunny. Molly and I fetched the bread. Mr Crousaz had nothing to say at all. I went in to see Katty. She was in one of her most aggravating moods, now

---

[244] See 5 October 1943.

doesn't think she will be turned out, mustn't speak of it. I cheerfully told her that Cyril had told James the next morning after she had told me that she might be turned out. She was furious and said, 'That was how mischievous rumours were started, that Cyril had probably heard the Russians marching and singing Georgian chants and so he concluded that Miss Connellan would be turned out of the Manoir!' My bewildered brain could not see any connections. Before I could say anything, Amy le Tissier came in and Katty gave her an enormous bundle, or rather pulled it out of a cupboard and they both staggered downstairs with it and Amy trundled it away in a wheelbarrow. I could not help thinking of crime stories and the disposal of the dead body! Katty would not answer a single question, but sat there with a faraway look in her eyes and so I took my departure.

Wednesday October 27th   N.S.W.
Boots! Boots! Boots! All day long.

Another lovely day and so warm. James has gone to a States meeting. I went to fetch the remainder of my onions from the de la Rue's. On my way I went into the Hazells. Mrs Hazell went round to see Katty on Monday. Katty said to her, 'Have you heard about me?' so Mrs Hazell told her, 'Yes, Mrs Carey had told her.' Katty was furious. Of course I realise what I have done. I have spoilt Katty's dramatic story which is a great pity. Katty wants to tell everybody herself! Mrs Hazell said Katty can't expect to keep it secret when she *does* tell everybody she meets and Amy le Tissier going back and forth with a wheelbarrow taking away great bundles.

Thursday October 28th
Boots! Boots! Boots! In the middle of the night now.

About a hundred Russian soldiers have just passed (8.30am) singing lustily. By Jove, their singing is very different to the Germans' dreary singing. James was told hundreds of them were being drilled by German officers on the Fort Field and they did not pay the slightest attention to anything the officers said. They were laughing and talking. Their own officers are 'White Russians'.

I had a lovely walk in. I took my tea with me and left here soon after two. The temperature was just right for me.

Maud and Olive told me about Marguerite Carey. They have to get their water from a spring near their house. Marguerite was filling a small jug at the spring and there were some soldiers standing by and they made kissing noises and she turned round and threw the water at them. The next day the German police arrived and wanted to see her. She was out so they interviewed Mabel and asked her all kinds of questions: how much money she had, did she own the house, etc., etc. They came the next day and Marguerite was in bed, she had to come down in her pyjamas and they questioned her very closely and said she had to go with them to Grange Lodge. She said she could not do that because she was acting in a play and had to go to a rehearsal. They said very well, she could go to the rehearsal, but after the play was over they would come for her again because she had insulted the great German Army!

Saturday October 30th   N.W.
Another beautiful day. What a wonderful week of weather we have had. Molly and I fetched the bread.

Mrs Mauger told me we were going to have a service in our church on Christmas Day. I wonder if that is true.

James came home with a different version of Marguerite's story. He heard that the soldiers had put ammunition and equipment in the Careys' garden and that Mrs Carey had thrown it all out into the road and said she would not have their stuff in her garden, and that she was in prison!

We have very little salt now. We are given a small quantity of salty dust on which we have to pour a pint of water, let it stand for twenty four hours and then we must pour the water off and use that pint of salt water for a fortnight for two people. We have our own brine factory at the Piette and the townspeople can get brine whenever they want to at a penny per gallon. They also make eight cwt of beautiful salt out of the sea water for the States dairy to use in butter making. Every day when the tide is high enough, salt water is pumped into the tank at the Piette Mill to keep the salt making process going. In these tanks the water is boiled by steam pipes that pass through it and convert it into brine. This brine in turn is pumped into large vats and also boiled by steam, but it is first tested with a hydrometer. By this test it may be found to be too strong for making good salt crystals as it would not dry properly, so instead of wasting it, other chemicals are added which after much boiling and purifying, turn it into magnesia carbonate, baking powder and other commodities.

They also have been making fish oil in the mill, extracting the oil from the livers of ray or dog fish. They have managed to produce an oil of the best possible quality and supplied it to chemists for medicinal purposes.

I do think it is wonderful how our people have managed to carry on and achieve so much. The way they mend bicycle tyres out of the queerest material is wonderful. It is extraordinary how calmly we go on doing without things or making do with substitutes. For instance, paint pots as saucepans. The way people have continued to make clothes out of anything is miraculous. Violet wore the prettiest jumper the other day, she had made it out of a black swimming suit and all the different coloured little bits of wool she could find in the house. My dish I wash up in has a big hole in it mended with a piece of rag and one of our big kettles also is mended with a piece of rag. Whatever we break can't be replaced and so we go on learning to do without more and more and really not minding very much.

November 1943

Tuesday November 2nd   S.W.
A finer day and very warm. Molly and I fetched the bread. Mr Crousaz had heard on Saturday that Marguerite Carey was going to be sent to Jersey to be questioned about her heinous offence of insulting the great German Army.

I am quite surprised how expert I am in the dark now. I used not to be able to do anything in the dark and now I can do all sorts of things. It is truly diabolical to cut off our light on the dark days, but it shows how things are going.

Thursday November 4th   S.W.
The wind went to the south-east yesterday but it is back again in the south-west and it is another 'pet day', perfectly beautiful and such a hot sun. Molly and I fetched the bread and we went to the Manoir but it was all shut up.

The Electricity Rationing Order has come into force. We are only allowed four units per household a week and forbidden to use electric irons, toasters, water heaters, refrigerators. They don't mention 'kettle', so I shall use mine if I want to.[245]

Guernsey grown tobacco costs 4s. 3d. an oz and the States have taxed it 8d. an oz and my word there is a lot of chat about it in the papers. It is retailed at £2 8s. 4d. per pound and States tax is 10s. 8d. on the lb. The States expect to get £5000 from this years crop.

Poor old Katty came in very upset and tired. She is supposed to leave the Manoir tomorrow and she has not found a house yet. She was offered one in de Beauvoir Terrace. There were no grates in it, no door handles or locks, no electricity, no gas stove, no water laid on!! She would not have it. I don't know what she is going to do.

Friday November 5th S.E.
A typical 5th of November. Still, grey, dark and dull. Mrs Hazell came in the morning to say she had been to the Manoir and Katty was not there and every place and room were locked up. Young Smith was there and said he did not think the vans were coming today. Fuzzey had been out some days ago and packed all the china. Georgians are supposed to be going there and the soldiers who were there told Katty they thought it was madness to put Georgians where all the ammunition is! It is extraordinary. Katty arrived quite late to say she had found a house, 57 Hauteville. It is the house the billeting officer wanted her to look at in the first place and she wouldn't. She is very pleased with it. It is at the top of Hauteville, the Rougiers' old house, has a beautiful view and also beautiful shutters for every window. She is sleeping at the Manoir tonight and then moving tomorrow. She has Georgian soldiers in the house. I am sorry for her because she has tried so hard to be able to hand that mouldy old house back to John Hayes with the furniture complete. I do think it is better for her health to be out of it.

Katty told me she saw Marguerite Carey, who said the case had been sent to Jersey and she did not know what was going to happen to her.

I am suffering from lack of vitamin C now. My suffering takes a most unpleasant form. I suddenly have no saliva in my mouth or throat and nearly choke. I am told I ought to eat a lot of tomatoes and fruit, but as I am suffering from 'occupational' from lack of vitamin B, and can't *touch* tomatoes or fruit, what on earth is a poor lass to do? James says, touch wood, that he has never been so free from indigestion as he is now, certainly I bought packets of Macleans stomach mixture and he has not used them. I am sure he ate too much meat. Mother always said he did, he ate such a lot. Now he has 2s. worth of meat once a fortnight. In peacetime, I was thankful when the butcher's book was under £1 a week!

Saturday November 6th S.E.
It is pouring with rain. Molly and I fetched the bread. I saw Katty for a minute. She was very hurt and upset because 'her soldiers' as she always called them had stolen from her right and left. I asked, what did she expect? She said she never thought they would behave like that! Mrs Hazell says Katty is getting a kick out of all this and it certainly is true.

Mrs Mauger met Mr Finey and asked him about the service for Christmas Day. He said it all rested with the Dean, but he added he did not know if he would be able to come out and hold a service in the Forest because there were so few clergymen in the Island he might be

---

[245] *La Gazette Officielle*, the *Star*, Saturday 30 October 1943: 'ELECTRICITY RATIONING'.

wanted elsewhere. A curious reason for a Rector to give to account for his inability to hold a Christmas Day service in his own Parish!

Sunday November 7th
Raining this morning and much colder.

We say the three worst years are behind us and it is true but we in this Island have to go on helplessly watching the wanton destruction of our Island, see them take away furniture and destroy anything they want to destroy. It is heartbreaking when one thinks what a happy prosperous little Island this was. Such a contented community, no unemployment, everybody having enough of the necessities and of leisure and enjoyment. It was the rarest thing to have a child crying. Everybody was so generous to appeals and to charity, the Freemasons alone sent away a staggering amount of money a year. Aunt Edith told me she was always writing and telling her relations how generous Guernsey people were to English charities as well as their own.

Will ye no come back again? Will ye no come back again? Better loved ye canna be. Will ye no come back again?

Thursday November 11th   N.E.
Molly and I fetched the bread. I met two Russians, one wished me good morning with a cheerful grin.

I left here at a quarter to two. I called in at Peggy's on the way. I have been so often and they have not been there and I have been so disappointed. This time I saw them through the window. I felt so pleased that I knocked hilariously with the knocker and rang the bell as well. Bertie opened the door to me with a face of fury and Peggy was hiding in the back. Of course, they thought I was a German! It was stupid of me because we are all so much on edge, However, they forgave me and Peggy was delighted to see me. She said she felt it was her duty to work in the garden, but now I had come she would light the fire and we could have a lovely gossip. Peggy soon had a glorious fire going and we did have a good gossip. She told me about an officer in the bar of one of the hotels who drew out of his pocket a huge wodge of notes and he said, 'I have just received my pay, this is it and I will bet all of this that there will be peace before Christmas. Another officer was in another bar and he was talking in English to a brother officer, who said to him, 'Isn't your leave due?' He answered, 'Yes, my leave is due, but I am not going on leave.' The other man said, 'Why not?' He replied, 'Because there is going to be the bloodiest revolution the world has ever known in Germany at any moment now and I shall be much safer over here.' We know now where all the rumours of 'peace before Christmas' come from.

Peggy had had a message from old Sue, a rather disturbing one. Sue was enquiring anxiously after her clothes and hoped the moth had not got into them because she expected to be home soon and wanted her clothes very badly! 'Gosh,' says Peggy, 'Sue's clothes are all over the place. I have two skirts which I have completely altered and a pair of shoes.' I said, 'Yes, I think Mabel Kinnersly gave away a dozen pairs of stockings. Most of Sue's clothes have been disposed of. Sue's sealskin coat is quite all right and free of moth. It is rather silly of Sue expecting to find her clothes, if we had been free after six months she could, but after four years she ought to realise how desperate her friends are for clothes.

Saturday November 13th   S.W.

Olive rang me up this morning in joyous excitement. She had the news last night that Hugh John's[246] wife had twin daughters in September. I am thrilled. Darling old Hugh. They wanted a girl, so now they have two. Olive did give me time to tell her that the next would be triplets, following the tradition of my great-grandfather who had twenty-eight children. There is a story in the family that when he was told the first little girl was born, he made the doctor have a glass of wine to drink the health of little Miss de Sausmarez. When he was told the second little girl was born, he again made the doctor drink the health of the second little Miss de Sausmarez, but when he was told of the arrival of the third little girl, he rushed upstairs saying 'He must stop this, he really must stop it!'

Tuesday November 16th   North wind. Ugh! Ugh! Ugh!

Bitterly cold and very dry. Molly and I fetched the bread. Olive told me on Thursday about the arrival of that last boat that escaped.[247] Maud and Olive have read the letters an Internee has sent telling the safe arrival of the boat in England and the surprising reception they had. They were not welcomed at all, they are treated as aliens and have to report to the police every day and have been told that if we have suffered any reprisals through their selfishness they will be punished. They were told they ought to have stayed and stuck it like we are doing!

Friday November 19th   N.E.

Bitterly cold and hail showers. Fine later and the sun came out. The man came to read the meter for the electric light today. We have burnt 30 units and we were allowed 85 units. This next quarter we will be allowed 65 units, so we ought to be all right. There is a water curfew now. Strange to have it in the winter. The water is turned off from 2pm to 5.30pm and 8pm to 6am.

Monday November 22nd   N.E.

I don't think anybody who isn't a farmer can possibly realise what poor farmers have to put up with. James engaged two extra men to help pull the beetroots. They came punctually at 8am. They hadn't been on the field any time when the Germans came and said they wanted the field for gunnery practice and turned them all out. As a matter of fact it poured with rain this afternoon, but they could have pulled the beetroots all the morning.

December 1943

Saturday December 4th   E.

An awful day. High wind and deluges of rain all day. Molly and I fetched the bread.

A high German official who came over here some time ago said, 'The devastation the Germans have done in this Island will always be a blot on German Military History.'

I am feeling full of mortification. My pride is in the dust. For over 62 years I have boasted that I have never had *a chilblain*, that I have never known what it was like to suffer from chilblains and privately and silently hoped that I *should* never have the ugly things on my hands! Today I have three chilblains on my hands, they are as ugly as possible as well as being

---
[246] Hugh John is Olive's son.
[247] See entries for 16 and 18 August 1943.

painful. Last year I remember I had a queer thing on my little toe and went to Miss Ross and showed it to her. She laughed and said, 'That is a chilblain'! That one went away very quickly. My hands are miserable.

Monday December 6th

A perfectly beautiful day, no wind, calm, sunny and mild. It rained in the early morning but cleared up afterwards and was fine all day. Violet came in the afternoon. I have bartered a dozen boxes of matches for 10lbs of flour.

Violet told us they know a farmer who has a number of turkeys and he takes all of them up into his bedroom at night. Mrs Hazell has trained her fowls to come in at night and sleep in boxes provided for them in the hall. The Tostevins had a goose and a gander stolen from them and they have one goose left and she asks it to come into the house and it knows exactly where to go. People dare to say animals are not intelligent.

Friday December 10th   N.E.

A fine morning. I went to St Stephen's. Maud and I walked down to Town together. Boots has asked for people to bring them as many books as they can and they pay a very good price. Maud was taking down several books in very good condition.

I had to leave my little cart to have spokes put into the back wheels. After 3½ years of hard work the little cart needs repair. I left it in a shop in Victoria Road and proceeded to go down to Town with a rucksack on my back, a loaded basket in one hand and a loaded chip in the other.

I met Aunt Edith in Boots who told me it was ten to twelve. We had a chat and I changed my book and sat down at the table there for a little rest and looked at my notebook and found I had an appointment with Miss Ross at 12. I had completely forgotten it, so I managed to arrive in time.

Miss Ross told me about her cow. She bought this cow before the Occupation and since has allowed a young farmer to have it and give her a pint of milk every day. She pays for all the roots and the hay and the grass, the cow sleeps in the farmer's stable. The inspector went to inspect this man's farm. He arrives at 7am, watches all the milkings and follows the cowman about the whole day. He saw this farmer carrying a pint measure of milk into the house and asked him what he was doing with it and was told it was Miss Ross' milk and she had it every day! The something something fool! Miss Ross went to see Ernest de Garis about it and stated her case and he told her she would not be summoned but she must sell her cow because it was illegal for people to keep less than three cows now. If she liked she could buy two others. She has sold her cow and she says bitterly she has not even had a milk pudding from her. Nowadays, the eleventh commandment holds good all the time: 'You must not be found out.' Others get away with pots of milk.

I met Gay Brock who said she had been looking for me to have lunch together at Berthelot Street and she had brought some potatoes for me. The perfect angel. We went there and had a very good lunch. Poor Gay is dreadfully worried about Mildred. Dr Gibson says Mildred is absolutely starving, this vegetable diet does her no good whatever. The only hope for her is to go to the Emergency Hospital for rest and food and Mildred won't go. They will not give the people the food in their own homes because they don't trust the people to give the food to the invalids. Mildred's feet and ankles are swollen now and she is very ill indeed. It is awful for Gay because she can do nothing.

When I got home I went to look for a message and there was the lovely azure envelope and I had two lovely messages, one was from Iris.

It was the tenth message from Iris sent on August 25th 1943: 'Don't worry about Jim. He is all right. Spent an evening with Michelle this week. She is upset you haven't been receiving her messages. Love Iris.'

Oh what a joy to hear Boy is safe, so I presume he is still in England. I wonder, he might be anywhere else where there is no fighting, Palestine or Egypt. Poor darling old Baba, I am sorry she is upset, if I don't get her messages I can't answer them. I do hope she will go on sending regularly because every message we receive is worth its weight in gold to us. I don't think anybody can understand what messages mean to us, only we ourselves who have gone through this Occupation can understand the awful desolation it is to be cut off from all our people. What a joy to come home and find those messages.

Saturday December 11th   N.E.

A dull cold glowering day. Molly and I fetched the bread in a hailstorm and returned in a snowstorm.

Mrs Mauger told me that on the bus going into Town on Tuesday when she went in there was a single soldier on every seat. They have been ordered to sit like that she thinks so civilians will be forced to sit beside them!

I was told on Friday of a farmer who has a pig weighing over 200lbs. He was given a permit to kill it and he was so afraid it would be stolen, he took it into his house every night for the week before it was killed and it is killed and he has his half pig. The things we have to do now.

I realise I write this diary in a fearful hurry. I am always afraid of them taking it away and I am only comfortable when it is safely hidden away. I wonder how soon we will be able to lose our sense of fear that we have <u>all</u> the time, except perhaps when we are in bed. Will we always look over our shoulder right and left before we say anything. Will we always be listening, listening?

Tuesday December 14th   N.E.

Another fine dry day but oh so cold. Molly and I fetched the bread. I spent the day doing up my Christmas parcels. Such a pathetic few. When I think of all the cards and all the presents I used to send! And yet I took such a long time doing them up. We are all suffering from having *NO TIME*! just like de la Field's book, *The Provincial Lady in Wartime*! Everything takes so much time now. Mrs Mauger told me she lights her fire at 2pm to get her husband's supper ready for 6pm and she is bellowing all the time. The coal is such poor stuff. Certainly fires now fill all our minds. The poor men spend all their time chopping wood and most of them have never chopped wood in their lives. It is a hard life now for everybody.

Thursday December 23rd   S.W.

A fine morning. Maud and I went to St Stephen's Church at 8.30am.

Olive dare not use her electric toaster or kettle now. She says anyhow she burns a unit of light a day and her allowance is only four units a week.

I went to Town as early as I could. Carrying my heavy basket and with my rucksack on my back I struggled down to the shop in Victoria Road where my push cart was being mended.

He said it would be ready by 2pm, so on I went with my baskets to Town. In the beginning I had good luck for the shops I went to were empty, and luckily I went to the bank first and the Guille Allez because they both closed at 12 and I did not know they were going to close.

Before lunch I went to Le Riches wine department. The manager there is a man who is all over the Germans, calls them 'Sir', is so glad to see them, hopes they will come again soon, etc., etc. I asked for a bottle of Benedictine, of course I could not have one, so I asked for any liqueur, I was told that because I had not bought one bottle of liqueur during the Occupation I would not be able to have any liqueur during the Occupation! There were a good many people in the shop and I relieved my over-charged feelings. I said, 'I have not bought one bottle of liqueur during the Occupation because every time I have asked for one I have been refused. I only come into Town once a fortnight and therefore have been unlucky.' He said, 'You can't have asked for a bottle very often Madame.' I said, 'You are quite right, I have not asked very often because I so dislike being refused but I want to get the position clear in my mind. I hoped to have a bottle of liqueur to offer my friends on Christmas Day, but I now understand from you that in spite of being an old customer, I shall never have a bottle of liqueur until peace is declared, because I have been too unlucky to have one during the Occupation?' He looked very confused and said, 'If you will call again this afternoon I will ring up the Association and see what I can do.' It was left at that. I wondered what association he was talking about. Also, before he attended to me, a woman and he had a whispered conversation and she paid 18 marks and was handed a basket already packed with bottles wrapped up in napkins. I have a very shrewd suspicion that if I were to hand him bottles of milk packed in napkins I would be given all the wine and liqueur I wanted! I would see him in a very hot place first!

I went to lunch at Berthelot Street and had lunch with the woman who keeps the barter shop in Collenette boot stores. She told me a remarkable story. She said she knew a man who earned his living by barter. He seldom was at home at night but was all over the country helping people in different ways and being paid by barter. I did not enquire very closely why he should be helping people at night! He was helping some people to kill a pig and the pig got away and they could not find it. He slept in a haystack that night. Early next morning, before curfew, he saw the pig trotting back, followed by a German soldier. The pig trotted into its own sty and the soldier knocked up the farm people and told them the pig had come back. Amazing story. She said, 'Lots go on that we know nothing about.' I said, 'Small blame to them, we are all pirates.'

Another woman picked up my glove for me which I had let fall and gave me my heavy basket and picked up her own and said, 'I say we are all Guernsey donkeys and have to carry everything.' I *do hope* all this friendliness will be the same after this Occupation, it is so nice.

After lunch I went back to Le Riche and was allowed to have a bottle of Anisette. I fetched my rations and at half past two I went to pick up my baskets at Mr Ware's and left Town at a quarter to three. I went partly up Mill Street and discovered I had left my cover at the butcher's. Carrying my heavy baskets and rucksack I wearily plodded back to get it and then I realised that it did not matter how tired I was, how exhausted I was, I *had* to walk those five miles home, beginning with that long hill up from Town, that if I stayed the night at Olive's, she literally hadn't a scrap of food or drink to give me.

I struggled up to where my push cart was and it was ready. How thankful I was. I dumped all my baskets on it and toiled up Victoria Road to the Bungalow and arrived there at ten to four and sank, completely exhausted, on my bed. I rested till 4.30 and started off again, was half way up Ville au Roi and found I had left my bag with all my money in it and back I had to go. By then I felt I understood and could apply the two words 'grim and dogged' to myself! When I hung it over my shoulder, I thought, '*Now* I hope I can start for home.'

And so ended my day in Town. My last day in Town this year. How strange it is. It is not just a day in Town. It is an adventure.

Saturday December 25th   S.W.
Fourth Christmas Day in captivity
A beautiful day and not cold at all. Mrs Mauger came in good time and James went to the Catel Church. I made some mulled wine. I have drunk this wine mixed with raspberry cordial and it has no effect on me whatever. I boiled it with raspberry cordial, sugar and cloves. I filled two thermi with it and Mrs Mauger and I drank the rest, nearly two tea cup fulls each. I drank mine straight off without anything to eat with it. My word, my wish came true, I was drunk for quite a long time.

James arrived about one and we had a lovely dinner, a beautiful joint of meat from one of our own animals. A perfect pudding made with flour, apples, carrots, home made raisins, sugar and sugar beet syrup. It was delicious.

Mrs Mauger gave me a Guernsey biscuit and we had a little cheese, so we ate that with the mulled wine and drank the children's health and the King's and absent friends'. I was *not* drunk again.

After dinner, as usual on Christmas Day, we did not want to eat much. Katty gave us some real tea for a present and we had that for tea. I gave James a pound of sweets and myself a pound of sweets. I had to take the sugar and butter to Collins and they made the sweets. We had a peaceful, quiet day and I finished my mulled wine in bed!

Friday December 31st   N.W.
A lovely day for the last day of 1943. It is very cold. I think my own special fairies were about today. It has been a day of days. Molly and I fetched the bread and while we were walking along I wished the RAF would fly over and, as soon as I reached the depot, I heard the hum of those beautiful engines and knew the darlings were up there and I saw the dainty trails they make. When we were walking home they came again. The Germans put up balloons over the airport. After I arrived home they seemed to come over all the morning and all the afternoon. Waves and waves of them.

I was told that the command here are full of jitters because they are sure the second front will begin in two or three days time. How those planes exhilarated us. I trod on air coming home and I found Mrs Renault bursting into song! If they only knew what it means to us to have them flying over. Of course we long for them to drop papers, to see an English newspaper would be *too* marvellous. The men were in the field watching them and I was at the back door and I thought I would be an awful fool if I ventured out across the yard because I could see the shrapnel flying and I am glad I didn't go, we picked up such a nasty bit just outside the hot plate door! I longed to join the men. All day they were flying over. It has been a wonderful day.

I have been walking on air all day and the perpetual pain in my side, through Occupational, has completely gone. They certainly have wished us a happy new year.

And so 1943 is ended and we are still in captivity, unable to do a single thing for those dear boys who are doing so much for us.

The Diaries of Violet Carey, 1944

January 1944

Wednesday January 5th   N.E.

A bitterly cold day. A heavy frost. Fine and dry. James went to a States meeting about the children's allowances. They passed everything so people with large families will have 4s. a week for each child instead of only four children in each family having the allowance of 4s. per head.[248] After the States meeting the Bailiff and Jurats met in the Jurats' room and wished the Bailiff and each other a happy new year and the Bailiff told them the German authorities wanted to cut down the butter and fat ration in October to 2½ oz per head and Sir Abraham Laine refused to sign and the whole Essential Commodities Committee threatened to resign. Now it is 3oz of fat per head per week. The German uuthorities say we must have 36 tons of butter in reserve and we have nine tons at present.

Tuesday January 11th   S.W.

Another foggy day. Molly and I fetched the bread. We had fog and drizzle all day. Dr Cambridge came about 7pm and I told him of my trouble. He did not tell me anything I did not know, but he hopes to give me medicine to help me. He told me I was starving for fats and to make James give me cream! He was very flattering because he thought I was much younger than I am. He said mine was a most interesting case, that he hadn't had one like it and was very pleased to meet me. I said I had met him before. 'Oh,' he said, 'I mean medically.' I said, 'I am not at all pleased to meet you medically. I like meeting you socially very much.' He laughed very much and he said he would be very upset about the reduction in the fat ration but he was sure things here will be different very soon and so he wasn't worrying. And so once more we are all buoyant with hope. But I don't want a second front.

Thursday January 13th   S.W.

Much more wind and a finer drier day. Molly and I fetched the bread. There are no ships coming just now, that is why we are having such small rations. Only 1½ oz of sugar per head this week and a ¼lb of pork per head this week. We don't care, it only means things are moving! All the time we are living on hope. Well, it helps us to get through the winter and not mind if it is cold.

---

[248] The *Star*, Thursday 6 January 1944: 'More families will now get children's allowances. States approval of needed reforms.' The States had abolished the veto on parents who are not compulsory contributors under Contributary Pensions Law 1935, therefore rendering many more children eligible for family allowance. The means test limit was also extended. Violet would probably have heard of this through James which is why she writes the day before it was published in the paper.

Mrs Hazell still has her fowls sleeping in the hall. They come in at a certain time and she arranged them in their boxes and they stay as she puts them. The cock crows twelve times in the early morning, finishes crowing about 7am and gets Mrs Hazell up to let them out.

The tanks officers and men are breaking down hedges in all directions and poor Fred Cattaroche has had one of his biggest fields taken from him for drilling Russian soldiers. Where they haven't taken the hedges down they have cut huge gaps in them. Whether it is for tank practice or because they expect tank battles over here we don't know.

Sunday January 16th

A calm, dull day. The birds are singing so beautifully. I am suffering from occupational dottiness. I carried James' hot water bottle as far as the chair in the dining room from the study and left it there and never put it in his bed at all. I put it down to pick up my book to carry upstairs, went happily to bed with my book and never remembered the bottle *at all* until James talked pathetically about his cold bed! Maud and Olive are quite worried about themselves behaving like that, but as we *all* are like that I don't think it matters. We will all recover when we are free. I love Dr Cambridge's prescription for me when I can get it, to eat basins and basins of cream! Yum yum! And as much butter as I can. I certainly shall.

Wednesday January 19th   S.W.

Gay came to see me today. I was so glad to see her. She says poor Mildred is very ill and Dick Gibson gives them no hope that she will be better until she gets the proper food. He doesn't mean that she will die, but she has not got the use of her legs and won't have it until she is fed properly. Gay was so disappointed because she managed to get two eggs for Mildred for her breakfast. They had pork and a steam pudding for lunch and a bean for supper and Mildred was violently sick. That just shows how careful we shall all have to be when we do have food.

Sunday January 23rd   N.W.

Although the weather is so bad just now, I realised walking home on Friday that the worst part of the winter is past, because of the light. I need not worry about the light and being later now. As I was walking down the Grange I met a woman talking furiously to herself and I realised with horror that was what I looked like now, muttering to myself. Olive joined me and I told her my horrible discovery and she said, 'Never mind, I have just seen myself in the looking glass in the Grange and I looked slightly senile with an imbecile smile on my face. *I* am feeling depressed about myself too!'

February 1944

Thursday February 10th   N.E.

A very cold bright sunny day. Molly and I fetched the bread.

I feel exactly as if I was catching a train. I am going by the bus this afternoon instead of taking my little cart. All yesterday afternoon I was packing my baggage! At least that is what it seemed like. I took two books, and a bottle and a tin of anti phlogisine for Miss Ross in one bag. In a chip basket I took bottles and bottles of milk, I dare not be seen with a can! In my rucksack I took my food and a bottle of coffee and other oddments. We had lunch sharp at twelve and so I was able to wash up and dress in comfort, not being hurried. I left the house at 1.15, successfully dodging Molly. I had to wait there a long time, but it was no use going later for the bus because it may come up very early from Leree. Two tank men and a soldier were waiting there too. At last the bus came and I got in and sat down on the front seat. The bus was full of tank men and soldiers and sailors. I wondered if I had got into one of their buses by mistake, there wasn't another civilian in it. However, it was too late. There I was driving to Town with them all and dreaming to myself about the dear boys in the sky and thinking what a wonderful target the bus would be with all those faces looking out of the window, when I suddenly woke up with a start to the inconvenient fact that Violet Mary's lovely face was looking out of the window too! However nothing happened and I arrived safely.

Nelly Welch came at three and we had such a lovely afternoon of M-J[249] and gossip. Nelly brought me such a delicious piece of her birthday cake. It was sweet of her, she said she knew I could not get to her so she brought the cake to me. Olive gave us delicious little maize cakes flavoured with almond and sugar, they were good and real TEA, fresh tea too. Oh, the aroma of it, 'smell' isn't good enough, *and* the taste of it *and* the stimulating effect of it. Oh! Oh! Oh!

They told me an intriguing story. A man riding on the wrong side of the road rode into another man at the Vale. Neither were hurt and they had a chat and the stranger told the Vale man all the news and when they parted the Vale man said, 'Don't you know we ride on the right hand side of the road now?' The other man replied, 'All right mate, I won't forget.'

They told me the story about Leonie Trouteaud and her interview at Grange Lodge. Leonie Trouteaud is the head of the Red Cross Bureau. A woman brought in a revolting message saying we had plenty of food, that the Germans were so kind to us and all sorts of things like that. Leonie refused to send the message and the woman reported her to Grange Lodge and Leonie was sent for and questioned by the German authorities. The man who interviewed her asked her why she would not send the message. She answered, 'When I was made head of the Red Cross Bureau you made me take an oath I would not send any message of propaganda. Reverse our positions. Would *you* send a message like that? He read the message again and looked at Leonie and he said, "No, if I was in your position I would not send that message. You were quite right not to send it."' *Good* for Leonie.

The next story is about a young assistant at Dubras. A German officer came in and tried to push himself into a chair before another man, a civilian. The assistant said, 'Excuse me, sir, this gentleman was here first.' The officer glared and said, 'If it was Anthony Eden would you tell him to wait?'

'Oh no sir, it would not be necessary,' answered the assistant.

'Why?' snapped the officer. 'Because Mr Eden is a gentleman,' was the answer. Dubras himself was in such a flat spin because he is so terrified of the Germans. They haven't heard of any reprisals being taken on that boy.

Tuesday February 15th   S.E.
Another perfect day, cold but such a warm sun. Molly and I fetched the bread. I heard a lark singing so cheerily. Mr Tuke and Bougourd were at the depot talking about a spy who haunts the buses and after they described him, I realised he was on the bus with me last Friday. A pleasant youth who never sits down but stands up talking to the driver the whole time and gets in and out for everybody, helping them with their baskets, etc. He also sits in bars at public houses, listening for people to tell the news.

Bougourd told us a long story illustrating the German police methods. He said he was rung up on the phone and told, 'German police calling'. They asked him if he had a cow, he thought they were talking at cross purposes and asked them if they meant a motor car and they said,

---

249 M-J refers to the game of mah-jong.

no, a cow. He told them he had no animals and then they asked him about another Bougourd, had he a farm? He said, 'I don't know if you would call it a farm, he has a bungalow and a field and a cow.' He said all the time they were becoming politer and politer and they said, 'You have answered quite correctly, we have examined his place and have been all over your place, did you know that?' Bougourd said he did not know it. That is the way they find out everything and then question you to try and trip you up.

Sunday February 20th   N.E.

I was sitting upstairs quite late in the afternoon yesterday and I heard Mrs Mauger shouting, 'A Red Cross message, a Red Cross message.' I rushed down and it was a reply from Michelle, only the second reply I have received from her. It was in answer to a message I sent her on November 27th *1942*, answered by her on August 8th *1943* and received by me on Saturday February 19th *1944*. Needless to say it was a bombshell!

'Home again. Engagement off. Just finished grand course. Was chosen to represent firm by the Chief Officer special interview. All my love to you both.'

I *am* so sad she has broken off her engagement. I wonder what the rest of the message means? Is the Chief the King? Was she chosen to take part in a special review of the nurses? Or has she been decorated? Anyhow, it is a thrilling message and she has received an honour. I am proud of her.

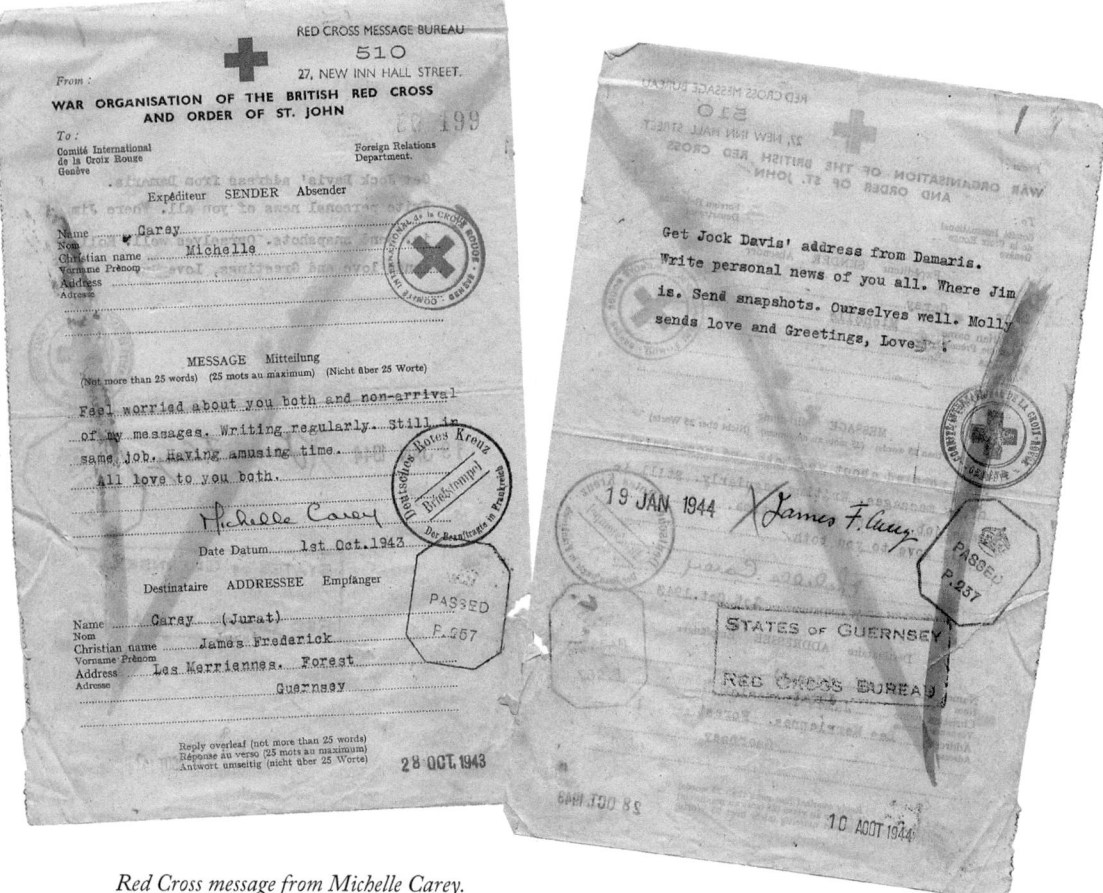

Red Cross message from Michelle Carey.

Tuesday February 22nd   N.E.
There is a notice in the paper ordering us to give precedence to all German soldiers in the shops and that severe punishment will be imposed on any who disregard this order. We are puzzled by that order. Why haven't they given that order before? Now when everything is so strictly rationed, it doesn't matter whether they have precedence or not except in the matter of time. Or are they wanting to punish us and any excuse will do? A solider can say a civilian has been served before him and his word will be taken whether it is true or not.[250]

Thursday February 24th   E.
New moon, 2.59am.
A very fine day, bright sunshine and blue sky and a *foul* east wind. Molly and I fetched the bread. Old Crousaz was not there. Molly gave me *such* a fright. On the way I saw her eating something. I had a stab of fear that it might be rat poison. Immediately after she began to carry on, writhe and wriggle, stretching herself, tying herself up in knots, every semblance of agonies of pain. After we came home she ate her dinner quite happily and was quite all right. I am certain she knew she had been making a fool of me.

After I got back I spent my time getting ready to go to Peggy's. I wonder, when we are free again, if I shall ever cease to feel that going out to tea is an adventure and a great event? Now I have to take my bread and butter and milk, etc. and identity card. I left home at twenty to three and after battling against the foul east wind I arrived at ten past three. I thought, I am thankful I am not walking into Town today.

Mabel Kinnersly was there and shortly after Elsie de Coudenhore arrived quite unexpectedly. We were so glad to see her. How she has altered. I wonder how many stone she has lost? Her spirits are as gay as ever. Olive and Maud came too, Maud having walked. Peggy had a lovely fire and the room was so pretty with flowers. Olive had brought a resume of Churchill's speech which she left on the table in view of everybody, when suddenly the dining room door burst open, a German soldier. He saluted and asked if his washing was ready? We all answered in chorus that we knew nothing about his washing and waved him to go to the Jehans. He apologised, saluted and disappeared. It is extraordinary, but we are all so used to that sort of thing that we hardly noticed it. Peggy had such a lovely tea, lovely little cakes and real tea. O … h! We took it in turns to play M-J. It was fun and before we all left, Peggy gave us a cocktail made of white wine, Cointreau and a dash of bitters and we all felt so happy. I didn't leave until nearly seven.

Poor Elsie told us their dire straits of having one candle per week for five people and no other light. I simply can't imagine how they manage at all.

Will we be free this year? Will we have to endure another winter? On my messages I put, 'Facing fourth winter cheerfully.' I would like to put 'Enduring fourth winter bravely.' Our people would never let that be sent. I feel if we have to endure another winter that the war will go on for years and years. And I think I had better write this diary as briefly as possible because I have no more books to use up, so what I shall do when this one is finished I *don't* know!

---

[250] *La Gazette Officielle*, the *Star*, Tuesday 22 February 1944: 'NOTICE: I am directed by the Feldkommandantur to warn all concerned that he has ordered that members of the German Forces must be given prior attention in all shops and other establishments frequented by them and that severe punishment will be imposed on any who disregard this order.' John Leale

Saturday February 26th   N.E.

Just as cold, no wind at all and leaden skies. James went to Town.

Mrs Mauger told me three sacks of swedes were brought into the market and the soldiers bought them all. This new order is going to be very grim about the soldiers precedence. If six soldiers come into the barbers, they must be served before civilians. That young assistant from Dubras was had up to Grange Lodge and was fined.[251] Machon who sold sheets with the news typed on it has had a terrible time with the German police. They have knocked him about dreadfully. He sent a number of the sheets of news to Sark.

Tuesday February 29th   N.E.

A fine day but cold as ever and sleeting. Molly and I fetched the bread. It was a lovely afternoon, bright sun and blue sky. I went to fetch Peggy. I arrived about three and Bertie and I had a good gossip waiting for Peggy to dress. He told me the story about the woman at St Saviours. The German police went to a cottage at St Saviours and said to the woman, 'You have a wireless?' She said, 'I have no wireless.' They showed her an anonymous letter and said, 'We must search your house.' She said, 'Certainly, you may search anywhere you like but I have to go out to fetch my rations and to take my child out, so if you will excuse me, I must go now.' She picked up the child and put her in the pram and went out with the child *and* the wireless in the pram!

Bertie also told me about a man called Le Cheminant who has been fined heavily for killing and keeping a pig. He gave milk and butter to a woman for the whole of the Occupation without charging her one penny. He became hard up, so he said to her, 'I must charge you for the milk now because I am short of money.' She said, 'I won't pay you a penny.' He said, 'Then I can't let you have any more milk.' She said, 'All right, it will be the worse for you,' and she reported him to the police for killing his pig.

Peggy took me down the water lane and believe it or not, although I have lived all my life in Guernsey and thirty years in the Forest, I have *never* been down that lane before! It is so pretty, of course very wet. When we reached the Petit Bot road we could not feel the wind at all. It was so hot in the sun. We climbed up the hill to the de Coudenhore's and looked down on poor little Petit Bot.

Elsie was as amusing as ever. They have letters from relations in France. France is in a very divided state. When the British win, France will go communist. The communists now are assassinating Germans and French. A great many French want a united Europe. They say Petain, aged 84, is a very very great man. No one knows what a burden he is carrying and how well he is managing. We over here know nothing.

Elsie said the officers in the fine weather regard their garden as a public garden. They are always walking about in it and trying to be friendly. One of them tried harder than the others and she talked to him and asked him when he thought the war would end? He replied, 'As long as Germany hold the Ukraine the war would go on indefinitely, but if they lost the Ukraine, that would shorten the war tremendously.' Well, they have lost the Ukraine!

Elsie told us a lovely story about Goebbels. He is supposed to have died and is waiting for St Peter to open the gate of Heaven to him. He looks down and sees the most lovely place, gardens and bands playing and restaurants with lovely food and drink. When St Peter opened the gate, he pointed down below and asked if he could go there? 'Oh yes, certainly,' says St Peter, 'but you must understand you can never leave again.' He didn't mind. He wanted to go

---

[251] Violet gives more details of the young assistant in her entry for 10 February 1944.

there, so down he went and knocked at the door and the devil opened it and he asked if he could come in. 'Oh certainly,' said the devil and stood aside to let him pass and he went in and the gates clanged behind him. The devil led him past the beautiful place, put him in a cell and locked him in and for several days fed him on bread and water. Goebbels asked why he was put in the cell and not allowed to go to the lovely place. 'Oh,' said the devil, 'this is where you are going to stay. The beautiful place in only propaganda!'

March 1944

Saturday March 4th   N.
Due north and colder than ever and sleeting. Molly and I fetched the bread.
At 5 o'clock I went to Bertie and Peggy's silver wedding party. I wore my new brown hat and brown dress and red cardigan and well polished brown shoes and felt very saucy indeed. Everybody looked so well dressed. It was fun and I got so drunk! I drank everything I was offered. I don't know how many glasses of cocktail, a lovely glass of champagne and a chocolate liqueur. We were all so mellow and so cheerful. Everybody was interested in Michelle's message and so sweet about her. Bless her. They are all sure it is a decoration and that she jolly well deserves it.[252] James and I stayed a little while after everybody had gone and then I got up very gingerly from my seat and came home, being very unsteady on my feet all the way, but quite clear in my head and able to talk distinctly! It was a lovely party, we will all remember it.

Friday March 17th
Another beautiful day, much warmer. We all went to church. There were seven people there. I went down to Town early. Everybody is very tense. I met Goulu and asked for his opinion; he said he was terrified they would try to land in northern France, he thought it would be disaster if they did and then he said hurriedly in a low voice, 'I don't talk about anything now, I would not even trust my own sister at this critical time,' and went away, leaving me aghast with astonishment because he has been so much the opposite before.

Maud and I were talking about Miss Andoire. I met her for the first time in the Occupation. She was looking very well, she told me she was 76 and was looking after the Income Tax offices and Barclays Bank and it was very hard work. It is wonderful how some of the people are carrying on and words fail me in admiration of our gallant little Town. How the shops are *still* keeping open.

Everybody is expecting the invasion to begin next week, they think if it doesn't, it won't begin until after Easter because of the moon.

I had a *lovely* walk home. I see they are making A.R. shelters in the thick hedges in the lanes.

Saturday March 18th   N.W.
No wind at all and a lovely day. Molly and I fetched the bread. Molly has not eaten her dinner for two days but looks very well. Old Mrs Baleine told me the Russians were feeding Molly. I hope they will continue to feed her.

Wednesday March 22nd   N.W.
Another lovely day. I left at a quarter to eleven. I arrived at Sausmarez Manor at twelve and went in to see Cousin Annie who was delighted to see me. I think Sausmarez Manor is the

---

[252] This refers to a message Violet had received and recorded on 20 February 1944.

saddest house in Guernsey. All my entire life I can only remember pathetic sick old people there and no young people at all and it is still the same. Certainly the curse has been fulfilled up to now. For 300 years the de Sausmarez held the Manor, then the Androz had it. A Miss de S. married the Androz owner and they had no children. They had been married several years and her brother offered to buy Sausmarez Manor and the Androz sold it to him. He had a son. Some years later Mrs Androz produced a son after ten years of marriage. Mr Androz wanted to buy the Manor back and Mr de S. wouldn't sell it to him and he cursed Mr de S. and said after his son there would be no direct heir and there hasn't been. A very unfair curse I think. Mother was *thankful* when my grandfather sold the Manor to his brother and so my father never inherited. It is a melancholy house.

Thursday March 23rd   Still N.W.
Another lovely day. Molly and I fetched the bread. I went by bus this afternoon, it was full of soldiers. I arrived at a quarter past two. We all went to Candie Library to see Grace Durand's play. Grace has written it and it was very clever. It was just all of us and how we talk about food all the time and she brought in the black market and anonymous letters very cleverly. We say we hope they will be able to broadcast it afterwards, because it is so typical of our life.

After the play I took my tea to Maud who as usual was very cheerful and very sweet. After seeing Maud I went to see Aunt Edith. While I was there we heard distinct machine gun firing and planes.

Two men have been sent back from Laufen camp. They are quite well and don't know why they have been sent back. One has been told to work at the gas works and the other somewhere else. They tell us that if they had no Red Cross parcels our people in Germany would starve to death, there is no doubt of that. When they first went there before their parcels came they all had a terrible time.

Friday March 24th
New moon, 12 noon.
Another lovely day. We all went to church. Maud and I went to Town early. Walking down we wondered what our people will think of the broken gates, railings and walls and the absence of paint everywhere and the poor shops and all the German notices. I want them all to be left for them to see.

Wednesday March 29th
A beautiful day. I caught the 1.30 bus. I wore Michelle's coat. I don't know what it was, if it was my beautiful figure adorning Baba's coat or Baba's coat adorning my beautiful figure? Or Baba's personality adorning us both? I forsee quite an interesting controversy coming between Michelle and I. I look so very elegant, smart and young in her clothes. She will want them *all* back again, of course I shall reasonably point out that they must *all* be very old fashioned and it is only my lovely figure that makes these clothes look so smart. I wonder how she will answer that? But the fact is that nine German soldiers and three women stood back to let me get into the bus before them! And thereby I got a front seat in a terribly overcrowded bus.

Violet and Mrs Martel got in. They were going to the Vale and were going to walk back. More and more soldiers got in all along the Forest Road. I was thankful to get out at the Old Post. I walked through Sausmarez Manor and past Nellie's and through the de Putron estate. I could not remember where Cissie Brock lived so I went to a house on the top of the hill and knocked at the back door. A delightful voice said 'Hullo' and this was such a pretty parrot. A lady came out followed by two lovely cats and a black Scotch terrier. She told me the parrot was twenty years old. Cissie lives at the bottom of the hill. Olive and Maud arrived soon after and we played M-J. Cissie gave us such a gorgeous tea including real tea! O … h. After drinking several cups Maud said she felt quite drunk. So did I! Cissie made the tea pretty strong.

Maud walked with me as far as the Old Post and I walked from there in twenty minutes! That was the tea. James met me at the Epinel and said a German officer had just been demanding a room and James had sent him on to Cambrai. Oh dear, it does make me feel ill when they come like that.

April 1944

Sunday April 2nd   E.
A thick mist and the wind has gone to the east. Here we are in April and no invasion. I wonder if Churchill is playing this game. Forcing the Germans to keep divisions all along the French front and enabling the Russians to press their advantage. Keeping the Germans guessing all the time, sending ammunition and supplies to Russia all the time and in the end have *no* invasion.

Tuesday April 25th   N.W.
Another beautiful day. Molly and I fetched the bread. Planes flew over twice in the day. They fired their big guns out to sea last night. After tea Peggy came to see me.

Peggy told me the personnel on the airport are packing up and the Commandant has ordered packing cases to be made very well and very strong to take to Germany. He wants to say they were made for him in Guernsey. We think they will leave some runways on the airport open for their getaway planes. The second in command has been here from the very beginning of the Occupation.

Bertie went to see Victor about the opening of our church and Victor said, 'I am quite willing to order it to be opened and I can do so as Lieutenant Governor, but do you think it is wise at this stage of the game?' and Bertie said, 'Oh yes, let us have it opened.' So Victor said, 'You must tell Mr Finey he must write me a letter asking for permission to open the church.' Bertie told Mr Finey and Mr Finey said that he had written a letter to the Dean asking for permission to hold evening services every Sunday and a Communion Service once a month, and if the Dean refuses he will write to Victor. He also told Bertie that he had had a letter from Mr Frossard telling him that if he opened the church on his own responsibility he would have the support of all the Rectors so we shall see what happens.

Wednesday April 26th   E.
Another beautiful day. In the afternoon I walked to Ethel Falkener to play M-J with her, Maud and Mabel. I have to walk because the bus won't stop now by the Old Post. My walk was marred by the niggly east wind because I had no hat pin and my hat kept blowing off. I carried it most of the way.

Poor Ethel looks very weary, Lyon looked very comic in his patched clothes. They were all very excited about that bombardment on France the other night. Mabel saw all the flashes, she said the sky was lit up and her house shook to pieces.

Mabel told us about May Sherwill's boy. The Germans have tunnelled under Havelet and the boys are always playing in the tunnel. The Germans lost a bag of tools and a Non Com.

Officer came to May and accused the boys of stealing it. She said they hadn't and the officer shouted at the boys and one of them kicked him. May called the officer a coward and a brute and he seized May by the arm, hurled her across the room and locked her in and took the boys aged nine and eleven and questioned them for two hours! The next day May went up and complained to the Kommandantur at Grange Lodge who had the Non Com. Officer on the mat and went for him and took May's part absolutely and said any good mother would stick up for her boys. May has a frightful bruise on her arm which she showed him and May said the boys had not stolen the tools. Victor is very upset about it because he is trying hard to get Sherwill back from Germany and Knackfuss promised him he would do his best to get Sherwill sent back. Unfortunately May sent him a letter through one of the men returning to the camp, an indiscreet letter, and Sherwill is very upset because the Germans got hold of the letter and made a great fuss about it and now this fun with the boys has put the lid on Sherwill being sent back.

Thursday April 27th   E.
Another lovely day. Molly and I fetched the bread. I went in by the bus. I arrived early to Olive's. Olive had a letter which said, 'Michelle was abroad'. Where is she? Oh it is so awful not knowing anything.

Everybody is very excited because Red X parcels are coming to the Island through the efforts of the internees who have been interceding on our behalf. Victor has known of this for a long time and has allowed the notice to be put in the paper because the news has leaked out, but Victor is very sad because he thinks it is now too late and the parcels will never be brought here owing to the difficulties of transport. I fear he is right. Today boats went as far as Jersey and had to come back and no boats are leaving the Island now. How wonderful it would be to receive a parcel oneself.[253]

May 1944

Monday May 1st   N.W.
A cloudy day. Violet came in the afternoon. We were playing poker patience and suddenly about five soldiers passed the window and came into the house. James had unfortunately left the back door open. One was drunk and the others were trying to get him away. He rushed into the drawing room and I heard James telling them he would frighten the Frau. The Frau was not in the least frightened. He snatched up my photograph of the Prince of Wales. I clutched hold of him and we staggered back into the kitchen where the others were and I then spouted all the German I knew. I was quite surprised I knew so much. He gave me back my photograph and at last they all went. James said they tried to make him stand to attention. One of them came back and apologised, he was very pathetic. He said, 'I am Deutsche soldier, unlucky war, my kamarade drink taken, nix gut, alcohol. You forget him. I friend. You friend. When Deutsche soldier come to your place, stop indoors, take no notice.' I said I would and he went away. The drunken one had taken my notice of 'Kein Durchgang' off and flung it into the tank and also the bucket.

The drunken soldier kept on saying the photograph was der Kaiser. I kept on saying, 'Nicht der Kaiser, der Bruder der Konig.' He shook me by the shoulders, I shook him back. They had

---

[253] The *Star*, Thursday 27 April 1944: 'Food coming from Red Cross for the Island … Glad news sent to Bailiff.' The Bailiff had received a letter from the camp captain, Mr Garfield Garland, at the Channel Island camp in Germany: 'I am glad to be able to inform you that our efforts with the International Red Cross have at last succeeded in arrangements being made for consignments of food to be sent to the Island.'

all passed through before and Molly had raged at them and one of the soldiers crossed the yard to go by the front. James was in the hot plate and shouted out at him. Suddenly, in the middle of my row with the drunken one, this officer turned on James and said, 'You were mauvais to me.' James looked completely blank as if he did not understand a word. Oh dear, oh dear. 'It was a pantomime and a picnic,' as Nan-Nan used to say. They all kept shouting and pointing at James and saying, 'Officer.' I said, 'Nicht Officer, farmer,' and I touched James and I said, 'Der Herr', and myself and said, 'Die Frau', and one of them stooped down and held his hand about a foot above the floor and said, 'Die Kinder'. I said, 'Ja, ja, ja, Die Kinder,' trying to give the impression there were at least ten children in the house! My one idea was to focus their attention on me and not on James. I knew they would not do anything to me. The drunken soldier and I kept on shaking each other, but he didn't hurt me, he was quite gentle. At last they managed to persuade him to go.

Later on James came in and when he looked for the bootjack Hedley made, it was gone. However, about ten o'clock there was a loud knocking on the door and one of the soldiers brought it back.

Thursday May 4th   N.E.
A dull day with a bitterly cold wind. Molly and I fetched the bread. Molly barks so furiously at the soldiers now, I am quite frightened they will kill her.

James inspected the prison today. He says the conditions now are disgusting, they are so overcrowded that they can't lock the doors, they must leave them open for ventilation. All the prisoners are given to eat beside their small bread and butter ration is a portion of cabbage a day.

Sunday May 7th   N.W.
The Forest Church re-opened.

Such a cold night and a heavy white frost and such a cold wind. I went to church in good time. There were quite a good congregation and the choir sang beautifully although there were not many. The service was choral communion. Mr Finey gave out the processional hymn and in his excitement forgot the others and we have no board our side. I cannot sing a note but I can make 'a joyful noise unto the Lord'. Mrs Fred Heaume who sits next to me can do the same. I suddenly realised that if I wasn't making a joyful noise unto the Lord I was weeping copiously and so I preferred to do the former. Two of the hymns I knew and found the right ones, then they played 'When I survey the wondrous cross'. I began to sing that lustily when I discovered they were using the tune to another hymn, horrified collapse of Violet Mary! To my delight they chimed the bells and rang the last bell. Mr Finey prayed for ourselves and for the freeing of all prisoners speedily. It was a beautiful service and we had a long chat with everybody, people whom I haven't seen for a long time.

Mrs de Garis from the Vilette was at church this morning and she told me poor Mr Finey had been fretting dreadfully because the church was closed and she thinks that helped to make him to ill, so I must retract all the hard things I have written in here about him and said about him!

Tuesday May 9th   N.E.
A lovely day but still very cold. There were planes over in the night and this morning.

Another lovely day with a bitterly cold wind. Molly and I fetched the bread. On the way home I saw the Forest School outside drinking milk out of straws out of jam pots. There are eight children and the school is at 'Sherwood', the first house in the lane through which I go for the bread. Incidentally, 'Sherwood' is the Gouffre public house after six o'clock! The children did look so well and happy, their teacher looks very young and they all love their school. We are derelict no longer. The Post Office has come back and the school and the church are opened.

Although it is very cold and my hands are very cold, they don't hurt me, that awful pain in my hands I suffered in the winter. I did not have *one* cold this winter and James only had two slight ones. Cold houses in the winter, if uncomfortable, seem to be very healthy.

Thursday May 11th
A beautiful hot day and no wind. We have heard that the boat sunk off Sark had ammunition and 3,000 mines on board. No wonder she shook this Island when she blew up. It is too lovely to think those 3,000 mines are all gone instead of being planted all over Guernsey. I told old Crousaz this and of course he did not believe me and moaned away about a sanitary cart which the States had bought for £3,000. Why on earth the States want to buy a sanitary cart which costs £3,000 *now* I can't imagine. If only I had been quick I ought to have said, 'I don't believe it!'

Maud and I were talking about witchcraft in Guernsey and she told me two most interesting stories. The de Vic Careys had a coachman in their family for years. One day he was driving Edith Carey home and he turned round and said to her, 'I will say goodbye to you now Miss Carey because the General is going to kill me tomorrow.' Edith soothed him and they had the doctor for him who said he had gone mad. Mrs Carey who firmly believed in witches said he was not mad but bewitched and she knew who the witch was. She consulted a white witch who said the coachman had been bewitched and the only cure was to send him across the water. They sent him and his family to England for a holiday and he came back quite cured. When Maud's foreman's mother was a girl she was bewitched and became a complete cripple. Her mother took her to Jersey to a white witch there who told her the witch was going to die and her daughter would recover. The witch died and the daughter quite recovered. The mother took her daughter to show her to the doctor who had been able to do nothing for her and he said at once, 'The witch is dead!'

Saturday May 13th and Sunday 14th
Another boiling hot day. Molly and I fetched the bread. Mrs Mauger told me a remarkable story about a Red Cross message. A woman in England sent the following message to her husband, 'Forgive, have a baby boy.' The husband replied, 'Forgiven, have a baby girl, let us forget what happened and make the best of it!'

I was dreadfully tired all day, had a heavy sleep after dinner, woke up shivering, shivered all the evening. Went to bed, woke up shivering and burning hot and then streaming with perspiration and fainting over and over again and of course violent attack of Occupational. Undoubtedly I had picked up a germ. I was ill all night, fainted in the morning again. Fortunately I had some rice so made rice water. I felt too ill for words all day. Had another awful night. Did not sleep at all.

German planes going over all night. James went to church. It was packed again.

Saturday May 20th   N.E.
Still a bitter wind. James went to Town. Molly and I fetched the bread. James rang up about 2pm and said poor Maud had had two awful haemorrhages and was not expected to live. He came home about six and said she had made a wonderful rally. This morning she was unconscious and quite pulseless when the doctor saw her. James had left her quite conscious

and clear and talking strongly. Dr Sutcliffe said her recuperation powers were miraculous. She had the first attack at 8am so why Mabel did not ring James up is extraordinary.

Thursday May 25th   S.W.
A lovely day and much warmer. Molly and I fetched the bread. I did have a piece of luck. I had 6lbs of peas in my basket beside the bread. I dragged the basket as usual behind me. When I took out Mrs Baleine's loaf I found I had dropped a loaf! Horrors! My loaf. I hastily left my little basket cart at home and hurried back, and by the Cas Rouge there was my loaf in the middle of the road! What a relief.

Mrs Renault this morning said to me, 'There is an old maid in St Andrews aged 43 and she is going to have a baby by a spaniel and I know it is true, Mrs James!' I laughed and said, 'I don't believe it.'

'It *is* true, by a foreigner.' I said, 'Oh, you mean a Spaniard!'

'Yes,' she said, 'A Spaniel,' and nothing could make her call him anything else!

I started my walk into Town at 1.30pm and arrived at 3pm. I had a lovely walk. Mabel Kin, Peggy and Maud and I played M-J and I won again.

Friday May 26th   S.W.
Dark lowering clouds but the glass is very high.

About 10 o'clock a soldier came and wanted to buy peas. He could talk quite well and he wouldn't go, so James began to saw some wood. The soldier threw off his belt and said, 'Let me do that for you,' and he sawed up a huge amount of wood, talking all the time. He cursed Goering, Hitler up and down. He said he was a farmer's son and that he had been billeted on a farm in France and the farmer died and only the wife and three daughters were left so he and some others got leave to work and help them and they got all the hay in for them and helped them in every way. Another pathetic story of friendliness.

I had a message from Iris yesterday. She said she had two messages from us in January and the Boy was well and optimistic and she had heard from Michelle. I wonder if Michelle is in Italy. Oh dear, it is *awful* not knowing.

Sunday May 28th   S.W.
We had such a beautiful service today, the church was packed. Mr Finey preached a beautiful sermon. He told a story of a German soldier coming into the church one day in the beginning of the Occupation and asking him for a New Testament. He gave him one and he told the soldier the only force that had real power in the world is the Holy Spirit and that all other forces only created chaos and misery and the soldier agreed with him. I wonder whether that soldier is alive or not. Mrs Rose sang 'O for the wings of a dove' divinely. How beautiful her voice is. It is not a woman's voice, it is a boy's voice. Those pure high notes. I think that it would be a very good thing for congregations and for clergymen if every church was forcibly closed for at least a year. It has made me realise not to take things so much for granted. McCartney prays for 'Patience, courage and unwavering faith in the ultimate liberation of these Islands, victory to our sovereign and to the whole world a great and lasting peace,' and he doesn't care how many soldiers or Gestapo are in the church. He is grand. In the beginning of the Occupation each clergyman was sent a written command that they should not pray for our King in church. The others started the prayer for the King and left silence for the finish of the prayer. Not Mr McCartney, he burnt the paper publicly and prayed for our King louder than ever.

June 1944

Monday June 5th   S.W.

It tried to rain in the night but the glass is still very high. Those darlings came twice before nine. Mrs Renault had to shelter twice on her way here. It is exhilarating.

The 'Spaniel's' baby has arrived. The woman is 41 and the Spaniel was 21. He wanted to marry her, the Germans won't allow foreigners to marry Guernsey women. The baby is a little girl.

They have been over again and, horrible to relate, one American plane was brought down near Castle Cornet and crashed into the sea. They think the pilot was killed.

The American pilot who was at Happy Landings told Noyon, who rescued him with a boat, that he did not know when the invasion would start, but he was quite sure he would not be a prisoner for long.

I have never felt so tired before as I feel today and so depressed. The prospect of enduring another winter is grim, grim, grim. I don't know how we will go through it because we are starving now. There is no getting away from it. I am starving and this beastly germ making me do without food after 5pm makes me worse still. Everybody calls me a fool for eating so little but what *can* I do? *Anything* is better than diarrhoea I think. I can't bear it any longer, I do feel so weak and faint.

Cyril Gorvel has just told James that John Sebire has told him a German soldier told him that if the wind stays where it is the invasion will begin tonight. I wonder?

Tuesday June 6th   N.W.

I have never slept so soundly. I did not wake until 6.30pm to the sound of guns and the steady hum of planes. Has the invasion begun?

The Invasion has Begun![254]

What a day of days. Over went the planes all the morning. Mrs Renault said they started at 11pm and never stopped. I slept all night.

Molly and I fetched the bread and we met Mr Tuke in the lane and we stopped and beamed at each other. Mr Crousaz told us they had landed in three places. Simultaneously Mr Tuke and I said, 'I don't believe it,' and we roared with laughter. Mr Crousaz was not at all amused and shouted at us that it was true and had come from a German source. Rumour says Cherbourg, Havre and Belgium. Thousands and thousands of planes must have passed over in the night. Mr Tuke saw three fighters flying very low and his boy saw a black and yellow plane. There was a rumour they fired at two German planes this morning but it was not true, they were British planes.

I slept like the dead this afternoon, I felt much better. I had tea and then felt if I did not talk to somebody I would burst, so I went to see Peggy.

All the schools are closed and places of entertainment. They have taken a quarter of the butter ration this week and the potato ration. Dick thinks we shall all be very hungry soon. Who cares! They have taken over the Post Office and telephone exchange and have machine guns posted over the Town.

A soldier said to Mr Gorvel, 'You Breetish do not understand what it is to be beaten, you have never been beaten, you do not understand what it feels like in the stomach!'

---

[254] The *Star*, 6 June 1944: 'Invasion begins at 5.30 this morning … "Germany will fight with her whole might and passionate resolution in order to protect Europe, her culture and the life of her people from Barbarism."'

Dick drove me home, I can't remember when I was last in a motor car! Oh dear, oh dear, how sick with excitement we all feel.

Thursday June 8th   N.W.
I still feel all churned up. Molly and I fetched the bread. Planes went over while we were going and they fired at them. I left early for Town, it was cloudy but it did not rain. The thing that struck me was the uncanny silence and emptiness of the roads, I hardly met a soul and very few lorries. All their cars and lorries are camouflaged.

Maud told me she went to Town and in the Grange she took shelter in a doorway with other people because of a barrage and a woman said, 'They have landed in six places,' and Maud did not believe her. She went to have her hair done and was told there. Olive came in to see her and had a chat and said nothing about the invasion and after she had gone Maud realised that Olive knew nothing about it and cursed herself for losing the thrill of telling Olive. Olive did not hear until late in the morning. The patients have all been moved from the Vauquiedor Hospital to an underground hospital under St Helene, they say it is a beautiful hospital they have built.

Olive and Maud quite surprised me by their warm welcome when I arrived, they thought it was so brave of me to come. It is so nice to be praised for courage I did not know I had! It *never* entered my head not to come, I was counting the hours. They say everybody is afraid to go out.

We kept hearing planes and the barrage. One plane *was* brought down near Castle Cornet, people saw it come down in flames.

Friday June 9th
Maud and I went to church. It is a grey day. I went to Town early. It is quite true, people are afraid to go out, there is hardly anybody in Town.

I met Peggy who told me Mabel Kinnersly was so desperately ill, she is in the Emergency Hospital and they are awfully anxious about her. What a curse that they have shut off all the phones.

I had lunch at Berthelot Street. Katty was there and Miss Abbott. The latter has a barter shop and she said business is as dead as a button, everybody thinks we shall be free in a fortnight! and will be able to get things from England soon. One *dare* not think of it. Olive says she wants our Occupation to end tidily on the 1st July, the exact four years.

Grace Durand came to tea and told us of a woman at Torteval who is weeping her eyes out because her darling German soldiers had told her they were going away! One soldier has said, 'In three weeks time I shall be in England.'

Victor was terribly worried about our food but a ship came in last Friday with flour, enough to last for four months, gas coal. Now we will have until the end of September and potatoes for the Germans. They took thirty tons of ours last week and were going to take thirty tons more this week.

I had a good deal of rain on the way home. Again I was struck by the silence and emptiness of the roads. The buses have all been taken off and so now *all* those fat German soldiers will have to walk like I do. Chee! Chee! Chee!

I don't think we can realise the smartness of our soldiers after seeing these soldiers in their sloppy untidy patched clothes with their fat backs and fat necks and fat hands. We will simply blink our eyes in amazement at our own boys when they come, except I think the tears will be flowing so fast, will we see them at all?

Gay said to me, 'Doesn't the thought of the Invasion make you feel absolutely sick?' And it does, of course, it is too awful to think that boys have to go through that awful ordeal to set us free. I can't eat, I feel sick all day long, I can't help thinking that Baba is in a hospital plane. I am sure she is and where is Boy, is he in India? If only they had told me. They could have told me.

Thursday June 15th

Thirty years ago today, I achieved the supreme triumph of my life. I produced Michelle. From henceforth I shall be known always as Michelle's mother, the mother of Michelle. It was such a hot day and today is much hotter again. Up to now this has been the coldest June on record. I should think we have all gone back to our winter clothes.

Planes attacked the harbour this morning. There is a U-boat in the harbour. They did not get it, they bombed and blew up an ammunitions dump. The U-boat was covered with nets and between two ships. The two ships were set on fire and a crane was knocked over on to one of the ships but the submarine was not touched. She came in damaged. After each raid they kept moving her to another part of the harbour.

Molly and I fetched the bread and a large number of planes passed over and they fired at them. We took refuge in a house. After fetching the bread we fetched brine from Timmers and again planes passed over and they fired at them. Molly and I sat side by side in the hedge.

I started very early for my walk and there were more people on the road. I counted ninety bicycles between here and the bungalow and arrived in time for tea. No planes came over to my great disappointment. I went in to see Markie who told me poor Mabel was very very ill with blood poisoning. The doctors now suggest it is her teeth, though matron says her gums are very healthy and her teeth are very firm. She is only allowed fruit juices and tomato juice. It is awful, if she died we shall all miss her so dreadfully.

After supper we drank darling old Baba's health in Benedictine. Olive managed to wangle a bottle out of Mackaye by telling him she wanted it for her mother's birthday in July when her mother would be 89. Darling old Baba, she was such a lovely baby, so fair and without a single mole or spot of any kind. What a sensation she caused, of course she showed her impatience as early as that by coming two months too early. Mother and Teddy and Annie and Carr and old John were all there and now they are all dead. No wonder I am so lonely.

Monday June 19th   N.E.

A fine day and a very high wind. Planes came over before nine and dropped three bombs in the harbour. The blast blew the glass out of the shop windows even in Bordage and Fountain Street. They were American planes. They did not hit a ship in the harbour.

I wish we were not in the charge of the Americans, but were in the charge of the RAF. We always felt so secure and safe with the RAF. Planes came over all the morning and they fired at them. Violet came to tea. It was very brave of her.

It really looks like rain. Violet says we have had no real rain since February 9th. The scarcity of hay is awful and nothing is growing.

Tuesday June 20th   N.E.

A strong east wind is blowing. I fetched the bread and Mr Crousaz told me he went into Town yesterday afternoon. He said it was a shambles and nobody was hurt! The breakages reached up to Trinity Square. One bank could not be used at all and the other had to use their strong room. The Town church windows are all broken on the sea side.

Maud and Peggy and Ethel Falkener came out to play M-J. Olive had been in the Town this morning. She said it was indescribable. Hundreds and hundreds of men were working, clearing away the glass and boarding up the windows. There were some miraculous escapes. One family in Hauteville were having their breakfast and the windows were smashed, the glass flew all over the room and not one was hurt. Apart from the blast, a German plane that was dropping mines was chased over here and dropped one mine in Kinnel's yard, one in Hauteville and one in the Bosq lane. They were eleven feet long. None of them exploded. The poor Special Aid was absolutely wrecked, the sink was blown into the middle of the room. Parson's window was wrecked. It *was* miraculous that not one single person was hurt. If it had happened later the casualties would have been too terrible.[255]

I saw poor Jack de Lisle this morning looking for grass for his cattle. The drought is appalling. He said his cows were milked last night and he was five gallons short. Two of his hens had been stolen and his potatoes had been dug. He thrust his hands savagely into his pockets and he said he had no heart to grow anything, he felt just like keeping his hands in his pockets and doing nothing. Can we blame him or any other farmer?

And oh I do feel so *hungry* tonight and I daren't take a potato, there are barely enough for our breakfast tomorrow. I simply *long* for white bread and butter tonight.

Saturday June 24th   N.E.
Another beautiful day. Molly and I fetched the bread. There is another school of thought here, this one thinks that the British will free Alderney and Jersey and leave us alone. An *unbearable* thought. They think because we are so heavily fortified and Jersey and Alderney are not, that the British will think it is better for us to starve than to have thousands killed and the Island destroyed. We certainly are between the devil and the deep blue sea. Poor little Sark and Guernsey.

Sunday June 25th   S.
James and I went to church. There was not quite such a large congregation. Mr Finey gave us a beautiful service. I really think the man is inspired. All of us who used to call him a coward and a rabbit must certainly eat our words in lumps. The prayers he says, prayers for our deliverance, protection for the King's forces in our sea and land, victory for our Sovereign. In his sermon he could not have been more outspoken. He certainly is a different man.

Poor Mabel Kinnersly has para-typhoid. At last they have found out what is the matter with her.

Thursday June 29th   S.W.
A dull day. Molly and I fetched the bread. There is a rumour that the BBC has said Alderney and Guernsey are the last strongholds the Germans have in the Channel. I wonder what that means?

Poor Mabel Kinnersly died last night. She passed into a coma yesterday morning and died quite peacefully. She knew she was going and said she was quite happy to go and had had a very happy life. How we shall all miss her. Somehow we never thought she was ill, she was always so gay and gallant. Dick Gibson never held out any hope because of her heart. She must have been failing for months and months and suffering and never let anybody know.

---

[255] *Guernsey Evening Press*, 21 June 1944, reported 'Anglo-Americans convert our shops into shambles'. The paper stated that the Anglo-American raid began between 8.30 and 9am on Monday 19 June. Bombs were dropped in the old harbour. 'Few shops escaped' but 'no one was injured.'

July 1944

Wednesday July 5th   S.W.

Pouring with rain this morning. James managed to get some of his hay cut with a team of oxen. I don't know what the farmers are going to do.

It cleared up in the afternoon. People who have been to Town today have come back bursting with excitement and rumour.

1. That we are going to be declared an Open Town.
2. Curfew will be until 11pm.
3. The schools are going to be re-opened.
4. Fishing will be allowed.
5. Tomatoes can be sent to Jersey.
6. Red Cross messages have arrived.
7. That there has been a big air raid on Jersey.

Peggy came in the evening. She said the Town was humming with excitement. If the Germans agree to us being an Open Town they must leave the guns and ammunition and cranes here intact and we must give them a safe crossing to France. One thing she knows is a fact because Stead the fish controller told her. The fishermen are now allowed to go freely where they like and when they like. There are no patrols and no supervision at all. He said what is to prevent the Sark fishermen running down to Carteret, they can get there in under an hour, or our fishermen going to St Malo?

If we are an Open Town we shall be freed by the International Red Cross. Diesel oil has arrived and we now have electric light until the end of October. That is a fact.

Anyhow, if there is no truth in the rumours, they relieve the deadly monotony of our lives and give us a pleasant thrill and something to talk about.

We have had no meat for three weeks.

On one of those bits of silver paper the RAF dropped was this message: 'Cheer up Guernsey. We shall relieve you soon,' and it was signed Sergeant Ross.

Saturday July 8th

A fine day and very hot. Molly and I fetched the bread. In the afternoon Maud, Olive and Bobby came to play M-J. I gave them little cakes and real coffee. We had such a jolly afternoon. I did enjoy it.

I have heard a fearful thing, that they have gassed 100,000 Jews in gas chambers holding 6,000 human beings, and trains of little children taken to be gassed. What can be done with such a diabolical nation? If I was the one who settled things after the war I would make both Germany and Russia reservations like they do in America with the Indians and I would have our Army, Navy and Air Force kept up to full war strength. I would gorge those two nations with food until I had made them so lethargic they would desire to eat and sleep and then the world might have peace.

Thursday July 27th   W.

Maud told me a German went to Mrs McCartney and asked for eggs, she had none and told him so and apparently he went off. She left her kitchen and when she came back she found he had taken her precious jar of salt and we are going to have no more. We are completely blockaded now.[256]

---

[256] Following the D-Day landings and the Liberation of France in June 1944 the food shortage became extremely serious as there was no access to food supplies from France. (Cruickshank, *The German Occupation*, p.123)

August 1944

Tuesday August 1st N.E.
A boiling hot day. Molly and I fetched the bread.

In the afternoon I walked over to the Vallon Cottage to Nelly's. Peggy and Maud were there and we played M-J. They told me that the Count von Schmettow had allowed Victor to write a letter to Switzerland telling them about our conditon. The Court wrote the letter for Victor in German and Victor wrote it in French and English. He has told them we have enough food until the end of September.

We think there are nearly 40,000 soldiers altogether in the Islands. Ships are supposed to be coming to take them away, but I don't think they will ever get away.

Maud and Olive are not too well. Olive has got dreadfully thin again. They are both doing too much. We all are. I am not going anywhere else except to Olive's and Town every week while the hot weather lasts. Of course *now* we are all living under a fearful strain. We are wild with impatience, our nerves are at breaking point. We feel that each day we cannot bear our conditions any longer and so it goes on.

Saturday August 5th
Another boiling hot day. Molly and I fetched the bread. There is a rumour people are making wireless sets as small as a matchbox to be used with headphones! They reqire a teeny little wire which they call a cat's whisker. One woman wanted one made and was asked for a 'cat's whisker', she replied she only had a kitten, would its whiskers be too small?

The girls working for the Germans received £2 10s. a week for five hours work and also three meals in the five hours! No wonder domestic service is dead in Guernsey.

Monday August 7th
Another boiling hot day. Perfect weather for the holiday, perfect weather for the children's holidays and for visitors for the bays and for the cliffs. There are no children, no visitors, no bays and no cliffs available to us and so it goes on.

Wednesday August 9th
A thick mist this morning but it cleared off and it is another perfect hot summer's day. It is James' 64th birthday. While we were at breakfast a German officer came to see him.

Mr Finey came to call. He told me that when they first came, he was afraid they would break into the church, so he went to call on the Commandant at Happy Landings. He met two soldiers on the way and asked them if he could see the Commandant. The soldier spoke perfect English and said he was sure he could, so Mr Finey asked him to come and interpret for him. To his surprise, both soldiers turned and ran away as fast as they could. He went to Happy Landings and a Lieutenant took him to the Commandant and the Commandant could not talk much English. Mr Finey said he thought the only universal language in the world was music, so he asked the

John Finey.

Commandant if he could play the organ. The Commandant replied, 'Yes, and I will come now.' To Mr Finey's surprise, they got on each side of him, grasped his arms in a grip of iron, drew their revolvers and marched him to the church. They took off their hats as they entered the church, clanked up the aisle. Mr Finey opened the organ, started the electric blower and the Commandant began to play church music most beautifully. He played for about an hour. They both crept out of church, shook hands with Mr Finey and went back to Happy Landings. He said the difference in their demeanour was remarkable.

Thursday August 10th   S.W.
I had a lovely walk in. I went through St Andrews. It was beautifully shady and all downhill. At the Vauxbelets, in two fields, soldiers naked to their waists and with bare feet were doing physical drill. How different to the beautiful precision of our men. They were jumping up and down in twos and threes and working their arms and pretending to boot, but all anyhow.

Friday August 11th   S.W.
Another fine day. Maud and I were nearly late for St Stephen's. I went to Town early. Everybody was so happy and joyful and the Town was full of rumours.

I had lunch at Berthelot Street with Bertie, Peggy and Cissie and Katty joined us. I had my hair shampooed today by Mrs Langlois for the first and I hope the last time by her! I felt as if I had stepped into a complete chapter of one of E.M. Delafield's books. I have never seen Mrs Langlois before. She has a harsh, gruff voice like a man's, very plain and no manners. I saw her goggle eyes looking at me when I removed my hat and two large fig leaves fell out. I use them to protect my poor head from the sun. I suppose she thought I was a disguised Bacchaute. She gave me a towel to protect my eyes from the soap and when I tried to use it, harshly bade me put my hands down. I felt she had taken a violent dislike to me on sight. I said, 'The weather is very hot.' She said, 'The weather is beautiful,' and conversation died. I also think she realised that if she disliked me, she positively *loathed* my hair. Never has it been treated with such brutality. I thought of kind Mrs Wallace and I thought never again! Never again, although I have to make an appointment a month or six weeks ahead, I will do that. She finally got a girl to finish drying it and we parted with mutual and fervent silent hopes that we will never see each other again!

Monday August 14th   S.E.
Another beautiful day. Yesterday was perfect because there was such a cool breeze and the same today. About 1am there was terrific firing on the sea. I was hanging out of the window watching the flashes. Mrs Renault said it was a wonderful sight, the sky was lit up by four searchlights from Jersey, they were throwing up huge star shells and there was a naval battle going on, they could see the ships drifting along in the red glow. After that was over, they kept firing the guns from here although there were no planes.

Everybody is saying the Americans will relieve us. If they do I shall be bitterly disappointed. I have just been *longing* to see our sailors and marines and soldiers marching down the High Street. I don't know what I shall do if it is the Americans.

Friday August 18th
Another fine hot day. I went to church. I got down to Town early. Everybody was in the highest spirits. In fact we are all sick with excitement. I have been feeling sick and queer for several days

now and I thought it was just the heat. I went to Miss Ross today and she told me she had been downright ill and had been to the doctor who told her it was nerves through excitement. He told her he had had a great many people ill like that lately. She said she could not sleep or eat. My head is so terribly overheated. Never mind.

Wednesday August 23rd
Sixty-four years ago today I came into the world and certainly never thought I would spend my 64th birthday in captivity. *But* what a day! Just before 2pm Mrs Renault arrived, bursting with excitement.

Peggy, Micky and Mrs Sherbrooke came to M-J. How hilarious and joyous we were, our play was almost erratic. I gave them a lovely tea. Apple tart and little cakes, real coffee and melon. How we all enjoyed it. We were discussing what our behaviour will be like when we go out to dinner or lunch parties again. After we have had our soup, we will automatically retain our spoons, exclaiming, 'I must use this again.' We have to wash up in cold water, then we will ignore our knives and use our spoon. Also we will watch each other all the time and if anybody leaves anything, we will say, 'Are you to leave that, I will finish it up.' If we see anybody crumbing *white* bread, we will scream at them, 'Don't do *that*, bread is more precious than gold. Then we will look at the food and say, 'O … h, don't talk, I want to get down to this and enjoy it,' and then the only sounds we shall hear will be 'O … .h, u … m!' At tea we shall say, 'Let me smell the tea pot, what a delicious smell,' and to each other we shall say politely, 'Do lick your knife, would you care to lick the jam spoon, of course, lick up your crumbs!' I'm sure that is the way we shall go on. Mrs Sherbrooke said her husband will go to her mantlepiece and say, 'What is all this muck?' and she will meekly say, 'Those are my cigarette ends, dear, I am drying them!'

Saturday August 26th
Another roasting hot day. Molly and I fetched the bread. Olive and Maud went to tea with Mrs Frossard last week and Mrs F. told them this story. A young farmer had made great friends with a Pole. They had been friends for a long time, for nearly a year. the farmer had been very good to the Pole in every way. Last week the Pole was seen going along the road looking very pleased with himself. He was going to the German police to report to them that the young farmer had a crystal wireless set! Jim always used to laugh at me because I used to say 'Beastly foreigners!' I say it now with more conviction than ever! The Countess says the Poles always claim that her family, the Radziwills, are Polish and she says they are *not* Polish, they are Lithuanian. She says the Poles are awful, *I say*, 'What foreigner isn't?'

We are only to have 2oz of sugar now. It is remarkable how the difference in men and women is so clearly noticeable now. The less food the women have, the harder they work, while the men won't work at all. Olive can't stop Rita working. Mrs Mauger is doing far too much, but James is in despair of getting any work out of the men at all.

There is a lovely story about Mrs Burnett. She was plucky. She had an officer billeted upon her. One evening, he brought a girl in who stayed all night. When that happened a second time, Mrs Burnett was determined to stop it. The officer went out and Mrs Burnett noticed the girl's bicycle was still there, so she proceeded to sweep down the stairs and she continued to do so until he came back, then she went into the kitchen and the girl escaped. She then asked the officer to come and speak to her and told him she would not allow such goings on. He expressed surprise and asked where the girl was?

'I waited until you came back and then I allowed her to go,' replied Mrs B calmly. He said, 'Are you aware I am the head of the Gestapo here?'

'What difference does that make?' said Mrs B. 'You showed me the photographs of your wife and daughters. Would you like them to know about that girl, and would you do such a thing in your mother's house?' He admitted he wouldn't. She said, 'I will go to the General if this happens again.' It has not happened again.

Thursday August 31st   S.W.

A fine day with a strong wind. Molly and I fetched the bread. I started early for Town and walked through St Andrews.

Olive's Rita will *not* wash up with cold water. Olive always washes the tea and supper things in cold water, and as *nothing* is greasy nowadays it doesn't matter. Olive says, 'Rita is much too valuable to lose,' so she hasn't argued with her but let her have her own way. However, she showed Rita that they were overdrawn with the gas and implored Rita to tell her what they were to do. Rita said nothing and went away. About an hour later she called Olive to come and see. Out in the garden, Rita had filled an old battered enamel basin with little sticks. On top of it she had balanced two old pokers and on top of the pokers was a kettle boiling away merrily. Since then Rita has built a turpie with bricks and Olive has found two bits of iron and Rita has put all her saucepans and kettles on it and not used the gas at all. Certainly we have proved that necessity is the mother of invention.

September 1944

Friday September 1st   S.W.

A fine day with a strong wind. Before I went to Town I went to Cambridge Park to see Mr Breton about Jim's cheque from the States for his motor car. Mr Breton told me they would credit him with it and called him an 'honourable evacuee' because he joined up. He said the States were going to pay out £36,000 to honourable evacuees. I was so relieved.

It was a pleasure walking through the markets. I did not *see* a German, I did not *hear* a German and I did not *smell* a German! It was wonderful, it might have been pre war except that the markets were so empty and silent. Never mind.

I had lunch at Berthelot Street with Bertie and Peggy. A young man at the next table handed us one of the leaflets and we looked at it quite openly. Then he showed us the following poem:

> 'An Indictment' written in June 1944 by Winter le Brocq.
> Illustrated by Edmund Blampied.
> First and only edition, Jersey 1944.
>
> Rumours of Carteret taken
> And Coutances …
> Of splendid death
> Of swift and violent carnage …
> But in the markets
> We,
> With anger on our lips,
> Cry at the price of strawberries.

"OUR BOYS!
WAIT FOR THE BRITISH BOYS!"
The Germans dig in the Parade,
Bivouac on the bowling-greens …
But on the peninsula,
At Bayeux,
There is death –
A thousand deaths …
And at Caen
Young boys,
The loveliest,
Lie bleeding.

Strawberries are like drops of blood.

When will the British come?
Release us from the prices?
Bring us cigarettes?
And tea?
(Ah, a good cup of tea! …
Life will be worth living again!)

At Carentan they are dying
And at Saint Lo!
Have they chocolate for us?
And butter?
Will they bring music –
Wireless sets?
Do they know what we pay for strawberries?
That tea is a pound an ounce?
Will they bring us the latest film?
The comedians?
The tragediennes?
NEWS REELS?

In the Seine Bay
The ships' carcasses
Rot …
Bodies are washed up at Honfleur,
At Trouville
They are buried.

The tomatoes have no flavour,
The potatoes are full of water,
Our diet is unvaried …
We are obsessed,
Stifled with ennui …

No news!
Not at Granville yet!

Yes! ... Yes!
Granville is flat!
Ah!

They will not strike here!
They are our people!
They love us!
If they knew of our sufferings!
They have heard ...
Be assured!
Someone has told them
That tea is a *guinea* an ounce!
The tomatoes are flavourless!
Potatoes watery!
Our diet unvarying!
And the price of strawberries
Incites them!
Shall we grow flowers
Or potatoes for the English markets
After?
Which will pay us best?

At Valognes they die,
And at Barfleur ...
Why don't they take Cherbourg?
Ah, if only they'd take Cherbourg!
What are they thinking of?

Strawberries are like heavy drops of blood
And
At such a price
Blood
Is cheaper.

That Indictment is absolutely true. We *are* like that. Instead of being thankful because our sufferings are so negligible compared to the sufferings of the boys. When planes fly over, instead of being filled with sick horror and terror, we are only exhilarated, the siren makes us laugh, we sleep in our beds every night without a thought of doing anything else. We have so much to be thankful for.

Sunday September 3rd   S.W.
Last Sunday, after the evening service, we all noticed a soldier waiting outside the church. When we were all out, he went in. The Brocks and we were talking and suddenly Peggy said, 'Hullo, somebody is giving an organ recital,' because someone was playing the organ. We did not stay or go back into the church. It was the soldier playing the organ. He had asked Mr Finey if he could play the organ, he played several tunes and finally he said to Mr Finey, let me play something you choose. Mr Finey put a hymnbook in front of him and said, 'Please play hymn 707.' Mr Finey and Wilson stood at attention, the soldier grinned all over his face and played 'God Save the King'!

Tuesday September 5th   S.W.
A fine day and the wind has gone down. Molly and I fetched the bread. While I was having tea, Mrs Renault called me and said someone wanted to speak to me. I went out and found the man that used to deliver our bread. I said jokingly, 'Have you brought me some lovely white bread? Or are you calling for orders?' To my astonishment he replied, yes he was calling for orders and he expects to be able to deliver us white bread very soon. He stayed and told us all he knew. He said the German bakers used his ovens but they gave him bits and pieces. He said he had seen one German baker breaking 56 dozen eggs making cake for the soldiers but *not now*! He also told us that the German flour has all gone bad, they stored it in the schools and then when they feared a landing they took it out of the schools and stored it in tunnels and of course the tunnels were too damp and draughty and he thinks they only have flour for a very short time and he said it is quite true, all that bread they buried in sawdust has gone bad. The Germans are having exactly the same ration of bread as we are, 4¼ lbs a week.

Friday September 8th   N.W.
We all went to church. Mr Collard actually said the prayer 'in time of war and tumults'. Maud and I went down to Town early. A leaflet was dropped at the Vale. I was shown one in Berthelot Street Restaurant. Otherwise I was not told anything local or otherwise and Maud and Olive heard nothing.

People are criticising poor old Victor again because he either has dined with Count von Schmettow or is going to. The silly fools, why can't they realise that Count von Schmettow wants to see Victor absolutely alone and talk over things with him and that is the only way he can do it. Count von S is supposed to have said that the sooner he can say the civilian population are starving, the better he will be pleased and then he can put up the white flag. What a mercy he isn't a Nazi. If we had that awful General Muller here now, I tremble to think what would have happened, I am sure he would have shot somebody.

Sunday September 10th   N.W.
A lovely day, but cold. More leaflets were dropped last night. A cowman who lives at Vazon picked up thirty-one in his garden. He brought three papers to his master. He hid them in his socks and it was lucky he did because he was stopped and searched, the papers were not found.

There is a new G.U.B. in Guernsey. The old one is the 'Glasshouse Utilisation Board'. The new one is the 'Guernsey Underground Barbers' and they are seizing girls who have been friendly with Germans, and men too, and they are shaving their heads. There are both men and girls members of this new organisation. How I wish they could get hold of the people who sent anonymous letters.

Our hot plate is really a great success. I call this the public bakehouse. I don't know how many people we cook for, the Gorvels, Mrs Baleine, Mrs Renault and Mrs Mauger and others.

Mr Finey let himself go in his sermon tonight against the girls who went with the enemy. He did not mince matters, but said what he thought in the plainest language. There were several soldiers in the church. We walked out to the tune of the 'Old Brigade'.

Wednesday September 20th   N.E.
Another perfect day. Mrs Sherbrooke, Peggy and Micky came out for M-J. It was lovely having them, they told me Brest had fallen. *Now* what will happen to us?

We have sent medical supplies and gas coal to Jersey. People are buying hot water there now.

Micky told us a lovely story. A man was listening to his crystal set and some Germans came to the door. He hastily put his set in his pocket and opened the door. The soldiers stared at him and one of them said, 'You have a crystal set.' He denied it and invited them to come in and search. 'Oh no,' said the soldier, 'we do not need to search, if you are not using your crystal set, will you give us those headphones you are wearing!'

Mrs Sherbrooke was very funny at tea. Micky suddenly said to her, 'Don't wipe your fingers on that table cloth, it isn't done.'

'But,' she protested, 'my fingers are quite clean, they are really clean, Mrs Carey, I have licked them all!' And none of us minded!

Saturday September 23rd N.E.

When I came down at about 8.15am, James, greeted me with 'Tremendous news, twelve American ships, flying the white flag, passed St Martins Point yesterday afternoon. They came as near as they could to the harbour and a boat came ashore flying the white flag and a party landed and went up to Grange Lodge and had a conference. They went back to the ship and all the ships went away outside the range of the guns and hauled down the white flag!' I didn't know whether I was going to be sick or cry! I rushed to the phone and rang up Olive and told her. I rang up Peggy, they had heard it very late last night. I rang up Gay and told her.[257]

James went off to Town and I fetched the bread and Old Crousaz had heard it too. Mr Tuke had heard that the American ships had all their guns ready for action.

Rumour I: That the landing party were blindfolded and taken to Grange Lodge in cars.

Rumour II: That there was only one American ship, the size of the *St Julien*, flying a Red Cross flag.

The Truth: Olive met Bobby Seabrooke who had watched the ship arriving with powerful glasses. She was flying the stars and stripes and the white flag at the mast head, a boat went out to her from the harbour. This boat was flying the white flag, no party landed and the ship went away.

Rumour III: That they had come to discuss medical supplies and food.

Rumour IV: That they have brought an ultimatum and the Germans have rejected it!

Gay came in to see me for a few minutes, she said she hadn't had her breakfast when I phoned and she was so excited she could not eat any breakfast. On the contrary, I ate my breakfast with gusto!

James came back corroborating Bobbie's statement about the American ship. Anyhow we have had a tremendous thrill out of it all. I expect we will have many more.

I went to Miss Ross on Friday. We were talking about the new G.U.B. and the letters. She said what made her feel perfectly sick was that she is sure all these girls who have been with the Germans will put on red, white and blue ribbons and will be all over the Americans when they come. She says she intends to slap the faces of all those she knows! I hope she will.

Peggy went into de la Mares and the assistant said to her, 'Come and see what we are making,' and took her to the back of the shop and there were lots of girls making red, white and blue ribbon rosettes by the dozen. It is all so *cheering*.

---

[257] Canadian Major Alan Chambers of SHAEF (Supreme Headquarters Allied Expeditionary Force) requested a rendezvous with the German Command on 22 September 1944, intending to try to start negotiations. Chambers did go aboard a German vessel but von Schmettow refused to discuss the situation, so Chambers was not allowed ashore. (William Bell, *Guernsey Occupied but Never Conquered*, pp.302-4)

Sunday September 24th   N.W.

There was a plane in the night and leaflets were dropped. It is blowing a gale and such a cold wind. We went to church for the Harvest Festival. I have never seen the church look so lovely.

After church I met Frank Renault who stopped me in a low voice, asked to speak to me and told me that two Germans had told him the American ship had brought an ultimatum, that the boat that went out to her returned and went out again, and they stayed on board for another quarter of an hour besides the first hour they stayed on board. Of course, we are all brimming with curiosity to know *why* she did come? Anyhow, it is a glorious thrill!

Peggy told me one of the sailors in the picket boat that went out to the American boat had said the conference took place in the picket boat between German officers and American officers. The Kommandant stayed on the pier. The conference lasted eighteen minutes only. The American officers offered cigarettes to the sailors and the German officers would not allow the sailors to accept the cigarettes. There were forty cars on the pier and great activity. Oh dear, oh dear, my curiosity is absolute torture! I wonder if we shall ever know. I suppose the Kommandant was afraid of being kidnapped. If it is an ultimatum they have sent it too soon, because we have food yet, such as it is, sufficient for our needs.

October 1944

Thursday October 5th   N.E.

A very cold wind and a gloomy day. Molly and I fetched the bread. I left at half past one for Town.

Micky Kinnersly came to play M-J. She told us the story of her arrest. I had never heard it before. She said she had not told people because Mabel was so upset and frightened about it. It happened when our wirelesses were taken away. One day the German police arrived at Peter's house. They asked Peter if he had a sister-in-law. Peter replied he had four sisters-in-law. They asked him how many were in the Island, he replied, 'One.'

'Mrs George Kinnersly,' they said, giving Micky's address.

'Yes,' said Peter. The police went away and Peter rang Micky up and told her about it. About four days later, it was Micky and George's wedding anniversary and Micky was expecting Mabel and Mrs Kennedy and Mrs Gordon to lunch. She was in the middle of the preparation of the lunch in the morning, a thundering knock came on her door. She opened the door and there were the German police. The officer said to her, 'You are under arrest.'

'What for?' said Micky.

'You have been circulating enemy propaganda.'

'How?' said Micky.

'By typewritten sheets of paper and by a transmitter.'

'I have no wireless, no transmitter, no typewriter and I cannot type,' said Micky. The officer came in and sat down and proceeded to ask Micky the usual irrelevant questions. How old was she? Where was she born? She told them she was born in Switzerland. In between the questions, the officer kept saying, 'But aren't you afraid?'

'Not at all,' said M. 'I have done nothing, what have I to be afraid of?' He asked her if her husband lived there?

'Don't be silly,' she said, 'of course my husband lives here.' She asked them why they thought she had been transmitting news. They had received an anonymous letter. She asked to see it but he would not show it to her. He was very truculent and rude in the beginning, but became quite civil. After about an hour he said again, 'You are under arrest.' M replied, 'If you want to take me to prison, you can't take me now, you must come and fetch me later because this is the anniversary of our wedding day and I am expecting my mother and brother and mother-in-law to lunch and you must excuse me now because I *must* go and see to dinner.' She got up then and went into the kitchen. He followed her. There was the most appetising smell in the kitchen, she had a rabbit roasting in the oven. The officer sniffed and looked around and then he said, 'This is too tempting, I must go before I yield to temptation,' and turned around and went out of the house! And Micky hasn't heard another word. As she says, she may still be under arrest for all she knows. They did not search the house.

Friday October 6th   N.E.
A fine day. I went to Mrs Carey to fetch my coat. Poor soul, she could hardly crawl, she has shingles and is so weak. Up to now she has been so well. People are suffering now.

Everybody is furiously angry with that statement Mr Eden made about us in Parliament. There are so many versions given by people who declare they heard it themselves:
  1. That the Germans had refused to surrender and were not treating the people improperly.
  2. That the people in the Channel Islands were being reasonably treated.
  3. That the Germans had been requested to surrender and had refused and as far as it could be ascertained, the Germans were not treating the population badly.[258]

As we truly say, they have only got the Germans word for it. O … h, how I wish they would leave us alone, if they can't free us. These silly statements do us no good, only harm. They could help us *enormously* if they would only send over two or three planes, two or three times every week, let them fly just out of range and draw their fire and use up their ammunition. By doing that they would send the Germans' nerves to pieces. This deadly peace over here is sending up their morale and bringing ours down to breaking point. We can endure anything but this desolate feeling of being completely forgotten.

Yesterday, when we were playing M-J in the afternoon, we heard a loud noise. We whispered to each other, 'Do you think they are bombarding Alderney?' We waited in breathless suspense and it came again, much nearer. We looked at each other in absolute disgust and we all spat out simultaneously, 'Thunder!'

Sunday October 8th   N.E.
A fine day. I have been so ill all day with Occupational. I really have had it constantly for four years. I could not go to church. James had gone and Cyril had gone up with the milk. I never thought of locking the door. I heard someone in the kitchen, went out to see and there was that detestable soldier who came last Sunday. There was a bucket of apples under the table. He asked for some and I had to give them to him, so now I shan't be able to boast any longer that I have not given the Germans anything, it is *sickening* but I was absolutely alone. He took three large ones, peeled them and put them in his pocket, he kept saying, 'Sehr gut, sticky.' I suppose

---

[258] According to *Hansard Parliamentary Debates* volume 403, p.952, Mr Eden made no comment about the Channel Islands in the September to October session of Parliament. The comment which probably fuelled this rumour is: 'October 4th 1944, Mr *Thorne* asked the Secretary of State of War whether the Germans still occupied Guernsey and Jersey, how people are being treated and if German soldiers had been called upon to surrender. *Mr A. Henderson* replied that the German garrison is still contained in the Channel Islands. No information received by the War Office which suggests that the behaviour of the German garrison is other than correct. The German garrison has been given the opportunity to surrender but has not accepted.'

he did not want his lovely comrades to see he had apples! He asked for matches and milk and I said, nix milk and nix matches. He held out his dirty hand for me to shake but I avoided that and showed him out, and he went away quite peaceably. They are pests.

Friday October 13th
A fine day. I went to Town early. Everybody is talking about the notice in the paper today. Here it is:

> Re: Supplies for the Channel Islanders
> In order to keep the population informed about the question of supplies and to stop injurious rumours, the Commander of the Channel Isles has authorised the *Evening Press* to publish the following information:
> The Channel Isles had virtually been cut off from all supplies already a month before the Invasion. From that moment, the population lived on the produce of the Island and from stocks which had been formed according to instructions from the Occupying Power. In view of the possibility of the state of siege, agriculture and industry had been adapted as far as feasible to make the fortresses self supporting.
> As the population, however, cannot be supplied indefinitely from the stocks of the fortress or from the produce harvested or manufactured within them, the Commander of the Channel Isles some time ago took the precaution of getting in touch with superior authorities and has informed the German Government of the situation.
> His action was appreciably facilitated by reports about the most essential commodities, supplies of which were running out in the near future, submitted by the States of Guernsey in the interest of the population of Guernsey.
> The German government has intimated its intention of taking the necessary steps in this matter with the Protecting Power. For this purpose the Commander of the Channel Isles has submitted a report about the Island's monthly requirements of essential commodities. Any action the Protecting Power may decide to take on this information is now, of course, beyond the control of the Occupying Authorities.[259]

Some people immediately think we shall each have a 10lb Red X parcel every month! Others that food will come in bulk. Others that the Germans are only protecting themselves and there is nothing in it at all. Others hope no food will come and then they will *have* to give in! I don't think any food will come.

Book IX

Thursday October 19th   S.W.
I never thought I should have to use this book as a diary. I *did* think we would be free before I had finished the last book.

The Germans came and chose nine of our beautiful trees and they are going to cut them down. they graciously allowed us to have three!

It is not blowing so hard. I had a lovely walk in and no rain. We played M-J with Gay. Maud heard the Germans were loading up ships with ammunition to take it away. Will they get it away?

---

[259] *Guernsey Evening Press*, 13 October 1944. Also documented in William Bell, *Guernsey Occupied but Never Conquered*, p.307.

Thursday October 26th   E.

There is a rumour that 'the man in the street' is supposed to have said, 'Something must be done about the Channel Islands.' I do hope that is true. In a broadcast they have said that furniture has been taken from the Channel Islands and northern France to Germany as a gift to the Germans whose homes have been devastated by air raids. *A gift*, ye Gods, the old fashioned name is 'loot'!

November 1944

Wednesday November 1st   E.

Pouring with rain. James went to a States meeting. He phoned in a furious hurry telling me to hide the potatoes because they are searching the farms for potatoes, poor farmers are never left alone! Mrs Mauger and I started filling up sacks and Bill and Cyril came back and finished the job. It is all so dreadful and upsetting, especially as we are all feeling so depressed facing the fifth winter and we never *dreamt* we would not be relieved by now.

James came back from the States meeting very late. He said the reason he had phoned was because he had met several men with yellow brassards on their arms and these men are allowed to search any house for food. At the States meeting, the Controlling Committee gave the dates when everything will be finished. All food except flour and sugar will be finished by the end of December, also all fuel and electric light. Flour and sugar will last until the middle of January and then everything will be finished. The only operations doctors can perform are life and death ones, the medical supplies are nearly finished.

Everybody says, 'Surely England will do something now.' Will she? Does she know? Or care? I know I am a 'dismal Jimmy' but I have the dismal feeling that England is always so casual and callous about her own people. All through history it has been so. After the last war look how the ex-servicemen and merchant seamen were treated? *If only* we had prepared ourselves to endure another winter! But when the invasion started, how hopeful we were, how we made jokes with each other, that we could only accept invitations provided we were not in England, how gay and cheerful we were with *everybody* whether we knew each other or not, and as each Channel port fell, our spirits rose higher and higher. *Now* we simply feel abandoned. How I sympathise with the unemployed, that awful feeling of being cast aside, not wanted and of no use.

Saturday November 4th   S.W.

A lovely day and much warmer I am glad to say. Molly and I fetched the bread. I was tired and I slept like the dead after lunch until 4pm. Mrs Mauger brought the rumour that Captain Noyon and another man have escaped to France. Captain Noyon was at the States meeting on Wednesday and he took notes of all the statements. They are supposed to have gone last night. It was a beautiful, calm night.[260]

---

[260] A group of private individuals thought the Controlling Committee were not taking a strong enough line with the Germans over the food situation and noted the statement made in the States on 1 November about the shortages. Captain Fred Noyon and a single companion left Guernsey at night after 'a normal afternoon's fishing expedition'. They arrived in the UK on 12 November. Noyon was interrogated but did not add to what was already known in Britain. When Red Cross supplies reached Guernsey it was wrongly assumed it was due to Noyon's efforts. Actually, the Germans allowed Victor Carey to send an appeal on 7 November as they realised that 'the supply of food to the civil population has great bearing on our own ability to hold out'. (Cruickshank, pp.272-3)

Monday November 6th   S.W.
That awful wind has dropped, I am thankful to say. It is a mild warm day. Violet came to tea. She told me a man with a yellow brassard had been to them. He told them he hated the job and that he was fed up with the war and everything. He asked questions and wrote it down in a book but did not search anything. He asked how many cows they had, how much roots, etc. As he was going, one fowl came round the corner, so he asked how many fowls. Frank waited and, of course, the whole blooming five had to show themselves, so Frank had to say five!

There is an order in the paper tonight that the Germans can requisition *everything*, the authorities I mean, and that farmers cannot dig their roots.

Thursday November 9th   N.E.
A lovely day but cold. Molly and I fetched the bread. I left at half past one for Olive's and arrived at three. I had a beautiful walk in. Poor Olive has had a dreadful attack of 'the Germ', she has been in bed for two days. She is so bad the doctor has ordered her a pint of good milk every day and also brandy.

Old Hutch and Gay came to play M-J. They told me about Victor's letter. He wrote a splendid letter to the German authorities and received a perfectly beastly one in reply. They practically asked him if he knew there was a war on, that the people in the Channel Islands did not know what a war is. They wanted to know what he thought they had brought all the guns here for?[261] After that, last Sunday, they sent for Victor and John Leale and Sir Abraham Laine to Grange Lodge and told them they could send a message to Geneva. Victor asked if he could send the message himself. Oh no, they would send it. So those three made up a message, but whether it will be sent we don't know.[262]

Saturday November 11th   N.E.
Armistice Day
It was raining this morning, but it cleared up. James went to Town all day. Molly and I fetched the bread.

James came home with the news that the Germans have taken a great deal of our flour and now our bread will be finished by December 15th, instead of lasting over January. Also they have taken tons and tons of potatoes and now the ration is cut down to 5lbs per head a week. He has seen Victor's letter and the German reply. In the paper tonight, there is the following:

> Notice
> The German Authorities have allowed me to send a radio message to the International Red Cross at Geneva stating the present serious shortage of many essentials in the Island, and asking for immediate help and a visit from a Red Cross representative without delay.
> I am informed that the message was despatched last Monday morning.
>   Victor G. Carey
>   Bailiff[263]

---

[261] Victor Carey and John Leale wrote a letter to von Schmettow requesting a meeting about the civilian food situation and asking to be allowed to communicate with England. Von Schmettow refused to meet them, and said that direct communication with England was impossible. (Island Archives, BF 13-17)

[262] According to Cruickshank, Count von Schmettow made an error of judgement when he refused to let Victor have any communication with the protecting power. MOK West overruled him and ordered that Carey's message should be allowed through, as it was politically desirable to do so. (Cruickshank, p.273)

[263] *Guernsey Evening Press*, Saturday 11 November 1944.

Among other things the Germans told Victor was that the Guernsey people planted tomatoes to make money instead of planting essential foodstuffs. Victor was able to show them the truth of that statement. He sent them a copy of their order making us put two thirds of glass in tomatoes.

We are sending an appeal to the Red Cross at Geneva asking for a Red Cross representative to come and visit us. *Why* hasn't England already sent a Red Cross representative to visit us? France sent one to visit her people over here. There are American prisoners in Jersey so everyone is hoping America will do something about them. Oh, it is galling to think that England will do nothing.[264]

Wednesday November 22nd
An awful day, blowing hard, thick fog, clammy and muggy. The banisters are streaming wet and the walls are streaming too. The whole house is reeking with damp.

The notice about the Red Cross ship is in the paper tonight. I wonder when the food will actually come and how?

> *La Gazette Officielle*
> Notice
> Following up the negotiations brought about by the Occupying Power as regards the provisioning of the civilian population of the Channel Islands, a supply of medicaments, soap and parcels of foodstuffs has been promised as a beginning.[265]

Thursday November 23rd   S.W.
Much warmer but drizzling. Molly and I fetched the bread. I went off in good time to Town and had a lovely walk. I went by the Forest Road and did not speak to anybody. Also I met practically nobody but walked along empty roads. I arrived very early.

Gay came to play M-J. Of course we were all very excited about the Red Cross ship. Our bread is going to be cut down next week, we are all going to have only 3lbs a head per week.

Maud and I philosophically say how wonderful it is that we can get used to anything. Another wonderful thing is that whenever we are in the lowest depths of depression, something happens to cheer us up. That has happened all through the Occupation, always a hope and it really doesn't matter whether it is true or not. Olive and I are planning to go to London together. We don't expect to be able to go at once, but we don't mind that because we want to be here in the beginning of our freedom to see all that happens here. We intend to enjoy ourselves in London, but I will stipulate very firmly that I must be made a tremendous fuss of and be taken care of. Olive feels the same. Olive expects to have many bilious attacks. I don't think she will because even if she imagines she is going to eat a lot, she won't be able to do so. We have all been warned not to attempt to eat large meals, to avoid bulk and overloading at any cost. Oh, won't Olive and I enjoy ourselves. She is going to help me choose my coat and skirt. That is what I am longing for. I haven't had one since I married but now I have this beautiful sylph-like figure with a lovely waist, I must have one. Olive says grimly, 'What will you do when you

---

[264] Britain was approached for help on 19 September. Chiefs of Staff, Ministry of Economic Warfare and Home Office wanted to send food, but Churchill disagreed and endorsed the proposal that the garrison should be starved out. He wrote in a marginal note, 'Let 'em starve. No fighting, They can rot at their leisure.' He meant the Germans, but this had obvious implications for the Islanders. However, Churchill overcame his scruples about helping the garrison on 7 November. (Cruickshank, pp.264, 269)

[265] *Guernsey Evening Press*, Wednesday 22 November 1944. This notice shows how the Germans had won a bloodless victory in making the British provide food so the garrison would be able to prolong its existence. However, the Islanders who had gone hungry for two months longer than necessary were brought back from the brink of disaster. (Cruickshank, p.269)

put on weight again?' I say I won't put on weight again. I wonder? I mustn't, because in so many ways I am so much better. My feet for instance, I don't need my supports now, I don't have any rheumatism and if it wasn't for this cursed germ, I would be perfectly well. And also, of course, I have neuritis sometimes.

Thursday November 31st   S.W.
A rainy morning but no wind. It cleared up about eleven. I went off about eleven taking my lunch with me. On the way I met Bertie so I went in to see Peggy who was cooking. We exchanged gossip. Bertie says that rumour that Count von Schmettow has resigned is quite true. He sent a message to Berlin saying how terrible the situation was here, that the men were starving and what was he to do? The answer he received was 'Resign, and the Admiral will take your place.' Unfortunately the Admiral is a fierce Nazi.[266]

I had a lovely walk in and arrived in very good time. For the first time as I was walking in, I thought the soldiers looked ghastly ill and Micky said she thought the same coming from St Martins, other people have said they thought so before. Until today I have thought the soldiers were all looking very well indeed, but not today. There is no doubt they are suffering.

December 1944

Friday December 1st   S.W.
A doubtful day but it became fine later. I went to Town early. I met Goulu, also in very good spirits. He is sure they will crash before Christmas and we shall be free. He says the Admiral will give up and will hand over to a lower rank and it will go on until a private is in charge and he will give in!

Everybody I met was talking about the Red Cross ship and the parcels. The Germans have ordered that neither Victor or the Controlling Committee should have anything to do with it. A Committee has been formed of St John's people and the Committee is meeting this afternoon. The St John's Ambulance men are to fetch the parcels and no docker will touch them to prevent stealing. Le Riche has been told to make a list of their customers and of course all the other grocers. The ship is supposed to come in either today or tomorrow or on Wednesday. Rumour says one ship has arrived in Jersey.

Saturday December 2nd   S.W.
A drizzling rain and mist. Molly and I fetched the bread. It does look an awful loaf and it is so heavy. Rumour says the bread may give out any moment now.

Eleven soldiers and foreigners have died from poisoning, through eating bulbs in mistake for onions.

Maud told me yesterday that the Controlling Committee are very sorry for the farmers and would like to help them, but the Germans interfere so much they can do nothing.

How wonderful the moonlight is. I never realised what an asset it was, if one had no other light.

And so we go on from bad to worse. Will that Red Cross ship come?

---

[266] Admiral Friedrich Huffmeier had been von Schmettow's Chief of Staff since October 1944. He did take over from von Schmettow but not until February 1945. He was a fervent Nazi and was determined to hold on to the Channel Islands for as long as possible. (Bell, *Guernsey Occupied but Never Conquered*, p.345)

Tuesday December 5th   S.W.
A fine day. Molly and I fetched the bread. Mr Crousaz told me such a good story, it must have come from the Germans. Hitler and Goering were discussing the situation together and decided it was very bad, very bad indeed. In fact, so bad they decided they had better get away. First of all they said they must disguise themselves, so Hitler said he would disguise himself as a farmer and Goering said, 'I will disguise myself as your Frau.' Goering got himself up as a gigantic German Frau with frills and furbelows and Hitler shaved off his moustache and disguised himself as a farmer. They decided they must test their disguises and see if anybody recognised them. Arm in arm they went into a restaurant and ordered tankards of beer. The barmaid put the tankards down in front of them and said 'That is for you, Herr Hitler, and that is for you Field Marshal Goering!' They were dumbfounded and after they had drunk their beer, they went outside and looked at each other and Hitler said to Goering, 'But your disguise is perfect, Herman.'

'And so is yours, Adolf,' replied Goering. 'Let us go and ask her how she knew us'. Back they went, arm in arm to the restaurant, and they sat down and ordered more beer and when she brought the beer, they said, 'Tell us how you recognised us my dear?' And what do you think she said?

'I am Goebbels,' was her reply.

The bread is awful. The bakers say they can't stand the smell of the hot bread made with musty oats.

Wednesday December 6th   S.W.
A lovely day but very cold. I have heard a foul story. A soldier asked a farmer to barter some wheat for a rabbit. The soldier said he had a fine, fat rabbit. The farmer agreed and the soldier gave him the rabbit, cleaned and skinned and it was a fat rabbit. The farmer and his family ate it with much enjoyment. Two days later, the soldier came with a parcel which he left with the farmer. The farmer opened it and discovered it was the head and skin of his own beautiful cat which he had lost. In one way it served them right for having dealings with the Germans. The poor cat.

Friday December 8th   N.W.
Such a cold day. I went to pay the tax at Cambridge Park. The scene in the office might have been a picture in *Punch*. About five young men sitting and lounging and smoking like chimneys, gossiping. A very nice girl attended to me. They certainly have very little to do.

We had a great many hail showers in the morning. Of course we all talked about the ship. Some think a ship about the size of the *Courier* would be large enough to bring the cargo and others are of the opinion that a ship about the size of the *Queen Mary* would be necessary. There have been the most elaborate arrangements made to prevent pilfering. Men are going to guard the cargo night and day until it is safely delivered. The school children have been given a holiday to go and see the ship. Of course, they won't be able to go on the White Rock, but they will be able to gaze on her from afar. She is expected to arrive on Sunday. I think the whole of the Town population will be on the pier or the Weighbridge to see her arrive. Some say the grocers will deliver the parcels, others say we shall have to fetch them ourselves, that they will weigh 10lbs, that we shall have two parcels weighing 12lbs each, that it won't be parcels at all, that we will have to give up coupons for them, that it is all a gigantic bluff on the part of the

Germans and no ship is coming at all and has anybody heard it mentioned on the BBC, that we hope it won't be mentioned on the BBC because our people will be in a flat spin when they hear it, that they are in a flat spin about us anyway and it will relieve their minds when they hear relief is coming to us, that the Germans will take it all, that the Germans won't dare to touch a thing. Anyhow, if the boat never comes, she has helped to raise our spirits out of black and awful depression.[267]

I felt awfully weak in the Town and thought I would never get up to Olive's. After my dinner I was all right. I left at 4.30 and it was bright and dry and sunny. I arrived home about six. They have taken one of our cows today.

Tuesday December 12th   N.W.
Colder than ever. Molly and I fetched the bread.

This evening James came rushing in, he had just heard our Red Cross ship had been mentioned on the one o'clock news. That they are sending a relief ship to the Channel Islands loaded with medical supplies, soap and parcels like the ones sent to the prisoners of war and that she was a Swedish ship and would start in a few days. Mr Morrison had said so. What a relief.[268]

Thursday December 14th   S.W.
What a different temperature. It is much warmer. I left at 10.30am. I arrived at Olive's in good time.

Maud and Olive were very excited because they had heard the Red Cross ship was bringing thousands of letters. O … h. Rita told them that the Germans at the Catel were roaring with laughter at us over the Red Cross ship, they said it was all a bluff and the ship would not come at all.

This was announced in Parliament by Mr Morrison and broadcast on December 12th:

> The Home Secretary announced yesterday morning in the House of Commons that the German government have given a guarantee of safe conduct for a ship to take medical supplies, soap and food parcels such as are sent to prisoners of war, to the people of the Channel Islands. He stated that International Law demanded that the Occupying Power should feed the people in occupied territory. *In view of the report that has been received of conditions prevailing there*, the British Government has decided to send supplies to the Islands and the German Government has guaranteed safe conduct of the ship. The supplies would be similar to those sent to prisoners of war and a representative would go to the Islands to find out conditions of the hospitals there. Arrangements are not yet complete. It is expected the ship will leave in few days.

We think the sentence, 'In view of the report, etc.' is due to Noyon's report. A friend of Noyon has now told that Noyon told him not to expect any news of him for a long time. When he had

---

[267] *Guernsey Evening Press*, 8 December 1944: 'Red Cross ship sails for C.I. – The *Evening Press* is authorised by Victor G. Carey, Esq., the Bailiff of Guernsey, to announce that he has been informed by German authorities that an International Red Cross ship was sure to set sail from Portugal for the Channel Islands yesterday.'

[268] Mr H. Morrison, Secretary of State for Home Affairs and Home Security, said, 'His Majesty's Government have decided that it would be right to supplement the rations of the civil population by sending supplies … on the basis of those supplied to prisoners of war.' *Hansard Parliamentary Debates*, volume 406, pp.1055-6.

seen everybody and made his reports and given over all his papers, he would ask the BBC to put in one of their talks the words 'Yes George,' and those two words have just come over the wireless.[269] Noyon deserves the George Medal, he risked his life by drowning or being shot. He said he was a widower and had no one belonging to him and so he was the best man to go.[270]

The soldiers are falling about through weakness, they do look bad now. I found one in the kitchen yesterday calling out 'Chef, Chef'. He wanted tomatoes. They seem to think tomatoes grow all year round.

Saturday December 16th   S.W.

A beautiful day and really warm. As I walked along to fetch the bread I sang a song of thankfulness that my hands and ankles were not aching with the cold. I certainly know the meaning of that sentence 'My bones are suffering from the bitter aching of the cold.' How our lives are completely absorbed by primitive things, warmth, food and light, cut off as we are from the rest of the world.

The Controlling Committee have practically told the men not to work. It is awfully stupid of them, now the men don't come to work until nearly 10 o'clock and they leave early. How the women are managing to live I simply don't know. They are giving most of their food to the men and children, they are doing all their work, standing in queues, bellowing the fires, chopping wood, gathering sticks and the men take the women's food quite complacently. Talk about guts, the men are puling infants compared to the women. Of course there are exceptions, but very few.

Monday December 18th   S.W.

A lovely day and so mild. Violet came to tea and brought the news that the gas will be cut off on Thursday December 21st at 9am. It does look like devilish cleverness to have timed to cut the gas off on the shortest day. What *are* people going to do?

Three more planes came in last night and one more later. They left again and were chased back and I don't know if they have gone yet.

No news of the Red Cross ship, I am longing for the letters yet I am sick with apprehension at what I shall hear. No news from Baba and Boy since February. I felt so depressed yesterday, I didn't know what to do.

Tuesday December 19th

A beautiful day. A spring day. Molly and I fetched the bread. James went to a meeting of the Dairy Committee and came back with the joyful news that they have found some more oil and we shall have electric light for six weeks longer. James has managed to get some paraffin, bartered for eggs. My hands are smelling of it at the moment, I never thought I should ever be pleased to find my hands smelling of paraffin but I am!

---

[269] Actual words were 'Personal message to George. The answer is yes.' Broadcast in Allied Expeditionary Forces Programme at one minute past 8am on 9 December. (Cruickshank, p.273)

[270] Cruickshank points out that the decision to send the Red Cross ship had been made before Noyon reached England, on 7 November 1944. See entry for 11 November 1944. The report Mr Morrison mentioned is probably information received through secret sources, namely a report from von Schmettow to MOK West recording that there would be nothing left for the civilian population after January 1945. (Cruickshank pp.269-70)

Wednesday December 27th   N.E.
Such a lovely day, a thick sparkling white frost, not a breath of wind and so cold.

A rumour has come that the Red Cross ship came last night. I rang up Olive and she said she did not think that was true, but she would let me know. At half past twelve, Maud Carey rang up to say someone had just rushed in to tell them the Red Cross ship was sighted and would be in in an hour. At twenty to one, Mrs Renault was rung up by Eunice Renault at Torteval in great excitement to tell her the ship was passing and they could see the red crosses on her, those Torteval people have eyes like hawks. Mrs Renault, James and all the men have rushed to the cliffs to see her. Maud Drake rang me up and said the Town was in a ferment of wild excitement, everybody rushing down to the seafront. I just sat at home and wept copiously. I can't think why I have started this awful habit of sobbing over every bit of good news. It is too idiotic for words. When we had that awful letter telling us we were to be evacuated, I was filled with horror and fury but did not cry. I can't understand it.

James came back, they could not see the ship because a thick mist had come down. He went again and came back at twenty to two and said they had seen her, plainly passing the Fond du Val, so she has *really* come.

Red Cross ship, HMS Vega, *30 December 1944.*

Thursday December 28th   N.E.
I went off nice and early and I went straight to Doris. I found her very well and cheerful. I arrived at the Bungalow about 12.30. Olive had seen the ship, she is lying at the London berth, she has three red crosses on her and 'International' written in large characters on her.

There is a meeting between the representatives and the Germans. The Bailiff of Jersey has been brought over here like a prisoner, they call him the guest of the Germans! He and Victor and Sir Abraham Laine are at the conference. When the ship arrived last night, there were crowds to meet her and the cheering could be heard in Kings Road. Some say it could be heard in St Sampsons! (What *will* it be like when our own first boat comes in?)

Friday December 29th
A damp day and not so cold. I went off to Town early. Everybody was one big beam. Our only topic was the ship. I went down to look at her. My feelings are indescribable. I saw the train puffing out with New Zealand parcels and two German guards sitting on the parcels and two St John's men with them. We all looked at each other in the crowd and laughed and laughed and laughed and we said, as we looked at the German guards, 'Chee! chee! chee! You won't have any of that food you are guarding!'

I walked up the Bordage with Leonie Trouteaud, the head of the Red Cross bureau. She was at the meeting yesterday and said she wouldn't have missed it for anything. There were all the High Command of the Germans there, all dressed up in their best uniforms with their belts polished and their revolvers all loaded and the representative completely unarmed. Then the row began. The Germans could be heard shouting from the Royal Court, all over Smith Street and St James Street. Didn't the representative tell them off! He told them, 'You Germans never will co-operate with the Red Cross properly.' They wanted to handle everything and make an inventory. He told them they could not touch a parcel, everything must be done by the St John's people and the Red Cross people here. They wanted to take twenty-five per cent of the parcels. He said, 'You are belligerents and the parcels are for the civilians.' He told them our conditions were the worst he had seen. He analysed our bread and said it was unfit for human consumption. The first thing he did yesterday was to wireless for 500 ton of flour. He said we were not to have any more of those awful oats. They had taken 500 ton of our beautiful wheat for themselves and replaced it with 500 ton of oats that were so musty they would not feed them to their horses! He told them the ship was 'international' and if they would not give in he would go straight back with the ship and would not leave a parcel, and he said to them, 'And you know what that would mean to you.' He spoke fluent German and shook his fist and they gave in like beaten schoolboys. The scorn he poured upon them, Leonie said, was wonderful. He is a Colonel Iselin, a Swiss Colonel. This conference took place yesterday.

The Germans said they must put armed guards on the train to guard the parcels. The rep said, 'Certainly, but there must be St John's men on the train too, and the Germans can guard them as far as the Piette but they cannot go into the Hall.' The Germans said they must put their police to guard from Well Road to the Piette in case the civilians tried to rush the train. 'Certainly,' said the rep, 'but the civilian police must be there too.'

How I wish I had been there. It is really like a comic opera. The soldiers on the train guarding the parcels from the cheering civilians and the St John's men guarding the parcels from the armed guards. The Germans hadn't a leg to stand on. They were sick.

I walked home. I did not have a lift. As I was walking along that silent and empty road, I thought of the divine wonder of that Red Cross ship. What a manifestation of the Almighty Power of the living God and his Son. In this Island are ten to twelve thousand trained German soldiers fully armed with revolvers, rifles, machine guns, many of them trained over the harbour. The Germans had to sweep away their mines and send out an E-boat to escort that unarmed

Smith Street.

ship in. The Germans are in absolute power here, completely isolated. What was there to prevent them murdering all the personnel of that ship, taking all the parcels and painting the ship another colour and telling their own story to the world. They have committed so many hideous and brutal crimes in this war that one more would not make much difference to the sum total. They fire on the Red Cross hospital ships, they used their own to bring guns and ammunition here and their Red Cross planes to bring high-up officers here. What *was there* to prevent them doing what they liked? And yet they *dared* not and that unarmed representative could talk to them as he liked and they *dared* not answer him and they had to meekly obey his orders. It was the most marvellous revelation of the Almighty Power of the Living God, but if his dear son had never come and lived and died for us on this earth, that Red Cross ship would never have come to bring us those parcels and in a very short time we would all have starved to death.

The ship has only just come in time; in about a fortnight, people would have been falling about the streets and unable to get up through the weakness. They are all wonderful because they never grumble, the people who have already died of starvation were always cheery, always laughed and said, 'Goodbye, another day nearer victory,' and 'It won't be long now.' They tried to walk up to the last.

The sufferings of the Townspeople now are too awful. No gas, no fires and in this bitter cold weather. From Mount Row and Ville au Roi they have to go right down to Trinity Square to their nearest comunual kitchen, they fetch their dinners and that is the only hot meal they have in the day and it is not hot by the time they get it home. Old people over eighty have to walk down and back again or they won't have anything at all. The distress is terrible. It is all too awful to think of.

Sunday December 31st   N.E.
I am so excited, I could hardly sleep all night. This is truly a red letter day. It is a beautiful sunny day, but bitterly cold, nobody minds. Violet fetched me at a quarter to two and we set off together. I met a dear little girl, wheeling home her parcel in her own little green wheelbarrow. We met women hugging their parcels, men on bicycles with five or six: 60 lbs! Vans galore. We arrived at Le Riche and there was no queue at all. I went straight in. They had letters up all over the shop. I went straight to 'C'. There was one man in front of me, old Crousaz was there. I deftly slipped in front of him when he wasn't looking. I said, 'Isn't it lovely having the parcels?' And he said, 'Yes, but we have had to come a long way for them!' He came in a van. I signed for mine and a kind man carried them out for me to my push cart. He had a van outside which he was filling full of parcels. Violet got hers and we started for home. Fair stood the wind for Forest, we met such cheery people who all called out to us, and the vans and the bicycles and the push carts and the soap boxes all carrying parcels. 'Oh frabjous day, calloo callay I chortle in my joy!' How sourly and enviously the German soldiers looked at us and at our parcels.

And 1944 has come to an end and we are still in captivity. But what a difference the arrival of that ship has made to our morale. No longer do we feel utterly desolate and deserted; apart from the horror of starvation, we felt that no one cared a scrap about us. This year has been very very grim, but our hopes are high for 1945. And that is one of the most striking examples of God's love for us. Every time we were more depressed, something happened, a rumour, whether it was false or true, would come and lift us out of depression. Or we would hear a piece of good news. We were always being carried along like that. And yet *everybody* felt on no account must they show their feelings.

Everybody laughed and was as bright as anything in Town or when they were together. Nobody grumbled, everybody made the best of our really appalling conditions. The universal motto has been right through the Occupation, 'We will show the Germans we can take it.'

The Diaries of Violet Carey, 1945

Book X

January 1945

Thursday January 4th   N.E.
A fine day but with such a bitter wind. I had the coldest and most disagreeable walk I have had for years!

Olive and Maud were in very good spirits. They have heard on very good authority that another ship is coming with flour and yeast and clothing for every one of us, a complete new outfit from top to toe. It is too wonderful.

Neither Victor nor the Bailiff of Jersey were able to say one word to the Representative, they were not allowed to dine on the ship and the Jersey Bailiff was taken back in another ship, not the *Vega*. Dr Symons was allowed to send a written report of medical needs and the two Bailiffs were allowed to write a list of requirements.

Friday January 5th   N.E.
Another bitterly cold day. I went to Town early. We had our last fat ration and my ration from Le Riche for two people for a fortnight cost 1s. 7d. and was oat flour and macaroni!

I met very few people to speak to, it was so cold in Town everybody was hurrying away. After lunch we were playing M-J and someone came to the door. Olive answered and we heard her say, 'How perfectly awful.' She came in and told us she had been cut off electric light for three weeks. She was completely shattered and worrying about Mrs Fisher. I suggested Mrs Brown Clarke should take her. Olive went to see her, they would willingly have taken her, but they were cut off themselves!

Saturday January 6th   N.E.
Pouring with rain and bitterly cold. I rang up Olive and she told me her mother was going to a nursing home that has just been opened this afternoon for three weeks. Poor Olive, it is dreadful for her. We were allowed 15 units in the six weeks and have used 12, only two people using the light and we go to bed so early. I do feel tired today and my eyes ache dreadfully.

At the bread depot they told me that men were bartering their parcels for drink and one person had taken 400 marks (£42 4s. 8d.) for their parcel. If only they could really prove it, those people would never be given a parcel again.

Monday January 8th   N.E.
Another bitterly cold day with a foul wind. I came down about 8.30 to find the cupboard and cake tin wide open in the kitchen. I keep all my bandages, etc. there and I immediately thought James had had an awful accident. Presently he came in and I asked him.

'No,' he hadn't opened the cupboard. I looked for his bread, gone! I looked for the rations, gone! We looked at each other and said simultaneously, 'Somebody has been and taken everything!' They must have come in while James was milking. They also took a dish of bean paste. I am very sad losing the dish, so that's that.

Thursday January 11th   N.E.
Another bitter day. I went to Town.

It is such a relief to Olive to have her mother warm in a nursing home. Mrs Fisher is very happy and comfortable and being well fed, much better food than Olive can give her. Rita is being tiresome, she thinks it is awful to have sent Mrs Fisher away, as if she had been sent to the workhouse. She had to acknowledge Mrs Fisher was much warmer there than she would be at home. Olive goes to see her every day.

Friday January 12th   N.E.
Same old bitter wind. It was horrible in Town. It is heartbreaking to see all the white pinched faces and poor naked legs. This awful weather makes it worse for everybody. Our own miseries are so intense the war seems to have receded from us. No planes come over and we hear no bombardment and very little news. It must be *too awful* for our poor soldiers at the different fronts.

Sunday January 14th   N.E.
Same old wind, same old cold only more so. Neither of us are going to church. I spent all yesterday afternoon attending to fires. I shall do the same today. This morning I searched my drawers for my parcel things which I had hidden, as usual, too effectively! Yesterday I had a gorgeous tea with jam. I was just like a happy child, I had jam all over my face, my hands and the table! I did enjoy myself.

Thursday January 18th   S.W.
First of all it was raining but it cleared up and I had a lovely walk with the wind behind me.

The Germans are offering 20 marks, £2 2s. 8½d. for a cat and 100 marks, £10 13s. 8d. for a cat to eat. They are savage with starvation now.

Poor Olive fainted five times yesterday. She went to early service at St Andrew's. Mrs McCartney thought she had had a stroke, she was brought home in the ambulance and was better in the afternoon, she is looking awfully bad I think. Of course it might be reaction from the long strain of looking after her mother. Mrs Fisher is very happy and they like her very much and are willing to keep her indefinitely, they charge 3½ guineas a week. Mrs Fisher is completely senile now. Rita is terribly disappointing and keeps repeating she would not send her mother away, although she has to admit that Mrs Fisher is much better there and much warmer. She was dreadfully upset because Mrs Fisher didn't know her.

Friday January 19th   N.W.
The wind has gone to the N.W. and it is blowing hard.

James rang me up just after nine. He said, 'I have bad news for you, your room has been ransacked in the night. Everything is upside down and your parcel has been taken.' I just felt like stone. I did not *dare* to think. My parcel was the least thing. I thought of my jewellery and *my diaries*!

I went to Town feeling stunned and of course did everything wrong. I forgot the banks shut at 12, so could not change my cheque and had to borrow from Olive. I came on home. Mrs Renault had stayed for the afternoon. The thief or thieves had opened every drawer in my room and left them all open about three inches. They had taken my tins of butter, jam and salmon. They hadn't found the tea, raisins or prunes or sugar. They had also taken three cakes of golden glory soap. They hadn't turned anything out onto the floor, the floor was strewn with matches, their own, there were two boxes of mine and two candles and they did not touch them. They had not touched anything else, they were evidently after my parcel.

What I think is uncanny is, why my room only? They did not open Jim's room door or go past James'. The bread tin was on the table and they did not touch it. I had a precious bottle of camp coffee on my dressing table and they did not touch that. They must have had heaps of time and the drawers were not turned out or roughly handled. They smashed the window by the sink and came in that way. They took all James' precious sugar beet syrup and evidently drank one whole pound because the jar was on the sink and a clothes brush was in the sink and two packets of dried carrots. We don't know if it was one man or two, Germans or civilians.

Saturday January 20th
Violet came to see me and we tidied up and Peggy came to find out how I was, darling Peggy. She told us a pitiful story about two old ladies in the Town who were discovered tearing up their own linoleum with their fingers, trying to make a little fire. They were sitting on the floor and there was no furniture in the room at all as they had burnt it all. They had nothing else to burn. Dr Rose had discovered them and had reported the case. Violet knew of another case where an old lady had a chair and a table left to burn and nothing else. Others are burning their banisters and the floors of their attics and the weather still is abnormally cold.

Sunday January 21st   N.W.
A fine day. I went to church in the morning.
   And now I am going to tell the story of the pig:
   We brought him from Mr Ware and he was such a nice friendly pig. When he was only five months old James decided to kill him, before he was stolen. He asked for a permit and the Controlling Committee took over a week to send the permit and every morning we thought the pig was gone. On Tuesday the permit came, on Wednesday the pig was killed and on Thursday Mr Ware took him away at 4pm and that night thieves came in but they did not go into the larder where all the bits and pieces and half pig's head was left. On Friday night I shut the old grey cat in the larder and I found pig's head on the floor and the old grey cat with a piece in her mouth. On Saturday morning, Mrs Renault shut little Tommy, the black and white cat, up in the larder and he had a nice chop. The old grey cat must have told Molly where

the rest of the pig was because just before I went to church, Molly came running out of the house with a nice chop in her mouth and I met the old grey cat on the stairs with another in her mouth, all the doors having been left open. I rescued the rest and put them in Jim's room. (to be continued).

Monday January 22nd   N.W.
Quite a fall of snow, ice everywhere and bitterly cold. James had to go for Chief Pleas.

The story of the pig continued:

Mrs Renault fetched the remains of the pig about 11am and she and I were at the larder door, she having put the basin down on the table, she had the pig's ear in her hand and was just going to hold it up to show the ravages when we heard a sharp knock, the kitchen door opened and there was an enormous German officer standing there. I went quickly to him and stood on the lower step, so he had to look down on me and could not pass until I removed myself. I had to give Mrs Renault time to hide the pig in the larder. He asked for the telephone. I became a dear deaf old soul. I said, 'Pardon, je ne comprends pas.'

'Telephone madam, telephone madam,' he said. I bent nearer to him and said, 'Pardon! pardon!' and then I heard the larder door shut. He shouted 'Telephone!'

Ah,' I said, all smiles, 'telephone, oui, oui, regardez voila,' and stepped aside and pointed where it was and he swaggered down to it. Mrs Renault and I returned to the kitchen, she peeling potatoes, I cutting up vegetables. We were close together, she whispered, 'He is talking beautiful French.' I whispered, 'Translate.' She, 'He is talking to a girl, he is saying, "You are nice, you are kind." He is asking for her father, he is asking him to get him something and he will fetch it this afternoon between two and four and he is going to tea with them on Sunday at four.' He came out frightfully pleased with himself and paid and went off.

Violet came in the afternoon and I told her all about it and I am thankful all that is left of that pig is in the saucepan!

Friday January 26th   S.W.
Mrs Fisher has quite gone back to her girlhood and thinks she is in Durham and Olive is her mother and is quite happy. Rita keeps repeating she would never have sent her mother away. This is a striking example of the difference in environment and way of living of the classes. In our class we have our own bedrooms and we sleep alone. In their class, their mother would not sleep alone and would never be alone and would get up early and be down sitting by the kitchen fire and peeling potatoes and using their hands all day long. They would not be allowed to stay in bed as long as they could be useful.

The treatment of the prisoners, civilian and German, is absolutely fiendish. They are given one small meal a day of watery soup and they are literally dying in their cells. The German soldiers are dying anyway. The other day a family heard a knock at the door. They answered it and found a shivering German soldier there who asked if he could come in and warm himself at their fire. He looked awful and so ill. They took him to the fire and presently he said, 'Will you ring up the German hospital and ask them to fetch a very sick German from your house?' They went to the phone and gave the message, came back and found the soldier dead! There is a story that the General has once more reported to Berlin the pitiable condition of the soldiers here and said they are dying of starvation and cold and the answer he received from Berlin was 'Let them die'.

Saturday January 27th   S.W.
The one good thing we have achieved in this Occupation is that lovely camaraderie that exists between us all. I do hope we won't lose it. We are all suffering alike and everybody helps each other. When I walk into Town and I meet other people with push carts, we mutually stop and ask each other pathetic questions about each other's wheels. They always notice my wobbly back wheel and the other with the thin tyre. We none of us know each other by sight but it doesn't matter.

February 1945

Thursday February 1st   S.W.
A beautiful day, such a soft wind and sunny. I decided I would not go until after lunch. I was washing up and three soldiers appeared and told us they had come to search the house for a 'radio'. They were a sergeant and two corporals. They made one corporal go out with James to search the stables and the sergeant and the other came with me. The sergeant was very thorough, the corporal was much more casual. They searched the kitchen thoroughly and the other two downstairs rooms. In the larder they found the pig! O … h, the to do they made over that. The sergeant spoke very little English. They came upstairs and searched my room, looking particularly in small drawers. I asked, 'Why?' and they said they were looking for crystal sets and again I asked, 'Why?' and they said Grange Lodge had had a letter telling them *all* farmers had crystal sets! In the end I did not believe him, they were looking for food and stores. They found two packets of matches and said they hadn't a match, so I gave them one packet between the three of them. They spotted Michelle's photograph and Boy's. The darling Baba, they said, 'Pretty girl! pretty girl!' I worked Baba's photograph for all I was worth, I kept showing them new ones and at last got them out of my room. In Baba's room they found my tins, a lot of chat over that. In Baba's drawer which they opened was her Viennese dress, that was a grand discovery, they talked and talked about that! Baba's photograph in the dining room delighted them. They discovered eggs in the larder, more chat. But I managed to prevent them going up into Hedley's room where all the seed potatoes were. I was very proud of that. I jollied them all the time. They wanted the keys for two boxes and James' identity card. He went to fetch them and was gone ages, to keep them quiet I asked questions about their uniforms, wives and children, when would the war finish. We were all in the conservatory and they discovered James' diesel oil. O … h, more trouble there. At last James came back, they had forgotten all about the keys and chatted about the oil! James said he had bartered two cock birds for it. I had to fetch my dictionary to find out the German for cock bird. I was in a fever to know how James had got on with his corporal. James said he never searched the stables much, but he was a farmer and he and James discussed farming in all its aspects in Germany and Guernsey and agreed most amicably on the subject. At last they went. Ten minutes after, the sergeant came back and talked more about the oil and eggs and so we knew what he wanted. James gave him three eggs and he accepted them! We hope we shall be left alone now. If they don't break in again three eggs and four boxes of matches was cheap. James doesn't think they will. I feel absolutely exhausted.

Saturday February 10th   N.W.
Very cold but dry. James came back and said they are still having a meeting about the bread with the Red Cross representative and they are all going at it hammer and tongs. I don't think

the Germans will give in. That Admiral has said he hoped to see us all on our hands and knees through starvation and, as he is the head of civil administration, he is able to do what he likes with us.[271]

This notice was in the paper tonight:

> Our Flour – Important notice to the people of Guernsey
> To my deep regret I have to inform you that the supply of flour will be exhausted after next Tuesday's bread issue but I have received a letter from Colonel Iselin, the International Red Cross Representative in Lisbon, who visited us six weeks ago, in which he states that on her next trip, the *Vega* will bring flour. This has been confirmed by Mr Callias, the International Red Cross Representative now in the Island. The *Vega* is expected back about the 5th March. The position has been considered in all its aspects and in order to alleviate suffering as far as possible, arrangements are being made for the distribution of Red Cross parcels on the 15th and on the 1st March. We hope to issue increased rations as far as our resources allow.
>
> Victor G. Carey, Bailiff

Poor poor Victor. How distressed he must have been when he composed that notice. Of course this confirms my dismal conviction that England is completely callous about the sufferings of her own people. Six weeks ago, our desperate S.O.S. was sent for flour by Colonel Iselin and he himself was able to tell about our situation, and yet no flour has come. Why should we expect England to care about us, we are just her own people? She is too busy helping Greece! I don't dare to think of the suffering of so many people, it is *too awful*.

Sunday February 11th   S.W.

What an awful day. We take everything up at night now, or hide the things and either Mrs Mauger wails or James bellows that the potatoes have disappeared, that someone has stolen them. It is only me who has hidden them and am suffering from temporary loss of memory and I cannot think where I have hidden them!

Ash Wednesday February 14th

In the morning I went to fetch salt. When I came back there was a German examining the bull books. All day long they have been asking questions. The climax came. James was dressing to go to church and three men came to take a heifer for the German Forces. Poor James had to come down without a collar and go with them, they wouldn't let him choose the animal or have any say in the matter whatever. James came in swearing about it, that they had taken his best heifer. I have never seen him so upset and depressed all through the Occupation.

He went to church. I stayed at home, but I am thankful to say no more Germans came.

Saturday February 24th   N.E.

A lovely day. James went to Town. He came back with the dire news that the electric light goes off tomorrow night. Poor Gay is in despair, we all are except that we believe that nothing is so bad as we think it is going to be and that we can get used to anything and *I* always add now, 'It won't be long'! But it is so grim.

---

[271] The Admiral is Vizeadmiral Friedrich Huffmeier. He was appointed as Chief of Staff to von Schmettow in December 1944 and relentlessly campaigned to oust von Schmettow. Huffmeier took over as Commander in Chief in February 1945. (Cruickshank, p.283)

The cows were milked again last night, always the best cow. We think it is the German inspector who is always coming to watch the cows being milked and comes and milks her. They say the Germans are searching the houses for sheets to make shirts for the soldiers.

Monday February 26th
Another thick fog and cold drizzle. It is awful without electric light. I carried a lantern everywhere, we used one of Violet's little paraffin lamps. It is miserable.

Wednesday February 28th
A lovely day, no fog and the birds are all singing and the gulls are screaming, 'Hark! Come ye back oh Violet Mary, come ye back to dear old Sark!' and that is just what I am *aching* to do, to go to Sark and stay with Aggie and Reggie instead of living in this nightmare life. Bertie was saying that we have gone back to our grandparents' period. But I said, 'Nonsense, our grandparents had coal, heaps of food and heaps of servants.' Bertie agreed. He said when he was a boy they kept four servants and so did we and how little they were paid, £10 a year probably and they slept in and did everything. Now I pay Mrs Renault £52 a year, she comes at 9 and leaves at 12 on Sundays, Mondays, Thursdays and Fridays and comes at 9 and leaves at 12 and returns at 2 and leaves at 5 on Tuesdays and Wednesdays and does not come at all on Saturdays.

I have to carry up 12 gallons of water twice a day to the bathroom from the little well in front of the house.

The officers say one man dies a week of starvation and that is nothing. Other people think the average is seven per week. There have been a hundred soldiers' funerals in the Jerbourg cemetery this year.

It is devastating to have to hide all our food. I hid my tin of jam so successfully I *could not* find it. At last, when completely exhausted, I found it in my waste paper basket.

March 1945

Saturday March 3rd   N.E.
I went to see Katty this afternoon. We were talking about starving people and how difficult to find them! Katty said Amy le Tissier is always saying how hungry she is, so Ilsa who is always so generous spread butter on two slices of her precious bread and gave it to Amy and told her she must eat them at once and not take them home to her boy. A week later Ilsa opened a drawer and found a mouldy slice of bread, so she called Amy and asked her about it. Amy said she was called away when she was eating the slices and must have forgotten this slice. Ilsa gasped and so did I when Katty told me! Ilsa said, 'I would have finished that slice as soon as I could,' and felt very sad she had sacrificed her precious bread in vain. That class are all alike. To them everything is just food.

Monday March 5th   N.E.
Another calm fine cold day. No news of the *Vega* yet. A plane left last night and the General is supposed to have gone on it to Berlin to interview Hitler about giving up here, that is the rumour in the country, but I fear the truth is the Admiral had the General's dismissal in his pocket for a long time and was ordered to give it to the General when the time was ripe

and apparently it is ripe now because the notice has been put in the soldiers' paper that the Admiral is now in Supreme Command. I am sure it is to have a severer discipline over the soldiers.[272]

At 6pm young Raymond Tostevin came down to tell us the *Vega* had been sighted. She passed our cliff at 8.30pm. Crowds of people were on our Big Glie watching her pass. She looked lovely on the calm sea. We think we shall have bread, a 2lb loaf on Thursday. Last week people had 4lbs of root vegetables and 5lbs of potatoes a head and 2½ of macaroni and flour and that was *all*! And ¼ pint of separated milk. It is too awful.

Thursday March 8th   N.E.
A perfectly lovely day. I gave Bill the bag and told him to call in for the bread on his way here. James said it was useless because the bread would not be given out until the afternoon. However, I persevered and Bill went off with the bag yesterday. Just after breakfast I heard everybody shouting so I rushed down to the kitchen and there were James, Mrs Renault, Bill and Cyril gazing at five loaves of bread which were spread out on the kitchen table. Such loaves as none of us have ever seen in Guernsey in our lives. They were enormous and so light and white. Never have we had such pure flour in Guernsey, first grade Canadian flour. We have always had blended flour. Two loaves for us, two for the Renaults and one for old Madame Baleine. I stood there silently with the tears streaming down my face and they were all silent too except Bill who said 'Cooo' every now and then. It was a real miracle to see that bread. 'Give us this day our daily bread.' That prayer certainly takes on a new meaning for us.

I had some of our homemade heavy bread made with washing soda for baking flour and vinegar and took it with me as well as the lovely bread. As I walked along the air was full of cheerful happy sounds and I discovered that every Guernseyman I met was whistling his loudest and the birds seemed to be doing the same. Several men stopped to show me their bread.

I arrived in very good time. Gay came to play M-J and of course we all talked about the bread. At tea, to my utter amazement, Olive and Maud asked me to exchange my heavy brown bread for their perfect bread! Both of them have been so well all through the Occupation and now they are fearful they won't be while *I* expect to be cured at long last of 'occupational'!

Monday March 12th   N.E.
Mildred Brock has been examined by the visiting German doctor and he told her she was the worst case of malnutrition he had seen. Mildred is awfully proud of herself.

I met Mrs Douglas on Friday who openly blew her nose on a piece of packing paper and we all take that as a matter of course. It is amazing how we have got used to everything. I could not bear to see all the poor folk with no stockings in the winter and their purple legs, it was *dreadful*. They don't look so bad now.

I walked down the stairs in the dark this evening, turned giddy, missed the last step, fell heavily to the ground and twisted my left foot under me and crawled up again in agony. I could not put my foot to the ground and the pain was awful all night.

---

[272] According to Cruickshank (*The German Occupation*, p. 283), that is exactly what did happen. Admiral Huffmeier took over from von Schmettow on 28 February 1945.

Tuesday March 13th   N.E.

A white frost again and very cold. I am going to stay in bed for four days and have fomentations. It is terribly swollen, I am so afraid I have broken it. Olive came in the afternoon. She was sweet and wants me to go in there and I am going on Monday!

Monday March 19th   N.E.

Another lovely day. I got up. My foot is painful, Miss Ingrouille arrived at a quarter to three with the van and Mrs Hazell came to say goodbye and Mrs Renault came with me and me and baskets of potatoes and food and a can of milk and a few clothes set off. I did enjoy the drive. Olive received me and she had my room so sweet. Maud was out. Olive and I had tea together. We had a lovely evening together.

Tuesday March 20th   N.E.

Another lovely day. I rang up Mr le Page the bone setter and he came out at 12.30. He did hurt but did it good at once. He said it was not broken but very badly bruised and the muscles badly wrenched.

   I had 'Occupation joy' for tea, that tinned cafe au lait made into caramel. It is too delicious for words. Olive said she could eat a whole tin at a sitting! I ate as much as I dared.

Friday March 23rd   S.E.

Another beautiful day, no sign of rain. My legs are still paining me a great deal. Maud is very shocked at the way Olive and I manage our own food supplies. Poor Olive has nothing to put on her bread today having eaten up her butter, etc. Maud is most careful and eats bread and scrape all the time. Olive and I have orgies and then cheerfully go without. Yesterday I saw Maud settle herself on the veranda and I tiptoed into the kitchen, cut myself two slices of bread, covered them thickly with Occupation joy and proceeded to enjoy myself! Maud woke up and decided to get her tea early and caught me nicely! Olive had taken up a small slice of bread and her tin and a spoon and was blissfully having a private orgy on her own on her bed and Maud came in! Olive managed to secrete the tin and spoon and Maud only saw the bread but she said her piece all the same, just like a blinking governess. At supper she pointed out to me that I had eaten a whole tin of butter and a whole tin of cafe au lait, and at that rate how long did I think my parcel was going to last me, etc., etc! I retorted that it was *my* parcel and that was all I could say.

Saturday March 24th   S.E.

A lovely morning. Olive came in while I was having breakfast. I was blissfully starting my second tin of Occupation joy and generously gave Olive a spoonful. We both felt like schoolgirls and agreed that Maud was too governessy for words and equally too silly not to get the enjoyment we did out of her food!

   Le Page came and did my foot and it is so painful, that awful bruise. Olive went to fetch the precious parcels. She had a New Zealand one and I had a new Canadian one and Maud had one too. We had corned beef and liver sausage and jam and Quaker oats and apple sauce, biscuits, chocolate and a small tin of cheese, raspberry jam, nestle milk, coffee, sugar, vitamin B and salt and half a pound of butter.

Wednesday March 28th   S.E.
A thick fog all day. The news is wonderful. Fifty miles into Germany and Russia and Allies closing in on every side. When will it end? Probably suddenly and soon.

I consider there are two Island disasters, the Admiral being in command and my foot! The former has come back from Alderney very glum and depressed. We all speculate on what *will* happen here when there is an Armistice, he says he *won't* give in. I think all the soldiers will flutter the white flags they have already made. What he ought to do is to hand over command to Victor, a proud day for Victor. We shall all go mad with impatience for news and contact with England. Oh dear, oh dear, I feel sick with impatience now.

April 1945

Friday April 13th
A beautiful day and so warm.

Maud and Olive have been to Town and have come back with more tragic and horrible news. A poor old couple living in the Hubits lanes have been murdered for their Red Cross parcel. Poor poor little Guernsey.

Monday April 16th   S.E.
Another boiling hot day. We are having a heat wave.

Certainly things are gradually worse and worse for us and this awful drought aggravated everything. Our hunger is getting more and more grim. All the roots have come to an end. Involuntarily, we can't help thinking more and more about food and how to ration ourselves. We have been advised to divide our food so as to have four small meals a day, meals which are getting smaller and smaller. Our precious parcels can only provide snacks now because of the grim uncertainty of the arrival of the next parcel and if there will be enough to go round. Certainly, 'hope deferred maketh the heart sick.' We try to kid ourselves that this excessive heat makes us less hungry, but it doesn't really and yet everybody is so cheerful, people are wonderful and the Germans remark on it.

Tuesday April 24th   S.E.
No rain. Fine day, bitter wind.

Violet came to see me and brought me some things. She told me poor Mr Gorvel had had a cow stolen out of the field, poor man, he was crying bitterly about it. Poor Frank had a heifer stolen out of the stable, she was just about to calve. Things get worse and worse.

Rita told me that people say it has been said on the wireless that 25,000 men have volunteered to come and free us. I can't bear to think of any of them losing their lives, but if they *are* coming, they ought to come now while the soldiers are falling down with weakness; later on they will be much stronger because they have planted the greenhouses with all kinds of food for themselves and they will have any amount later on. We are all getting weaker and weaker and I wish I could get accustomed to being hungry, I can't.

Wednesday April 25th
Another fine day but the weather looks on the change. Maud and Olive went up to play bridge with Nelly. Last week Nelly was wakened by a noise and called Mr Welch. Of course he said it was nothing. Again she heard it and called out to him and he went to the window and found two Germans trying to get in. He shouted every name he could think of at

them and Nelly leant out of her window beating a gong violently. In one minute the din in the neighbourhood was terrific: police whistles, gongs and bells and screams. The terrified Germans ran away. All the people there had agreed to make as much noise as possible simultaneously and they did. The next night the Germans came again and again the Welches shouted at them and again everybody started the din and again the Germans ran away. It is such a good idea.

Thursday April 26th   S.E.
Micky Kinnersly told Olive a German had come to their house asking for food, and when he opened his pocket and showed her it was full of live wriggling worms and dead young birds, and he told her he was going to eat them. The soldiers are eating grass. How hungry we *all* are. It is an awful sensation and it goes on and on. Olive and I both say we shall think of food more than anything for the rest of our days!

Friday April 27th   N.E.
A fine day but a bitter wind. It is so cold, I have put on my beloved Guernsey and rug skirt again. The news is marvellous and breathtaking. We have heard that the Laufen camp have been freed but no news of the Biberach camp.[273]

Saturday April 28th   N.E.
A bitter bitterly cold wind and icy showers. Olive is fetching the parcels today.

Tremendous excitement over the news. The Russians and Allies have met. Mussolini has been captured. Milan, Turin and Genoa have given in. We are using the docks at Bremen. And what is going to happen to *us*!

James arrived about 6pm. He was breathless and quite incoherent. At last he managed to tell me that the Parsons had listened to the 4 o'clock news and had rushed over to Maud to tell her that Himmler had offered unconditional surrender to the Americans and us but not to the Russians and had been told nothing doing until they did so.[274] I went cold all over. Mildred Henderson came to leave a parcel for Maud and I whispered the news to her, that is how it took me, I wanted to whisper.

James arrived when I was struggling to boil some milk on the turpie. I had been puffing and blowing it for over half an hour. James got it to boil in five minutes! We all sat round that turpie and discussed everything. James exchanged his butter with Doris for sugar. Maud and Olive came in, they had heard it too and how will it affect *us*!

May 1945

Tuesday May 1st
Still a bitter cold wind. Snow fell yesterday and a little is lying today.

I heard that the Cabinet and War Council had had an all night sitting and Parliament was meeting at 3pm today and that we would not be told anything for 48 hours. Also that the

---
[273] These were the two camps that non-native Channel Islanders had been deported to in 1942.
[274] On 22 April Himmler, in command of the Rhine and Vistula Armies, met with Count von Bernadotte, a Swedish Red Cross official involved with negotiating with the Western Allies. Himmler offered to surrender to the Western Allies but not the Russians. He explained that Germany would continue to fight the Russians 'until the front of the Western powers has replaced the German front'. However, the Western powers had no intention of turning against Russia and refused to accept anything but total and complete surrender of all armies on all fronts. (Martin Gilbert, *Second World War*, pp.643, 670)

Admiral had had a meeting at the Regal here and said he knew some soldiers did not want to fight but that others did and he was prepared to fight to the end and would not give the Islands up, so that's that. However, the Germans at Mrs Burnett's were destroying their papers all Monday and are packed up, ready to give in. Olive, Maud and I were discussing our meetings with our children, poor darlings, what they will look like after all they have been through. We wonder what we will look like to them, but they have been through much more than we have.

Thursday May 3rd

Bitter cold wind. Rita brought the news that an ultimatum has been given to Alderney. There is wonderful news: 'All enemy land, sea and air forces in Italy have surrendered unconditionally to Field Marshall Alexander.' Nearly a million men are involved. The terms signed on Sunday called for the cessation of hostilities at 12 noon Greenwich Mean Time. Yesterday, in northern Italy and Western Austria, Mr Churchill giving the news to the Commons last night said, 'The surrender brought to conclusion the work of as gallant an allied army as ever marched!'

German resistance in Berlin ended yesterday afternoon after a house to house battle lasting just over a week. Hamburg has been declared an open town. British are to enter the city today.

The Germans' radio commentator has declared that Hitler and Goebbels have both committed suicide. Over 1,000 tons of food and fuel have been taken in Holland.

And what about us? All this wonderful news seems to leave us more desolate and hungry. They must regard us as a tiny little pocket, probably a tiresome tiny little pocket, and yet so big and so tragic for ourselves.

Mr Le Page came to do my leg. I really think he has got it into place at last, but the pain is still awful and he says it is weakness and won't be better until I have more food and I am sure he is right.

Friday May 4th   S.W.

It poured in torrents most of the night, blessed blessed rain. This morning I heard Rita talking! talking! and I thought there must be some exciting news. I heard her go up to Maud's room and continue talking, talking and I waited in a fever of impatience. At last she came but it was only to say the *Vega* was alongside, that people had said she was in yesterday, but she wasn't, but she is now. The thrice blessed *Vega*. Victor is not going to allow a single delay, we shall be given the parcels as soon as possible and, oh, we can really think that this is the last voyage under these conditions.

Saturday May 5th   S.W.

It rained most of the night and it is raining hard this morning and blowing as well and very very cold.

James came in about 2pm. He was breathless with excitement and quite incoherent. He said, 'It is all over, we shall be free now or at 5 o' clock this afternoon, they have had a meeting at 12!' I felt cold all over and then I said, 'I won't believe we are free until I hear the church bells.' And then James said very incoherently, 'I believe 500 are arming, or they only have arms for 300.' I said, 'Who are arming?'

'The civilians, of course, to get their own back on the Germans.' I felt colder than ever as I visualised 300 civilians against 14,000 armed Germans. However, I rallied myself and thought that is only a rumour. Now we are all so excited. Poor Maud could only eat a few mouthfuls and then felt so dreadfully sick she could not eat any more.

Dick Mansell came with a message and said all the babies in the prams were waving Union Jacks and the prams were decorated and queues were waiting outside the shops to buy red, white and blue favours. He told us also that the Admiral had asked the Bailiff to come to a meeting this morning at 12 noon. All yesterday we heard explosions and he said they were exploding mines.

Sunday May 6th   S.W.
It is raining this morning but it is much warmer. We hounded Olive to ring up Victor last night and she had a talk with him. He was non-commital but said he was very happy. That tells us everything. Poor Victor, what an awful time he has had and how well he has done everything. I do hope in time we shall all know exactly what he has had to put up with.

Olive went to St Andrew's church. Mr McCartney told them the hours of the services when we are free. He also prayed for 'our loved ones in England and elsewhere, for their anxiety over us to be relieved'.

Ralph Durand came this afternoon. He had heard the cable had been mended and Victor was in touch with the Home Office. I bet he will tell them how we are starving over here. Ralph was in Town yesterday afternoon and saw all the children with their Union Jacks. He said, 'One lady was carrying two flags and dropped them at the feet of a German officer. Of course, the paper came off and he saw the flags. She was very upset. He said to her, "Don't be embarrassed Madame, we are just as pleased as you are"!'

Maud went out and when she came home at about half past six she said, '*The war is over!*'[275] I suddenly realised that that moment was, and will always be, the happiest moment of my life. Winnie Harvey had met Maud and told her she had heard it. I thought, I don't care a bit about my leg, I must go and see someone, so after supper I went to see Eileen who HAD NOT HEARD THE NEWS! What a thrill for me. Eileen really thought I was a ghost, she was so surprised to see me. I stayed with her until after nine and Guille the gardener came in and told us the nine o'clock news, that Mr Churchill had broadcast they were laying down their arms in Europe and that Norway, Czechoslovakia, the Channel ports and the Channel Islands had to surrender in the next forty-eight hours. Walking home, I noticed the soldiers looked the same, I don't think any of them knew it.

Monday May 7th
Such a hot day. Rita said a German soldier told them he had heard the news from a civilian. The soldiers have not been told a thing yet. The secretiveness and lack of co-operation has to be seen to be believed. The plane that came over last night dropped leaflets for the soldiers. The Admiral *did* ask Victor not to allow the church bells to ring, or flags to be put out, because he was afraid of his men, and Victor replied that he too would be unable to control the people and prevent them showing their joy by hanging out flags and ringing the church bells![276] The

---

[275] The unconditional surrender of the German High Command was signed at 1.41am on 7 May. (Martin Gilbert, *Second World War*, p.689) The BBC announced that Victory in Europe Day would be celebrated on 8 May. (Bunting, *The Model Occupation*, p.247) The Bailiffs of Guernsey and Jersey were officially informed that the war was over by the German Command at 10am on 8 May.

[276] Cruickshank records that the Germans asked the Bailiffs not to allow flags to be hoisted until after the Prime Minister's speech.

Admiral went to Jersey yesterday and rumour says he has gone on to Granville which means the Americans will take the surrender. *What* a bitter disappointment, o … h and I have been *dreaming* of seeing marines and soldiers marching through the Town.

We heard the news that there will be a general holiday in England tomorrow and Wednesday and that Churchill will speak at 3pm and the King in the evening tomorrow.

I rang up Victor and he told me he was counting the hours to our deliverance which he thinks will come in a few days time. Good old Victor, he certainly deserves any honour that is given him. What a terrible time it has been for him and how well he has done. No one will ever know what he has had to put up with.

Book XI

Tuesday May 8th   S.W.
Very warm and raining in showers. I hardly slept all night. No plane has come over and Rita has brought the gloomy news the Admiral has refused to surrender.[277] They are mining the coast feverishly and putting bombs on the posts in the fields. She also told us a corporal arrived yesterday with his mattress and settled himself in a greenhouse full of potatoes and told the owner the potatoes were theirs and he was going to guard them. Such a wave of bitter disappointment and desolation came over me as I felt the national holiday inside the fortress of England is today and we are outside that fortress.

James has just rushed in (11am). The Admiral has given in. We can put our flags up at 3pm. We are free at last.

In the afternoon I went down to Town. First of all I went to Miss Ross. No ships have come yet. I walked down Smith Street and met Major Scott and after that Muriel Agar. While we were talking, Mr Orde from Boots[278] came to us and said, 'Would you like to hear the broadcast?'

'Wouldn't we!' we said. He said, 'We have a set in the library.' So we went up to the library, it was full of people, and sat down and listened to patriotic music and then, 'London calling …' Oh! I shall never forget it. And when Mr Churchill said 'Our dear Channel Islands' the tears streamed down my cheeks quite unashamed.[279]

After the broadcast I went down to the pier with Lily Carey. I started to walk on to the White Rock and the *German* sentry who was there called me back and very unwillingly I came back. I asked what he meant by calling me back and he said I must have a permit. Two St John's men came up and I appealed to them and one of them said, 'It is because of the mines, you have to be shown the way.' I said, 'I don't mind you turning me off, or one of our policemen, but why is *he* the sentry now?' The St John's men said the sentries are for their own people really. And

---

[277] Admiral Hüffmeiner, the German Commander in Chief of the Islands, sent Zimmerman, a junior naval officer, to the arranged rendezvous with a party of British officers aboard HMS *Bulldog* and HMS *Beagle*. Hüffmeiner had only authorised Zimmerman to discuss terms of armistice. However, he was told there was no question of armistice and a properly accredited representative must come and sign the surrender document. Eventually, at 7.14am on 9 May, Guernsey's surrender was signed on the quarterdeck of HMS *Bulldog* by General Major Heine, the Commander in Guernsey, just outside St Peter Port. (Cruickshank, pp.295-6)

[278] The lending library.

[279] In this broadcast, at 3pm on 8 May, Churchill announced that 'Hostilities will end officially at one minute past midnight today, but in the interests of saving lives the "ceasefire" began yesterday to be sounded all along the front, and our dear Channel Islands are also to be freed today.' (Bunting, *The Model Occupation*, p.248)

National anthem at States meeting, 8 May 1945.

of course, we are in the most peculiar position. Free, with the enemy also free in our midst, it is extraordinary. All the soldiers I met looked very cheerful.

Wednesday May 9th   S.W.
A heavy day. We heard there were two destroyers in the harbour and a minesweeper and American, Canadian and *Guernsey* soldiers in the Town. They met the Bailiff this morning at 10am. What a glorious moment. Oh what a day of days this is. The Town was crowded. The banks are changing RMs into good money again, so the queues outside the banks are enormous. The Post Office are taking letters and stamping them, there are no more stamps. I could not go to Town because of my leg.

Nelly Welch told us yesterday that she rang up poor Victor before 10.30 and asked when we could put up our flags. He nearly bit her head off and said, 'Not yet'. He had already had a most disagreeable half hour with the German authorities over the premature display of Union Jacks by the babies on Saturday! and he didn't want another.

About 1.30pm today we heard the sound of beautiful engines and flying low over the Island they came. The planes! The planes! Oh! What another moment of pure bliss. They have been flying over every ten minutes. I really think I shall blow up with emotion.

Thursday May 10th   S.W.
A fine day with heavy showers. More lovely planes flew over this morning. They flew over yesterday protecting the soldiers landing. Crowds were down on the White Rock to meet them. Men of the Hampshire Regiment came, the advance guard, the rest come on Saturday. I went

Royal Court, 9 May 1945, hoisting Union Jack.

down to Town early. I went to see Bertie who told me there was a ceremony at the War Memorial this morning. I waited for over an hour to get into the bank to change my money into real British money!

I was tired when I came home. Gay came to play M-J. I told her I had kept Jim's wireless and she told me she had one too. When I think of all the fits I had when they were searching the house! We seem to be it in the news, poor desolate little Guernsey. There is a rumour going round that Winston Churchill is coming over on Saturday for the hoisting of the Standard and the King's speech.

I rang up Peggy, she was completely overwhelmed. I asked her how many handkerchiefs she had used? She had lost count. I said I let the tears stream down my cheeks naked and unashamed! I wish I could feel better and not as if I was going to blow up at any moment.

I saw the soldiers this morning. How well they looked and how fat. I shook hands and they said, 'Pleased to shake hands I'm sure.' I was determined I would not come home until I had shaken hands with a soldier and seen khaki instead of that *awful* uniform. I don't know where the German soldiers are, there are practically none about.

Friday May 11th
Such a hot day. I went down to the States Office to get my ticket for the service on Sunday. I also changed the rest of my marks. I went to Miss Ross who said the rumour going about was that 1,000 planes would fly over the Island on Thursday and that Winston Churchill and the King were coming! The King wouldn't come like that, but I quite believe Mr Churchill will come. Everything is too overwhelming. We either burst into tears when we greet each other or else we roar with laughter, but coherent speech, *never*!

Mrs Hazell and James came to tea. The cows have been milked three nights running. However, all the Germans are prisoners today. I met Mr Ridge who told me our people intended to invade us on Monday. They were going to land at L'Ancresse and sweep up to the Fort. They have been training volunteers since September and 18,000 troops and 1,500 planes were going to take part. Also that the Admiral had decided to blow up the harbour and electric light on Wednesday, could anything be nearer?! It is a miracle how blessed we have been. We say if people don't believe in God in Guernsey they are damn fools. The Germans made as many difficulties as they possibly could, they would not let prisoners be freed until after midnight, they objected to the gunboats staying outside the harbour, said they would regard it as an act of hostility as war was not over until after midnight, so the boats went away until midnight. They sent a lieutenant in a filthy minesweeper, he stepped on the snowy deck of the Destroyer leaving the dirty mark of his boots on that deck. He was taken to an Admiral and a General and he asked for the terms of the armistice; he was told, 'No armistice. No terms. Unconditional surrender. Go back.' And back he went and a General returned and signed the paper at last!

Of course I have never heard anything so much touch and go as it was on Tuesday. The situation has never been so critical and ugly all through the Occupation as it was on Tuesday morning between 10 and 10.30am. The British have been preparing and training 18,000 volunteers to come and relieve us and they were coming in August 1944 and then changed their plans. 1,500 planes were coming too and if they made the attack they say three quarters of the Island would have been destroyed with a great loss of life, but they said, if they had to drive them out of here, they were going to make the invasion here on Monday and the Germans intended to blow up the harbour and public services on Wednesday. What we have been spared. The Germans would not let prisoners out until after 12 midnight on Tuesday.

Saturday May 12th   S.W.
A boiling hot, cloudless day. I have hardly slept all night. I am that restless I don't know what to do. All yesterday the planes were flying over in beautiful formations and this morning too. Olive and I just drop everything and rush out to look and wave at them. Life is simply overwhelming now.

Rita didn't come today so we each got our own breakfast which meant boiling a kettle and eating two slices of that divine bread and butter. I went down to the depot to fetch the bread for Olive. Mrs Raven was there. She said she saw a soldier disarmed yesterday. There was a sentry outside Belmont and a soldier came out on a motorbike. The sentry told him to 'Halt' and took away his rifle and ammunition and then let him ride away, they were all officially prisoners yesterday. O … h to think that we will never see that hideous uniform again or hear those *awful* boots. I can't believe it. Yesterday they were rushing about in lorries and cars and motorbikes all day just like they used to do the first days they came.

I had a very early lunch and went down to Elizabeth College and was there just after 12. Soon Peggy arrived, I *was* so glad to see her. I have been longing to see her. We sat side by side in perfect harmony having the identical reactions. And then we heard the band, a British band. O … h Peggy and I clasped hands in silence. To see those brawny, healthy, clean, strong soldiers marching in amid cheers and hand clapping. It was just, just … I murmured, '*Peggy*, a British word of Command.' Peggy muttered, 'Vi, the Navy, the Navy is coming,' as a car drove up and the Admiral got out of it. Then more cheers and we saw the British Legion standards coming in. The Bailiff drove up and the Royal Court in their robes stood on the top of the steps and the Union Jack was broken and 'God Save the King' was played and we all sang it lustily which I suppose was quite wrong. Colonel Snow[280] read the Proclamation and the King's message standing in the middle of the steps. It was just immense.

It is interesting to see the people who have kept their wireless sets. I kept Boy's 'Phillips' and it is working beautifully.

Sunday May 13th S.W.

It is not quite so warm. I went to the Thanksgiving Service at the Town Church. All the way up Mount Durand they had Red Cross lorries going up filled with brown faced healthy laughing boys. One called out to me, 'It is a long pull Missus.' At the top they had all stopped, I don't think they knew their way. I talked to lots of them. They told me only twenty men landed to take possession of Guernsey! How like the English, and there were 14,000 German soldiers here![281]

I am sure we will always be saying, 'Isn't that British?' or 'Isn't that like the Germans?' I had one wish satisfied. I have been longing to see soldiers and marines walking through our Town and I have today. I spoke to a young marine who told me it was awful their not getting any mails. Poor darling, I didn't impress upon him that we had been without mails for nearly five years! But all the same I can't understand why no mails are coming here, nor papers.

The Admiral was taken away last night, they made him walk down to the pier, they didn't let him swank down in a car. There is a rumour he tried to do himself in but I don't believe it. I am convinced that if he had had the guts to do himself in he would *never* have surrendered, he would have fired those awful guns and the Destroyers, he would have carried out his appalling programme here and *then* would have committed suicide. We have been spared a lot.

About 450 cases of starvation will not recover. We are dreadfully worried, no diesel oil has arrived yet and the lack of water in the Town is making conditions appalling. The oil they are using for the electric light is their iron ration they were keeping as a three week supply. We are hoping to have our telephone restored. No one can realise unless they have experienced it what it means to be without a phone in the country.

---

[280] Brigadier Snow was commander of the liberating forces.
[281] *The Times*, Friday 11 May, reported that 'Twenty-two men of the Royal Artillery went to St Peter Port, Guernsey to take over the Island with a garrison of 10,000 Germans.'

Monday May 14th   S.W.
Blowing very hard and colder but fine. I rang up Violet this morning. She said when Frank went in with the milk he saw thousands of German prisoners marching down to the pier.

James and Bertie came about 5pm. Poor dears, they were absolutely worn out, they had been to the ceremony at the Royal Court to hear Mr Herbert Morrison, the Home Secretary. He arrived by a destroyer. Both Bertie and James were feeling sick with horror because they had heard of the torture camp at Castle Cornet for the first time. The first place the British asked for was the horror camp. There were no Guernsey people in it, foreigners and Germans. Some of them have been so maltreated they won't live, there was also one at the Vale. It is awful to think that was happening over here.

Another horror we have found out here, they had three enormous concrete halls in the Island into which they were going to put all of us over sixty years of age and they were going to gas us if the occasion arose that they wanted to reduce the population on account of the lack of food. Some say if they had won the war, they would have gassed us, made everybody under sixty work and would have taken all the young girls to Germany.

Tuesday May 15th
A very foggy day and only a week ago and all this happened. I rang up Eileen this morning. How she made me laugh. This morning she was having her hair permed and it was all screwed up and another khaki giant arrived and sat with her for an hour and a half and told her all about her son Henry. I went down to meet her at Le Noury and how we laughed. I said we have discussed imaginary meetings with our people and thought of all sorts of situations we might be in but *never* being at the hairdressers!

Tim Scott joined us, he told us that these men were very frightened of their reception over here because of the great fraternisation that had gone on with the Germans. That hurt me like anything, to think these boys should have doubted their welcome here. Anyhow, they say they could not have had a warmer welcome. Eileen and Tim were talking about the girls who went with the Germans and people are warning the soldiers against them. Tim said the girls are marked down, that the Secret Service know who they are and also the names of the men over here who had black market dealings with the Germans.

All day yesterday the German prisoners were marching down to the boat. They were

Violet Carey, late 1940.

collected in groups and girls were waiting about to say goodbye to them. The Tommies ordered them away and asked them if they would like to go for a holiday. People think they are going to be deported. They are going to send German prisoners over here to clean up the mess. I was hoping I would never hear those boots again.

We are being told that an abundance of food is coming over. I wish it would hurry up because we now have nothing but bread. Everything is finished. A man today gave me a sweet, he said, 'Do have this sweet Mrs Carey, you look as if you need it very badly.' The soldiers are giving sweets away all the time and naturally to the children, but really we want sugar dreadfully too. The pain in my leg is awful now and my ear is beginning to ache. With all this excitement I have not been able to eat even the food I have got.

Thursday May 17th

Another boiling hot day. We hear there is a mail today. I feel sick with excitement. I wonder when I shall be able to eat again. Except for more bread we have not been given anything to eat. Most of us are unable to eat so perhaps it is as well.

I heard a thundering knock on the door and there was old Dyke with a packet of letters. 'There,' says he, 'go and sit down and read them, that will keep you quiet for a long time.' O … h. I yelled for James and we sat down together in the dining room and there was one packet marked 'photographs'. I tore it open. Darling Boy and Iris. Boy looking exactly the same, except for a fine moustache, and Iris looks so sweet. And then the letters. I read that Boy had been in Africa and that filthy Greece and was now in Italy. How *thankful* I am I did not know it. He has been well all the time. Thank God for that. Baba was in France and is now in Germany near that horrible Belsen concentration camp. She says, 'We have heard terrible things from people we have met who have been there. We are getting in quite a lot of X P.O.W.s and some are nearly dead due entirely to exposure and starvation.'

Tuesday May 22nd   S.W.

Raining. I got up in plenty of time and went down to the Regal to see the 10 o'clock performance of the *Battle of Britain*. It was a marvellous picture. When we came out we said, 'We must not grumble, we must not think we have had a bad time here. After all we have slept every night in our beds and have had no air raids at all.'

After the broadcast was over, the post came. O … h. And at last a lovely letter from darling Baba from Germany. What a joy and the darling sent me £50. It was too adorable of her. She is longing to come home, she seems very well. She sent a photo of Jim and herself at last. She is in khaki now and has a medal ribbon and two stars on her shoulder and wears a beret. I wonder why they put the nurses in khaki.

Baba asks if the German prisoners are herded into iron cages like they are in Germany? I should think not, very much the reverse. As I limped home the five miles, seven cars each full of German officers dashed by, I thought, why not make those officers walk like we have to walk and use that petrol for buses for us?

It is such a joy to have Baba's letter. I read it over and over again. I am still dazed with happiness.

Sunday May 27th

A lovely day. I went to church. Peggy told me Booty and Mildred and twelve others were taken away by plane today at 9am. The doctors sent by the Home Office went with them. Mildred had a label round her neck with the words '"Starvation" to go to Dr Swinburne, St Annes.' They regard her as the worst case of starvation they have seen in the whole of Europe. They also regard her as a most interesting case and nine specialists are going to see her. She will have nothing but injections. The doctors told us that we hear of terrible cases in Holland but they are not nearly as bad as the cases they have seen here. There are 2,000 medical and surgical cases waiting for a ship to take them away.

Monday May 28th

We are more excited than ever, the King and Queen are flying over next Wednesday June 6th and they go to Jersey first and come here after. I spent all day writing letters and I cannot catch up.

Jurats meeting the King and Queen.

Tuesday May 29th   N.E.

A very cold wind. Peggy and Eileen and Micky came to M-J. How we all talked, our M-J was very sketchy.

Mrs Mauger is certainly seeing the soldiers out here are not picking girls who have been with the Germans. If she sees one with a soldier, she goes straight up to the soldier and tells him. Everybody is doing the same.

Wednesday May 30th

A warmer day. I had the most wonderful letter from Baba yesterday. She had received mine, so now we are linked up at last after those five desolate weary years. I could never go through it again. I feel as if she and I are quite close to each other, it is a lovely feeling. The darling seems to be having a very interesting time, but they have to still round up Germans and Michelle drove five miles with a German prisoner, levelling a revolver at him the whole time.

[Violet did continue to write in her diary until November 1945. However, the entries begin to get very sketchy after this point and mostly record her daily activities. Included in the suitcase which the diaries were kept in was the first letter which she wrote to her daughter after Liberation.]

Les Merrienes
La Forest
Guernsey

FREE

Friday May 18th

Darling.

At last I can write to you after all this long weary time. Oh Baba, it has been awful and I don't believe any of us would have stayed if we had realised how long it would be, but still, we are glad we have saved Guernsey. I am quite incoherent, so I will write down everything as it comes.

I can't describe our feelings on Sunday evening, May 6th when I heard the war in Europe was over. We all say we don't think we shall ever know such a moment of pure happiness again.

I was staying with Auntie Olive. Some weeks ago I fainted on the stairs from weakness and fell and sprained my foot horribly. I came into the bungalow to be able to have treatment from the bone setter. He made my foot well in three treatments, but occupational neuritis set up in my other leg, and it has been dreadful. I am told I can't get any better until I get more sugar and am advised to walk as much as I can even if it is painful and so I do. I have walked everywhere. I bought a little push cart to carry all my things.

Daddy has been very well all the time, except that he had neuritis in his arm, but was able to have treatment for it. Auntie Olive has been very well too, and darling Molly, who has been the grandest watchdog. She *loathed* the Germans and always warned us by her particular savage barking when any of them were about. They were always round us, walking all over the house and searching the house for the wireless. They did not find it and it is working beautifully now.

I got the most tremendous kick out of fooling the Germans, the whole bally lot, men Officers, Gestapo Gendarneice. We had them all in turn and, darling, I played my role of being a dear, helpless, old soul to perfection, except I had an inspiration straight from Heaven, and I became a dear, helpless, *deaf*, old soul and that took much more time. Daddy and Mrs Renault were splendid at hiding things as long as they had plenty of time, so my job was to keep them talking which I did. I always pretended I knew a little German, and then asked them to translate for me. They all seem to know a good deal of English. You were my greatest asset, they all fell for your photograph in Austrian dress and I told them you had been in Austria, etc., etc. with my ears stretching to hear Daddy or Mrs Renault give me the all clear signal. We were always hiding something, potatoes, wheat etc. They used to look at your photo and say, 'Pretty girl, pretty girl,' and I smiled fatuously and said, 'Meine Tochter' in a die away voice. It was most exhausting, but such a thrill when they went away and said solemnly to me, 'We have found nothing.'

What a hectic time we have had the last 10 days. We have laughed all the Occupation, we weren't going to let the Germans see they could get us down. Now we seem to do nothing but cry for happiness, it is too fantastic. We meet each other, shake hands and gulp and depart hastily. I said to Peggy, 'I don't mind the tears chasing each other down my cheeks, naked and unashamed, and gulping all the time for a time, but I want to know when will I be normal again? Ever?' and Peggy agreed with me, but we are all alike.

When we heard that the war was over in Europe on the Sunday, I think that will be the happiest moment of my life. On Monday and Monday night, the Germans were running everywhere feverishly and dragging heavy guns down to L'Ancresse. The Admiral said he would fight to the last. On Tuesday morning at 10am he refused to surrender. That was the ugliest and most critical moment of the whole Occupation. At 10.30 his officers made him give in. He sent a lieutenant on a filthy minesweeper whose dirty boots fouled the white deck of the gun boat. The lieutenant was met by an Admiral and a General. He gave an exaggerated Nazi salute and demanded the terms of the armistice. He was told, 'No terms, no armistice, unconditional surrender, go back,' and he scuttled back and finally a Colonel signed at 12 midnight. We put up our flags at 3pm and I heard the broadcast in the Town. It was wonderful and every day has been wonderful ever since.

If the *Vega* hadn't brought us parcels, I really think we would all be dead. We couldn't have gone on, we were three weeks without bread anyhow, and we certainly realised the meaning of the prayer, 'Give us this day our daily bread.' I suffered all the time from diarrhoea, 'the germ' we called it, caused by the bread. The Germans took our wheat and gave us oats that were so bad, they would not feed them to their horses. When the *Vega* brought that divine white Canadian flour to make our bread, I was well in two days. I was one of the worst cases. I have lost over 3 stone, and weigh less than 9 stone, I have never been so light. I was considered one of the best dressed women here, wearing your clothes darling!

Yesterday was another thrill. We had our first mail. I had 22 letters and the next thrill will be seeing you my Baba. I expect you will fly over sometime soon?

Reggie has written and told me Aggie had been so ill, but he says she is better again. We don't know *when* anybody will be allowed to come over to live, or when any of us can go away. The medical and surgical cases haven't gone yet. Auntie Maud is very well and just as cheerful and wonderful as ever. Poor Uncle Perdy died in August 1940, quite suddenly from heart, no one knew he was ill.

We have had to cut down a good many trees and the Germans have taken a good many, and they have dug trenches in our fields and put posts up with mines on them. We have not been turned out of our house and they have not been billeted on us, so we have been very lucky. And oh, best of all, we were not sent to Germany. We were ordered to go, but Daddy was exempted being a farmer. That was an *awful* moment, when we had the order.

I have had a lovely letter from Iris and such good photographs of her and Jim. *Do* send me yours, I am longing for one of you.

Now I must write to Jim. All love darling and we both say, Thank God you are safe. Daddy is so happy and excited, he says he doesn't know what to do. You can send some chocolates and sweets. We are starving for sugar.

Appendix

Index of People mentioned in Violet Carey's Diaries

Major Bandelow was appointed Comandant of Guernsey in October 1940. He succeeded Dr Lanz.

Bertie and Peggy Brock were friends of Violet's who lived on Queen's Road in St Peter Port. They moved to the Forest later in the Occupation.

Clem Brouard was a tomato grower. His greenhouses were behind Les Merriennes.

Aunt Edith Carey was James' aunt. She lived at Les Gravees in St Peter Port. Violet often visited her on her trips to town. Her daughter was Vera Carey, who lived with her.

Maud Carey was James' sister. She suffered from epilepsy and so had a companion (Mabel) who lived with and looked after her. They lived in St Peter Port and Violet often went to visit them when she went to town.

Perdy Carey was James' youngest brother. Doris was his wife. They lived at Le Hurel in St Martins. He died in July 1940.

Victor Carey was Bailiff of the Island during the Occupation. He was a distant relative of Violet's, being a member of a different branch of the Carey family. Violet often visited him and his sister-in-law, Mrs Swete, during the Occupation and had the utmost respect for the way Victor handled the Germans.

Herbert Cheeseborough was originally from Yorkshire, lived at Le Panage in St Martins. He was an assistant at Le Riches and was renowned for collaboration.

Katty Connellan was an Irish lady who lived out on the cliffs in the Forest. She is remembered as being rather eccentric with a very dramatic nature.

Olive de Sausmarez was Violet's sister-in-law. She was the widow of Violet's brother, Teddy. She lived at Pre au Puit, often referred to as the 'bungalow' on King's Road in St Peter Port.

Maud Drake was a friend who had been at college with Violet. She lived in St Peter Port and the diaries suggest she stayed with Olive de Sausmarez in the later years of the Occupation.

Lyon and Ethel Falkener were friends of Violet who lived in St Martins.

Mr Raymond Falla was a member of the Controlling Committee and was responsible for agriculture. He was sent to France in August 1940 to buy food supplies for the Island.

Mr Finey was the rector of the Forest parish.

Mrs Fisher was Olive de Sausmarez's mother. She was very elderly at the time of the Occupation and lived at Pre au Puit with Olive.

Mabel Frere was a friend of Violet's and was married to Macleod Frere and they lived in St Peter Port. She was deported to Germany in September 1942.

Miss Gaudion owned a bookshop in town.

The **Gorvels** were neighbours who lived at La Roberge, near to Les Merriennes.

Mr Guille was the rector of St Peter's.

Hedley Hamon was Sarkese. He was the widower of Violet's nanny, Annie. When Annie died, Violet and James had taken him in; he lived with them at Les Merriennes and helped run the farm. His daughter was Violet Martel.

Reverend Hartley Jackson was the rector of St Stephen's church in St Peter Port.

Mrs Hayes was a friend of Violet who lived at Le Manoir, in the Forest parish, near to Les Merriennes. Mrs Hayes evacuated to England in June 1940.

Mr and Mrs Hazell were friends of Violet's. They lived at Les Villets in the Forest.

Mr W.G. Hubert was a seed trade expert and local seed merchant. He accompanied Raymond Falla to France in August 1940 to buy supplies for the Islanders.

Admiral Freidrich Huffmeier came to the Channel Islands in June 1944. He became Colonel Count von Schmettow's Chief of Staff in October 1944, was made Vice Admiral in January 1945 and succeeded von Schmettow in February 1945. He was a fervent Nazi and held on to the Channel Islands for as long as possible.

Mr Johns was a member of the Controlling Committee.

Ilsa had come over to Guernsey before the Occupation as an au pair and got trapped there. She looked after a house called Fontenelles in the Forest.

Mabel Kinnersly was a great friend of Violet's. She was widowed and lived at 'Calais' in St Martins.

Knackfuss was the Feldkommandant in October 1941.

Sir Abraham Laine was a member of the Controlling Committee.

Dr Lanz was the first German Commandant in 1940.

Mrs le Masurier, Philip Martel's half sister, was deported in 1940 for helping to shelter spies (Mulholland and Martel) although allowed to return in January 1941. See footnote for 29 August 1940.

Mr le Page owned the Old Forge Stores. He often gave Violet a lift in his van when Violet was walking to and from town.

Dr Maass was Dr Lanz's Chief of Staff.

Helen Marquand, known as **Markie,** was the schoolmistress of the Dame School and lived in Ville au Roi, St Peter Port. Violet often visited her when she went to Town.

Philip Martel was an Islander who had joined up and left the Island before the Occupation. He and Desmond Mulholland were sent to the Island with orders to meet and guide commandos who were due to arrive on 12 July to carry out a raid on the German military. However, no commandos came; unbeknown to Mulholland and Martel, the raid had been postponed and consequently they were stranded on the Island. To begin with they hid, sheltered by their families. However, aware of the trouble they could cause their families, they eventually went to Sherwill to say they wanted to give themselves up. Knowing they would probably be shot because they wore civilian clothes and were technically spies, Sherwill found them uniforms. The Germans interrogated them and sent them to France. They were kept there as prisoners of war until the end of the war. Their salvation was probably due to the sticking to their story about landing in uniform and stealing civilian clothes and their genuine ignorance about the actual raid attempted on 14 July. (Cruickshank, pp.89, 91) See 29 August 1940.

Violet Martel was Hedley's daughter. She had worked for Violet as a maid, but then married a farmer, Frank Martel. They lived at Les Blicqs in St Andrews.

Mary had been Violet's cook. She was married to a grower, Cliff Cherry.

Mrs Mauger was Violet's charlady. She lived at Les Villets in the Forest.

Mrs Michael, Desmond Mulholland's mother, was deported in 1940 for helping to shelter spies (Mulholland and Martel) although allowed to return in January 1941. See footnote for 29 August 1940.

Michelle (Baba) was Violet's eldest child. She had trained as a nurse and had joined QAIMNS. She was posted on HMHC *Worthing*, a hospital carrier, and was sent to West Africa later in the war.

Mrs Milburne was an acquaintance of Violet's who lived in the Vale. Violet often mentioned speaking to her in Town.

Molly was Violet's dog, a black spaniel.

General Müller took over the military command of the Channel Islands in October 1941, with headquarters in Guernsey.

Desmond Mulholland – *see* Philip Martel

Natie was Bertie and Peggy Brock's maid.

Hubert Nicolle and James Symes were sent on a reconnaissance trip to Guernsey on 3 September 1940; they had been ordered to gather information about the situation in the Island. Their rendezvous did not appear and they were stranded on the Island. They managed to hide for about six weeks, firstly with their families, and then in the games pavilion at Elizabeth College. They were treated as prisoners of war. Those who helped them, including Sherwill, were also deported, but were released three months later and allowed to return to Guernsey. (Cruickshank, p.99)

Booty Ozanne was a friend that Violet often saw when she visited Olive.

Captain John Parker was another spy that the British sent to Guernsey. There are two suggestions as to his mission. Cruickshank claims he was sent to gather information for another raid, particularly information about the airport. (Cruickshank, pp.95-7) According to William Bell, however, he was sent to find two other spies, Nicolle and Symes, who had been stranded on the island. (Bell, pp.24, 67) Either way he fell into a German trench and was captured. He was interrogated by the Germans and sent to a prisoner of war camp for the rest of the war.

Pierre de Putron was a Jurat in the Royal Court and became Air Raid Precautions Commandant.

Mr Rannsson lived in the old coastguard cottage in Torteval.

Mrs Renault was Violet's maid and came daily to do most of the housework and some of the cooking. She lived at Les Villets, Forest.

Colonel Schumacher became Chief of Staff when Dr Maass left in August 1940.

Bobbie Seabrooke was a friend that Violet often met and spoke to in town. She lived in St Martins.

The **Sebires** were a farming family who lived in the Forest.

A.J. Sherwill was the Attorney General and an elected member of the Royal Court. He was elected as President of the Controlling Committee which was set up as a kind of war cabinet just before the Occupation. He was released from this duty in late 1940 following his involvement with two spies and then deported to Germany with other English-born islanders in February 1943.

Aggie and Reggie Sowels lived in Sark but evacuated to England before the Occupation. Aggie was one of Violet's cousins.

Mrs Swete was Victor Carey's sister-in-law. She came over to be his housekeeper when Victor's wife died.

James Symes – *see* Hubert Nicolle

J.E.B. Tetley was viewed by many Islanders as a collaborator as he associated freely with the Germans. (Bell, *Guernsey Occupied but Never Conquered*, p.225)

Mr Timmer was a Dutchman and a grower for export. He supposedly collaborated outwardly with the Germans during the Occupation.

The **Tourtels** were a family who lived in the Forest.

Mr George Vaudin became Guernsey's permanent representative in Granville for buying supplies.

Colonel Count von Schmettow was the German Commandant for the Channel Islands, replacing Major Bandelow. His headquarters were in Jersey.

Mr Ware was the master butcher and often gave Violet a lift home from town.

John and Nellie Welch were friends of Violet's who lived in St Martins.

Gouliot Williams lived in Doyle Road in St Peter Port and was a General. Violet often recording having conversations with him on her trips to town. Violet spelt his name as 'Goulu' as well as 'Gouliot' and I have been unable to ascertain which is correct.

Bibliography

Manuscript Sources

Imperial War Museum, London, Diary of Cecil Bazely
Island Archives, Guernsey, AS/LC 16-01, -02, -03, Diaries of Ken Lewis
Island Archives, Guernsey, AQ 368/01, Occupation Diary of Violet Carey, 1940
Island Archives, Guernsey, AQ 368/02, Occupation Diary of Violet Carey, 1944
Island Archives, Guernsey, AQ 368/03, Occupation Diary of Violet Carey, 1940
Island Archives, Guernsey, AQ 368/04, Occupation Diary of Violet Carey, 1945
Island Archives, Guernsey, AQ 368/05, Occupation Diary of Violet Carey, 1945
Island Archives, Guernsey, AQ 368/06, Occupation Diary of Violet Carey, 1943-1944
Island Archives, Guernsey, AQ 368/07, Occupation Diary of Violet Carey, 1943
Island Archives, Guernsey, AQ 368/08, Occupation Diary of Violet Carey, 1941
Island Archives, Guernsey, AQ 368/09, Transcripts of Letters from Michelle Carey and Occupation Diary 1942
Island Archives, Guernsey, AQ 368/10, Occupation Diary of Violet Carey, 1941-1942
Island Archives, Guernsey, AQ 368/11, Occupation Diary of Violet Carey, 1942
Island Archives, Guernsey, CC/RI, Occupation Registration Files
'L'Enseigne De Noble Homme De Sausmarez Fût Dressé Sur Le Pinacle De St Martin AD 1199'. The de Sausmarez Family Tree. Consulted by kind permission of Patricia Paxton.
Letters of Violet Mary Carey. Consulted by kind permission of Patricia Paxton.
The National Archives, HO 45/22399, Extracts from the *Daily Herald* and *Daily Worker*
The National Archives, HO 45/22399, Letter from Brigadier Snow to the Home Office in response to the MI5 Report
The National Archives, HO 45/22399, MI5 Report, 'The Channel Islands Under German Occupation'
The National Archives, HO 45/25844, Mr J. Chuter Ede, the Home Secretary's statement about the Channel Islands in the House of Commons, 17 August 1945
The Greffe, Guernsey, *Billet d'Etat 1940-1945*
The Greffe, Guernsey, *Ordonnances*

Interviews

Diana de Jersey, Liz McIntyre and Pam Browne, 20 October 2001
Richard Heaume, Director of the German Occupation Museum, Guernsey, 19 October 2001
Sheila James, 28 December 2000
Susan Marks, 23 August 2001
Michelle Nixon (Violet Carey's daughter), 30 March 2000, 26 July 2000
Patricia Paxton, 27 November 2000, 31 December 2000, 9 May 2002
Ken Tough, HM Greffier, Guernsey, 23 May 2001

Newspapers and Periodicals

Contemporary European History
Critical Inquiry
Current Sociology
Quarterly Review
Transactions of the Royal Historical Society
The *Guernsey Evening Press*
The *Star* (Guernsey)
Women's History Review
Victorian Studies

Contemporary Articles, Books, Pamphlets and Speeches

Channel Islands Occupation Review
John Dalmau, *Slave Worker in the Channel Islands*
John Leale, *Report of Five Years of German Occupation*. Jurat Leale's address to the States of Guernsey, 23 May 1945 (Guernsey, 1945)

Published Secondary Sources

Allport, Gordon and Postman, Leo, *The Psychology of Rumour* (New York, Henry Holt and Co., 1947)
Bachmann, K.M., *The Prey of an Eagle: A Personal Record of Family Life Written Throughout the German Occupation of Guernsey* (Guernsey, Guernsey Press Co. Ltd, 1972)
Bell, Anne Oliver (ed.), assisted by McNellie, Andrew, *The Diary of Virginia Woolf* (London, Hogarth, 1984)
Bell, William, *Guernsey Occupied but Never Conquered* (Exeter, Studio Publishing Services, 2002)
Bell, William, *I Beg to Report: Policing in Guernsey During the German Occupation* (Guernsey, Guernsey Press Co. Ltd., 1995)
Bell, William, *The Commando Who Came Home to Spy* (Guernsey, The Guernsey Press Co. Ltd, 1998)
Bihet, Molly, *A Child's War* (Guernsey, Guernsey Press Co. Ltd, 1985)
Binding, Tim, *Island Madness* (London, Picador, 1999)
Bremmer, Jan and Roodenburg, Herman (eds), *A Cultural History of Humour* (Cambridge, Polity Press, 1997)
Browning, Christopher, *Ordinary Men: Reserve Police Battalion 101 and the Final Solution in Poland* (New York, Harper Collins, 1992)
Brownstein, Rachel, *Becoming a Heroine: Reading about Women in Novels* (New York, Viking Press, 1982)
Bunting, Madeleine, *The Model Occupation: The Channel Islands Under German Rule, 1940-1945* (London, Harper Collins, 1995)
Calder, Angus, *The Myth of the Blitz* (London, Pimlico, 1992)
Cannadine, David, *Class in Britain* (London, Penguin Books, 1998)
Carey, Edith, *The Channel Islands* (London, A. & C. Black, 1904)
Carey, William Wilfred, Carey, Edith Frances and Curtis, Spencer Carey, *The History of the Careys of Guernsey* (London, J.M. Dent and Sons, 1938)
Cesarini, David, *Britain and the Holocaust* (London, Holocaust Education Trust, 1998)
Cohen, Frederick, *The Jews in The Channel Islands During the German Occupation 1940-1945* (Jersey, Jersey Heritage Trust, 2000)
Conkin, Paul K. and Higham, John (eds), *New Directions in American Intellectual History* (Baltimore, Johns Hopkins University Press, 1979)
Cook, Chris and Sked, Alan (eds), *Crisis and Controversy: Essays in Honour of A.J.P. Taylor* (London, Macmillan, 1976)

Corfield, Penelope (ed.) *Rethinking History* (London, Routledge, 1997)
Couch, Michael, *My Friend is my Enemy* (Guernsey, Guernsey Press Co. Ltd, 1991)
Crosby, Travis, *The Impact of Civilian Evacuation in the Second World War* (London, Croom Helm, 1986)
Cruickshank, Charles, *The German Occupation of the Channel Islands* (Guernsey, Guernsey Press Co. Ltd, 1975)
Delafield, E.M., *The Diary of a Provincial Lady* (London, Howard Baker, 1972)
Delafield, E.M., *The Provincial Lady in Wartime* (London, Macmillan, 1940)
Earle, Rebecca (ed.), *Epistolary Selves: Letters and Letter Writers, 1600-1945* (Aldershot, Ashgate Publishing Ltd, 1999)
Edwards, G.B., *The Book of Ebenezer le Page* (London, Penguin, 1982)
Falla, Frank, *The Silent War* (Guernsey, Burbridge Ltd, 1994)
Felman, Shoshana, *What Does a Woman Want? Reading and Sexual Difference* (Baltimore and London, Johns Hopkins University Press, 1993)
Flint, Kate, *The Woman Reader: 1817-1914* (Oxford, Clarendon Press, 1993)
Fraser, David, *The Fate of the Jews in the Channel Islands, 1940-1945* (Brighton, Sussex Academic Press, 2000)
Freud, Sigmund, *Jokes and their Relation to the Unconscious*, translated by James Strachey (London, Routledge and Kegan Paul, 1960)
Gildea, Robert, *Marianne in Chains: In Search of the German Occupation 1940-1945* (London, Macmillan, 2002)
Goldhagen, Daniel, *Hitler's Willing Executioners: Ordinary Germans and the Holocaust* (London, Little, Brown and Company, 1996)
Guelff, Richard and Roberts, Adam (eds), *Documents on the Laws of War* (Oxford, Clarendon Press, 1982)
Guppy, A.W., *Stone De Croze! The Original Guernseyman Volume Two* (Guernsey, Guernsey Evening Press, 1979)
Hartley, Jenny, *Hearts Undefeated: Women's Writing of the Second World War* (Great Britain, Virago, 1996)
Harvey, Winifred, *The Battle of Newlands: The Wartime Diaries of Winifred Harvey*, edited by Rosemary Booth (Guernsey, Guernsey Press Co. Ltd. 1995)
Hawthorn, Jeremy (ed.), *The Nineteenth-Century British Novel* (London, Edward Arnold, 1986)
Hocart, Richard, *An Island Assembly: The Development of the States of Guernsey, 1700-1949* (Guernsey, Guernsey Museum and Art Gallery, 1988)
Johnston, Peter, *A Short History of Guernsey* (Guernsey, Guernsey Press Co. Ltd, 1994)
Kaplan, Cora, *Sea Changes: Essays on Culture and Feminism* (London, Verso, 1986)
Keiller, Frank, *Prison Without Bars: Living in Jersey Under the German Occupation* (Wiltshire, Seaflower Books, 2000)
Knowles Smith, Hazel, *The Changing Face of the Channel Islands Occupation: Record, Memory and Myth* (Basingstoke and New York, 2007)
The Definitive Edition of Rudyard Kipling's Verse (London, Hodder and Stoughton, 1940)
Light, Alison: *Forever England: Femininity, Literature and Conservatism Between the Wars* (London, Routledge, 1991)
Loveridge, John, *The Constitution and Law of Guernsey*, second edition, edited by J.H. Loveridge Junior (Guernsey, La Societe Guernesiase, 1997)
Mahy, Miriam, *There is an Occupation* (Guernsey, Guernsey Press Co. Ltd, 1992)
Mandler, Peter and Pedersen, Susan (eds), *After the Victorians* (London and New York, Routledge, 1994)
Marwick, Arthur, *Class, Image and Reality in Britain, France and the USA since 1930* (London, Macmillan, 1990)
Marwick, Arthur, *War and Social Change in the Twentieth Century* (London, 1974)
Merriman, John, *A History of Modern Europe from the Renaissance to the Present* (London, W.W. Norton and Company, 1996)

Mitchell, Margaret, *Gone With the Wind* (London, Macmillan, 1936)
Neubauer, Hans-Joachim, *The Rumour: A Cultural History*, translated by Christian Braun (London, Free Association Books, 1999)
Ozanne, Beryl, *A Peep Behind the Screens 1940-1945* (Guernsey, Guernsey Press Co. Ltd, 1994)
Palmer, Bryan, *Descent into Discourse: The Reification of Language and the Writing of Social History* (Philadelphia, Temple University Press, 1990)
Parker, Sheila, *An Occupational Hazard* (Guernsey, Sausmarez Brook, 1985)
Paton, George and Powell, Chris (eds), *Humour in Society: Resistance and Control* (London, Macmillan Press Ltd, 1988)
Perks, Robert and Thompson, Alistair (eds), *The Oral History Reader* (London and New York, Routledge, 1998)
Piette, Adam, *Imagination at War: British Fiction and Poetry, 1939-1945* (London, Papermac, 1995)
Purvis, June (ed.), *Women's History, Britain 1850-1945: An Introduction* (London, UCL, 1995)
Riley, Denise: *War in the Nursery: Theories of Child and Mother* (London, Virago, 1983)
Sauvary, J.C., *Diary of the German Occupation of Guernsey 1940-1945* (Guernsey, Guernsey Press Co. Ltd, 1990)
Sheridan, Dorothy (ed.), *Wartime Women: A Mass-Observation Anthology 1937-1945* (London, Phoenix Press, 1990)
Sherwill, Ambrose, *A Fair and Honest Book* (Lulu, 2006)
Smith, Harold (ed.), *War and Social Change: British Society in the Second World War* (Manchester, Manchester University Press, 1986)
Steedman, Carolyn, *Landscape for a Good Woman* (London, Virago, 1986)
Struther, Jan, *Mrs Miniver* (London, Virago, 1989)
Summerfield, Penny, *Reconstructing Women's Wartime Lives: Discourse and Subjectivity in Oral Histories of the Second World War* (Manchester and New York, Manchester University Press, 1998)
Toms, Carel, *Hitler's Fortress Islands: Germany's Occupation of the Channel Islands* (Guernsey, Burbridge Ltd, 1996)
Ward and Lock, *Illustrated Guide and Popular History of the Channel Islands* (1881)
Warren, J.P., *Our Own Island* (Guernsey, Guernsey Press Co. Ltd, 1926)
White, Luise, *Speaking With Vampires: Rumor and History in Colonial Africa* (Berkley, Los Angeles and London, University of California Press, 2000)
Wood, Alan and Mary, *Islands in Danger* (London, Streamline Publications, 1955)
Woolf, Virginia, *A Room of One's Own* (London, Penguin, 1945)

Unpublished Papers and Theses

Kate Chilton and Alice Evans, 'Mixed up and Muddled: The Private Testimony and Public History of the German Occupation of Guernsey, 1940-1945' (Joint paper given at 'Texts of Testimony' Conference, Liverpool, August 2001)
Sheridan Russell, 'Their Dearest Friends: Women's Writing and the Educational Importance of Adolescent Girls' Journals' (University of Sussex, MA dissertation, 1989)

INDEX

air raids: on St Peter Port June 1940, 3; other, 10, 28, 92-4, 117, 170-1
anonymous letters, 115-17

Bandelow, Major, 20
Blucher, Countess, 35, 42, 70, 73, 77
Brock: Bertie, 98, 119, 213; Mildred, 127, 134, 151, 156, 163, 202; Peggy, 30, 35, 67, 87, 106, 108, 122, 128, 135-6, 142, 144-5, 149, 210
Brosch, Dr, 36, 69

Carey: Doris, 6, 39, 55, 72; James Frederick, 1, 2, 9, 34-5, 46, 72, 90, 94, 120, 135, 139, 142, 164, 184, 200, 213; Jim (Boy), 65, 91, 152, 214; Michelle (Baba), 2, 68, 92, 130, 214, 215-16; Perdy, 6; Victor, Bailiff of Guernsey and England, 5-6, 24, 27, 41, and the Germans, 17-18, 38, 81, 99, 173, 185, 207, and the Islanders, 25, 115, 124, 138, 163, 164, 179, 207, 208, public messages to Islanders, 50, 52-5, 200, V-sign campaign, 52-5, *see also* V-sign campaign
Cherry, Mary and Cliff, 7, 77, 133
Churchill, Winston, 82, 89, 107, 206, 208
clothes, *see* rationing
collaboration and fraternisation, 21-2, 37, 46, 71, 73, 115, 213; Islanders' disapproval of, 179, 180, 38, 215
Connellan, Katty, 1, 2, 28, 59, 83, 88, 114, 125, 127, 130, 145-6, 148
Controlling Committee, 51, 63, 98, 141, 187, 190

damage to Island and property, 6, 26, 56, 69, 76, 85, 91, 135, 142, 149, 162
demilitarisation, 2, 41
deportation of Islanders: first considered, 62-3; first deportation, 97, 103; reports from camps, 111, 115, 124, 162; second deportation, 120-1
de Sausmarez, Olive, 12, 30, 40, 43, 64, 82, 150, 156, 176, 186, 203

escapes from the Island, 17, 83, 98, 136-7, 150, 184
evacuation, 2, 50

Falkener, Ethel and Lyon, 42, 144, 163
Falla, Raymond, 14, 46
Finey, John, 2, 124, 148, 163, 165, 167, 171, 173, 178, 179, 196
Fisher, Emily, 196, 198
food: black market, 71; malnutrition, 61, 71, 80, 127, 138, 202; prices, 78, 127, 131, 133, 136, 195; shortages, 78, 202, 204, 205; starvation, 71, 127, 130, 134, 138, 201, 212, 215; weight loss, 15, 64, 217; *see also* rationing
foreign workers brought to the Island, 66, 67, 72, 76, 80, 86, 89, 106, 126, 128, 145, 175
Forest Church, 67, 82, 163, 165
Frere, Mabel, 67-8, 118

Gaudion, Miss, 16, 56, 58
George VI, King: messages, 16; speeches, 41; visit to Guernsey, 215
German authorities, 42, 118, 157-8, 185
German building and fortifications, 70, 129, 132
German invasion of Guernsey, 3
German soldiers: compassion towards, 7, 134, 187; interaction with Islanders, humorous, 6, 19, 75, 79, 178, 198, negative, 34, 56, 69-70, 92, 95, 139-40, 160, 164, 165, 182, 188, positive, 4, 5, 73, 77, 86, 90, 101, 107, 138, 167, 173-4; occupying property, 40, 56, 63, 104, *see also* damage; searching property, 137, 160, 184, 199; suffering, 35, 190, 196, 198

Hamon, Hedley, 1, 70-1
Hayes, Mrs, 1
Hazell, Ethel, 12, 53, 108, 119, 156
Hitler, Adolf, 135, 188, 206
Hubert, W.G., 14
Huffmeier, Admiral, 187, 200, 201, 206, 208, 212

invasion (British) of France, 163, 168
Islanders: dignified reaction to Germans, 8, 42, 72, 107; heroic endurance, 8, 10, 87, 100, 147, 159, 161, 194, 204, 217; optimism and camaraderie, 85, 87, 106, 130, 138, 140, 155, 186, 189, 194, 199; resistance or remonstration with Germans, 78, 90, 146, 157, 164, 175-6; suffering, 193, 197, 200; working for Germans, 73, 125, 128, 139, 173

Jackson, Reverend Hartley, 68
Jews, 41, 172

Kinnersly, Mabel, 16, 36-7, 107, 119, 135, 169, 171

Ladies College, 7
Laine, Abraham, 18-19, 155, 185
Lanz, Dr, 9
laws introduced during occupation, 9, 40, 155, *see also* orders
Leale, John, 98, 185
le Masurier, Mrs, 13

Maass, Dr, 9
Martel: Frank, 89, 95; Philip, 13; Violet, 74, 77, 108, 122
Mauger, Alice, 8, 66, 96, 107, 125, 140-1
memory loss or 'occupational dottiness', 140, 156, 200
Michael, Mrs, 13
Mulholland, Desmond, 13

Nicolle, Hubert, 22-23
notices, 17, 40, 65, 69, 82, 85, 91, 110, 159, 183, 185, 186, 200

operations and reconnaissance, 6, 13, 22, 103-4
orders, 4, 5, 15, 18, 20, 23, 25, 61, 128; *see also* laws
Organisation Todt, 122, 134-5
Ozanne, Booty, 64

police scandal, 74, 75, 78, 80, 83

RAF: leaflets, 16, 29, 56, 172; planes, 28, 60-1, 69, 97, 154
rationing: clothes, 9, 87, 140, 143; food, 9, 37, 43, 46-7, 58, 128, 185, 195; *see also* food; fuel and electricity, 65, 81, 113, 148, 150, 152, 195, 200, 212
reconnaissance, *see* operations
Red Cross: messages, 91, 92, 130, 152, 158, 166; parcels, 164, 185, 187, 194, 204, *see also* Vega
Renault, Emely, 2, 8, 30, 167
Ross, Miss, 37, 81, 145, 151, 175
Royal Court, 2, 9

Schlier, Ilsa, 79, 201
Schumacher, Colonel, 10
Sherwill, Ambrose, 8, 20, 24, 25, 27, 33, 164
Snow, Brigadier, 212
States of Deliberation, 9, 51, 155
Symes, James, 22-3

Tetley, J.E.B., 11
theft, 12, 66, 110, 111, 126, 129, 171, 172, 196, 197, 201, 204
Timmer, G.J., 8, 59, 73

UK government, 2, 81, 182, 186, 189, 205

V-sign campaign, 52-5, 58
VE Day, 208
Vega, 186-9, 191, 202, 206, *see also* Red Cross
von Schmettow, Colonel Count, 20, 173, 179, 187

Welch, John and Nellie, 61, 84, 98-9, 124, 138, 204-5
Williams, Gouliot, 94, 109, 161

Visit our website and discover thousands of other History Press books.

www.thehistorypress.co.uk